PIETY
&
POWER

PIETY

&

POWER

MIKE PENCE

AND THE TAKING

OF THE WHITE HOUSE

TOM LOBIANCO

DEY ST.
An Imprint of WILLIAM MORROW

DEY ST.

HarperCollins books may be purchased for educational, business, or sales promotional use. For information, please email the Special Markets Department at SPsales@harpercollins.com.

FIRST EDITION

Designed by Paula Russell Szafranski

Library of Congress Cataloging-in-Publication Data has been applied for.

ISBN 978-0-06-286878-7

19 20 21 22 23   LSC   10 9 8 7 6 5 4 3 2 1

For Angelica and Maria Alessandra

CONTENTS

AUTHOR'S NOTE

Vice President Mike Pence declined to be interviewed or answer questions for this book, per multiple aides. They gave a handful of reasons for why he wouldn't talk, largely that he doesn't participate in interviews about himself for profiles or books about him. I hope he changes his mind and that policy. He has an innately fascinating story to tell about his career in politics, and there are many things only he can answer. In the places where I couldn't get a clear read on the situation from his friends, advisers, and others, I tried to make it clear that there was no obvious answer.

The rest of the book is based on interviews with more than a hundred people around Pence throughout his life—as well as my own interviews with him from over the years in my role as a reporter for the Associated Press. Some folks I spoke with almost daily, as I reported this, and others I sat with for hours at a time. Many wished to remain anonymous for various reasons, and I have noted this in the endnotes.

As I began writing, I had to decide whether to write the entire book in the third person, including my own reporting, or to jump between the third person for most of the material and the first person for my own. In the end, I elected to use the third person for the entire work (and to refer to myself as the "AP reporter") because it better focused on the true subject of the book—Pence, not me.

To everyone who gave generously of their time, wisdom, and candor, I say, "Thank you." I hope this book reflects the most complete and accurate picture of the vice president, and it would not be possible without you.

Throughout my reporting I came across numerous inconsistencies in the vice president's life story—perhaps naively, I do not attribute these to any malicious intent, but instead often found them to be a product of the fog of history and a repeated trend of confusion about what Mike Pence himself actually said or meant. (Ironically, Pence has occasionally wavered on key facts about his background in various interviews.) In the cases where I felt confident in a particular version of events, judged largely on each source's direct knowledge of the situation, I tried to go with that version in here. In cases where I was unsure which version was accurate, I tried to present as much information as possible and let the facts sit out there.

PIETY
&
POWER

INTRODUCTION:
THE CARETAKER GOVERNMENT

The cherry-red, faux-antique phone sits on the top-left corner of the Resolute desk. President Michael R. Pence sits behind it, papers neatly arranged across the desk. The gold curtains that former president Donald Trump hung from the windows around the Oval Office have been replaced with something a bit more traditional, a bit more austere. But the painting of President Andrew Jackson remains, and therein lies the reminder that Pence now straddles the divide between the American tradition and the wild chaotic populism that ultimately put him in the presidency.

A small coterie of advisers attends most of the meetings in the Oval Office with the new president, Pence #46. There's Marc Short, the master of pulling levers on Capitol Hill; Kellyanne Conway, Pence's longtime political consultant who miraculously survived the entirety of Trump's presidency. There's Josh Pitcock, the onetime chief of staff from the vice president's office who had been deemed too wonkish and operational in 2016, but whose talents are back in vogue now that Pence has won the big prize. And then there's the one adviser who's never in the room, but always present, a reminder reflected in the high gloss of the red phone: Karen Pence.

Pence's victory at the polls in 2024 wasn't resounding, but it was a victory—a testimony to his long-term strategy to ride the wave of the political moment, but never lead it. He just held on tight until Trumpism's bitter end.

His signature achievement in eight years of carrying Trump's water was the establishment of a strong network of antiabortion pregnancy centers—centers that curbed abortions (and access to prenatal care) by undercutting Planned Parenthood clinics across the country. For pro-life activists who view their crusade in terms no less grand than the effort to end slavery, this was a resounding victory after decades of chipping away at the constitutional right.

The irony is that Trump still gets all the credit for being the strongest antiabortion president in the nation's history. And now, after Trump made a total of four appointments to the Supreme Court, jam-packed the federal courts, recorded seven video messages for the annual Right to Life March, and beat back allegation after allegation of infidelity, Pence has almost nothing left to take credit for. Which he is okay with, honestly—he's always been the caretaker, the one who comes in after a big change and tidies up. When he was governor, he toiled in the shadow of Mitch Daniels and now that he's president, he's left dealing with all that Trump has left behind.

But none of that matters. He's president. Number 46.

—

This, of course, is an imagining of what the Pence presidency would look like, but it is rooted in the reporting throughout this book. It is based on an assessment of his political style, his executive abilities, his tight-knit circle of advisers, and the values at his personal core. Kellyanne Conway surprised me once by turning the tables and asking me what my assessment of Pence's time in the White House was: Is he a glorified coatrack, or the Svengali, secretly tugging the strings of Trump and the U.S. government? I answered that he seemed to fall somewhere in between. He is the ultimate political shape-shifter; by turns, neither Dan Quayle nor Dick Cheney, but he can inhabit the persona of either if required.

To truly understand what a Pence presidency would look like, his governorship is the best model—it was the only time he was stripped of all protections and left to decide things flatly for himself. Which leads us back to the red phone at the corner of the desk. With Trump in such a weak position as president, unaware of the deep details and complex issues that swarm the president every day, schizophrenic in his decision making, the question inside Washington has often been, "Is Mike Pence the shadow president?"

The problem is, anyone asking that question is asking it about the wrong Pence. Second Lady Karen Pence rules the roost, and that faux-antique red phone in the vice president's office is more powerful than anyone knows. She stayed on the phone with him throughout the day, every day; when he was governor, even though she worked from an office across the hall. She didn't walk over to his office, because then all the spies that dotted the statehouse would have seen her hand. Instead she stayed on her phone, and he on his.

Smart lobbyists in Indiana and Washington would occasionally use a trick to get through to Mike Pence—they would go through Pence's former chief of staff Bill Smith, who was close with Karen, and he would pass the message to Karen who, if they were lucky, would pass it to Mike. There was all manner of cloak-and-dagger to it, buttoning up the actual message inside pillows of praise for Smith, packed with plaudits for Karen, and, finally, complete reverence for Pence. But the power of getting to Karen was undeniable—which was part of the reason that Pence's aides fought to show who had true access to her.

One former Trump White House official put it this way: Pence is philosophical, his thinking meanders sometimes as he weighs his options, and Karen is the one who usually keeps him looking in a singular direction. &

But is Pence's flip-flopping one of his most powerful political tools? The Trump presidency has tested this theory and given it credence. Pence was a free trade supporter for decades, part of what used to be a core principle for him—in his first successful run for Congress in 2000, he beat back opponents who said that NAFTA was destroying Indiana communities. He said laid-off workers would need to learn new job skills to keep up with the changing economy. In 2016, as Carrier manufacturing was shutting down its Indianapolis plant, Pence refused to provide state subsidies to try and keep the manufacturer there. Just a few weeks after the 2016 election, Trump upstaged Pence in his home state and said he would do everything possible to keep the Carrier jobs there. An Indiana official bumped into Pence at the big announcement that they would provide state funding to keep Carrier there and asked him why the about-face? And Pence just smiled and slapped him on the back, "Now we're with you."

In Washington, some veteran Republican lobbyists and lawmakers said they were confident that Pence was actively fighting Trump on his efforts to impose tariffs on China—something they said was guaranteed to wreck the economy. But a senior Democratic aide who had watched Pence work the halls on behalf of Trump offered this withering assessment, "He's all hat and no cattle." Which is to say, when Pence jaunted down Pennsylvania Avenue, to do Trump's bidding at the Capitol, lawmakers weren't buying what he was selling because they knew Pence's messages were empty and did not carry the full weight of presidential decision.

But there remained a core set of values, core principles that Trump couldn't touch and, indeed, that Pence drove as his hallmark issues inside the Trump administration: pro-life and religious freedom, or, put another way, antiabortion and antigay. Inside Trump's White House, he carved out a niche filling the Department of Health and Human

Services with longtime aides who built out a department dedicated to curbing abortion. Pence welcomed longtime antiabortion activists to the White House for regular meetings and they worked closely to place new limits on access. And, of course, cutting taxes. In Indiana he wanted to do away with the state's income tax entirely and replace it with a usage tax similar to an inflated sales tax. And in Washington, he helped push through Trump's sweeping tax cuts while easily dropping previous concerns about federal debt.

Throughout the Trump presidency, Pence has shown a seemingly endless ability to bend and contort himself, to swim with the political power tides. And, by bending, he has won long-sought goals at the hands of the "porn star presidency." So, what about when the reins come off, when he no longer must carry water for Trump? Make no mistake: the Oval Office is his ultimate goal, and if he achieves it, it will be the truest test of Pence's loyalties. ❧

His foreign policy would very likely be a return to the neoconservative policies sought by President George W. Bush (and Vice President Dick Cheney). A President Pence would hold Israel in the highest regard, the result of his mixture of neoconservative-light and his deep evangelical faith that calls for unflinching devotion to restoring Jerusalem entirely to the Jewish people. As president, he would not clean up "the swamp" or take a hard line on money in politics. A former Trump White House official noted, "Mike is absolutely in awe of people who make money. If you see him around (billionaire Republican donor Paul) Singer, he is absolutely enthralled." He's also a major beneficiary of Koch family money.

What's clear is the public would be the last to know about his decision-making process. In his long political career, Pence has always been happy to talk about others, almost always warmly, and deliver the party line, unfettered. But when it comes to his own role and decisions, he becomes deeply uncomfortable, resorting to a tactic of railroading questioners rather than answering directly. When a reporter confronted him at the 2018 Winter Olympics in Seoul about the appearance that he was "out of the loop" in the Trump White House, he turned beet red in the face.

But despite his attempts to lie low, to stay off the record and to disappear into the shadows, there is much we do know about Mike Pence, and it paints a clear picture of how he has operated as one of the most secretive vice presidents in history, and how he would rule if he should ever achieve his ultimate goal of becoming commander in chief. Of course, it will also depend upon the state of the world and the nation . . . and what Karen says on the other end of the red phone.

PROLOGUE:

THE CORNFIELD IN PENCE'S BACKYARD

When I started covering Mike Pence seven years ago, he would occasionally mention that he had grown up in a small town in Southern Indiana with a cornfield in his backyard. There was nothing terribly stunning in that statement; he sounded like a standard rural conservative politician—there were plenty of them in Indiana. But I had been to his hometown—Columbus, Indiana—a few times, and it wasn't a rural, cornfield kind of place. It was a gorgeous medium-size city, with a rich history. I assumed the cornfield bit had been an embellishment, a detail added to create a folksier persona. Pence certainly wouldn't have been the first politician to employ such a tactic.

So I was plenty surprised when, on a trip to Columbus in February of 2018, I came across the very house Pence had grown up in—right where Hawcreek Boulevard dead-ends at Thirty-First Street on Columbus's northside. A light snow from that morning covered the ground, but the land behind the old Pence house was plowed. Old stalks from row upon row of corn poked their way through the light dusting. Pence had left some detail out of his story, however, such as the fact that he had grown up in the city's newest subdivision, one built to support Columbus's booming manufacturing industry and an influx of middle-class families. The Pences were one of those upwardly mobile families living in the shiny suburb, in Middle America, in the middle of the postwar American dream. He hadn't lived the life of a farmer, but when he'd mentioned the cornfield, he'd been truthful. His details were accurate, but the whole of the story was not. It was the very first clue, a small detail, but also a small window into who he really is.

Later, I learned much more about where Pence grew up, and how he grew up. There was far more to the story and more that would explain this man, the unlikely vice president to Donald J. Trump, than could be explained by that cornfield.

Pence was the fourth governor I'd covered in my career (two in Maryland and two in Indiana) and one of dozens of politicians I've written about regularly. But among all of them, he was the most vexing. No matter how often I wrote about him, bumped into him, chatted with him, I never felt like I had my finger on his pulse, that I connected with him or even understood what drove him. Other reporters would often tell me that he was such a "great quote" when he was in Congress (before I started covering him) but by the time he returned to Indiana to run for governor, something seemed to have switched off—he was more hidden away. Or at least that's how I rationalized it until the fall of 2017, when I bumped into a friend who had covered him extensively before. I asked my fellow reporter if he felt like he ever truly understood Pence, could get to his purpose, his motivation, his drive. His answer? No.

The general public is now well aware of some of Pence's evasive peccadilloes; his unerring ability to wash away Trump's latest insanity unfazed (or at least outwardly unmoved); and his almost robotic handling of every new disaster, now firmly ensconced in the popular

arena by *Saturday Night Live*'s Beck Bennett. There's also the stereotypes and hyperbolized caricatures of him as antigay, antiquated,
stiff, theocratic—all have fragments of truth to them, but none fully
capture him. In another universe, where Trump never descended his
golden escalator into the 2016 race, this probably wouldn't amount
to much more than barstool pontificating among reporters and political hacks. But through a variety of forces I'll reveal here, and a
dash of (apparently) divine intervention, Mike Pence now sits a breath
away from the Oval Office. And, given the inexperience of the current chief executive, Pence is an important sphere of influence in the
administration—although not in the ways that a stream of hot takes
and speculative paranoia from Trump loyalists have pushed out there.
He is neither Svengali, pulling the strings of Trump, nor glorified
coatrack, merging with the background of every meeting—though
there is a common thread in those polar opposite assessments, which
is his hidden nature.

   As I reported and researched for this book, I grew more empathetic of Pence, his religion, his politics, him as a flawed human. I
also had the same nagging feeling that I had when I covered him in
Indiana. I was missing something about him; I was misunderstanding
him. (That nagging itch was so constant that on another reporting trip
back to Indiana, in August 2018, I drove back again to his old home
near Hawcreek Boulevard. I had to see if there was actual corn growing there, to make sure I'd been right. I parked my car at the end of
the road, and there it was, rows of it so thick I couldn't see across the
field. Some stalks were seven feet high. I walked over and plucked a
golden-brown tassel from the top of a small stalk. I carried it with me
while I wrote this book—proof that I hadn't been so off the mark after
all.) But I had never gotten through the layers, mined facets that developed over four decades, to see him for what he is—a man with the
political skills, more often unseen than explicit, and the impervious
discipline that he's always had, which seem to shine brighter in the
Trump White House. Through my work, I came across two general

camps: those who had been friends and associates of Pence but felt like they never knew him, and a small clutch of devoted loyalists who had been invited into his inner sanctum and believed entirely in his talent and his purpose.

One of Pence's earliest benefactors, Chuck Quilhot was immediately enthralled by the young Pence after the first-time congressional candidate made a cold call to him in 1988 looking for a campaign donation. They talked for hours and formed a lasting friendship. But decades later, Quilhot still puzzled over how Pence had changed, noting that he had a Forrest Gump–like quality—showing up in all the right places: "I mean, it's a remarkable story, but he's a, he's an altar boy, isn't he? You know, I keep wrestling with it. Is he really that simple and you know, Forrest Gump kind of a personality? Or is he just, is he a real controlled and ambitious guy? And I don't know. I can't decide." A former longtime neighbor put it more succinctly, "I've known him for thirty years and I still don't know him."

The man who made Pence a household name throughout Indiana, Scott Uecker, said the young radio host he hired in 1994 was gregarious, warm, funny, and open. He was open to both conservative and liberal guests and heard everyone out—he was a great listener. But when he went to Washington, he changed, he hid his humor and open personality. He became more strident in his political views, and colder in his outward appearance, flatter, more fake (or was it careful?). Veteran Republican operatives in Indiana who ran across him periodically over the course of three decades described him as a "Zelig"—the main character from Woody Allen's mockumentary of the same name. Zelig is a mysterious character who pops up in black-and-white photos through history, sometimes as a jazz musician, other times in a Fu Manchu outfit with a wispy white mustache down to his toes. The presentation in the film is hilarious and vaudevillian, but the point is inescapable: this man overhauls his appearance almost seamlessly to fit his environment. Can he so easily shape-shift because there is no core? How else could he so effectively adopt the styles of the strongest personalities around him? This, as it turned out, would be an incredibly accurate model for Pence—he did change his colors every decade or so, adapting to his ever-shifting environment and taking on the traits he thought would make him successful.

Washington operators who worked for Ronald Reagan laughed at Pence's comparisons of Trump to Reagan because Trump wasn't the one who reminded them of Reagan—it was Pence. The slight laugh, the mild deprecating style of humor, the squinted eyes and knowing head nod—it was all Reagan. And there was Pence, emulating every tic of his political hero. In his career, his friends laughed at his uncanny ability to do impersonations, from Bill Clinton, which he did on-air during his radio days, to George W. Bush at Republican fund-raising dinners. ("'Mike, I'm here to encourage you. I wanna be your encourager.'") He even occasionally does Trump impersonations. Pence once acknowledged that he seemed to unwittingly take on other people's quirks and defining characteristics. "I've become more myself on radio," he said in 1998. "There is a temptation, intentionally or unintentionally, to imitate people you respect. You invariably think, 'I need to be like someone who is interesting.' After a while, you develop a certain comfort level with doing your own thing."

This was a defining trait of his career—his chameleon properties, stretched over decades. In his first two runs for Congress, he was a standard-issue Republican candidate—not taking sides in the split between conservatives and the establishment of the party. In the '90s he became a full-throated conservative and changed into a declawed version of Rush Limbaugh. In Congress, a decade later, he became a leader of the hard Right, a blend of Christian Right conservative and Tea Partiers that one broadcaster dubbed "teavangelical." But he dropped that image with breakneck speed in 2011 to run for governor of Indiana, this time becoming a conservative technocrat in the mold of Indiana's popular governor, Mitch Daniels. That's nothing new for any politician, of course (think of John Kerry's flip-flopping, Hillary

Clinton's transformation from an accented Arkansas political wife to nonaccented secretary of state and presidential candidate).

No, the interesting part about Pence's shape-shifting was the lag time—he never led the wave, he always caught it after it was cresting. That was never clearer than in April 2016, when the tsunami of Trump was about to break, washing away Reagan's Republican Party and the hopes of conservatives who had spent decades building the GOP into an ideological force. Pence couldn't decide between his past, represented by movement conservative Ted Cruz, and his future, represented by raging nationalist Donald Trump—so he picked both. And shortly after the wave broke, with Trump's victory in the Indiana primary a few days later, Pence was on his way to his latest evolution at Trump's side.

In a normal administration, there probably wouldn't be any need for a biography of the sitting vice president. Interest in the last Hoosier to become vice president, Dan Quayle, seemed to start with a grievous spelling error and end with a cultural skewering on *Murphy Brown*. And Pence is nothing close to the shadow presidency of Dick Cheney. But since the inauguration, Mike Pence has seemed seconds from taking the throne. The FBI began investigating the president's campaign in July of 2016 for possible collusion with Russia to win the election. Trump's personal lawyer, Michael Cohen, flipped against him in August 2018 in exchange for leniency in court. And the special counsel investigating Trump and his campaign has convinced almost a half-dozen Trump aides to testify in his sprawling investigation. The peril to Trump from multiple federal investigations likely matches his own threat to himself: his steady diet of Filet-O-Fish sandwiches, chocolate milkshakes, cable news, and Twitter.

The lag time in Pence's identity changes led many throughout his career to question not just who he was, but where his loyalties lay. Not least of whom was President Trump himself. After Democrats won the House in 2018, Trump began asking aides and confidants whether he could trust Pence—and whether he should keep him on the ticket in 2020. Trump denied this publicly, but Pence and he had never developed a close relationship.

The Democrats had overtaken the House, heightening the threat of impeachment. As Democrats made their political calculations, one question was inescapable: If they got rid of Trump, who would they be getting instead?

———

But one thing hadn't changed throughout Pence's long political career, his strict religious devotion. There was still a core, buried deeply in his center.

Pence's self-affixed Christian-first label has never been seriously parsed. Christian is a sweeping term; Catholics were the first Christians, but some Protestants insist that Catholics don't count as Christians—and they fought vicious wars throughout Europe hundreds of years ago to prove that point. The split goes further among Protestants; many Fundamentalists—who take the Bible to be literally true—still distrust so-called Modernists, with their more interpretive approach. And none of that accounts for evangelicals, a broad and amorphous group that crosses all the worlds of Christianity and yet is often presented as its own unique bubble. So where did Pence fall in that sweeping panoply of religion? Well, everywhere and nowhere. His own religious identity seems strangely amorphous, even as he puts it out there as his chief defining characteristic.

Like the cornfield, the story of how he came to God was not quite as simple as he presented in public (nor should it have been). Religious conversions often take years, if not decades, and Pence's was no different. He had his first savior experience with Jesus in 1978 but kept attending Catholic Church through the '80s into the early '90s. After they had children, Karen and Mike Pence opted to attend a nondenominational church in Greenwood that could best be described as a reformed Baptist church with an evangelical bent. In DC, the Pences attended a nondenominational megachurch popular among Christian conservatives in Congress and the Bush White House. Pence's pastor there trained at seminaries steeped in Christian Fundamentalism and Dispensationalism (the study of the end of the world), but those topics were rarely addressed in his more broad-based sermons.

And what of Pence himself? Just because he attended a Fundamentalist megachurch didn't necessarily make him a hard-core Bible-thumper. Pence's close political aides and allies, formed during his time in Congress, describe an unshakably pious man. But his friends in Indiana rarely saw the public displays of religiosity before he went to Washington in 2000. And those displays disappeared again when he returned to Indiana to run for governor, a dozen years later. The culture warrior who had once threatened to shut down the government in the name of stopping abortions was left behind, somewhere inside the Washington Beltway. So, what happened with his deep faith?

The answer to the question of which style of Christianity Pence espouses and how that influences his policies is not as clean-cut as either progressives or conservatives would present, but there are important clues to be gleaned from both his personal and political life. And those answers have everything to do with why he stands so firmly by Donald Trump. That's the piety part of this book, and it explains the power.

—

When Pence secured his place by Trump's side, it created a rift in his circle of friends and associates. Like Mike and Karen, most of them saw a calling from God, but a small and vocal minority saw it as a complete sellout, a scandal—it was Pence's ambition calling, in the form of Trump. One friend summed it up simply, "He sold his soul." This is the central issue that a handful of us Pence-perts have been parsing for two years now: Was he answering the call from Donald, or from God?

In another way of putting it: Is Pence a fraud? By every indication he has been faithful in his marriage (a stumbling block that has tripped up many other Christian conservative leaders over the years). He has scrupulously avoided the soft corruption of political handouts to his friends and has even voted against their personal interests at times. He reads the Bible, still marks it up with a highlighter, attends church as often as he can, prays before meetings, and consults God routinely. But his ambition is paramount—reflected in the supreme honing of his political skills, the tools that have gotten him where he currently sits. His signature line, that he is a Christian, a conservative, and a Republican—in that order—is strikingly honest. But the unstated quality that pulls rank on all others is that he is a politician first and foremost, with skills sharpened over a lifetime. It's not a role he was born to play; his family was no political dynasty. Instead, Pence fashioned himself to fit the role, immersing himself early and completely in the milieu of politics like the finest method actor. And it worked.

But the reason he is in the White House, serving next to a man who made a living breaking almost every Christian bromide, someone so amoral that Pence once said anyone fitting that description should be immediately impeached, is because, in the end, ambition and the hunger for power outweighed anything else.

So who is Michael Richard Pence? The answer is like that cornfield—there's a tassel of truth to the carefully crafted public persona, but so much more underneath the layers.

CHAPTER 1

IDYLLIC

Michael Richard Pence was born into a blustery family of second-generation Irish Catholic immigrants, so rambunctious that he was almost lost in the mix when he came along. His maternal grandfather, Richard Michael Cawley, left civil war in Ireland in 1923 when he was just twenty years old. He emigrated to the United States with only $23 in his pocket and quickly made his way to Chicago, to meet his uncle and an older brother. In the early 1920s, America was embroiled in vicious immigration debates and Cawley's type were not in favor—Irish Catholics, who the British American and German American Protestants viewed as radicals and, in some corners, "papists"—a slur for Catholics, meaning they were puppets of the pope, unable to think for themselves.

Cawley found a safe haven in the Irish Catholic immigrant community in Chicago. He quickly married, had children, and found stable work driving a streetcar. In 1931, he married a first-generation

Irish American woman, Mary Elizabeth Maloney, and in 1932, they had a daughter, Nancy. Two decades later, Nancy met a young soldier at the USO, just back from the Korean War, Edward Pence Jr. Pence was descended from Irish and German immigrants. The two soon married, and in 1956 Ed Pence found work as an oil salesman, servicing territories south, in Indiana. They packed up and left the city for the country.

When Ed and Nancy Pence moved their family from Chicago to Indiana, they had just had their first child—a boy, Gregory—in 1956. Another boy, Edward, soon followed. Their first stop was Indianapolis, then, in 1959, they moved an hour south to Columbus. They moved into a small apartment, a box of a house in a long row, known as "the Dunlappe Apartments"—their neighbors were the other young families who were pouring into Columbus to take jobs with the city's burgeoning diesel engine maker, Cummins. Ed Pence was doing well, rising through the ranks as a salesman at Kiel Brothers Oil Co., a regional distributor of gasoline through Southern Indiana and the Ohio River valley. On June 7, 1959, their third child—another boy—Michael Richard Pence was born. Michael was named for his maternal grandfather. The Pence family continued growing at a clip akin to Columbus itself—another boy followed, and the brood was forced to find a home large enough for six. "My mother and father were the American dream," Pence said. "We had some lean years, times when I can remember sleeping in the same bed with my brother or when Christmas meant only one present, but they worked hard to succeed, and they tried to instill that in all of us." The Pence's second home was a modest ranch house in the newest, most modern development in a rapidly growing town. Columbus was gobbling up cornfields in short order, and the Pences now had their own humble plot.

As the third child, Pence struggled for attention with his two older—and more aggressive—brothers. His grandfather, Richard, took a shine to him and taught him "Humpty Dumpty" in Gaelic. Richard revered Franklin Delano Roosevelt and the other Democratic leaders who had helped Irish immigrants like himself. And, like millions of other Irish Americans, he was thrilled when one of their own made it all the way to the White House, despite nationalist attacks alleging that John F. Kennedy would be a puppet of the Vatican. Michael's grandfather's political leanings skewed to the Democrats; his grandson followed suit.

The Pence household was strict, devout, Irish Catholic, and more or less Democratic—although politics was not an important family issue. Ed Pence Jr. was a stern patriarch; the children were not permitted to speak at the dinner table. "If you lied to him, you'd be taken upstairs, have a conversation, and then he'd whack you with a belt," older brother Greg Pence said. Nancy Pence had a sharp Irish wit and knew how to deliver a humbling chiding with a wink and a dash of love. The Pence children developed a similar style—dry, clean humor matched with a quick tongue and the kind of verbal roughhousing that comes from having to compete for attention without being punished. Greg Pence, the oldest of the clan, earned the nickname "General Harassment" and Michael, in the middle, became "Bubbles"—because he was both gregarious and a little pudgy. "Michael's hilarious," Nancy Pence said of her son. "I attribute it to the Irish. We're faith filled and have a good sense of humor."

What little politics the Pences did discuss revolved around the news of the day—big national developments and historical moments. "There weren't very many political discussions around the dinner table," Mike Pence said. "My mom grew up in a Democratic family. My dad was a small business Republican, but we never talked about politics." When he was just seven years old, Mike Pence was awestruck by the nation's first Irish Catholic president, Kennedy. He took photos of Kennedy and stuffed them into a time capsule. The young Pence viewed him not as a politician, but as a leader. Pence made a memory box, with news clippings and pictures of Kennedy. He idolized him, explaining later, "In my early youth I was very inspired by the life of John Kennedy. The heroes of my youth were John F. Kennedy, Martin Luther King Jr."

As Pence was developing his identity and an eye toward politics and public service, the East Coast elites had been picking up on someone special inside Columbus, Indiana—the town father, founder of the city's largest manufacturer and philanthropic leader, J. Irwin Miller. In 1967, *Esquire* magazine flew a contributor to Indiana to write about the man who was transforming Columbus, Indiana, into a small cosmopolitan island in the sea of cornfields. Irwin Miller read from his bible while sitting in his office in the center of the small downtown and picked out of his favorite passages in Isaiah 51: "Look to the rock from which you are hewn and the quarry from which you are digged." *Esquire* very much liked this quarry, "This man ought to be the next President of the United States," crowed the October 1967 issue, with a profile view of Miller dominating the cover.

The new developments eating into the cornfields surrounding Columbus's town center were packed with the young families of engineers, salesmen, and other white-collar workers being pulled into Columbus by Miller's Cummins and other major employers. And in the center of the city, Miller's family filled it with world-renowned architecture: a church and conference center designed by the Saarinen family of architects, whose other projects included Washington's Dulles International Airport, Lincoln Center in New York City, and the Gateway Arch in St. Louis. Fabled architect I. M. Pei redesigned major city centers in Dallas, Boston, and other metropolises. He envisioned the pyramid at the center of the Louvre and the John F. Kennedy presidential library in Boston. And he also designed the public library in downtown Columbus—a redbrick modernist masterpiece, with a wide-open plaza and an art installation specifically built to complement the First Christian Church across the street . . . which was designed by the Saarinens.

There was magic in Columbus.

Columbus was a blossoming oasis, but it also wasn't yet a metropolis. There was a movie theater downtown and plenty of restaurants, but the Pence family still found themselves without much to do other than drive around town for fun on the weekends. They also felt the cultural strife associated with first- and second-generation Catholic Americans moving into Protestant strongholds. Greg Pence recalled that the Protestant kids in Columbus would sometimes throw rocks at him and his brothers because of their religion. Indiana, at large, was home to some of the worst ethnic and racial clashes in the country. The Ku Klux Klan had been a powerful force in Indiana politics four decades earlier, but scandal—including the murder of an Indiana schoolteacher—largely drove the group out. In Columbus, vestiges of the group remained. Irwin Miller fought landlords who refused to sell to African Americans, but the town was still very white during Pence's childhood.

Pence lacked the familial pedigree that propelled Kennedy and, closer to home, Irwin Miller, to power. But he did have a spark, a gift that had been hidden away in his stern household but nourished by his family position as a middle child. "He was always talking," his mother, Nancy Pence, said. "What surprised me was how well he could talk in front of crowds." As a fifth-grade student at the Catholic school run by the St. Columba parish in Columbus, Mike Pence signed up for a speech competition put on by the local Optimist Club. He bested kids who were grades ahead of him, and he stunned his mother. "When it came his turn, his voice just boomed out over the audience. He just blew everybody away. I had a hard time associating the boy speaking up there with our son."

Sister Sharon Bierman taught him math, science, and religion in the seventh and eighth grades at St. Columba—she noticed the bright and meticulous student and suggested he again compete in the Optimist Club speech competition. In February 1972, as a seventh grader, he placed second in the Columbus Optimist Club contest. In his speech, the young Mike Pence cited John F. Kennedy's belief that the "courage of great men can inspire others to overcome obstacles." The next year, he took first place. He seemed to tap into some preternatural calm in front of an audience. Where some get nervous, shake, lose their footing, Pence found that even at that young age he was "able to channel a lot of that anxiety into the message I'm giving."

Sister Bierman also noticed a young man with a talent for understanding and internalizing the Catholic faith. "He loved memorizing the seven sacraments, the corporal works of mercy. I loved the way he knew all the mysteries of the rosary," Sister Bierman said years later. "He excelled in religion." The corporal works of mercy, Jesus's acts of charity, specifically called on followers to perform similar acts of charity. And Pence did his best, helping the children of migrant workers who attended school with him. One day, Sister Bierman asked him if he would consider joining the priesthood, but he answered no. He wanted to raise a family someday, when he met the right woman.

He stayed at St. Columba through the ninth grade, then transferred to the larger public school across the street, Columbus North High School, in 1974. By then Pence was a public speaking veteran. The Columbus North speech team drew a throng of talented students and competed nationally. The team and its pair of dedicated coaches took Pence to a new level. Pence's high school speech coach and mentor, Debbie Shoultz, said, "It wasn't just that it came naturally to him. He worked hard at it." Pence, self-effacingly, called himself a goof-off in middle school, but Shoultz saw more maturity in him, "By the time he came to high school he had developed a sincerity that showed in his speaking."

The First Run for Office

Pence, like the other neighborhood kids, went biking to the drugstore to buy candy and played touch football at the nearby farm. When he ran over to Tom Hodek's place down the street, he popped his head in the front door—ran to the kitchen, opened the fridge, grabbed whatever he wanted, and ran back outside to keep playing. And Hodek did the same at the Pences. Soon, that familiarity with his peers and in his neighborhood would pay off.

In 1975, Mike's dad connected him with a business associate, John Rumple, the head of the local Democratic Party. Through Rumple, the young Pence took a gig working as a youth coordinator for a local Democrat running for judge. His job was getting other neighborhood kids to go door-to-door with him, promoting the candidate. Rumple also started coaching him in speech contests, "He had a lot of energy," Rumple said.

Mike Pence might have been a smooth talker, but he wasn't a hotshot. He made the football team in ninth grade, but not by much. "I was the fourth-string center on the team," he said. "That means I was one grade above the blocking sled." It was, bluntly, because he was fat. "I had three brothers who were lean and hard and thin, and I was the exact opposite." Pence was, he said, "a fat little kid, the real pumpkin in a pickle patch." He changed in a big way the summer of 1975, after his sophomore year of high school. He had been overweight much of his young adult life; a doctor put him on a strict regimen. He lost 55 pounds. When he returned that fall, to start his junior year, other students walked up to him and asked, "Are you new?" In a way, he was. With a fresh shot of confidence, he promptly ran for vice president of the student government and lost.

Michael Pence was a newly crowned man about campus. He organized student Fun Day, with outdoor games—human wheelbarrow races, tricycle races—and put together a talent show. He began writing a comic for the high school paper, the *Triangle*. "The Adventures of Mortimer" was imminently safe, bland in its writing, but decent in his artistry. In the November 19, 1976, strip, Pence's "Mortimer" and a fellow student sit by the swim lane at the pool watching girls compete. "Wow, look at those girl swimmers in them there new 'skinsuits'! They're outta sight!" Mortimer's friend says, gawking. Mortimer plays the straight man, "Yes, and I hear they cut down on water drag and allow one to actually swim faster!" Then Mortimer's buddy drops the surprise on him, "Did I tell you I tried out for the girls swim team??" Gàsp! "Sure, what with women's lib and everything going around, I thought, 'What the heck!'" Mortimer's jaw drops, then he asks his buddy if he made the team. "Na. . . . I couldn't fit in the suit." Womp, womp.

Mike also pumped gas at the local Marathon gas station, saved his money, then headed to Tom Pickett's music shop for a guitar and some lessons. There were still a few imperfections to his polish: throughout his senior yearbook his smile looks forced at times, his lips closed tight—a certain sternness on his face. But when he was with the speech club he couldn't hide his joy—a snapshot shows him with a natural, wide grin as he received the award for the state's best public speaker—and there peeked out a full mouth of braces.

"I think he became interested in politics in high school. He had come across a book on the Constitution. He read that book over and over and it obviously had an influence on his life," Shoultz said. "Even when he was a senior he talked to his classmates about one day being president."

His peers saw he was focused in a way that nobody else their age was. "He had a bigger plan for himself, unlike most of us who were happy to make it to the next weekend," said Vic Thompson, one of Pence's closest friends and a colleague on the speech team. He also flashed his natural sense of humor. He would head over to Jeff Brown's house, whose family owned the local newspaper, the *Columbus Republic*, and he would put on a one-man comedy show for the family. "He could've been a stand-up comedian; he'd have my mom in stitches," Brown said. "He's always had political ambitions and worked hard at it. I think God poured his blessings on him, and his family." ✤

By the summer of 1977, Mike Pence, eighteen years old, was polished, trim, gregarious, loquacious, energetic, and ambitious. Pence was personifying his heroes, people like Kennedy, who used politics to shape U.S. history—the news clippings he'd stuffed in a time capsule a few years earlier formed the first public role model for him. By the time he left high school, he was a politician through and through— now he just had to go figure out exactly what he stood for.

CHAPTER 2

CONVERSION

Pence left Columbus, Indiana, a modest star—the president of his high school class (although the title was neither valedictorian nor connoted most popular student). He had transformed from a pudgy, gregarious young boy lost in the middle of his family into a charismatic figure at one of the state's largest high schools. But for college, Pence went smaller than his own high school, picking a small liberal arts school near the bank of the Ohio River in Southern Indiana, Hanover College.

Hanover was a Presbyterian school, generally viewed as more conservative than some of the other small colleges around the state. Pence moved from Columbus to the dorms of Hanover in September 1977. In an instant, he was yanked out of a well-built, comfortable world into one of anonymity. As he went looking for his footing in a strange new world, he started attending meetings of a small Christian group at the school, Vespers. It wasn't for any specific denomination;

Catholics and evangelicals were in the mix of about twenty students who went a few days during the week. The group met in the small Hanover chapel. A rotation of older students would get up, deliver a short reading from the Bible, then they discussed the passage and sang a few songs. It was like church service lite. No communion or big sermons, but still worship.

What drew Pence to these gatherings? For one thing, there was a girl he liked. But they also offered some comfort as he ached for home and felt the pain of adjusting from being a fairly popular high school senior to an unknown college freshman.

The shepherd of the Christian fellowship, John Gable, was a bright, charismatic senior, just a few years older but infinitely more wizened than the freshmen around him. He smiled brightly and strummed his guitar as the group sang in praise, Mike Pence on the riser behind him, strumming backup. Gable led them all, but occasionally he plucked one of his favorites from the flock to take over. In 1978, he picked Pence. "He had taken an interest in me, and he was talking with me about faith," Pence said. "And I got to a point where I said, 'John, I've decided I'm gonna go ahead and be Christian.'" Gable had a gold cross he wore on a chain around his neck, Pence wanted one for himself—it would make him a Christian. He asked Gable to fetch the catalog he had ordered it from, so he could place an order himself. Gable shot back at him, "You know, you've gotta wear it in your heart before you wear it around your neck." Pence said that Gable seemed to cut straight through his BS, "I stood there for ten minutes because I felt like he just kinda pulled the curtain aside and he looked right at me and just said, 'I see ya. I see ya for what ya, where you really are.'"

Was he a pretender? Was he showboating? Lost? Pence wouldn't say, but he was clearly searching for something.

At the end of his freshman year at college, in April 1978, Pence went with his Vespers group to the evangelical version of Woodstock, the Ichthus Music Festival. Preachers from a hippie Jesus brand of Christianity took the stage in between Christian-rock versions of prog-rock bands like Rush and folk staples like Bob Dylan. The festival, put on by the Asbury Theological Seminary, was part of a growing number of spontaneous revivals in colleges around the country that merged the '70s spirit of shedding old institutional order with the deep vein of American evangelicalism. Standing in the pastoral hills of Wilmore, Kentucky, just outside of Lexington, Pence stood in a light rain, "My heart really finally broke with a deep realization [that] what had happened on the cross, in some infinitesimal way, had happened for me. And I gave my life—made a personal decision to trust Jesus Christ as my Savior."

In that moment, Pence became born again. He was now, in the loosest definition, an evangelical Christian. But that was a broad term for an amorphous world. Pence was just at the start of his religious journey.

Pence was stepping into a subculture with a deep vein in American history. He was removing himself from the regimented and hierarchical Catholic order and entering a world that was at once freewheeling in its interpretations and centered on taking the Bible quite literally. Pence had not only converted to becoming an evangelical Christian, he had joined the ranks of the blossoming Fundamentalist movement.

THE DISPENSATIONS

A century earlier, Darwin's theory of evolution, the Scopes Monkey Trial, and the public acceptance of reason and science created a conundrum for some Christians. The mainline denominations and their hierarchies, the Presbyterians, Methodists, northern Baptists, and other Protestant branches sought to square the new science of evolution with God's word in the Bible—perhaps seven days of creation meant seven eons of cosmic development. But another branch of Christianity emerged, one dedicated to the old ways of reading the Bible, literally. In 1909, the founder of Union Oil, Lyman Stewart, published what he called the five Fundamentals of Christianity: The

Bible is the literal message from God and is infallible as a result. Jesus Christ is the son of God. Christ was a real person in human history, not a parable, and the miracle of his virgin birth is real. Christ's real death on the cross stands in as atonement for the broader sins of humanity in the eyes of God, and Christ's resurrection was real. And, finally, Christ will return in person on earth and usher in the end of the world, God's final judgment on all humanity.

That final tenet, the belief in Jesus's literal return to earth, in the flesh, and the resulting End of the World, is derived from a very distinct brand of Christianity dating back a century earlier: Dispensationalists. The name came from the seven eras, or "dispensations," of human history that followers said were outlined in the Bible. Like many things related to the Bible, the finer details were greatly debated, but one thing was not: the seventh and final dispensation was marked by Jesus's return to Earth, the final judgment by God, and the end of the world. Stewart made it a key ingredient of Fundamentalism and, by 1924, it was ensconced in religious academia via the creation of the Dallas Theological Seminary and also the Asbury Theological Seminary, which hosted the Christian music festival where Pence converted.

For years the split between mainline denominations and the Fundamentalists remained a theological battle, limited largely to church hierarchy and theologians. But the Scopes Monkey Trial forced it into the open, and after the Fundamentalists lost, they were driven underground. They retreated from mainstream culture. They built their own universities, their own seminaries, even their own publishers. And for close to fifty years they worked quietly, away from the world.

Throughout the '50s and '60s, pop culture learned about evangelical Christianity from another source, someone slightly removed from the world of Fundamentalism: Billy Graham. Graham's massive crusades—the modern update of tent revivals, where he would save thousands of people in stadiums and arenas—shied away from the theological scraps that had driven Fundamentalists from the mainstream.

He was more concerned with winning over souls, no matter what flavor of Christianity they chose.

But little by little new threats from the mainstream world, liberalizing attitudes in postwar America, coaxed them back into the public arena. The nuclear family began falling apart, divorce numbers grew. Drug use expanded. And gay men and women slowly, cautiously, began coming out in public. Even the courts themselves seemed aligned against them. In 1962, the U.S. Supreme Court banned mandatory prayer in public school classrooms, and in 1963 it ruled that mandatory Bible readings were a violation of the First Amendment's promise of free exercise. Finally, in 1973, the Supreme Court—the philosopher kings of the secular world—legalized abortion. All of this, Fundamentalists believed, was evidence that the very fabric of civilized society was ripping apart.

Finally, after decades in seclusion, they were ready to reemerge. All they needed was the right kind of push.

ENTER THE DOOMSDAY PROPHETS

In 1979, the political activists at the center of the country's burgeoning conservative movement took a road trip from Washington down to Central Virginia, near the foothills of the Appalachian Mountains. Paul Weyrich, Morton Blackwell, and a few others went to meet with a popular Fundamentalist leader, Jerry Falwell. They were looking for, as Blackwell put it, "virgin timber" for their political movement. Falwell was a Fundamentalist evangelical force—he created one of the nation's largest megachurches and started a K-12 school and college dedicated to teaching Fundamentalism. As they sat with Falwell, Weyrich beckoned to the legions of evangelical Christians, "Out there is what one might call a moral majority." Falwell loved that, thus beginning the formal wedding of Fundamentalists and the political conservative movement. Falwell cribbed the name "Moral Majority."

The nascent coupling got its first chance to test their power with the 1980 race—Falwell, Pat Robertson, and other prominent televangelists, including a Southern California pastor named Tim LaHaye, pushed their flock to abandon the evangelical Christian in the race, Jimmy Carter, and embrace the film celebrity who had been married twice, Ronald Reagan.

Robertson, Falwell, LaHaye, and others didn't talk about it much in their political discourse, but their preaching was filled with a dark threat of doom and hellfire that fueled their viewers (and their donations) with stunning power. They often focused on the fifth of Lyman Stewart's five Fundamentals, the physical return of Jesus Christ, and the End of the World.

Jerry Falwell wrote "Nuclear War and the Second Coming of Jesus Christ," a pamphlet explaining, for the layperson, how the world would end. On the cover are the Greek letters Alpha and Omega—a reference to Jesus's declaration to John of Patmos in the Book of Revelation, "Behold, I am coming quickly, and my reward is with me, to give to each one according to what he has done. I am the Alpha and the Omega, the first and the last, the beginning and the end."

The biblical eras, or dispensations, were clear, Falwell explained: Two thousand years of "the Church," the reign of religion and the saving of souls for God, contrasted against the work of Satan, spreading confusion and sin. Then, God would rapture his saved into heaven—they would disappear without a trace from the earth, leaving a terrible battle for all that were left behind. Russia would invade Israel, the anti-Christ would arise as a new global leader, the Roman Empire would be rebuilt, God would scald the earth with his judgments—fire and demons would devour the unfaithful. Then the forces of the anti-Christ, their heads marked with the symbol 666, would march on the Holy Land in the Battle of Armageddon. At the final moment, Jesus Christ himself would return through the East Gate of the city of Jerusalem and lead his people to victory. Then Jesus would reign in person, for one thousand years, over a great peace on earth in which even the wildest animals would be as docile as a regular house pet. At the end of one thousand years, God would cleanse the earth a final time—not with water, because he had promised Noah no more floods, but with fire. The fire, Falwell offered, could easily be a nuclear bombing.

Falwell closed his pamphlet by offering a prayer: recite and it will save your soul—you will be raptured and not suffer through the great Tribulation of man. And then mail the attached coupon back to him, in Lynchburg, Virginia, so he can know you've come into the flock.

This was Falwell's own take on the End of the World theology, also called Dispensationalism. Among Dispensationalists, there was great debate and divergence over how and when the world would end, and Jesus would return. And whether Christians should hasten that biblical climax. But certain tenets were clear, for one: Jewish control of Jerusalem must be restored, the temple of King Solomon rebuilt a third time and all Christians and Muslims expelled from the holy city to bring Jesus's return, and the end of the world.

Robertson, another Fundamentalist preacher from Virginia, built a Fundamentalist broadcasting empire starting with "The 700 Club" and the Christian Broadcasting Network. He drew in millions from their living rooms. In a 1980 broadcast, he told his viewers precisely why Israel was so important to the Second Coming of Jesus. "According to my bible, the Jews must hold all of Jerusalem, or Jesus isn't coming back again." In real-world terms, this meant not carving the city in two and giving East Jerusalem to the Palestinians, he said. Robertson was angry at Jimmy Carter for allowing his diplomats and foreign policy aides to acquiesce, regardless the real-world consequences. "Jesus is coming, dependent on that. And I'm not going to let any of them hold him back."

Robertson and Falwell became the best-known faces of this new politicized Fundamentalist movement, but LaHaye would most successfully inject biblical prophecy into American pop culture more than a decade later.

The Next Step

If Pence believed in some of the wilder doomsday prophecies, he didn't show it. He had only been at Hanover a year and was just recently converted to evangelicalism—and the wild brand of Falwell and Robertson's religion had little to do with the festival where Pence was saved, according to his friends. Pence's new worldview fell more in line with Billy Graham–style crusades, itself an update of old American tent revivals. In this world, all that mattered was the ticket to entry, converting more souls to personally accepting Christ. The finer details, like whether individuals would consider themselves Fundamentalists or Modernists and whether they would subscribe to Dispensationalism, could be hashed out later. Salvation was the priority.

The bigger question was which side would Pence end up on—Graham or Falwell and Robertson? But it wouldn't be answered immediately. After all, he was still just eighteen years old and struggling to find his place around the school.

Hanover College was tucked away in the hills of Southern Indiana, near the Ohio River and more akin to rural Kentucky than agricultural Indiana in many ways. The mainline denomination churches of Columbus, Indiana, gave way to more fervent "low" churches that stripped away the trappings of religion and instilled more fire and spirituality. The First City Christian Church, designed by the Saarinens, gave way to the Point of Grace Family Praise Fellowship, a Pentecostal church, in nearby Madison; and Catholic churches all but disappeared in the deep countryside. Hanover was a conservative Presbyterian college, but it also was still a typical college, with typical college life. The student paper, the *Triangle*, covered the effort to let students drink on campus—Hanover was dry—and stayed hot on the trail of a male flasher who stalked women on campus. *The Amityville Horror* and *Doonesbury's Greatest Hits* topped the list of paperback sales on campus.

Pence kept up his cartooning, writing a regular strip for the student paper. His humor took on an edgier tone than he had in high school. In one strip, from that fall of 1978, a reporter corners the football coach to ask how he likes running the intramural league. The coach shrugs, saying, "Okay, man, but really, girls sports . . ." Just then, a giant, beefy arm cuts in the corner of the strip, dangling over the coach's head. In the next panel is the rest of the arm, attached to a beefy girl, who's livid. "WHAT?!" she yells, as she hoists the coach by his polo shirt. The coach tries to play it off, finishing, ". . . are probably the toughest on campus (gulp) . . . Isn't that right, Sylvia?"

In the group photo for Pence's fraternity, Phi Gamma Delta, Pence looked up from under his wavy-brown mop top and flashed the devil's horns with his right arm raised high. Not because he was a Satan worshipper, but because he liked rock. His fraternity, nicknamed the "Fijis," were considered to be one of the more staid fraternities on campus. They averaged a modest 3.14 GPA that year for the entire house, which was near the top of the pack—other frats and sororities on campus scored close to 2.8 GPAs on average.

But the Fijis weren't entirely bookish, and sometimes even came close to the iconic frat from *Animal House*. In the fall of 1978, they sat on probation for violating the school's strict rule against drinking. They had to deliver a presentation on "alcohol use and abuse across the country and at Hanover," and also develop a proposal of how they would police themselves. Shortly after Pence's frat pleaded their case to get off probation, Pence sketched a subversive comic strip for the paper, entitled "A Historical Note on the Alcohol Steering Committee"—it showed Thomas Jefferson presenting King George with the Declaration of Independence, followed by King George tearing it up. Pence ends the strip suggesting revolution, "Remember what they had to do?"

Later in his sophomore year, Pence was selected president of the Fijis. One day, his frat brothers rolled in a keg for a party, but the associate dean at the school found out. As the administrator stormed over,

Pence and his frat brothers hid the keg. Then Pence met the associate dean at the door . . . and he led him straight to the keg. Pence's close friend and frat brother, Dan Murphy, couldn't believe the guy who had advocated revolution just a few months earlier had ratted them out. "They really raked us over the coals," Murphy said. "The whole house was locked down."

By the fall of 1979, his junior year, Pence rose to another leadership role, as one of the lead students directing Vespers. He no longer appeared in the photos with his other brothers in the Fijis and instead grew more active in Vespers. Now it was freshmen looking up to him, the same way he used to look up to John Gable. A small group of girls sat in the grass with him as he discussed religion, wearing a visor and a T-shirt from the 1979 Ichthus Music Festival. Pence led the small group each year on an annual retreat to Ichthus, but not every student felt the same deep, personal experience that Pence discovered there in 1978. "Vespers provides a warm atmosphere where Christians and non-Christians can together explore the challenge of walking in the light of God's presence and love," wrote the editors of *Revonah*, the school's yearbook. "Prayer, sharing, and singing praises are integral parts of the unique and special ministry that enables its participants to gain a deeper understanding of their relationship to God and others."

Pence laid out his leadership of the group for the student paper, "Basically what we are seeking to do is draw closer to God and to each other through Jesus Christ," he said. "I originally went because I was checking things out, but at the first meeting I saw a girl that I was interested in asking out, so I kept going in hopes of seeing her again. . . . I can see now that God used that motivation to bring me back to the fellowship that played a big part in bringing me to Christ."

Falwell's Moral Majority stormed the Republican Party in the spring of 1980. They won coveted delegate seats in state party conventions across the country—including taking over Alaska's state Republican Party almost entirely—guaranteeing them formal seats at the tables of power.

Falwell, the Moral Majority leader, had prayed privately with Reagan during the primaries over the spring and then endorsed him. At the top of Falwell's list of concerns was banning abortion, and Reagan promised he would fight to ban abortions. When a reporter asked about Reagan's previous support for abortion, when he was governor of California, Falwell dismissed any concerns: "I don't care what a man was. I care what he is."

As Reagan locked in the nomination, the GOP establishment called for George H. W. Bush on the ticket as a check and guarantee in the White House. But the new Moral Majority troops enlisted by the GOP viewed Reagan's former primary opponent with a deep mistrust. They and others on the right sought a purist, somebody who wouldn't bend on key issues like abortion. They launched a petition drive to get Representative Jack Kemp on the ticket. The new troops in the GOP were energetic, but also volatile, and unwilling to simply go along with the way things had been done in the past.

In his senior year, the fall of 1980, Pence signed up for an intensive U.S. history course with George M. Curtis III. For his final year of college, Curtis took Pence on a libertarian tour of U.S. history. That November Pence cast his first vote for president, for a good and tested evangelical, Jimmy Carter—"There was a sense of 'Why would you elect a movie star?'" Pence said. But Curtis showed him precisely why to take the actor over the evangelical. He introduced Pence to supply-side economics and conservative fiscal policy. "He showed me that day that Reagan wasn't a vacuous movie star." Curtis gave a clear model to Pence's personal philosophy of politics and governance. Curtis said Pence came to Republicanism and conservatism naturally, "People latch on to the material. It isn't me." Pence, he said, latched on to two key principles: constitutional integrity and rule of law. Pence may have voted for Carter, but he now had a name for his ideology, conservative, and a political home, the Republican Party.

It didn't hurt that Reagan also won the election on November 4,

1980, in spectacular fashion—he crushed Carter, 489–49 on the electoral map, winning all but six states. Reagan was now the hero of the conservative movement and a new, amicable face, for Republicans—a fresh look after the pockmarked presidency of Richard Nixon. And, even more important, Reagan carried the imprimatur of the Moral Majority and conservative evangelicals everywhere. "When I accepted your nomination for president, I asked for your prayers at the moment," Reagan said in his brief victory speech. "I won't ask for them in this particular moment, but I will just say I would be very happy to have them in the days ahead."

On December 14, 1980, Pence turned in a senior thesis for Curtis examining the nexus of religion and the very foundation of the Republican Party, Abraham Lincoln. The paper, "The Religious Expressions of Abraham Lincoln," was long-winded and plodding, with a careful approach to the research but an apprehension to come to clear conclusions. Pence, at times, marveled at Lincoln's lack of religiosity and the very first Republican president's unwillingness to wear religion on his sleeve. Pence opened by quoting Lincoln's longtime law partner, William Herndon, "'Probably except in his scrapes, Lincoln never poured out his soul to any mortal creature at any time and on no subject.'" Pence then wrote, "The religious beliefs of Abraham were no more static than they were easily discernible." Indeed, Pence did a fairly exhaustive review of Lincoln's statements about faith and religion and came away with a man who was reserved, skeptical of organized religion, and highly sensitive to the power of religion in politics.

As much as Pence tried to crack Lincoln, he seemed to reveal more in the thirty-seven-page thesis about his own struggle to decide who he was. Pointing to Lincoln's start in politics, in the mid-1830s, Pence recounted how Lincoln almost published an essay skeptical of Christianity. "The essay included a defense of the ideas that the Bible was not God's inspired word nor Jesus God's son," Pence wrote. "The essay was quietly destroyed by his friend and employer, Samuel Hill, who recognized the impropriety of a young man harbouring such unsavory ideas." But a few years later, Pence wrote, "Lincoln proceeded in his own style of faith." Pence noted Lincoln's "defensive posture" when talking about his personal religion in public. In his retelling, Lincoln comes across as agnostic and almost liberal in his religious leanings. When the wife of a Confederate soldier wrote directly to Lincoln seeking his pardon because he is a religious man, Lincoln tersely replied: "The religion that sets men to rebel and fight against their government, because as they think, that government does not sufficiently help some men to eat their bread on the sweat of other men's facts is not the sort of religion on upon which people get to heaven."

By the end of the paper, and of Lincoln's life, Pence finds a man who grudgingly came to accept Christianity after three decades of wrangling with it in private and public. Pence had come to conservative Republicanism easily, but his religious journey would bear some of the same struggles Lincoln expressed.

Pence graduated from Hanover College in the spring of 1981. That May, he delivered the student address at graduation. Wearing his black graduation gown and oversized square reading glasses, with a mop of dark brown hair, Pence called on his fellow graduates to "get even" with their past, in other words repay their debts—to their hometowns, their families, and their schools, especially Hanover. Despite not being active in many activities and groups around campus, like student government, or having the most stellar grades, Pence won the speaking slot by submitting his speech to a panel of students and school administrators. They picked his out of a batch of other students. He was known around campus as the speech champion of Columbus, Indiana. He also shared the stage with President Ronald Reagan's national security adviser, Richard Allen, who delivered the commencement address. Pence was ready to enter the world. He had a girlfriend, a freshman he met at Vespers. But he broke up with her as he prepared to leave college. He considered applying to the priesthood and studying at Catholic University in Washington.

He was also eyeing law school. Given the choice between priesthood and law school, Pence family patriarch Ed Pence urged Mike Pence to go to law school. After graduating, Pence met with priests leading the archdiocese of Indianapolis, to consider joining the priesthood. But he decided against it, citing his desire to raise a family of his own someday.

Pence took the LSATs and applied to Indiana University's law school in Indianapolis, but his scores were terrible. Dejected, he stuck around at Hanover College helping recruit potential students. He traversed the state meeting with high school students, trying to get them to attend his alma mater. He stayed in Madison, Indiana, but did not seem to be getting any closer to his goal of attending law school.

Shortly after graduation, Mike's grandfather and namesake, Richard Michael Cawley, died. Cawley, who had plucked Pence out from the raucous pack formed by his three other brothers and taken him under his wing, was gone. Pence recounted later, "He got off the boat an Irish lad, he died an American, and I am an American because of him." His grandfather's death struck him, just as he was trying to figure out his path in life. Pence had undergone many conversions in the last four years, but he still struggled to find his own identity. So he flew to Ireland in search of his ancestry with one of his cousins, Trish Tamler. He traveled to Doocastle, the village in rural County Mayo that Richard Michael Cawley had left six decades earlier. Tamler said the experience was very emotional for Pence.

After he returned, Pence retook the LSATs, and this time scored well enough to be accepted to IU's law school. He moved north, to the big city, in 1983. Indianapolis was a sleepy city when compared with most other American metropolises at the time, but it was the center of action for the state. Pence moved into a small white house on Pennsylvania Street (he would sometimes joke about his residence, the white house on Pennsylvania).

Pence went to night school; the cool kids went to day school, and their paths rarely crossed with his. But Pence had a small cadre of close friends, fellow born-again Christians. They would stay up all night discussing law, philosophy, politics, faith. But his philosophizing was soon waylaid by love.

Karen Batten was just two years older than Mike Pence but had already been through a lifetime of experience by the time they met in 1983. She grew up in Indianapolis and went to college nearby at Butler University. She had married her college beau, Steve Whitaker—the son of an Eli Lilly Company executive—in a ceremony in Big Bend, Texas, in 1978. It was not a bad marriage, but it was a listless one that seemed to lack passion. Karen followed Steve to Seattle as he studied medicine, but after a few years they separated and eventually divorced. She returned home to Indianapolis.

Karen Sue Batten and Michael Richard Pence were made for each other—their personalities were a yin and yang: he was a pleaser and she was a "bulldog," as he once put it. But their shared experiences dovetailed—sometimes in very deep ways. Karen Batten had survived the regimen of Catholic high school in Indianapolis. Pence had suffered the wrath of the nuns at St. Columba's school in Columbus. He was a speech club champion—and she was a speech club champion. She was a lifelong Catholic now questioning her church, but not her faith. And he was a lifelong Catholic who felt a pull to something deeper in the evangelical movement. When they first met in the summer of 1983, she was playing guitar at St. Thomas Aquinas Church in Indianapolis, one of the city's most liberal Catholic churches. Heck, Pence played guitar, too.

Their romance was intense, purposeful, and almost immediate. Pence quickly discovered that Karen's sister was also attending IU law school, so in a unique show of reportorial style he called the registrar's office for the sister's number. He finagled the information from a skeptical university secretary and called Karen's sister at home. To his surprise, it was Karen who picked up the phone instead—she was babysitting her niece and nephew. Pence immediately recognized her voice and hung up without saying a word.

Then he called her back.

A few days later he came by for a dinner of taco salad. A few days after that they went ice-skating at the Pepsi Coliseum at the Indianapolis fairgrounds. The connection was clear. As they fell deeper in love, Karen said to him, "Oh, you're my number one." And Mike stopped her, bluntly, "You know, I'm probably going to disappoint you if you make me number one in your life." He was referring to Jesus, that God was the number one figure in his life. But he was also referring to their basic humanity, Karen recalled, that neither one of them could be perfect and that they should be understanding and accepting of their human failings.

Karen's niece and nephew made a bet that the two lovebirds would get married. Karen sensed the same thing and prepared her answer, etched on a golden cross necklace: "Yes." Mike asked a few months later, on a stroll along the canal that runs through the center of Indianapolis. He brought two loaves of bread to feed the ducks, hollowing out one loaf and placing a box with the ring inside. The second he also hollowed out and placed a small split of champagne, with the hope that his question would be answered positively. They married in June 1985 at a Catholic church near the Indianapolis Motor Speedway.

Pence had been a modest partyer during his stag life, but that all washed away after he met Karen. She took the young man with deeply philosophical views of politics and religion and lofty ambitions and focused him in a way that had been missing until that point. She pointed him on a path to making his dreams of being a politician, maybe even president, real. That path started with an important step: graduating from law school, getting a good job, and starting their family. He had just one more year of law school, and then, if everything went to plan, he'd land a serious job at a big firm and, God willing, Karen would be pregnant.

The year after his marriage, from 1985 to 1986, set the course for his political career, gingerly and methodically. Pence worked under the tutelage of a legendary Indiana professor known for rearing big-name Republicans, Professor William Harvey. Harvey had mentored Mitch Daniels, the ambitious chief of staff to Dick Lugar; he mentored U.S. Senator Dan Quayle when he was in school; and he mentored Quayle's chief of staff, Dan Coats. Harvey was a curator of Republican talent but found his own success blocked by partisanship—he was nominated to a judgeship on the influential Seventh Circuit Court of Appeals by Ronald Reagan but was rejected by the Democratic-held Senate. The experience led to some bitterness from his mentees, who said partisan politics derailed a good man.

Pence also kept up his cartooning with a strip for the student paper *Law Daze*, with a similar everyman theme from his strips in high school and college. Pence's drawing skills had improved a good bit since high school—his characters were more emotive and more consistent—but his humor was still a bit flat.

Paul Ogden, a classmate and editor of the paper, saw Pence every now and then at the school paper. One of Pence's buddies in the Christian Legal Society was running for student president against Ogden. That spring of 1986, Pence turned in his latest strip to Ogden; it was a screed against a William Randolph Hearst–style news baron with a penchant for yellow journalism. It was a screed against Ogden himself! Surprised, Ogden ran the cartoon anyway. Ogden later beat Pence's friend in the election.

A few months later, when Pence graduated from law school, the student election spat didn't matter much; he was on his way to a much bigger goal. He had a job working under Clarence Doninger at a respected Indianapolis law firm—it wasn't exactly blue chip, but it could take him to blue chip status if he toughed it out. The problem he faced, though, was he wasn't bringing in any business. "He wasn't serious about it," recalled a friend. "It didn't feel like he put his whole self into the law."

His work on the outside was the early makings of Pence's political career. When he wasn't lawyering—which was often—he was pounding the ground meeting Republican power players around Indianapolis. However, the politicking didn't pay the bills, so the couple would have to live off Karen's teacher's salary.

THE GRAND OL' PARTY

Indiana, for more than a century, was a rock-ribbed Republican mainstay, but it always maintained a tinge of the South to it. In the middle of the Civil War, Republican governor Oliver Perry Morton directed the Republican members of the state legislature to prepare to decamp to Kentucky—a parliamentary gambit designed to keep Indiana in the Union. That bit of Indiana history, among other events—like a steady, unmitigated run of Ku Klux Klan activity throughout the state well after the turn of the twentieth century—led some local observers to dub Indiana "The South's Middle Finger to the North," a rectangular digit of a protrusion that juts clean into the Rust Belt.

Indiana's position between the South and the Rust Belt also spurred another distinction—"The Mother of Vice Presidents." The state became a favorite for successful presidential candidates who needed some regional and political balance in their ticket to win the White House. As a bridge between the old Democratic South and the emerging Republican Midwest, Indiana was a critical swing state in elections through the mid to late 1800s and the early 1900s—and both parties went to the well there about once every thirty years. Republican Schuyler Colfax joined former Union general Ulysses Grant in office in 1867. In 1885, Thomas Hendricks joined Democrat Grover Cleveland (though Hendricks died just eight months after inauguration). In 1905, Hoosier Charles Fairbanks ran with Republican icon Theodore Roosevelt (although Fairbanks was a conservative, selected by the delegates of the 1904 Republican convention and who often fought the progressive policies of Roosevelt). And eight years later, in 1913, Thomas Marshall joined Woodrow Wilson's ticket. (Marshall, acting as Senate president, created the rule allowing for two-thirds of the senators to vote to end filibusters.)

But by 1986, Indiana had entered a dry spell in filling national tickets—a mark as much of the country's massive shifts in demographics and politics since the turn of the century as the Republican Party's own shift away from a patrician party more aligned with the North to a more conservative party guided by Nixon's allegiance with the old Democratic South. Indiana, it seemed, was no longer a swing state able to offer much to presidential contenders.

But the robust Indiana GOP machine still offered innumerable opportunities for young politicians, like Pence, climbing the ladder. Pence had a late start, trailing most of his peers in the arena by a few years—his life and career didn't come into focus until after he met Karen—but the machine still offered ample opportunity. Republican governor Robert Orr and U.S. Senator Richard Lugar brought up dozens of operators under their wing—the most famous among Lugar's young charges was a brilliant strategist named Mitch Daniels. And they could all thank the father of modern Indiana Republican politics for those jobs, Marion County GOP boss Keith Bulen.

But another Hoosier was cutting a new path for young politicos, a new style of candidate-centered politics and away from the old GOP machine politics. James Danforth Quayle—a scion of the Pulliam newspaper family—skipped the line in his first run for Congress. The big Republican brains in Washington gave him and his wife, Marilyn, a pamphlet telling him he'd have to get in line behind other veteran politicos. Marilyn Quayle took the pamphlet and tossed it in the trash, and Dan Quayle was elected to Congress in 1977. A few years later, Quayle picked off Indiana's long-serving senator Birch Bayh, becoming the youngest U.S. senator ever elected from the state. Quayle aide Greg Zoeller recalled, "It was expected you would work your way through politics, but it was starting to change."

Yet Pence fundamentally adhered to the old authority. His Catholic roots had instilled in him a respect for authority and conservative thinkers who championed order—he played by the old rules. So he went to work as precinct committeeman for the Indianapolis Republicans, the lowest foot soldier in the organization, because the best way to learn politics was still from the ground up. He represented his small college hamlet, Broad Ripple, a popular neighborhood where Karen grew up and close to Butler College. Mike and Karen lived together in a small house in Broad Ripple; she taught art at Acton Elementary School on the other side of the city.

Trailing behind his peers by a few years and new to professional politics, Pence started knocking on doors, meeting with everyone he could: How could he become a politician? "What does that mean? How do you get involved? Where do you start?" Pence asked one of his earliest advisers. "He studied up, and he was good at follow-through," the adviser said. "He's a good notetaker and he basically laid it out and tried to figure out what the next steps are." One acquaintance suggested he find Jeff Cardwell, the owner of a local hardware store and a prominent developer on the city's southside, who was tied in with the political brass. That summer of 1986, Pence and Cardwell met for lunch at the Dutch Oven, a local spot on the city's southside. Pence and Cardwell immediately hit it off; they were both young newlyweds, born-again Christians, and huge fans of Ronald Reagan. They talked at length about the 1986 tax reform package that Reagan was negotiating with congressional Democrats. By the end of lunch, Cardwell was convinced Pence should be in office. He agreed to plug Pence in.

Cardwell and some friends put on a modest fund raiser for the would-be politico—$25 a head, with coffee and pie. By the end of the fund raiser, Pence had in his corner a powerful group of local Republican all stars. What he didn't have, though, was a race toward which he could direct all that enthusiasm.

In 1986, Pence could afford to spend most of his time politicking—a job that didn't pay. He and his siblings all had substantial assets from when their father had sold several gas stations he owned around Columbus. Each sibling received close to $1 million—they weren't filthy rich, but they were better off than most. They each invested their money, socked it away for the future. Pence's closest friend, one of his frat brothers from college, Jay Steger, had invested most of Mike's share in a pair of privately held companies—an effort by an aggressive young stockbroker to diversify Pence's holdings. Then both companies went belly-up, and Mike and Karen Pence lost almost all the inheritance.

They were crushed, but what could they do, other than keep going?

The following year, Toby McClamroch, a young deputy in the Indianapolis GOP machine, went around the city trying to line up support for a run at the state senate. He set meetings with all one hundred precinct committeemen, the foot soldiers and activists who comprised the gears and girders of the party. In the fall of 1987, with just a few months left before the 1988 Republican primary, McClamroch met with the precinct committeeman for the Broad Ripple neighborhood, Mike Pence. They went out to lunch and like a good politician seeking a voter's support, McClamroch spent the meeting asking about Pence's own plans for the future.

Pence did have some plans. In the long run he wanted to move back to Columbus after a few years and run for Congress representing his hometown. McClamroch smiled and he told Pence that the Indianapolis Republicans had been desperate for a candidate to take on the Democrat representing Indiana's Second District in Congress. The district pulled in Pence's hometown of Columbus and also a slice of Indianapolis. McClamroch gave Pence the phone number for John Sweezy, the Indianapolis GOP chair. McClamroch then dialed up Sweezy and said, "This guy is going to call you and is sharp as can be and you need to convince him to run for Congress." Sweezy then called Virgil Scheidt, the GOP chairman for Bartholomew County, which included Columbus. Sweezy told him they had a sacrificial lamb for the Second District. Scheidt was on board.

Pence called Sweezy just a few hours after his meeting with McClamroch, and the very next day Pence walked up to Sweezy's office on the second floor of the Indianapolis GOP headquarters. Sweezy, a rotund chain-smoker with a slightly unkempt beard, didn't say much in his meetings with would-be candidates. But he did call the shots, and he liked Pence. He told Pence he was their guy for the Second District.

That next weekend, Mike and Karen went looking for a new house, one inside the Second District.

CHAPTER 3

CANDIDATE SCHOOL—1988

A century earlier, the Ball brothers of Buffalo, New York, went prospecting for new natural gas fields to fuel their glass jar business. The small towns that speckled north-central Indiana had only recently discovered they sat on top of an abundant natural gas reserve. To advertise their newfound bounty, town fathers drove pipes into the ground, sticking straight up into the sky—then they lit the top on fire, a perpetual beacon to all manufacturers that they were open for business. In the 1880s, the Ball family moved their glass-making business to Muncie, Indiana, and underpinned a boom in work and manufacturing for the small town. Forty years later they helped revive the old teachers college there, which became Ball State University. The unionized workforce that filled their plants elected Democrats to office, but the Ball family were patrician Republicans through and through.

When Indiana's mapmakers drew up the Second District, they

pulled in pieces that Mike Pence knew all about—a slice of Indianapolis where he and Karen had just bought a house, a swath of Columbus, his hometown. But what he didn't know about was the biggest voting center in the entire district, the one that consistently returned a Democrat to office year after year and was the bane of the GOP: Muncie.

In some ways Muncie was very much like Columbus—both cities were manufacturing spokes on the wheel that ringed Indianapolis— and the blue-collar workers of Cummins engine-maker in Columbus were very much like the UAW members cranking out parts for Chevy and BorgWerner in Muncie. And each spoke on the manufacturing wheel—Columbus to the south, Muncie to the northeast, Kokomo to the north, and others—provided enough well-paying jobs to build a thriving middle class throughout the state.

But as Pence entered the arena in the mid-'80s, Muncie's manufacturing was hollowing out—global trade and opening of markets, combined with a buccaneer corporate mentality in the upper echelons of Wall Street, left more American companies decamping and more foreign competition invading. Pence's hometown clipped along just fine, due to the work of forward-looking town fathers like Irwin Miller who invested heavily in global and advanced manufacturing. But Columbus was the exception and Muncie was more of the rule.

By 1987, as Sweezy drafted Pence to run to represent Muncie, the town neared its dusk. The earth began reclaiming unused buildings, weeds and vines poked through barren asphalt—in time they would engulf entire plants and abandoned warehouses. But the old teachers' college the Ball family had propped up hummed along, and a certain young academic there was about to collide with Pence.

SHARP POLITICS

U.S. representative Phil Sharp had represented the Second District in Congress since 1974; he was a "Watergate Baby," part of the wave of

Democrats swept in after Nixon resigned. He was lean, aquiline, and professorial with big glasses and a cool demeanor. Sharp earned his master's in foreign service from Georgetown University in 1964, then spent two years studying at Oxford University in England. He spent the late 1960s working for Senator Vance Hartke, a conservative Midwest Democrat, and eventually joined the faculty at Ball State, teaching political science. Like Pence, he was young when he launched his political career—in his late twenties—and by the time he took office he was married and had a new baby. Sharp had to run twice, unsuccessfully, before a wave carried him into office on his third try.

The Watergate scandal may have swept him into office, but staying there meant fighting constantly in a district that nominally held an edge for Republican voters. For a dozen years, Sharp beat back a retinue of Republican challengers with strong constituent work and a natural Hoosier aversion to raw partisanship. The Ball family heirs spent decades seeking strong Republican candidates to buck the union voting force—but Sharp bested every one of them. Through the late '70s and early '80s, Sharp trounced perennial Republican scrapper Bill Frazier. In 1982, former Shelbyville mayor Ralph VanNatta fell. In 1984, the Ball family tapped their company's own spokesman, Ken MacKenzie—he came within six percentage points of toppling Sharp. In 1986, Sharp defeated an unknown Republican challenger named Don Lynch by more than 22 points. As the 1988 race approached, the Republicans didn't have anyone, until Pence walked into Sweezy's office. ✿

NEWT'S CAMPAIGN SCHOOL

Paul Ogden, the old editor of the law school student paper, bumped into Pence on a flight out to Washington in 1987. They were both heading to the Republican Party's campaign school, a training boot camp for would-be politicos and operatives. The campaign school was the brainchild of a wily, but blustery congressman from Georgia,

Newt Gingrich, and his right-hand man, Joe Gaylord. Gingrich had taken over GOPAC, a political group launched by former Delaware governor Pete DuPont, after DuPont launched his White House bid in 1988.

Like Sharp, Gingrich ran twice unsuccessfully, in 1974 and 1976, on a liberal good government platform. And he lost twice to a conservative Democrat. By 1978, he changed his stripes and ran against his Democratic opponent with a simple message: "She's too liberal." It worked and he won a ticket to Washington. And when he got there, he kept up that strategy. Gingrich felt that the GOP would remain a permanent minority in the House as long as they followed decorum and gentlemanly conduct, so he dispensed with all of that. The *Washington Post* cataloged the best of Gingrich: House Democratic leaders formed a "trio of muggers," the Iran Contra hearings became a "left-wing lynch mob," and other Democrats were "sick."

Gingrich was easy to dismiss, because he was the odd man out among Republicans. The old establishment held the reins and maintained order under the direction of House Minority Leader Bob Michel. And Democrats maintained an insurmountable majority—through Reagan's eight years in office, they never held less than a fifty-seat lead in the House. The Gipper's popularity couldn't break the Democratic coalition of coastal liberals, Rust Belt populists, and heritage Democrats from the South. The dynamic generated the name "Reagan Democrats" for pockets of voters across the country.

But Gingrich and his GOPAC campaign school saw would-be Republican voters underneath the veneer of conservative Democrats. Gingrich, the ideas man, cooked up the strategy and Gaylord went searching for candidates to flip those House seats from Democrat to Republican. It could take years, maybe even decades. So they built a training camp, with its own training manual, *Flying Upside Down*—the essential guide to unseating Democrats using Gingrich's firebrand style of politics.

Under the heading "Fights Make News; Shyness Doesn't" they

wrote: "Republicans by nature are shy. And they tend to shy away from controversy." (This was certainly true of Pence—he'd have the occasional spat, like his comic strip blowing up Paul Ogden, but was generally affable.) "Frankly, some Republicans make the mistake of worrying too much about what friends and neighbors and the so-called country club set might think if they 'go negative' and get aggressive. . . . They discover they didn't have the stomach for confrontation and controversy, and, essentially give up the fight." Gingrich seemed to speak directly to young Pence, "To win, Republicans have to overcome their aversion to controversy and learn to take the fight to the other side."

Gaylord, meanwhile, groomed the young talent that flew into Washington—including Pence. "I was happy to see any warm-bodied candidates," Gaylord said dryly. Pence didn't exactly bowl people over with dynamism, bold thinking, or visionary declaration. But he did win powerful allies with an undefeatable smile, affability, and genuine warmth. And he knew what mattered to his audience in any given moment, including Gaylord. "Mike loved my book—so, of course, I loved him."

Pence flew back to Indiana with a campaign-in-a-box; he took his campaign manager, a youngish operative, Colin Chapman, from the Gingrich campaign school. He picked counsel from a short list of preapproved operatives and advisers. For polling, he took the shop run by Reagan's own pollster, Dick Wirthlin. For messaging, he took Arthur Finkelstein, who built a legendary career in the GOP labeling opponents as "too liberal." Pence left the strategy to the DC experts. He was more of a tactics guy. And, as it turned out, Mike Pence happened to be great at executing other people's plays.

Pence internalized the Gingrich campaign manual and ran a new Washington-style campaign, with tight, scripted messaging, big smiles, a polished look, and acidic attacks on Sharp. He accused Sharp of being in the pocket of "special interests" in Washington. He mirrored the attack-dog style of his Washington consultants, like

Arthur Finkelstein, "Many people just don't know how liberal he is," Pence said of Sharp.

But Pence faced a tougher opponent than Sharp: anonymity. Nobody knew his name, so, Pence began courting the press. He headed to the small newspaper offices in the basement of the statehouse—converted stables where legislators used to tether their horses for the day and journalists now hunkered. Pence walked up to the door of Doug Richardson, lead statehouse reporter for the Associated Press, and introduced himself. He handed Richardson his résumé, his political bona fides. Richardson flicked down the paper and stopped for a minute: "Mike, it looks like you've been living in Washington Township," which is well outside the Second Congressional District. Of course, he had, but Pence wasn't trying to highlight the fact that he just moved into the district a few months ago. So, he noted that he grew up in Columbus. Richardson reminded Pence that Columbus was largely represented by veteran Democratic representative Lee Hamilton. Richardson was tripping him up with facts and details, but Pence just wanted to get straight to the point: he was running for Congress and people oughta know about it.

Pence was clearly green, but he had help from Republicans dying to get rid of Sharp. GOP boss Sweezy pulled in national fund raiser Jeff Terp to help. Terp listened in on his fund-raising calls: Pence would spend an hour on the phone with each donor, talking about their lives and reminiscing—and never close the deal. Terp yanked him back and taught him the ropes: fifteen-minute phone calls and, just like *Glengarry Glen Ross*, remember your ABCs—always be closing. If Pence needed $2,000, ask for $4,000—$2,000 from him and $2,000 from the guy's wife. If the donor said yes to $1,000 and asked where to mail it, tell him you'll be in the neighborhood and can come by and pick it up.

Pence also went calling on would-be donors in person. On one of those door knocks he met Chuck Quilhot, an Indianapolis insurance salesman who was deeply plugged in with local and national political figures. Pence immediately connected with Quilhot and they talked for hours. Pence's core team of support came together nicely.

Pence's campaign apparatus was now firmly in place. But who was he exactly? Was he a Pat Robertson, religious Right social crusader? Dyed-in-the-wool Republican Party man, like George Bush? Conservative hard-liner? The answer, from Pence's Gingrich-trained campaign manager, was "I would say Mike characterizes himself more as a Hoosier." The reality was that Pence hadn't really thought through the details of his own image, how he wanted to present himself. That question seemed a tad ethereal given that he had only been running for office for a few months. But the civil war inside the GOP made it increasingly perilous to avoid taking sides.

Pat Robertson's Rumblings

After eight years of Reagan, the marriage of Fundamentalists with the GOP began fraying. Prominent leaders from within the movement had misgivings about whether politics was the right vehicle for what they wanted to accomplish. Falwell deputies who had come in at the very start of the Moral Majority, Cal Thomas and Ed Dobson, began moving away—even though they still firmly supported the goals and morals the group sought. Inside the movement, some leaders thought that by the embracing of political fund-raising and a pursuit of raw, terrestrial power, they had sacrificed their spiritual goals, even trying to replace the higher power of God. It was eight years after Reagan, their chosen warrior, had taken over, and not much had changed: abortion was still legal, drug use was up, and popular culture was promoting more and more debauchery with the rise of new powers like MTV.

The Christian Right was also racked by scandal. One of their own, televangelist Jim Bakker, had been accused of cheating on his wife with a twenty-one-year-old church secretary, Jessica Hahn. He then used money from parishioners to silence Hahn. Robertson, of

The 700 Club and Christian Broadcasting Network, decided that their failing was putting their political hopes in a vessel, in a professional politician. So in 1987, Robertson announced he would run for president himself.

Vice President George H. W. Bush had the backing of Reagan, but Bush's claim to the Reagan mantle wasn't strong enough to clear the Republican field. Senate Republican leader Bob Dole was in, so was veteran GOP ideas man Jack Kemp. Robertson ran to the right of all of them, the very embodiment of Fundamentalist ideals. Dole and Robertson both bested Bush in Iowa, coming in first and second place, respectively. Bush carried the patrician and establishment stronghold, New Hampshire, one week later, but Dole placed surprisingly well. The Republican base did not seem all that excited about Bush. Dole won a trio of contests in the Upper Midwest the following week, and Robertson won contests in Alaska and Hawaii. But the swarm of primaries that hit in March, necessitating a national campaign operation that only Bush had, tilted the playing field away from the upstarts. By the end of March 1988, Dole bowed out and endorsed Bush. But Robertson refused to leave.

That April 1988, Robertson flew into Indianapolis with a stark message: AIDS was God's punishment for the sins of homosexuality and drug use. Despite Robertson's assertion, Indiana already had an important role in disproving that attack. Ronald Reagan's eleventh-hour decision to address the health crisis was driven, in part, by a young boy from Kokomo, Indiana. Doctors diagnosed thirteen-year-old Ryan White with AIDS after he was admitted to the hospital with pneumonia. Teachers and parents at his middle school refused to attend school with him. White, they said, would infect them and their children.

In an instant, White became proof that the HIV/AIDS crisis was something far more pandemic. White was a hemophiliac, and he had contracted the disease from a tainted batch of blood. By the end of 1985, White had become the public face of the AIDS crisis.

Robertson marshaled the forces who stuck to the smiting argument, when he rallied at the Murat Shrine Theatre in Indianapolis. Inside, he promised that he was there to "make America great again," conspicuously nabbing Reagan's own campaign slogan for himself. "When you read about it, we realize that 92 percent of those who have the disease in this country are either male homosexuals or intravenous drug users. Both of those practices are unnatural and wrong," Robertson told his supporters. "Those of us in our population—240 million who are healthy and want to stay alive—have a far greater right than the sexual privacy of a few people who contracted AIDS. AIDS does not have civil rights."

The yells of Robertson and the Christian Right became louder than ever, but Pence was not yet aligned with them. He never had to pick a side, so he didn't. Like the Abraham Lincoln he detailed at length in his senior thesis at Hanover College, Pence didn't blend his religion and politics. He also had more immediate concerns than choosing sides in the GOP's civil war. The Republican primary for Indiana's Second District was one month away.

His dad, Ed Pence, had initially balked at Mike's run for Congress, contending that he was too green. But as Pence built his campaign, Ed became one of his son's biggest supporters. The GOP machine did a good job clearing the field for him; he had a nominal opponent from Greenwood, Indiana, but Pence had his eyes firmly trained on Sharp. But then, on April 13, 1988, on the golf course at the Harrison Lake Country Club in Columbus, Edward Pence died of a heart attack. He was only fifty-eight. Mike Pence was crushed. But he wouldn't quit; Mike knew he had to carry through. A few weeks later, Pence rolled over Ray Schwab, his Republican primary opponent, 71 percent to 29 percent. His first victory was tinged with sorrow, but it was still resounding. Mike Pence was now officially the Republican nominee for Indiana's Second Congressional District.

He promised a gentlemanly bout with Sharp in the general election fight. "This will not be a nasty, or mean-spirited campaign," Pence said. "We are going to take hard, clean punches at the man and what he has done in Congress. I hope to engage him as soon as possible." Just two days later, Phil Sharp sent one of his congressional staffers to Columbus to meet with constituents, a hint that Sharp planned to use the power of incumbency and his political savvy against the young GOP upstart. Sharp's campaign sensed danger, "For the first time in several years the opposition has a very reasonable and seemingly articulate candidate running against Phil."

THE SHARP EDGE

Joe Gaylord couldn't believe how strong Sharp's hold on the district was. He ran a focus group and tested an easy issue for conservative Indiana—Did Second District voters support the death penalty? They overwhelmingly said, "Yes." But when they learned that Sharp opposed the death penalty, they changed their tune. "Because people liked Sharp, whatever position he took, they could figure out a justification," Gaylord said. He'd hit the bedrock of Sharp's support: fourteen years of building strong relationships across the district. Sharp worked the ground hard, showing up at town halls and running a strong constituent service operation. Sharp was used to fighting for his life in every election, making him a nonstop campaigner and sensitive to his standing with Republicans.

With danger on the horizon, Sharp called in one of those chits. "As a conservative Republican representing Texas's Twenty-Sixth District, reducing the deficit while maintaining a strong and efficient national defense has long been one of my concerns," wrote U.S. representative Dick Armey, a staunch conservative, in a letter of support for Sharp. "Our success is proof that Republicans and Democrats can come together and put the national interest ahead of parochial interest."

Pence, meanwhile, still faced down the hurdle of anonymity. The Sharp campaign found out that 87 percent of voters said they either couldn't rate Pence or didn't know who he was. Sharp's polling team then asked the voters who could at least remember Pence's name where he stood on the issues—90 percent said they just didn't know. "Promoting family values?"—Dunno. "Holding down taxes?"—Dunno. "Reducing the budget deficit?"—Dunno. "Dealing with unfair foreign trade practices?"—Dunno.

Mike Pence?—Dunno.

Pence had to whip up some attention for himself and controversy for Sharp, so he proposed ten debates, in a pithy letter to Sharp. "I understand that with the time you spend in Washington, you rarely have the opportunity to return to the Second District." Sharp sent a patrician rebuttal on May 27: "Congratulations on your nomination. I look forward to debating with you during the fall campaign. It has always been my policy to do so."

Pence may have slashed at Sharp in the media, but he cut a different figure on the circuit of campaign stops and small fund raisers. He was personable and present and took his time with each potential voter. Karen joined him on most stops after she wrapped up teaching each day. They came up with a novel trick to gin up some interest: they would bike across the district to meet voters. Pence pulled out a fixed-gear bicycle and Karen got hers. He put on a short-sleeved, checked button-down shirt, shorts, sneakers, and tube socks. And a Mike Pence for Congress sticker. And Pence, the former fat kid in school, got on his bike and began pedaling down the highway.

John Schorg, a reporter for the *Columbus Republic*, biked with the Pences from Winchester, Indiana, near the Ohio border, down State Highway 27 to Richmond. "What on earth provokes a man to: go out on a day when the thermometer is scraping the 100-degree mark; decide to ride a bicycle; and make such a trip down state highways, complete with semis operating at full throttle, dust flying and leather-lunged motorists yelling, 'Get the hell outta the way, you knothead!'?"

Schorg reported that Pence biked 261 miles—broken into twenty- to twenty-five-mile segments. Mike Pence, on his retro, decidedly unfancy ride, was just what the farmers of Indiana's Second District were looking for, he figured—the perfect contrast to one of those high-gloss Washington politicians. "I think people respond well to someone who comes riding along down the street, straddling a bicycle," Pence said. Karen pedaled along with the team, faithfully. At every stop, Mike Pence shook hands, chatted briefly, and put on his best show. And Karen did hers, standing quietly by his side, smiling but hardly saying a word.

On the ground, Pence was in his element, earnest, steady, and genuine. All he had to do was walk over, shake hands, and say, "Hi, I'm Mike Pence. I'm running for Congress." But working the ground as a nice guy and packing the air with attacks created a perplexing duality.

Ryan Streeter earned $150 a month to drive Pence everywhere, between small towns, on country roads from campaign stops to fund raisers. The two became fast friends talking theology and politics. Streeter appreciated that Pence could talk for hours, in deep, meaningful conversations, with almost whoever he was engaging. Pence in turn marveled at Streeter's ability to recall and recite Bible verse. Mike and Karen identified as evangelical Catholics, and Catholics, Pence noted, were not very good at reciting scripture.

One summer night, as they drove back from a fund raiser, Streeter pressed him—he must know some verse! Pence relented. Sure, he learned a little at the Catholic summer camp he attended as a child. Romans, Chapters 8 and 9—what it means to be a follower of Christ. Together they tested Pence's religious dexterity. Pence mentioned that he kept the same verses he had been taught years ago in his glove compartment, laminated. "Let me see if I can pull it back up," Pence said, then he handed Streeter the laminated card—Romans 8—that he kept in the glovebox. As Streeter drove, he peered over the scripture, and Pence started reciting. "He's trying to recite the passage and he's getting quite a lot of it right!"

At this point in the Bible, the Apostle Paul had moved on from trying to win over the slightly easier targets—the idolatrous masses of Corinth, among others—and was shipping God's message directly to the people who had killed Jesus, the Romans. Paul's argument, in Romans 8, is a bedrock of Christianity, that God's and Jesus's love for humanity is endless and permanent. It is, in a sense, what it means to be a Christian. In this moment, Pence and Streeter struggled with that philosophical quandary. How do you live a Christlike existence in a field as dirty as politics? It was the same debate that led purists like Cal Thomas and Ed Dobson to leave the Moral Majority: How do you live in this world, but not be of it?

In the philosophical confines of their car, Streeter and Pence could be certain of their path. But outside Mike Pence faced a more practical problem, one outlined in perfect detail by the Gingrich playbook: Incumbents can be nice, they can turn the other cheek, ignore sleights, and float above the muck. But challengers must live in the dirt.

THE ATTACK

One distinctive political ad mailed to voters seemed to blend Nice Mike and Nasty Mike in a clever fashion. Pence hit Sharp as being a softie in the War on Drugs. "There's Something That Phil Sharp Isn't Telling You About His Record on Drugs . . ." read the mailer. Lying in the backdrop was a rolled-up $50 bill, a razor blade, one crack rock, and a small pile of cocaine. Flip it over, and the answer is spelled out in lines of coke: "IT'S WEAK."

But on the inside of the piece, Pence's warm smile greeted voters, with a nice photo of him. He detailed his plan "to get tough against drugs": first off, sentence drug dealers who commit murder to death; next, send the military to the border to stop the drug dealers pouring in from Mexico; then cut U.S. aid to countries producing drugs; and, finally, drug-test every federal worker.

Sharp took to the airwaves, in thirty-second spots, to defend against Pence. "Congressman Phil Sharp believes that drugs—and the crimes and tragedies that drugs create—are one of the most serious problems facing America today," the narrator says in one spot. Sharp also accused Pence of being a "Johnny-come-lately" on the issue, saying he had already voted for everything Pence said he was for.

The Pence campaign calculated that Sharp had taken $1 million in PAC money during fourteen years in Congress. They fudged the math to make it sound like Sharp had collected that much in just one year—a stunning figure. Pence then commissioned a plaque that he planned to present to Sharp, congratulating him on becoming the first Hoosier to collect $1 million in PAC money. (Pence paid $46.72 to Sutterfield Plaque and Trophy in Indianapolis. But he never made the presentation.)

As the race wound through the summer, Pence began to lose some of the polished demeanor he usually displayed in public. After a candidate forum with Sharp in Franklin, Indiana, he approached a man in the crowd who had asked some needling questions of him. When he saw that the man was wearing an armband supporting Sharp, he fired at him: "Ah, Hitler Youth, I see."

ANOTHER INDIANA SURPRISE

That summer, as Vice President George H. W. Bush secured the nomination for president, rumors swirled about who he would pick as his running mate. Conservative activists wanted Representative Jack Kemp on the ticket with Bush, to provide ideological balance and secure their support. Party operatives had also regularly been raising Lugar as a potential running mate to any Republican nominee since the 1980 race—his foreign policy chops and Midwest roots would make a fine balance to any ticket. As the Republican Party descended on New Orleans for their 1988 convention, Lugar worked the state delegations, delivering breakfast speeches and rallying the troops.

The morning of Tuesday, August 16, 1988, word slowly trickled out among the Republican delegates that Bush was traveling up the Mississippi with the senator from Indiana. That was odd, thought Lugar, because he was standing at the front of a roomful of convention delegates having breakfast. They meant the other senator from Indiana, the junior senator from Indiana—Dan Quayle had jumped the line again, like he did in 1977. Lugar's vast, loyal network was stunned—how could he get passed over for the kid from Fort Wayne? But Bush and his team were quite in tune with the balance they needed for this ticket—it wasn't regional or any experience, it was youth and ideology. Quayle, a Fundamentalist Christian, represented the ascendant conservative wing of the party—Bush was protecting his right flank.   ❧

Late that summer, House Republican recruits won an invitation to the White House. Mike Pence met his idol, Ronald Reagan. He walked in to meet the president and shook his hand. "For all the world it felt like I was talking to Mount Rushmore," he later recounted. As he looked at Reagan, he said, "Mr. President, I have something I'd really like to tell you. I just want to thank you for everything you've done to inspire my generation to believe in this country again." And Reagan blushed. Pence saw "real humility" from the most important man in the nation, even the world. Sitting for a picture with the president, Pence looked at Reagan with a radiant smile. Pence still looked like the young college freshman strumming guitar at Vespers, with a thatch of curly brown hair and a big grin. By the end of the summer of 1988, Pence was riding high. It felt like he was destined for Washington. The only thing left was the election itself, which was just a little under two months away.

PENCE V. SHARP

After circling each other from a distance for months, Sharp and Pence finally met on the debate stage. On October 11, they gathered at the WIPB studio on Ball State University's campus for their first of two debates. Pence was poised, clean—the model public speaker of his Columbus training—and he tore into Sharp. Increasing the minimum wage would cause businesses to lay off workers, he said, "When you raise the guy on the bottom rung of the ladder, you have to raise everybody else." He blasted Sharp and the Democrats on spending, "The answer to every social ill is to spend more money." One of Sharp's aides scribbled a note to his boss, "Stop being defensive." It was underlined repeatedly. Sharp had been in Congress since 1975 and fought through innumerable legislative debates, but Pence commanded the stage in the campaign debate. This was clearly the young Pence's arena, where he sparred with quick, pithy rhetorical jabs and parries. The next week, at their second debate in Columbus, Pence knocked Sharp and the Democrats for their protectionist trade policies—marred with nationalist overtones. The stance may be popular with Rust Belt workers, but Pence stood firm with the GOP stance supporting free markets. They "don't like Japanese coming to America. We in Columbus know what a positive impact foreign investment can be in this country," Pence said. Pence performed well onstage. But it wasn't clear yet whether that would translate into votes in a few weeks.

Early on Election Night, November 8, 1988, the returns looked good—shockingly good. Vote tallies coming in from rural Indiana and some of the smaller towns dotting the Second District favored Pence. Across the country, Vice President George H. W. Bush led a resounding victory for Republicans up and down the ticket—as he racked up wins reminiscent of Reagan's own near sweep just four years earlier. It looked like Pence was about to topple the mighty Sharp. But the early totals didn't include the swarm of Democrats who poured in from Muncie. Sharp squeaked a win by six percentage points: 53–47, the second time a Republican came within a hair of beating him. Sharp had won 116,915 votes. But Pence put him on notice, collecting 102,846 votes—and winning a handful of counties, including the home of Columbus, Bartholomew County.

Pence took the platform at his election-night party—the crowd was crushed, but Pence was already looking ahead. Karen, however, who had put their lives on hold for two years, was angry—it would be at least two more years before they truly settled in as a family again. Schorg, the *Columbus Republic* reporter, looked over at her and saw a withering growl building just under the surface. Other candidates' wives occasionally tell Schorg "Go fuck yourself!" But Karen would never say anything so brash, she just simmered.

Larry Shores, the editor of the *Muncie Star*, dinged Pence on his incredibly negative campaign—Shores noted he had never seen anything like it before—but wrote that the negative didn't outweigh the good for Pence. "Although the Pence campaign probably overstepped its bounds in a few spots, it succeeded in other respects. Pence proved to be a tireless campaigner and someone to be reckoned with if he decided to tackle Sharp again two years from now." Indeed, the 1990 election was two years away. But professional operatives, like the Republicans helping Pence, knew that real campaigns started the day after the previous election.

CHAPTER 4

BROKE—1990

Quilhot, the insurance salesman Pence courted in his 1988 run, could sense Pence was down in the dumps after the close 1988 loss, so he invited him to breakfast with some other young Republicans at Acapulco Joe's downtown. Bottomless coffee and giant plates of huevos rancheros, beans, rice, cheese, and hot sauce in giant red squirt bottles filled the booths. Pence was hurt, but not finished. "Pence didn't know which end was up," Quilhot said. "He was down in the dumps, [but] you could tell he wanted to run again."

Quilhot had big plans of his own, he wanted to start a think tank and a conservative journal in the style of Dinesh D'Souza, a flame-throwing conservative activist. The other guys at Acapulco Joe's didn't seem too hot on the idea. But Quilhot walked out convinced he was going to start the journal on his own. He looked over at Pence and asked him if he wanted to run the think tank and journal. It would give Pence a real job and some regular income. It would also keep him in the mix politically. Besides, Pence would have better luck in the 1992 campaign cycle, with a Republican presidential candidate at the top of the ticket lifting up all House contenders. ◦

At home, Mike and Karen Pence had been trying to conceive for three years, unsuccessfully. That took a back seat through his first race, and the couple never discussed it with anyone outside their family. They paid $10,000 for fertility treatments that were an alternative to in vitro fertilization approved by the Catholic Church. But they had no luck. And their money problems had continued—Pence hadn't been bringing in business for his law firm through the 1988 race and they were basically living on Karen's public-school teacher's salary. If he ran again immediately, Pence would have to find some way to scrap together more cash and put becoming a father on hold.

But Pence had momentum, perhaps enough to carry him straight through to victory on Election Day in two years. He was smooth, dashing, disciplined, and methodical—all qualities that indicated he could unseat Sharp on the second try. The trick now was figuring out how to make it look like he wasn't a professional politician. The hypocrisy would be glaringly obvious to most voters. In short, Pence had to run without looking like he was running—an invaluable skill for anyone heading to Washington.

Pence began making adjustments behind the scenes, starting with blaming the kid from Gingrich's campaign school for his loss. "I will freely admit my frustration with the fairly narrow scope that the last campaign took, and I attribute that to the folks we had," Pence said. Pence never fully trusted his first campaign manager, Chapman, and developed a habit of micromanaging operations. He replaced Chapman with a veteran of the Sweezy Indianapolis machine, Sherman Johnson. Sweezy, a man of few words but sage advice, told Johnson, "always keep the candidate's wife happy."

Next, Pence launched a media tour, with a fabricated quandary: Will he or won't he run again?

The theater was par for the course in the world of politics. He drove down to Columbus for an interview on WRZQ-FM with Tim Bonnell. Pence made his pitch for why the people of the Second District needed a Republican in Washington. Bonnell, a tall, lanky kid just out of college, said it sounded like he was running against Sharp again. Pence cautioned he hadn't made up his mind yet (even though he very much had) and then got back on message: Sharp needed to go. After the interview, Bonnell asked what he would do if he ran and lost a second time. Pence shrugged. Then Bonnell motioned around the studio—you could always do this, he said.

Pence's greatest weakness from 1988 was his anonymity. Radio could easily cure that ailment. And his chance came almost immediately— Sharon Disinger, the wife of a radio station owner in Rushville, Indiana, had watched Pence during the 1988 campaign and liked the way he delivered the conservative message to perfection. Disinger's husband, Louis, carved out a weekly spot for Pence on WRCR, a low-wattage station squarely in the center of the Second District where he manned "Washington Update," weighing in on the issues of the week.

Meanwhile, Pence kept the heat on Sharp. In a July 1989 letter to the editor sent to papers around the Second District, he said it was time to ban big money from politics once and for all! "Banning PACs and precluding the stockpiling of campaign dollars seems the only fair and, well, American thing to do," Pence wrote. He signed it, "Mike Pence, former candidate for Congress."

Finally, after spending a year running behind the scenes, he let the public in on the ill-kept secret. The 1990 race would be immensely better, "I think you'll sense from this campaign a different level of professionalism."

THE MOVING GROUND

Bush's big 1988 win could have been read as a resounding confirmation of moderate, establishment Republican values. He trounced Massachusetts governor Michael Dukakis, collecting an astounding

426 electoral votes to Dukakis's 111. But Bush's selection of Quayle as running mate spoke to the moving ground beneath the feet of all Republicans. The patrician party of Eisenhower was being supplanted by a band of activists—the offspring of Barry Goldwater–style conservative policies matched with radical left Abby Hoffman tactics. And a fateful decision by the nascent Bush administration in March 1989 only hastened this shift.   ❧

Dick Cheney, a cagey Washington operator, spent the '80s climbing the rungs of power in the House. When he entered the House in 1979, at just thirty-seven years old, Cheney was already a favorite of both the establishment and the growing conservative class. After eight years, Cheney translated that broad support into a position as the third-ranking Republican in the House. Two years later, with Gingrich's band of Far Right upstarts knocking at the door, House Republican leader Bob Michel picked Cheney to be his second-in-command, a move that would keep the Right at bay.

As Bush built his administration, he selected Texas Republican John Tower to be his secretary of defense. But the Senate spiked Tower's nomination 47–53, amid rumors of drunkenness and womanizing. So Bush turned to Dick Cheney, a veteran of the Ford administration and proven operator. When Bush plucked Cheney out of the House, Gingrich rushed in to fill the vacuum. The man who advised that "throwing grenades is easier than catching them" was now helping call the shots for the House Republicans. And the pipeline that Gingrich had spent a decade laying across the country now led directly to the upper echelons of power.

Then, in June 1990, almost as if to prove conservatives couldn't trust him, George Bush said he was prepared to raise taxes! The tanking economy had ripped open a new hole in the federal budget, but Bush had kept his own party in the dark about the decision. Gingrich refused to attend the bill signing at the White House, a stark rebuttal from inside the party. The crack before was now a gaping rift between the Republican Party and the conservative base.

Pence never took a side, but that rightward shift could still be felt, even six hundred miles from Washington. Few were as attuned to it as Sharp. Democratic strategist Alan Secrest warned Sharp that a new wave, like the Watergate wave of 1974, was building, "As I noted (we are seeing this phenomenon elsewhere, too), the shift that has taken place in your district's political topography is at least 80 percent context-driven (like '74) and at most 20 percent Pence-driven. (It's probably more like 95 percent vs. 5 percent)."

RUTHLESSLY SHARP

Sharp didn't need a pollster to tell him he was in trouble. He hired a pair of battle-hardened staffers, Billy Linville and Bob McCarson, to take the fight to Pence. His strategist, Secrest, decided Sharp would need at least one "hit" every ten days between the summer of 1990 and Labor Day. They'd need to ding Pence in the press regularly. This, as it turned out, would not be a problem.

On June 30, Linville ran over to the secretary of state's office and picked up a copy of Pence's latest campaign finance report. He sat outside on the steps of the statehouse, leafing through the pages, and quickly realized he had found "the silver bullet" for the Sharp campaign. Some aides thought it was a little odd when Pence registered his campaign as a for-profit business, but Pence said he did it because he was serious about running government like a business. Deep in the report, Linville found the real reason—Pence was spending campaign cash on personal bills. Pence had decided months ago to supplement Karen's teacher's salary with campaign cash. He spent $992 a month to pay their mortgage, $222 a month for Karen's car payments. He even used donations from friends and supporters to pay down a mountain of credit card debt. All told, he spent about $13,000 of campaign cash for personal use.

He'd gotten a taste of the campaign cash in 1988, making some of Karen's car payments from the campaign and nobody ever raised any concerns. So he went full blast in 1990. He never told anyone.

Pence's campaign manager, Sherman Johnson, didn't learn about it until a reporter called asking about it. In a pinch, he stuck up for Pence, "It's a full-time job to run a campaign against an incumbent of that tenure." As the news trickled out, Pence became defensive, "I'm not embarrassed that I need to make a living."

Practically, both were right. Campaigning full-time cut into the ability for most regular folks to earn a living. Unless they were rich or an incumbent, would-be pols would have to stop their primary line of work to run for public office. But politically, Linville's discovery condemned the Pence campaign.

With a fatal "hit" in the bag, Sharp eased back in the campaign and began sending Linville to smaller candidate forums in his place. On one side of the stage stood the Republican nominee, on the other stood the Democratic nominee's staffer. Pence's message never wavered; he stuck hard to attacking Sharp for taking PAC money—but his hands shook, nervously. When Linville pressed him on the campaign cash, Pence rolled through the attack using his legendary speech and debate training. But words couldn't cover his embarrassment and he blushed, Linville said, "He was just red in the face and didn't know how to deal with it."

Pence never grasped how damning it was. "I think it made sense to him. So, therefore it made sense to the world," Johnson said. "And that happened on a couple other things in the campaign—What he thought made perfect sense to him didn't fare well in the public."

The only thing Pence could do was move on with the plan; there were still four months left in the race. Pence and the team backing him in Washington doubled down on painting Sharp as a crony of special interests and Pence as the good ol' Hoosier boy. But Pence himself was slipping.

He promised that he would fight clean, "We will not deal with the personal character flaws of my opponent." But in a too-clever ploy, he attempted to cast Sharp as a "liar" in a spat involving the local prosecutor from Rush County, Indiana. The *Indianapolis Star* wryly noted in its headline, "Pence Urges Clean Campaign, Calls Opponent a Liar."

Pence's television campaign fared better. First, in late July, he ran a spot called "Enough"—"Mike Pence has been talking about the issues all across the Second District," the narrator intones, while on-screen Mike Pence strolls down Main St., Anytown, Indiana. But, the narrator continues, "Sharp has begun a negative campaign against Pence personally!" (That would be the Rush County fiasco.) "Enough is enough! If you want a congressman who will stand on the issues and won't make personal attacks, take a look at Mike Pence."

Two weeks later came the second ad, in which the narrator blasts Phil Sharp as a corrupt, crooked crony: "The S&L Bailout, increasing taxes, endless ethics scandals, a flood of special interest money! If you think it's time for new leadership . . . Take a look at Mike Pence."

By September, Pence found the balance between good guy and attack dog. In his third spot, he walked across a baseball field, bat in hand—he looked straight at the camera, "In baseball, both sides start the game even. . . ." He's dressed this time in khakis and a blue plaid shirt—a little bit Indiana and a little bit DC. "But in politics that's not the case. Big special interests pick who they want to win congressional races and then pour in hundreds of thousands of dollars to elect their candidate." Then the ad cut away to something more sinister, a gray screen patched with dollar signs and the corporate logos of all Sharp's alleged masters: Ashland Chemicals, Philip Morris, Exxon, more. And then it switches back to Pence, "If you elect me," he says, lifting his weathered Louisville Slugger, "when I come to bat. I'll be hitting for you."

As he pulled off his positive campaign ad spree, something darker simmered just beneath the surface. Pence had never been attacked like this before. Sure, he had been blasting away at Sharp for close to four years now, and turnabout was fair play. But his campaign staff noticed him withdrawing, becoming suspicious of campaign aides. He began withholding payments to certain staffers, declining to sign their paychecks. Pence started to wonder if maybe they needed something stronger on television, something that clearly stated what a corporate stooge Sharp was. The answer would have to wait until after the lone debate of the contest.

THE MUNCIE DEBATE

On September 28, 1990, Pence and Sharp took the debate stage at WIPB studios, on the campus of Ball State University in Muncie with just under a month until the election. The studio was small and packed with viewers sitting in folding chairs. Pence and Sharp stood at the front, with a panel of questioners ready to pepper them, just a little to the right. The animosity between Pence and Sharp had been building for years, and now they would face off for their only debate of the 1990 race.

Sharp stood square-jawed, with his large glasses reflecting the bright lights. He wore a gray-striped suit and red tie with blue stripe. He looked aquiline and a tad aloof—perfectly Washington.

To his left stood Pence, in a neatly tailored dark blue suit—with the bespoke stitching along his lapel—a clean white button-down and red tie with small white stars. His face was a little rounder than Sharp's, and like Sharp, he wore glasses. They were a new addition and Sharp's campaign staff joked that it was an attempt to make Pence look older, more congressional. He did look older than his thirty-one years with his poise, streaks of white running through his hair and Reagan-esque mannerisms. But Pence didn't need the shtick. In reality, he was a stone-cold killer on the debate stage.

Pence let loose the fire on the sea of perms, seated in folding chairs throughout the live audience. Drilling for oil in the Arctic? "I lived through that energy crisis on the gasoline station drive at Ray's Marathon in Columbus, Indiana," Pence said, personalizing his life for the audience. "I pumped gas there as I worked my way through college and I remember very distinctly people saying to me over and over again—'This must never happen again! We can never let ourselves become this dependent on the Persian Gulf for oil!'"

Strengthen the Clean Air Act? "I consider myself to be an environmentalist," Pence said. "My wife, Karen, started a recycling program in the second grade where she teaches." But then he added that a recent study found that "acid rain is not an environmental crisis."

Sharp, the veteran statesman, hung back and played it cool.

What would you do in the face of an expected recession, Mr. Pence? Cut the capital gains tax! "It's been said it's a tax cut for the rich, it's not—it's a tax cut for the families, the small businesses, and the family farms right here in the Second Congressional District."

Sharp spied his opening, "Mike, Donald Trump will be delighted to hear your commitment there—because 80 percent of the capital gains tax will go to people making well over $100,000 a year."

Mr. Pence, back to you, would you support a veto of new civil rights legislation?

"The first decision that would be made—maybe not by Donald Trump—but by a lot of the small-business people employed in this district would be that 'Well, we have to create some quotas to protect ourselves from charges of discrimination now that the burden has shifted on us,'" Pence said. "That the American free enterprise system should not be encouraged by Washington to create racist policy to hire X number of blacks, X number of women, X number of Hispanics."

Pence was getting under Sharp's skin. "There's a lot of dispute about that 'truth,' Mike, because a lot of people think that's blatantly false what you just said—the law does not require any kind of numerical quotas."

And then, Sharp brought out the big guns. You're against big taxes, Mike? Well, how about the oil fees you'd raise—the cost would soar to $300 a barrel!

Meanwhile, Sharp's arms have been creeping ever further above the podium—moving from calm, low-lying gestures, like the fall election breezes, into something a little wilder.

Pence watched, and smiled. As Sharp's arms descended, Pence nailed him, "We need limited terms for members of Congress." The whole room laughed, the timing and delivery was perfect. Then Pence promised, "You only got me for twelve years, then I'm out after twelve years."

At the end of the hour Pence walked off the stage with a smile. Finally, the campaign had played out squarely in his favor—the speech club champion of Columbus North High had schooled the nutty professor.

THE ARAB AD

The afterglow from the debate did not last long. The mortal wounding from Pence's campaign cash fiasco became more apparent with time. He was burning through more than he could bring in. He'd pulled in $367,000 but had spent $447,000. As of September 30, Pence only had slightly more than $5,000 in the bank for the homestretch. Adding to their woes, George Bush's popularity was sinking fast and he was taking down every Republican with him. Ed Rollins, the head of Republican National Committee, issued a warning to every candidate—they should distance themselves from their president.

Sharp's team rightly predicted that Pence would need more free press because he couldn't afford to buy TV time. Pence's spokesman, Ed Sagebiel, told the *Muncie Star* that Pence would join a "tea party" protest seeking tax cuts in Muncie, complete with crates of tea being tossed into the White River. But then Sagebiel called the paper back to say Pence wouldn't join the protest, because "it didn't really sound like a great idea after we talked about it."

They only had a few weeks until the election, and Pence needed to nail Sharp harder than ever. He stewed.

Not long after the debate, he ran into his campaign headquarters, early on a Monday morning. Sherman Johnson, his campaign manager, was already at work. Pence was "bubbly," saying he had a great idea for an ad. Pence was a big *Saturday Night Live* fan, and he had an SNL-type skit ready. They would open with a head-on shot of a man wearing a keffiyeh, a head scarf, and a traditional Arabic tunic. He was a sheik! Just like the ones who set the oil embargo a decade earlier. The man would wear aviator sunglasses and thank Phil Sharp for sending so much American money to Saudi Arabia—and then, halfway through the spot, he would pull off his shades . . . and reveal a second set of shades. Because Arabs are always wearing shades!

Pence acted out the ad for Johnson; he clasped his hands together and shook them in the air, just like he thought a sheik would thank a foreigner.

Johnson thought it was terrible, even racist. Pence didn't care, he told Johnson to make it happen. With just a few weeks left, out of cash and running out of time, Johnson scrambled to find donors to pay for the last-minute spot. Finally, he lined up the support of an outside group and they filmed the spot out of state.

On October 14, 1990, Pence let 'er rip. "My people would like to thank you Americans for buying so much of our oil," Pence's "Arab" says. Then he clasps his ringed fingers together, shakes them in the air, and exclaims, "Oh, thank you, Phil Sharp!"

The Indianapolis media couldn't believe their eyes. "Congressional candidate Mike Pence's television ad with the phony Arab oil minister is so bad it's perversely delightful," *Indianapolis Star* columnist Dan Carpenter declared. "It looks and sounds like something *Saturday Night Live* might have cooked up with the budget of (the local gunshop)."

The ad nabbed the attention of Arab American groups in Washington. The next day, Tuesday, protests cropped up around Indianapolis. But Pence acted like nothing was wrong, "If I felt the ad was racist or if I felt it was playing to stereotypes, I wasn't going to run it. So, they made sure the dignity of the Arabs was preserved. It does not invite you to laugh at Arabs, but it does invite you to laugh."

Jim Zogby, the executive director of the Arab American Institute was surprised; this was precisely the type of ad they'd fought in 1988, but by 1990, with Bush's alliance with Gulf nations in the Gulf War, the anti-Arab pandering had largely dissipated. Zogby was surprised how passé Pence's choice was. "This was, 'Here we go again,'" Zogby said. "But it was hurtful."

The protests engulfed the Pence campaign, sucking out the last of its remaining oxygen. President Bush himself delivered the coup de grâce, signing a budget deal with tax increases on Monday, November 5, 1990.

On Election Night, November 6, 1990, Pence and his team gathered together on the second floor of Jonathan Byrd's mega-cafeteria in Greenwood, Indiana. Byrd was a good Republican and held plenty of victory parties at his massive restaurant. But this was not going to be one of those parties. "We had a pretty good sense early on that it wasn't looking good," Jeff Cardwell said. Cardwell didn't have to stick around to know the result, it was a wash. Pence lost 59–40 to Sharp. Shortly after nine P.M., Pence conceded defeat and left.

He had poured himself into becoming a politician, a dream he curated over two decades. And now, instead of meeting his goal, he was lost. Pence had done almost everything by the book—even using the campaign cash for personal expenses was technically kosher, if not exactly smart. But 1990 turned into a far darker affair than he had planned. He wasn't connecting with voters. It wasn't just that nobody knew who he was. *He* didn't know who he was. And his personal life was coming apart at the seams. Mike and Karen's efforts to conceive had gone nowhere. He had a mountain of personal debt and was out of a job. Perhaps this loss was God's way of telling Mike to give it up.

CHAPTER 5

THE THINK TANK

Pence surveyed the loss; how could he have failed so spectacularly? As he tried to find a path forward, and some work, he called his network of donors and supporters, but they wouldn't take or return his calls. He couldn't understand why. He didn't grasp that using the campaign cash to make his mortgage and car payments was a clear violation of their trust. He'd also promised them a clean campaign, built on ideas and values, but instead delivered the most vicious fight Indiana had ever seen. "Mike burned a lot of bridges," his oldest brother, Greg Pence, said. "He upset a lot of his backers. It was partly because of immaturity, but he really was kind of full of shit."

The firm guidance he built in a decade of learning and exploring, from his faith to his conservatism, evaporated in the four years he took to become a professional campaigner. His ambition, and his studious application of that ambition, shredded his values. As he campaigned for Congress over the last four years, he never said who he was, he never let the public see that he was a good, principled man. Pence was stunned when a reporter asked him after the 1990 race if he was a conservative. He'd spent so much time attacking Sharp that the people who got paid to know about him, the reporters, didn't even know his values.

But not everyone was disenchanted with Mike Pence. Chuck Quilhot got his conservative think tank off the ground and it was still growing. Quilhot called Pence immediately after the election, ostensibly to check on him, but also to remind him that he could have a job at the Indiana Policy Review Foundation. Almost immediately, he got a fax from Pence with a list of everything he wanted: his salary requirement, a company car, and some very detailed questions about the health-care plan. Quilhot said he didn't think they'd be able to get him the car. But the rest looked fine.

Mike and Karen had been trying for five years to have children, unsuccessfully—their infertility woes had been overshadowed by his campaigns, but now starting a family was a priority. "We didn't tell anybody," Karen Pence said. "We didn't tell anybody we were struggling." Pence's own father went to the young Karen before he died, just a few years earlier, and asked her what was going on. "You know, there's never a good time to have kids. You've just got to have kids. They don't come out as teenagers. You'll have time to get ready for the teenager years," Ed Pence told her at the time. Karen admitted to her father-in-law, "You know what, we've gone through several procedures, we don't know what's going on, but we can't seem to get pregnant."

Mike and Karen were regulars at St. Barnabas, the Catholic church not far from their house. (The church, fittingly enough, was directly across the street from the home of longtime Indianapolis GOP boss Keith Bulen.) They were evangelical Christians, to be certain, but also Catholic. They were evangelical Catholics. But the pregnancy woes tried their faith. "When you go through a procedure, and you spend $10,000 and it doesn't work, it's really, really frustrating," Karen Pence said. "How can God put this desire in my heart and not bring me kids? . . . It made me question Him a lot."

After trying for years, they got on a list to adopt a baby. But not long after Pence took the IPR job, he and Karen got pregnant with their first child. After years of trying and praying, God answered their calls.

Being Conservative

The *Indiana Policy Review* journal could trace its roots directly back to the reactionary—and explosive—conservative journal started by fire-brand Dinesh D'Souza at Dartmouth College. Meanwhile, at the end of the Reagan presidency, Reagan and the founders of the Heritage Foundation—the premier national conservative think tank—began building a network of state-based conservative think tanks around the country. They wanted to move the dial right in the statehouses, city halls, and county boards nationwide. And they looked to a Hoosier, Byron Lamm, to start that network. In his home state, Lamm looked to his cousin, Chuck Quilhot, to start the *Indiana Policy Review*.

When Pence joined in 1991, the journal was already clipping along. Ostensibly Pence was a director of the IPR Foundation, but titles didn't mean much for the small group—they all pitched in, and it was a tight circle. Craig Ladwig edited the journal and wrote most of the essays and op-eds, Pence took on the fund-raising, Quilhot handled business oversight, and his cousin, Lamm, plugged them in with the national conservative movement.

Pence veered onto a new path. He left behind the tedious, grinding world of campaign politics and entered the world of conservative thinkers and activists in a way he'd only touched on in college. Ladwig called it Pence's "graduate school." The IPR and D'Souza's national think tank network gave Pence access to the most important ideologues of the modern conservative movement. They regularly hosted fund raisers and talks, with luminaries like William F. Buckley and P. J. O'Rourke.

The small group also reflected a central split on the right between libertarian-leaning conservatives, who wanted to focus on fiscal policy, and religious and social conservatives, who wanted to fly the banner on issues like abortion and religion. The Policy Review principals split evenly: Ladwig and Lamm voted to skip the social crusades, Quilhot and Pence said they had a moral duty to fight. The four eventually decided to drop the social issues, but Quilhot and Pence were never fully happy with the decision.

Pence settled in to work at IPR's small office in downtown Indianapolis. As he went out to lunch each day, he would bump into a veteran Republican hand he had met during the 1988 race, Bill Smith. Smith had been working for U.S. representative Danny Burton in Washington through the '80s. In 1989, Smith started up another local think tank, the Indiana Family Institute.

The Indiana Family Institute thrived exclusively on the religious and social issues championed by the Christian Right. Just as Lamm and the Heritage Foundation were starting their network of state-level think tanks, a conservative evangelical activist, James Dobson, was starting a Moral Majority–style network of state-level think tanks focused on fighting abortions, supporting religion in schools, and trying to curb divorce rates. They also sought a new way to square their position on AIDS.

The nation had finally come to terms with the HIV/AIDS crisis in a way that had eluded the Reagan White House for a decade. After Ryan White died in 1990, Reagan signaled the final shift for almost everyone on the right with his letter eulogizing White, "We owe it to Ryan to make sure that the fear and ignorance that chased him from his home and his school will be eliminated." The new answer from the Christian Right was abstinence—the safest sex was no sex. In full-page ads placed throughout the state, Smith's group wrote "In Defense of a Little Virginity," opening with, "The federal government has spent almost $3 billion of our taxes since 1970 to promote contraceptives and 'safe sex' among our teenagers. Isn't it time we asked: What have we gotten for our money?"

Pence didn't join Smith's group right away, but the two men

found they were simpatico on almost every issue. And so was Karen. On July 29, 1991, the *Indianapolis Star* tried to explain the often fatal stigma that gay teenagers felt—the paper highlighted that gay teenagers commit suicide at much higher rates than their straight counterparts. The paper interviewed four boys, ages sixteen to twenty. The paper clearly treated this as a touchy subject; the last names of the boys were not printed and the accompanying photo showed two boys holding hands—their backs to the camera, so their faces couldn't be seen. Nineteen-year-old Harold said, "I've known since I was eight years old. I had a crush on my math teacher. I was wondering why. I knew I was different from then on." Karen Pence, an elementary-school teacher, wasn't having it. On August 11, 1991, she wrote into the *Star*, "After seeing a whole page devoted to encouraging young people to accept their homosexuality, I have decided to no longer use the *Indianapolis Star* to teach newspaper education. Your implication that an eight-year-old having a crush on a teacher of the same sex means that child is gay or lesbian is absurd." She ended her note, "I only pray that most parents were able to intercept before their children were encouraged to call the Gay/Lesbian Youth Hotline which encourages them to 'accept their homosexuality.'"

With a child on the way and a new job, Pence moved on from the campaign life, but he was itchy. The work for the IPR Foundation didn't quite feel like a career to him, more like a job. Pence couldn't quite see five or ten years down the road. To fete out his plans, Pence and a few friends got together and studied Stephen Covey's masterwork *The 7 Habits of Highly Effective People*. Covey's book offered some sage advice for Pence as he searched for a path forward—be proactive (don't wait for things to happen), start with a goal and head in that direction, prioritize, look for options that make everyone happy, and listen carefully first before speaking. The latter point came naturally to Pence, he was very empathetic one-on-one.

He also got proactive, even if he wasn't running for any office. He used his new role to hang around the statehouse, like a hybrid gadfly and lobbyist. Pence bumped into Doug Richardson, the AP reporter, and groused about how incredulous he was at the fact that the current governor, Democrat Evan Bayh, was outflanking the Indiana Republicans on tax cuts! Bayh had some help, via a wave of gambling that was sweeping through Indiana. A few years earlier, Indiana voters approved the creation of a lottery—it filled the state coffers with billions in new dollars. It was like manna from the heavens, letting Bayh promise to increase spending on roads *and* cut the state's car tax. Pence and Smith were no fans of the new gambling push from Indiana Democrats. It seemed amoral, and craven, to take the money for state programs and look the other way on all the social ills gambling created.

As Pence wound through the summer, he found his footing. The disastrous campaign was a half year removed. He also had repaid personal debt he built during the campaign (despite paying himself from the campaign coffers). The Federal Election Commission also finally delivered clear rules about using campaign cash for personal expenses: don't do it. It may have been legal before, but Pence's debacle and a series of other races around the country spurred the FEC to outlaw it. Pence almost had his closure. There was just one more item left.

As Pence met with sage Republicans trying to plan out his future, he ran into Peter Rusthoven—a former lawyer in the Reagan White House and a well-known Republican around town. Pence sat in Rusthoven's office with a straightforward question, "What should I do with my life?" Rusthoven sensed that Pence was not done with campaigning. "You care too much about public life and public affairs. The way you were in that campaign is not the Mike Pence I know," Rusthoven said. After some pontificating, Rusthoven told Pence, "You need to apologize." Request absolution, he said, "Keep your oar in the water and see what happens."

Even if Pence never ran again for another office, he still had to bury the image of a vicious partisan attack dog. Hoosiers didn't take well to personal attacks in their politics (Indiana isn't New York).

Also, Pence let himself be swayed by the big-name Republicans and fell in line with their playbook. He sat down with his new buddy, Bob Massie, and they brainstormed: He needed to write a book! The book would be called *Confessions of a Negative Campaigner*. Pence started a book proposal and even worked up a draft chapter in short order. Chapter 1 was all about John Sweezy and how Pence had been recruited to run for Congress. Pence and Massie started shopping the proposal, but it fell flat. One religious publishing house answered, "This would be great if he had won. But nobody reads about a loser."

So Pence turned back to his new friends at the *Indiana Policy Review* journal. If an entire book wasn't in the cards, perhaps a simple essay would do. The *Indiana Policy Review* published Pence's confessional in its fall 1991 quarterly issue. Pence opened his five-hundred-word essay on page 5 of the review with the advice of St. Paul, "It is a trustworthy statement, deserving of full acceptance, that Jesus Christ came to save sinners, among whom I am foremost of all." He now knew that "negative campaigning is wrong. . . . The mantra of a modern political campaign is 'drive up the negatives.'"

Instead, Pence wrote, a political campaign "ought to be about three simple propositions: First, a campaign ought to demonstrate the basic human decency of the candidate. . . . Second, a campaign ought to be about the advancement of issues whose success or failure is more significant than that of the candidate. . . . Third, and very much last, campaigns should (not only) be about winning."

Pence wouldn't get down in the mud again, and neither should anyone else. Then he shopped the article to some op-ed pages and ginned up some interest for his apology tour. When a reporter asked him if he had apologized directly to Sharp, Pence stopped him—this was only a confession, not an apology, certainly not an apology to Sharp. "It is a confession, an admission, a personal indictment. That's the extent of it," he told the *Muncie Star*. "I don't mean to be disrespectful, but my opponent is really irrelevant to this equation. I'm talking about me. I'm saying what I did was wrong. I know that now."

Mocking Mullin

In November 1991, Karen Pence gave birth to their first child, a boy, Michael Pence Jr. After six arduous, trying years, God had answered their prayers.

With his oar in the water, Pence continued working for the Indianapolis GOP machine. Sweezy had a small mess for him on Election Day, 1991—the Republican councilman from the city's southside had been busted on DUI charges, was living outside the district with a stripper, and had tried to kill himself. Sweezy needed Pence to go down to the polls and see if they could salvage the race. Barring that, he should try to win over the Democratic candidate to support them.

Pence got to Southport Middle School early on Election Day, wearing a tweed coat and red tie. His Democratic target, Tim Mullin, was wearing the exact same thing. The "Republican uniform," Mullin joked; he needed Republican voters if he was going to win. Pence tried his hand at converting him, wholesale—on politics and religion. Mullin, an Irish Catholic Democrat, laughed at Pence. "You're more likely to get me to become a Protestant than a Republican." Pence began browbeating him, wanting to know if Mullin worshipped every Sunday. Mullin clipped his head off. "It's none of your business. My grandparents came to this country from Ireland, and we were escaping people like you!" Rebuffed, Pence shifted to righteously taunting Mullin. As Mullin spoke with voters heading into the polling booths, Pence positioned himself behind each voter and looked over their shoulders at Mullin—a glaring reminder that they were stuck together at Southport Middle School all day.

Mullin won easily, and he was still very much a Catholic and a Democrat. But Pence's entreaties would not be ignored. Shortly after Mullin took office, Greg Dixon, an extremist pastor from the Indianapolis Baptist Temple, called Mullin in for a meeting at his office. When Mullin arrived at Dixon's office, he found Pence there, too. And Pence asked him again: Would he join the movement? Mullin declined, again.

Enter Pat Buchanan and
the Bush Takedown

Conservative outrage at Bush was peaking just as the president's re-election bid was getting under way, and in a last-minute move at the end of 1991, hard Right conservatives found their champion: former Nixon speechwriter Pat Buchanan. Buchanan helped craft Nixon's Southern Strategy to lure Southern white voters away from the Democrats. Buchanan developed a reputation as a whip-smart politician, but also a virulent nationalist. Buchanan picked up where Pat Robertson left off in 1988. On February 18, 1992, Buchanan shocked the Washington crowd, edging up against Bush in New Hampshire with 38 percent of the vote against a sitting president! Buchanan promised more bloodshed as the primaries moved south, with contests throughout the Bible Belt. Internal polling, however, quickly found Buchanan losing steam—so he drew up a TV ad that nobody could ignore.

"In the last three years Bush has invested our tax dollars in pornographic and blasphemous art, too shocking to show," said the narrator. In the background, a shirtless man danced, the camera panned around him, showing his bare butt cheeks poking through holes in his leather pants. A gray mugshot of President George Bush partially obscured his right butt cheek. "This so-called art has glorified homosexuality, exploited children, and perverted the image of Jesus Christ." The narrator continues, while the film in the background rolls—it's a gay pride parade, awash in shirtless men, one wearing a leather chest harness studded with metal, and many, many mustaches. The footage stops on another man's ass, in tight blue jeans: "Send Bush a Message!" The stark background footage for the ad was taken from a 1989 documentary about the alienation of gay black men—ostracized from mainstream American life, from black culture, and from white gay culture. The film was produced in part with support from the National Endowment for the Arts, which gave Buchanan just enough string to say Bush was promoting homosexuality.

In one formative year, the political agnosticism of Pence's 1988 and 1990 races vanished—he emerged at the start of 1992 as a Christian conservative, and Buchanan was his guy. Early in the primaries, Pence pulled Quilhot aside and suggested Quilhot become Buchanan's Indiana state chairman. Quilhot declined. Pence said he felt the same spark with Buchanan that he felt with Reagan. In the heat of the 1992 Republican primary, Pence said he wasn't sure he could vote for Bush; if Buchanan lost the primary, he was considering sitting out 1992 altogether. It would all depend, Pence said, on how Bush treated Buchanan. If he called Buchanan a bigot, then "Bush will disenfranchise an enormous throng of Republicans."

But Buchanan was resonating with conservative voters for another reason. He was ringing a stark populist bell that no other candidate could—or would: The United States was losing its status in the world, and it was time to put America first; good American jobs were being outsourced and nobody cared about the average American. The economy suffered through a downturn in the late '80s, and the offshoring of manufacturing jobs started under Reagan had only continued unfettered during Bush's term. Bush easily won his remaining primary contests, but a sizable batch of Republicans registered their protest votes in every remaining contest.

Bush survived the conservative uprising and held on to lock in the nomination. As the national convention approached, chatter trickled out of the White House that Bush and his chief of staff, James Baker, were planning to dump Dan Quayle from the 1992 ticket. He had served his purpose in 1988 in helping keep the Right on board, but he never truly clicked with Bush or his management style, the rumors went. Quayle was at risk of being replaced by someone with a stronger relationship with the president: James Baker himself. Some White House aides felt the president needed a real partner, not just someone to keep the Right at bay.

"The struggles within the GOP will have less to do with winning the 1992 election than they will with finally resolving a long-running war between the two wings of the party: (a) the Rockefeller Republicans, the country-club and establishment wing whose policies and principles are purchased to complement direct-mail campaigns; and (b) the Goldwater Republicans, the wing of committed economic and social conservatives whose intellectual energy has powered the party for the past two decades," Pence wrote in Quayle's defense in the pages of the *Indiana Policy Review* quarterly journal. "Dan Quayle holds the mind and heart of the conservative, church-going voters who have created the contemporary Republican Party. George Bush does not."

On the other side, Democratic nominee Bill Clinton picked up on this populist disenchantment and simmered it down into one catchphrase: "It's the economy, stupid." Clinton, the young governor of Arkansas, radiated charisma and boiled intricate policy down to easy sound bites singularly focused on the economic pain felt by the country.

Quayle survived the threat and stayed on the ticket, and conservatives fell back in line with the Republican Party as they looked at the prospect of a Clinton presidency. With a few weeks left in the election, Pence turned his pen on Clinton, in an opinion piece for the *Indianapolis Star*; he equated the move with that of a spurned wife who checks in at the "no tell motel" to sleep around—revenge on her cheating husband. "She doesn't care about the suitor, he is merely a vehicle of her vengeance. The sadness comes the morning after, when she awakens soberly, to her indiscretion and shame. I submit that America is, at this moment, standing in the lobby of the motel while Slick Willie parks the car."

On November 3, 1992, Bill Clinton won the White House, with 370 electoral votes.

David McIntosh had been working for Quayle in the White House when Clinton swept into office. Out of a job, McIntosh moved back with his wife to Indiana. Soon he decided to make a run for office himself—he was ready to take on Pence's old rival, Phil Sharp, in the Second District. The GOP bigwigs told McIntosh they'd love to have someone credible running against Sharp again, but maybe he oughta talk with Mike Pence before deciding to dive in.

Pence planned to warn McIntosh against a run, after his own bruising experience. But when they met downtown, at Acapulco Joe's, they connected immediately. They talked for two hours. Pence asked McIntosh about his views on abortion and conception; McIntosh said life begins at conception—therefore abortion is the killing of a life. They also bonded over cutting taxes and drawing down spending.

Then Pence offered his new friend some advice. "David, my thought in coming here today was to warn you this isn't a good idea. You shouldn't run for Congress; Phil Sharp's just too hard to beat," Pence told McIntosh. "But you have shown me you're not running for Congress just to run, but you're running to propound these conservative ideas. And if you'll do that, and that's your goal, then you should do it because you'll be advancing the cause for these ideas." Pence then offered his youngest sister, Annie, to help run McIntosh's campaign. (Almost a dozen years after Pence's parents had Pence and his brothers, they had two more girls, Annie and Mary Therese, so young that they were almost a second family.) Pence also turned over his old roster of donors from the 1988 and 1990 races—Pence had no need of it.

Not long after that, Mike and Karen Pence had McIntosh and his wife, Ruthie, over to their house for dinner. Karen cooked up some chicken, and they parsed over the day-to-day operation of campaign life. Karen told Ruthie to keep her day job and then find David after work and meet up with him on the campaign trail. With the birth of his first child in 1991 and a second on the way, a new career and a stable home life, Pence gladly passed the torch to McIntosh. "I genuinely believe I have found something I'm reasonably good at and want to pursue a career through that. I don't know if I ever was good at being a politician. I don't know if I had the temperament for it. I found the restraints on my ability to be candid very frustrating."

CHAPTER 6

MIKE PENCE, INC. V. MICHAEL

Even after two years, the sting of loss was still fresh for Pence. "You couldn't talk to him about elected office, he just said, 'No way. I'm never going near that again!'" said Bob Massie, his friend who had studied the *Seven Habits of Highly Effective People* with him. Pence was concerned that he lost himself in politics and public life. The outside world wanted "Mike Pence, Inc." Pence told Massie once, but he didn't want to lose his core, his values, "Michael" as he put it.

At the start of 1993, the IPR invited Russell Kirk, one of the fathers of the modern conservative movement, to speak at a dinner. Other leaders of the movement had come through before, but none captured Pence's attention the same way that Kirk did. Quilhot recalled Pence was downright dazzled. For the first time, Pence heard a philosophy that had grown out of the values he knew from childhood. It felt like the same conservatism George Curtis had introduced him to more than a decade earlier—not bookish or aristocratic, like

Buckley, but earnest and straightforward, calling for conserving the traditions that Pence saw in the nation's founding fathers.

One day Pence drove down to meet Kirk after a speech in Columbus, Indiana. They sat in the lobby of the Holiday Inn and talked. Pence prodded him, much like he had prodded his early political advisers years earlier. Was he a neoconservative, like Buckley? A paleoconservative, like Pat Buchanan? Kirk shot back simply, "A conservative. . . . I wrote a book on it." It was classic Kirk, direct and understated. Kirk's *The Conservative Mind* defined a style of conservatism that did not resonate much in Washington or the East Coast, but picked up adherents throughout the rest of the country. The book itself was a collection of essays on the major conservative thinkers, from Milton Friedman to Friedrich Hayek. In it, Kirk writes, "Men cannot improve a society by setting fire to it: they must seek out its old virtues and bring them back into the light." And at the core of those "old virtues," he writes, is the Church and Christianity. To Kirk, the freedom of man was inextricably linked to God.

It became Pence's second favorite book, surpassed only by the Bible. "The conservative is animated by the principle of driving toward the ideal solutions that are grounded in economic freedom and individual liberty, but also understanding that compromise is part of the conservative approach to governance," Pence said later about his meeting with Kirk. "I don't believe in compromising principles, but I do believe in finding a way forward on the basis of authentic common ground."

That June, Mike and Karen had their second child, Charlotte. In the years since he quit campaigning his family blossomed. Just three years earlier Mike and Karen were sitting on a waiting list for an adoption, now they had given birth to two beautiful children. The further away he got from running for office, the more God seemed to provide for his family.

By the end of 1993, Quilhot found that the IPR was coming up short on money. Quilhot's parents bankrolled a fair amount of the effort, and they wanted another failed congressional candidate from Indiana, Rick Hawks, on the payroll. At the start, Quilhot had money for Pence and Hawks. Pence did a great job fund-raising in 1991 and 1992. Hawks was fund-raising, too, but it was for his own project, his own church. Meanwhile, Pence seemed to be slipping away, more into promoting himself than the IPR—spending more time on his radio show (he had started hosting "The Mike Pence Show" on WNDE in 1992) and starting his own newsletter, *The Pence Report*.

Quilhot was in a pickle. He liked Pence; so he put the decision in Pence's hands. "I had three really good years there and just came to the conclusion I wanted to go and do something else," Pence said. So as 1993 wrapped up, Quilhot gave Pence a few months to get a better footing in radio, then cut him loose from IPR.

But radio wasn't paying the bills for Pence. And now he had a family of four. Karen had taken off from teaching to raise the children, they had a mortgage to pay on a modest colonial in Indianapolis, and no discernible income to count on.

They were broke. Again.

A few months later, in February 1994, the perfect opportunity opened up. Phil Sharp announced his retirement; he saw the conservative wave building in the 1994 elections and got out before it washed him out. "Great decision, bad timing," Pence mused. "My impression on the campaign trail (four years ago) was he was really tired. He made a tough decision. In all respects he ought to be admired for that." The GOP power brokers immediately went to Pence; they wanted a tested warrior—not McIntosh. But Pence had made a promise to support McIntosh and he stuck by it—he was done running for office.

As Pence's career seemed to evaporate, his family and spiritual life flourished. He loved being a father and adored his growing family. And as a family, the Pences began a more concentrated journey to their evangelical Christian faith. Pence continued attending St. Barnabas Catholic Church, but Karen began attending a staunchly evangelical megachurch a little farther south, the Community Church of Greenwood.

The pastor of the church, Jim Dodson, noticed the young family and pursued Pence for a meeting. Dodson called, Pence would schedule a meeting, then cancel at the last minute, so Dodson would call again, and again, and again until he succeeded. When Pence and Dodson met for breakfast at the Bob Evans on the southside of Indianapolis, Pence said, "You're the most persistent person I've ever met in my life. You just don't give up."

Dodson eventually convinced Pence to help form a small prayer group that met every Friday morning to study the Bible. "In your faith, there's a Scripture that says 'Iron sharpens iron," Dodson said. "The idea is, if you have people you're around and you're challenging each other, you'll make each other better followers of Christ." The spiritual transformation that started sixteen years earlier, in the pastoral hills of rural Kentucky, culminated in Pence leaving the Catholic Church, reluctantly—pulled out by his family and a very persistent evangelical pastor. Mike Pence was now a fully active evangelical Christian.

Meanwhile, Pence's side project, working as a local radio talker, was about to become a fruitful endeavor, with the unintentional help of a raucous radio shock jock.

THE RISE OF RUSH

Rush Limbaugh got his start DJing in Pittsburgh, then found his way to Sacramento to replace a shock jock who had made his way to the big time, Morton Downey Jr. Limbaugh adopted much of Downey's style: goading, mocking, insulting, and pushing people, and soon he catapulted to WABC in New York and was quickly syndicated across the nation. By the early '90s, Limbaugh was a conservative juggernaut unlike anything previously seen.

In the heat of the 1992 contest between Bush and Buchanan, Limbaugh initially sided with Buchanan. Pence listened to Limbaugh every day and thought he'd be a great speaker for the Indiana Policy Review Foundation, so he faxed him an invitation to headline a dinner. Meanwhile, Bush's campaign team went to work on Limbaugh to get him to change sides—and he did, with the promise of some access to Bush. Pence couldn't believe it! So he faxed another letter to Limbaugh, this one rescinding the invitation. A short while later, Chuck Quilhot's sister told him to turn on the radio—Rush Limbaugh was destroying Mike Pence on the radio! He was lighting up the Indiana Policy Review for revoking his invitation!

Limbaugh played on the biggest station in Indiana, WIBC, 1070 AM, the major news-talk station. Pence said his modest weekend radio show on the much-smaller WNDE, "garishly rips off Rush Limbaugh's style, while focusing on Indiana." Pence liked to joke that he was "Rush on decaf," but even that was overstating it. Rush liked to talk, a lot, and fill the airwaves with his voice. Pence took more callers, did more newsmaker interviews, and was cordial on-air. He also didn't mercilessly mock people he didn't agree with. About the only thing they had in common was the conservatism and the microphone.

At the start of 1994, the executives of Network Indiana, a syndicated service that sold news and sports programming to small stations around the state, went looking for their own version of Rush Limbaugh to help sell more local advertisers on their product. Network Indiana serviced everywhere outside the Indianapolis bubble, providing news for the low-wattage stations in towns like Shelbyville, Muncie, Anderson. Pence's boss at WNDE knew that he had just lost his job at the think tank and was providing for a growing family, so she told her friends at Network Indiana she had just the guy. On April 11, 1994, he was given a statewide talk-radio show. *The Mike Pence Show* began airing around the state just as conservative talk-radio ensconced itself in the political arena as an unmatched cudgel.

Limbaugh's daily rampages fueled a true conservative revolution running up to the 1994 midterms. Buchanan's surprise run at the White House two years earlier hinted at the raw, populist anger of white Middle America, but with a Republican in the White House it was hard to unify the Right. That changed when Bill Clinton took the

White House; now the Far Right found it easy to marshal their forces against an obvious enemy—Clinton was a philanderer, he assaulted women, he was socializing health care, he wanted to raise taxes, he dodged the draft, he smoked pot and lied about it, and just, damn it, he was so damn slick.

And with the right unified, Gingrich's GOPAC was at the center of a wave ready to wash the Democrats out of Washington. Gingrich's overarching theme was squarely in the culture war; it harkened to American greatness, which seemed to have passed, using the tagline "Renewing American Civilization." "We must build a governing majority, founded on basic principles, that is prepared to do what we failed to do during the last twelve years: replace the Welfare State with an Opportunity Society, and demonstrate that our ideas are the key to progress, freedom and the Renewal of American Civilization."

On November 8, 1994, GOPAC's tactics worked, with some help from Limbaugh. The Republicans won fifty-four new seats—a landslide, more than enough to take control of the House for the first time in four decades. They cut into the South for the first time, destroying a critical flange of the Democratic coalition. Voters who had been going Republican for president, while sending Democratic good ol' boys back for another two years every year, decided they didn't like what those good ol' boys were doing once they left "back home" for their seats in Washington. The Democrats never saw it coming—the wave even swept out Democratic House Speaker Tom Foley. And in Indiana's Second District, David McIntosh got the ticket to Washington that would've been Pence's.

If Pence was angry, he didn't show it—he had begun a new life, as a pundit, not a candidate.

LEFT BEHIND—NOVEMBER 1994

There was another big winner on November 8, 1994, the Christian Right—the evangelical political army had proven its might in a big way, providing soldiers for the Gingrich Revolution. And Tim La-Haye, one of the early founders of the Christian Right with Falwell and Robertson, seized the opportunity. LaHaye and his collaborator, Jerry Jenkins, set to work on a series of action books all about the end times. The result was the Tom Clancy novel of biblical doomsday prophecy, *Left Behind*. Millions of people disappear from the earth in an instant, and everyone who was left behind struggles to figure out what the hell just happened. Book upon book in the popular series followed, mixing action and mystery with the suspense of Revelation itself. The important details were true to the biblical end-times prophecies, much like Jerry Falwell's *Nuclear War and the Second Coming of Jesus Christ*, but the story was gripping—and very popular among evangelical consumers. Jenkins knew each book had to be riveting and leave readers wanting more. "This is our message. But it has to work as fiction," Jenkins said. "We believe (the Tribulation) to be true and that it will happen someday. But if it looks like preaching or teaching, it would not work."

Among more mainstream evangelicals, LaHaye, Robertson, and Falwell represented the most extreme viewpoints on the right. And their conservative political colleagues saw them as a little nutty. (Bowls of fire from the heavens? Satan walking the earth? Literally?) But they represented an ardent wing of the Right, one that Pence had fallen in with at the Indiana Family Institute—the IFI's nascent website advertised a link to the forthcoming *Left Behind: The Movie*. And the politicians didn't mind their help either. Conservative columnist Kathleen Parker used the Christian Right megapastor John Hagee's influence over his congregation to explain the value to political figures: "If Hagee were urging his congregation to tithe money to fight global warming based on apocalyptic interpretation of Scripture, does anyone really think that Al Gore would decline the check?" This didn't happen, of course.

Pence might have bought into the Falwell brand of social conservatism, but he kept the hellfire and doomsday prophecies off the air.

In just one year, Pence built himself into a local media star. His radio show became a destination for state and national politicians—he put them on around the state, in markets where Indianapolis couldn't reach. He also planned to launch a Sunday-morning talk show, a roundtable roundup of the week's news. He grew into the role of Indiana's own Larry King, said Scott Uecker, one of the directors at Network Indiana. Pence explained his soft approach this way, "My obligation first as a Christian is to try to respect that person," he said. "There's a great misunderstanding out there about this. If you can't disagree and maintain some civility, then forget democracy."

He still attempted some Limbaugh-esque humor, but didn't always hit the mark. In September 1995, just days after Cal Ripken broke Lou Gehrig's streak for most consecutive games played—2,131— Pence deadpanned, "Somebody please call me and explain what the big deal is about a guy who shows up for work three or four days a week, maybe three hours at a time, six months out of the year, and gets paid $5.9 million to do it."

While he was out making the media rounds to promote his new television show, reporters wanted to know: It seemed like he was doing an awful lot to stay in the spotlight, was he sure he was done with politics? "I'm done dreaming," he said. "All my dreams today have to do with my faith and wife and three kids. I take all the rest a day at a time. I say that from the heart because my lifelong dream was always to serve in Congress."

Pence played it safe on the air, but he sounded more like Falwell and Pat Robertson at the local GOP fund raisers he headlined. "The epicenter of our cultural decline is the decline of the family. Welfare, regulation, illegitimacy, outcome-based education, too much government—all are directly related to the decline of the family," Pence said during a talk in Greenwood, Indiana, later in 1995. "There really is cause to become involved to head off this cultural crisis. Our nation is on the decline."

As the 1996 election neared, the Christian Right kept its collective eye on Pat Buchanan, as he mounted a second White House bid. He seemed to have kept his core base of support from 1992, and in February 1996, he stormed to a second-place finish in Iowa. Pence was elated.

On February 13, 1996, the day after the Iowa caucuses, Pence immediately leapt to his defense. To bolster his point, he brought on a Christian conservative activist, Chris Dickson. "I appreciate you leaving the pitchfork and the horns at home this morning. Don't you get frustrated with the way the media says, 'The Christian Right reared its ugly head with Pat Buchanan.' You ever get tired of being vilified for political activism?" Pence asked. Dickson laughed, "I get a kick out of showing up and people seeing I only have one head. But it is a little tiring to get portrayed as an absolute fanatic, we're just mainstream." Dickson wasn't entirely off the mark; veteran Republicans began noticing more and more Christian Right activists showing up to their town halls, pushing them further and further to the right on abortion, government spending, God in the public square, and every other cultural flash point.

GAMBLING IN INDIANA, TRUMP STYLE

The conservative groundswell and the Christian Right also had another battle to fight: against gambling. What started as a few casino boats in select locations in Indiana—gambling covered by a fig leaf—was now the third-largest casino industry in the country, behind only Las Vegas and Atlantic City. Naturally, it attracted the biggest gambler in the country with an abysmal record to match: Donald Trump.

Pence and others at the Indiana Family Institute may have been fighting gambling around the state, but inside the bubble of Indianapolis—the state's power brokers opened the doors for more and more casinos. Their latest pick was Gary, Indiana—the once-bustling manufacturing town just outside Chicago, now poverty-stricken and crumbling. The weeds in the vacant lots and buildings grew so tall they looked like trees.

The Democrats hoped a pair of casino boats would pump enough money into the city to restart its engines. And Donald Trump promised he would do just that, in grand style. While Pence was on-air that Tuesday, February 13, 1996, the statehouse illuminati readied an epic roast at their annual Gridiron Dinner—a comedic bash of inside jokes for all the politicians, lobbyists, and journalists. Trump was the big target this year, but the local handlers for Trump knew he didn't take kindly to insults, even if they were just friendly ribbings. So they found the perfect foil: a megarich billionaire who had been divorced twice, had a penchant for gambling, and met his current wife when she jumped topless out of a papier mâché cake two years earlier—Stephen Hilbert.

As the Gridiron opened, Trump and his second wife, Marla Maples, walked to the stage—waving, smiling. The Indiana press opened with an *SNL* Weekend Update–style "news" bit—"A Gridiron news quiz now: The number 13,500 is A. The capacity of the new downtown baseball stadium. B. The number of Marion County voters who actually turned out for the last election. C. The current circulation of the *Indianapolis News* or D. The number of Stephen Hilbert's ex-wives." Trump and Maples laughed.

The "newscaster" onstage offered up another joke, "IU Basketball Coach Bob Knight has taken a cue from (Democratic Party chairwoman) Ann DeLaney to author a book about the intricacies of his profession. The book will be titled, 'Basketball for Dumb Fucks.' Knight is offering free copies to the media." Trump yawned at some of the local trivia, although the scriptwriters tried to keep it from being too insidery.

Finally, they came to the Trump "roast." Republican Party chairman Mike McDaniel and veteran TV reporter Jim Shella took the podiums on opposite sides of the stage. "Ladies and gentleman, please welcome to the Gridiron Hot Seat, Mr. Donald J. Trump," McDaniel began. Trump walked around from the table, waved, shook their hands. He couldn't quite figure out where to sit, eventually landing in the conspicuously placed seat dead center of the stage—no table or podium in front of him. He smiled, stiffly. Before they started, Mc-Daniel motioned to him, bashfully. "I hate to act like a hick Hoosier and all that kind of stuff. But I'm kind of an autograph collector." Shella walked across the stage and gave Trump a copy of the program, then Trump whipped out a pen from his tux coat. But McDaniel cut in, "Whoa, whoa! Don. Don! I didn't say I wanted to get it from you. I wanted you to help me get it from Marla, geez!" Trump slaps the copy of the program down on the table in front of Marla Maples. "God! How presumptuous can you be, ladies and gentlemen?"

"The Gridiron committee determined long ago that we wanted to roast a famous tycoon, someone with a huge fortune, young wife, tied to gambling, a ruthless businessman with a reputation as a self-centered jerk," said Shella. "Steve Hilbert wasn't available, so we settled for Donald Trump." McDaniel hopped in from the other side of the stage, "The Trump name is everywhere, including on some previously unexpected places. Here are a few. Trump the watch: It has no power source, in other words, no one can determine what makes it tick. Trump the luncheon meat: it's made of highly refined bologna. Some people swallow it whole, others gag." Trump got a laugh with that last one. But what about the hair? "Just look at it this way: This is how (U.S. Senator) Dan Coats would look if he had a billion dollars."

After a grueling run, Trump got a rebuttal. "You know, many New Yorkers first discovered Indiana when we legalized riverboat gambling. I know I did. I remember to this day reading the story in the *New York Times* and I knew immediately what I had to do—I had to find where Indiana was." Ba-zing. Then Trump hit Hilbert. "The other day I met this fellow named Hilbert," Trump said. "He started out with a few thousand bucks, some undervalued insurance companies, milked them to death for huge profits. Found a lovely and talented young woman, started investing in gambling properties for entertainment, and flaunted the money and his beautiful bride on the pages of the glossy magazines, and I'm trying to figure out, who the hell is he trying to imitate anyway? And I don't like it." ❧

Hilbert wasn't even there for the show, but he had pulled almost as much stage time as Trump. Who was this guy? "It's simple. Hilbert has become Indiana's version of Donald Trump," veteran investigative reporter Dick Cady explained. Hilbert made some big bets in the mid-'90s selling commercial insurance and struck it big, but he was also aggressive—using every new purchase to leverage more borrowing power to make his next acquisition. Hilbert's wealth and power were skyrocketing, but so was the mountain of debt he owed. But debt didn't matter so much when you're en vogue.

Pence wasn't at the Gridiron, either; he didn't run in that crowd. Pence opposed gambling on fiscal grounds, citing it as taxation on the poor. Still, Hilbert was powerful, and Pence enjoyed his access to the most powerful men in Indiana. Four years earlier, Pence had put his name on top of a lawsuit challenging the powers that be in Indiana, trying to block state lawmakers from getting lifetime health insurance paid for by taxpayers. But, increasingly, Pence was joining the club of Indiana power brokers. Pence desperately wanted proximity to power, and that meant he wanted to meet Hilbert. Pence had just the vehicle; his new television program—he would go once every three months to a famous Hoosier's home and sit down for a light discussion with a small group of local big names. Sure, Hilbert and Trump had been through a few marriages, but Pence saw no reason to skewer them (unlike Clinton).

The Hilbert home was palatial, a $33 million mansion in the nicest suburb just north of Indianapolis. Le Chateau Renaissance, as Hilbert dubbed it, stood on forty acres with twenty-five thousand square feet of living space. The interior, lined with mahogany and marble, was befitting of Indiana's richest man. WNDY-TV aired the very first *Dinner with Mike Pence* TV special on October 27, 1996; it was filmed at Hilbert's house. They had an all-star cast, including

Eli Lilly executive Mitch Daniels, former Indiana lieutenant governor John Mutz, and of course, Hilbert. The group dined on fried ravioli salad, pan-seared salmon, and desserts.

A few weeks later, Bill Clinton won reelection to the White House, despite the cries of moralists like Pence.

THE RADIO PRO—1997

As 1997 started, Network Indiana and *The Mike Pence Show* moved into a nice new building directly across the street from the Indianapolis Motor Speedway. It was at the new studio where Pence confronted his longtime producer, Chris Pollack. Pollack had been with Pence from the start producing Mike's old weekend show at WNDE in 1994 and had come with him to Network Indiana to turn him into a star. Pollack not only knew how to run the boards, he knew how to book the politicians, he knew how to cue the issues. And just as they were about to hit it big, the wheels came off, right as they went into a commercial break. A colleague watched Pence through the studio glass; Pence stood just inches from Pollack's face—almost nose to nose—and yelled at him furiously. Pollack got the last word as he marched out of the building: "You run your own damn board!"

Pence sat utterly helpless. The seconds ticked by in the ad break in the middle of a program; he would be coming back on-air in a few minutes. Meekly, he got on the intercom and tried for help, "Russ Maloney. Russ Maloney to the studio, please." Russ didn't show. Pence had no idea how to run the boards. He panicked. "Scott Uecker. Scott Uecker to the studio, please." Uecker, the program director, didn't show up either. Pence was getting desperate, "Ernie Caldwell, Ernie to the studio, please," Ernie was the network president. Ernie didn't come. What the hell? Where was everybody? *The Mike Pence Show* was about to return from break! To dead air. "Anybody. Would somebody pleeease come to the studio??" Finally, Uecker and another tech ran in to save him.

Nobody quite knew what sparked the fight, but Pence's colleagues had been picking up on the modestly sized ego he had been feeding over recent years. Pence had rebuilt himself into a local media star. His radio show was carried on close to two dozen stations around the state, and he had his own TV show. Pence still joked that he was "Rush on decaf" but Uecker was right, Pence was more like Larry King. The big interviews and unfettered access inflated his head, gradually.

The next day Pence asked Dan Jensen, one of the producers at Network Indiana, if he could fill in on the show for Pollack. Pence and Jensen hit it off, and Jensen took over as producer full-time. Jensen was easygoing and let Pence cycle through the big three topics that would always light up the phones: whether Indiana should adopt Daylight Saving Time, Indiana should return to one division of high school basketball for the entire state (which produced the mythic story of *Hoosiers*), and Indiana University basketball coaching legend Bob Knight ought to be fired.

After close to eight years on-air, Pence was in his swing. The typical show ran like clockwork. Mike would hop on-air and say, "Did you see Bob Knight? Did you see what he did this weekend?" Then Jensen watched the phone line, about seven or eight of them, light up—the board went green. So Jensen would cue up the Indiana everyman, "Jim from Bedford," and Pence took the call, "Let's go to line two right now, and we've got Jim in Bedford. And, well, Jim, what do you think about Coach Knight?" And Jim would say, "Well, Coach Knight is an idiot." Then Jensen cued up a big Knight supporter, and he'd say, "Well, Bob Knight is basketball in Indiana." Jensen laid it out, "Sometimes you'd just let the callers drive the show."

If he did some obscure Washington item for an hour, the phones went dead. One morning, after a particular dud, Pence walked over to Jensen and said, "If we ever do that topic again, jam a sock in my mouth." The next day Jensen came in with one of his old athletic socks and hung it up in the production booth in easy view for Pence. Pence also had Jensen screen for the conspiracy theorists—the callers who talked about One World Government, blue helmets, and black helicopters. When Pence was out, Jensen teased the wackos himself: "Mike Pence isn't here today, he was picked up by an unmarked black helicopter. (Cue helicopter audio.) We hear he's being taken to a secret meeting of the trilateral commission of the Council on Foreign Relations."

A few months after Jensen took over production, national radio chain Emmis bought Network Indiana. Emmis owned the largest, most influential station in Indiana radio—WIBC, 1070 AM. What luck! Pence hit the big time! Now he'd finally be on the biggest AM talker in Indiana. The newly expanded Emmis team moved into a beautiful new radio studio in the center of downtown Indianapolis. Their main studio faced out to Monument Circle, but Pence's show would be taped on the fourth floor of the building. Then he learned why they'd have to tape it—because his show was going to play on WIBC at midnight, on a tape replay.

He wasn't at the big time yet, but opportunity surrounded him. Veteran producers and radio folks offered tips and guidance constantly. Jon Quick, the program director, listened in on Pence's show one day shortly after he started at Emmis.

As Pence wrapped up and walked out of the studio he saw Quick and asked him how it went. "Great," said Quick, "but stop doing your radio voice."

"What radio voice?" Pence asked. Pence hadn't noticed, but Quick had, that Pence sounded an awful lot like Rush Limbaugh when he was on-air, but not so much in person.

"Your radio voice—don't do it," Quick shot back. "Your callers are Hoosiers, you're a Hoosier, just talk to them like you would anybody."

By the end of 1997 almost everyone around Pence figured he was completely done campaigning. But Steve Simpson, the morning newsman for WIBC, caught a whiff of Pence's growing ego and wondered: Was this whole radio bit about something else? Simpson remembered covering Pence's two races for Congress in 1988 and 1990, and he noticed the stunning turnabout to on-air Nice Guy. This felt a little too convenient, like an image rehab that was in preparation for a second shot at politics. Simpson said, "The perfect way to do that is to be in people's homes Monday through Friday and have a radio show where you cast yourself in the role of a nice guy." ◦

As far as fodder for his new show, Pence didn't have to look far. The Clinton presidency was almost custom-built for conservative moralists on-air. The parade of female accusers from his time as governor and then his trysts in the White House itself seemed to multiply throughout his presidency. By his second term in office, the special prosecutor who had started out investigating a questionable insider land deal from Clinton's Arkansas days had expanded his probe into Clinton's affair with a much younger staffer, Monica Lewinsky. Pence wrote on the website for his radio show that the Clinton scandal "will be a perfect vehicle for those in the mainstream liberal press to deal a final blow to old-fashioned morality in America. 'The Age of Aquarius' generation now running most of the major news departments in the country have been pining for the opportunity to denigrate what remains of our old allegiance to marital fidelity."

House Republicans laid the groundwork through 1998 to conduct an impeachment of Clinton for lying about his affair with Lewinsky. But Republicans' own affairs slipped out in public, and the Clinton press team successfully spun the narrative that Republicans were overstepping into the president's private life. The president's party typically loses seats in the House in every midterm election, but voters chewed in to Republicans' House majority on November 3, 1998, flipping five seats over to the Democrats. In the wake of the loss, Gingrich announced he would resign his House seat. The man selected to replace Gingrich, who would preside over the Clinton impeachment, Louisiana representative Bob Livingston, had also been cheating. After Livingston bowed out of the running for Speaker, they picked someone seemingly unassailable, Illinois representative Denny Hastert.

At the end of 1998, the Republican-led House of Representatives opened its impeachment of President Bill Clinton—the first since President Andrew Johnson's trial 130 years earlier. Pence watched the proceedings and despaired; even though the House Republicans had enough votes to impeach Clinton, the president was likely to survive the Senate trial and even emerge stronger politically. Pence blamed Johnson himself. Shortly after the Civil War, Johnson argued for the popular election of U.S. senators, instead of by the state legislatures. Four decades later, the states ratified the Seventeenth Amendment. That popular election, Pence argued, led Republican senators to crumble under popular pressure. "After 14 months of presidential lying and obfuscation the only prudent conclusion is that the Constitution failed," Pence wrote in the *Indianapolis Star* in February 1999. "Bill Clinton owes Andrew Johnson a debt of gratitude."

The Clinton impeachment left another mark on Pence, observed radio colleague Kate Shepherd: words matter. Clinton tripped up trying to lie about his affair with Lewinsky, not because he had the affair.

Meanwhile, Pence's friend Representative David McIntosh eyed the governor's office from Washington for a few months; he was ready to move up and also move his family back to Indiana after six years in Washington. Democratic governor Frank O'Bannon looked vulnerable to a strong challenge. The Clinton years hadn't done much to help Democrats' brand in Indiana, and with the 2000 election cycle at the doorstep, McIntosh saw his chance. McIntosh immediately called up his old friend Mike Pence and asked if he would consider running for his seat, Indiana's Second Congressional District, when he vacated it to run for governor. Pence told McIntosh, "No, we've decided not to run for office." McIntosh pushed back, "Would you and Karen please pray about this?"

CHAPTER 7

RESURRECTION—2000

The offer from McIntosh jolted Pence—could it be, one decade after his dreams were crushed, that God was giving him a second chance? He'd paid his penance—he reformed himself into a nice guy in the public's eye. Pence's problem was that his life was now on a different trajectory. Just a few months after his 1990 loss for Congress, the Pences became a family. And, by Pence's own standards, families needed stability. Campaigns are demanding exercises; they open families up to public inspection, they demand massive amounts of time from the candidate and also tremendous flexibility from all involved. The prying press would pick at any perceived weakness or weirdness they found in the Pence unit. Was Mike Pence ready for that? Was his family ready?

There was also one other tiny complication: Mike Pence didn't live in the Second District. Mike and Karen would have to uproot their family from Indianapolis and move an hour's drive south just to run. Pence had done this once before, in 1987, in his very first run for office. But now they had three small kids—along with the perfect colonial house in a bucolic neighborhood at the southern edge of Indianapolis. Starting from Michael Jr., with each new child, they planted a small sapling in the backyard—and each tree grew steadily as they all grew as a family. They were rooted. Of course, the congressional mapmakers weren't thinking of Pence's own ambitions when they pulled the Second District out of Indianapolis in 1992.

He also wasn't sure he wanted to leave the media spotlight, just as he had hit his stride. Indeed, Pence had an easy way about him on-air, a comfortableness and light touch that made him a good interviewer. In one episode of *The Mike Pence Show*, Pence led an in-depth discussion of economic development policy in Indiana. One of the panelists noted that a "famous Hoosier" once said he robbed banks, "because that's where the money is." Pence laughed and deadpanned, "That's John Dillinger, folks." Pence's friends laughed when they saw it, it was classic Michael, easygoing and humorous.

Pence wanted to run, but he knew it would take some working on Karen to get her to yes. He asked Peter Rusthoven, who so wisely suggested he keep his oar in the political water with a public act of contrition, for a hand. Rusthoven and the Pences went to a small Republican fund raiser. Mike got up to work the room, and Rusthoven pulled up next to Karen to float the idea of another run. "You know, this is a great opportunity for the whole family. Think of how great it would be to have a U.S. congressman for a father to your kids. You know this was always Mike's dream; this is God giving him a second chance." Karen was open to the idea, but not yet convinced. They'd need to pray on it, she said.

That August of 1999, McIntosh ran into his friends Mike and Karen at a GOP donor's suite at the Indianapolis Motor Speedway, right across the street from his old radio studio. They were there for the running of the Brickyard 400. "Mike, have you thought any more about the congressional race?" he queried. Pence replied, "I haven't completely decided yet, but we've been praying about it and it looks like something we'd be willing to do."

Later that summer, Mike and Karen took the family on a retreat to Theodore Roosevelt National Park in North Dakota. They loved horseback riding, and as they rode up a hill, they reached a plateau and spotted two red-tailed hawks soaring effortlessly above them— not flapping their wings at all. Mike said, "If we do it, we need to do it like those hawks. We just need to spread our wings and let God lift us up where he wants to take us." Karen knew it was their sign. She was in.

They returned from their trip ready, but first they had to get their ducks in a row. For starters, they would have to find a home in the Second District. Next he needed to convince his broad network of supporters he really had changed from the vicious campaign brawler of a decade past. Third, Pence would have to leave his job to run for Congress, and Karen was working full-time at home raising their three kids. They would have to draw down their life's savings and live off credit cards for about a year. Campaign cash was very much out of the question.

As they embarked on their return to campaigning, Karen picked out one of their favorite verses and had it framed. Jeremiah 29:11, "'For I know the plans I have for you,' declares the Lord, 'plans to prosper you and not to harm you, plans to give you hope and a future.'"

Taken as a single verse, it clearly read like a promise of providence for God's followers. But pulling back, Chapter 29 of Jeremiah is the recitation of God's promise to the exiled Jews living in Babylon under the rule of the tyrant Nebuchadnezzar. And his promise to "prosper" his followers is a broader promise to return all the Jews to Jerusalem after seventy years in captivity in Babylon. Jeremiah 29, verses 10 through 14 read: "This is what the Lord says: 'When seventy years are completed for Babylon, I will come to you and fulfill my good promise to bring you back to this place. For I know the plans I have for you,' declares the Lord, 'plans to prosper you and not to harm you, plans to give you hope and a future. Then you will call on me and come and pray to me, and I will listen to you. You will seek me and find me when you seek me with all your heart. I will be found by you,' declares the Lord, 'and will bring you back from captivity. I will gather you from all the nations and places where I have banished you,' declares the Lord, 'and will bring you back to the place from which I carried you into exile.'"

Perhaps the exile of their situation was being forced to move their family, change careers, and live off debt for a year with faith as their guide.

A Different Kind of Evangelical—2000

Even as Pence moved closer to the Jerry Falwell–Pat Robertson wing of evangelicalism, he never quite ensconced with them, although his good friend Bill Smith lived in that world. At the same time, the broader evangelical community, the universe outside the politicized Christian Right movement, found a new champion from the unlikeliest of families. Texas governor George W. Bush, running that summer in the Republican primary, told a crowd in Iowa that his favorite philosopher was Jesus Christ, "because he changed my heart." "I was watching the debate with my wife and daughter in the room, neither of whom are political junkies," said Richard Land, a leader in the Southern Baptist Convention. "And when they heard that answer they both stopped what they were doing, looked at me, and said 'Wow.'"

W. was a different kind of evangelical—not a strict Fundamentalist. He had been converted late in life by no less than Billy Graham himself. One time his mother, former first lady Barbara Bush, and he got in a debate over whether you need to be born again to enter heaven. They got Billy Graham on the phone and he told them the answer was to just be good and follow the Lord.

If he was a cookie-cutter Republican in 1988 and 1990, Pence had moved clearly into the culture warrior camp by the start of the

2000 race. At the end of 1999, he went to Bill Smith and asked him to run his primary campaign. Republicans were flooding the race and he needed someone who knew the ropes—someone who knew both Indiana and Washington. "They had a whole peace about running," Smith said, after hearing Mike and Karen's story of seeing the hawks riding the wind. "He became the candidate who reflected the man he had become," Smith said. "He was the kind of guy that was the first to forgive somebody—he really had become a man who had a softer heart and a better idea of what civility looked like."

Shortly after Smith took over the campaign, he drove to Muncie to the campaign headquarters of Republican Luke Messer, one of a handful of other candidates already announced. Messer's staff were surprised to see Pence's campaign chief; Smith said he wanted to see Messer. As Luke Messer walked out, Smith told him, "If you ever see anything about Pence's campaign that lacks integrity, I want you to call me and we'll make it right." Meanwhile, Van Smith, the Muncie businessman who held the strings for almost all the campaign money in the district, put out word that Pence was the man. The heirs to the Ball family fortune were on board, and so went the rest of the GOP money class. Other Republicans could run, but they'd have a hard time finding money.

The table was set for Pence's big comeback. Then Pence reached back to his old playbook from 1989—he mounted a campaign without ever announcing it. On November 9, 1999, he filed an "exploratory committee" with the Federal Election Commission, to "consider" running for Congress. Pence said he wanted to support Indiana's farmers and supported "reversing our nation's moral decline." But he made it clear that his decision wouldn't come until after the new year. A few weeks later, Pence announced that he was moving his family to Edinburgh, Indiana—inside the Second District—another clear giveaway he was running. But he remained coy, "I won't make a formal announcement until January." Meanwhile, Pence went on-air daily, on close to a dozen radio stations throughout the Second District, and continued his weekly television roundtable. For all intents and purposes, Pence was a congressional candidate with his own slice of the airwaves.

His Republican opponents, who had announced months ago and were playing it straight, sniffed out his game. Jeff Linder, a state lawmaker running in the primary, noted that Pence had filed a "statement of candidacy" form with the FEC on November 9—Linder said that made Pence a candidate from then forward. Linder argued that he and every other candidate was owed equal airtime, close to one hundred hours each, for all the time Pence was on-air from November 9 until he quit his show on December 31. WIBC balked; putting on congressional candidates for a hundred hours each would be terrible for business.

The new year rolled around, the Y2K virus did not blow up the world, and Mike Pence continued stringing out his decision and stayed on the air. In other words, nothing changed. On January 10, he said, "I do intend to run for Congress in the year 2000." His new deadline for a formal launch was February, just three months before the actual primary election—Pence was running out the clock. He was already the clear front-runner in the Republican primary, with the backing of every local donor and power broker of note. And he wasn't even officially in the race.

On February 15, 2000, Pence scheduled kickoff rallies in Columbus and Muncie, Indiana. He never broke a sweat. On May 2, 2000, he clobbered Messer, Linder, and all his other GOP opponents, collecting 44 percent of the vote. Professional handicappers expected the seat to stay in GOP hands that November; Indiana's Second District was all but his. Jeremiah 29:11 may have been a bit dramatic, but he wasn't going to be in exile very long.

THE TWO MIKES

Now Pence had a deeper challenge. Dispatching with the Republican field via a shadow campaign was easy; now he would have to fix some of the big problems from his first two races, beginning with defining who exactly he was. He buried the persona of attack dog with his "Confessions" essay and the radio show, but now he had to say who stood in that place. The new Mike Pence was a good Christian with a consistent message: fiscal restraint, strong national defense, and traditional family values.

"Our campaign has committed itself this year to talking about Mike Pence, and about what Mike Pence believes," Pence said in his first TV ad, in a straight-on shot to the camera. The footage was gauzy, almost like it was glowing. Then Pence dropped the Bob Dole impersonation. "I've learned a lot in the last ten years; I've seen my children born, I've built a business." The business he was talking about was his radio show. "What I've learned is that negative personal attacks have no place in public life."

Another spot featured Karen walking through the front of the classroom, "Everything I know about public education, I've learned from my wife, Karen. She's been a public-school teacher, who's taught in the classroom for more than fifteen years." The footage was still gauzy as it panned over Karen in a royal blue dress talking with students. "She really believes in kids and taught me a long time ago there's nothing that ails our local schools that teachers can't fix, if we give them the resources and the freedom to teach."

A third spot featured a farmer walking out at sunrise, clicking on his radio—on came *The Mike Pence Show*, "Greetings across the amber waves of grain, this is Mike Pence." Then the narrator came on "Across farm field and town, highway and home, Mike Pence has spoken, from his heart to ours."

The Mike Pence of the finely crafted television spots was a good Christian who never stuck his neck out on divisive social issues. But the Mike Pence of the internet had no problem going there. His "Guide to Renewing the American Dream" spoke to a different audience, a more fervent crowd that wanted to go online to learn more about him. He sounded like Rush Limbaugh with the caffeine, he was almost Pentecostal in his fervor. The government should notify parents before their children are given any condoms, "homosexual" couples should not get marriage benefits or special protections against hate crimes, and taxes should be cut so that "one parent may choose to be a full-time at-home parent if they so desire."

Women's military service needs to be curbed: "While women have always made an important contribution to national security, we must resist the liberal impulse to use the military to advance the interest of women in civilian culture at the expense of military readiness and effectiveness." And gays should not be permitted in the military at all. "Homosexuality is incompatible with military service because the presence of homosexuals in the ranks weakens unit cohesion."

And Congress must "audit" the HIV prevention act named after Hoosier Ryan White, to ensure money doesn't go to groups that "celebrate and encourage the type of behaviors that facilitate the spreading of HIV." And Pence supported gay conversion programs: "Resources should be directed toward those institutions which provide assistance to those seeking to change their sexual behavior."

Something had emerged over his life and career: Pence had a propensity for being pulled in new directions easily by whoever had his ear at the moment. In college he was drafted into the evangelical movement, and later conservative Republicanism. After law school he was recruited into the ranks of mainstream Republican Party loyalists. After his failing congressional bids, he was pulled into the Libertarian-leaning world of the *Indiana Policy Review*, and then into an evangelical megachurch in 1994. But by the late '90s, Bill Smith, the head of the Christian Right–aligned group Indiana Family Institute, had grabbed Pence's ear—and Pence sounded more and more like the Christian Right.

Coming into the closing months of the race, it was impossible to tell which Mike Pence would show up to Congress if elected.

On the national level, Texas governor George W. Bush was running a close race against Clinton's vice president, Al Gore, for the White House. Bush put down an insurgent run by Arizona senator

John McCain months earlier and moved into Republican nomination mode. As part of assuming the mantle of the Republican Party's leader, Bush launched a search committee for his own running mate. He tasked his father's old adviser Dick Cheney with running the search. And, at the end of that search, Cheney came back with the name of the best candidate for vice president: himself. Cheney still represented the bridge between establishment and conservative Republicans, even though Bush himself had both wings locked up better than his father ever did. But Cheney also represented something new, a powerful force that could be almost more influential than Bush himself in shaping policy if they won in November.

THE 2000 DEBATE

The last time Mike Pence took the stage at WIPB's studios at Ball State University, he was thirty-one years old, he was overwrought— cocky and sharp, but also floundering at the penultimate moment before his political career evaporated. When he returned, a decade later on October 15, 2000, he was humbler, wiser, more confident, and more even-keeled. Now he wore a modest blue suit and a snow-capped do. Mike Pence, father of three, smiled as the camera panned to him—his wife, Karen, and youngest daughter, Audrey, now six, sat a few rows back in the crowd. This time he had nothing to prove, he had already won the race.

Moderator Steve Bell introduced the candidates for Indiana's Second District—Democrat Bob Rock, Pence, and Independent Bill Frazier.

All Pence had to do now was play keep-away. So which Pence would sit onstage that night, TV Ad Mike, with the picture so gauzy that he almost blurred right into the background? Or Culture Warrior Mike, who wanted to curtail gay rights?

As they worked through their opening statements, Pence dispatched his most glaring weakness. "I was born and raised here in the

Second Congressional District, but for the vagaries of redistricting would have lived my entire adult life in this district." Then, he quickly moved into his boilerplate, "I believe that I truly do represent the values of the Second District of Indiana. People who believe in limited government, less taxes, people who believe in a strong military and that that military has been cut, and people who believe in traditional moral values, like the right to life."

Then they moved to the questions. Where did Pence stand on the Middle East conflict? Firmly with Israel. "There's a lot of talk these days about the U.S. needing to be an honest broker and needing to be fair to all sides. Well, I submit to you that our relationship with Israel is precious and it's unique."

Okay, how about gays in the military? Clinton had approved the now famous "Don't Ask, Don't Tell" policy—a fig leaf that allowed gay men and women to serve as long as no one outed them. "Homosexuality and homosexual behavior is incompatible with military service," Pence said. "We simply need to end this social experimentation. We also need to end, quite candidly, the gender integration in basic training and the assignment of women to combat support units and ultimately into harm's way." Rock and Frazier agreed with Pence's stance.

Pence was sounding more like Culture Warrior Mike than gauzy TV Ad Mike. But then moderator Steve Bell served up a softball: economic policy. What would the candidates do to bring jobs back to Muncie, Indiana, and the rest of the Second District?

Rock immediately said he would kill NAFTA, the North American Free Trade Agreement, which many Hoosiers blamed for companies closing their factories and moving abroad. Then Frazier said he wanted it gone, too. "I'm a farmer and NAFTA was supposed to do great things for farmers," Frazier said, as he pulled a small piece of paper out of his pocket, unfolded it, and waved it in front of him, "This is a weigh ticket for a load of corn I took in two days ago. My net loss was two cents a bushel. I sold my corn at a loss." He added that he got into farming because he lost his auto plant job. "I know what it is to lose a job, and it's not pleasant."

Then they got to Pence, "Bill, I have to tell you I lost a job when Karen, who's with us tonight, was pregnant with little Audrey, who is here tonight and is six years of age. I understand how tough that is on families and how frightening that is." He wound his way through an explanation of how Hoosiers need to adjust to a new economy, and learn new skill sets, before Rock and Frazier finally pinned him down. Did he or did he not support NAFTA and free trade? "I do support free trade," Pence said. "I believe it's about the only thing that President Clinton's ever done that I've agreed with."

Pence tried to change topics, saying, "My Democratic opponent tries to put me in the extreme by saying global warming is a myth. The reality is there is a growing number in the scientific community who are questioning, just questioning, as scientists are called to do, some of the theories about the global warming, the erosion of the ozone layer." Pence then made a clever move, saying that his Democratic opponent must surely support the treaty to combat global warming supported by Democratic presidential candidate Al Gore. Bob Rock said he'd have to study more before making that decision. Then Pence cut him off, "Well, if I believed that global warming was real, then I would support the treaty."

Pence had successfully deflected his opponents and finally defined himself clearly, as what kind of politician he would be: Christian Right, economically conservative, pro–free trade and anti-environmental regulations.

On Tuesday, November 7, 2000, Mike Pence won his long-awaited, and hard-earned, ticket to Washington. He beat Democrat Bob Rock, 51 percent–38 percent (Frazier picked up a little under 10 percent). The race for the White House that year was far from over, however. A voting debacle in Florida left the nation unsure who won the state and, therefore, who won the White House. The drama played out all the way to the Supreme Court and left many Democrats declaring that

George W. Bush was an illegitimate president. The wounds from that divide would never completely heal and hinted at a new trend in national politics, where elections never truly ended. Mike Pence's long, winding journey to Congress, one that had started in 1986 with him making cold calls to local Republican bigwigs, ended fourteen years later with every major Republican kingmaker in his corner.

Now all he had to do was decide whether to take Karen and the kids with him to DC.

CHAPTER 8

THE UNKNOWN

Seven years after they first met, it was David McIntosh offering the advice to Mike Pence. McIntosh lost his bid for governor, and now he was the one finished with politics and staying in Indiana. After Pence's big win, McIntosh told Mike to take his family with him to Washington; they should stick together and he would be better for it. Almost as soon as they had moved into their new home just outside Columbus, Indiana, the Pences were packing up again, this time for Washington.

Karen and Mike and the family had some work to do adjusting to Washington. They left Indiana with upward of $30,000 in credit card debt—the result of neither Mike nor Karen holding paying jobs while they ran. They had to find a school for their three kids, ages nine, seven, and six. And they needed to find a church for their family. They quickly landed on Immanuel Bible Church in Springfield, Virginia, just inside the Beltway. The church was nondenominational, but spiritually and culturally conservative, much like the Community Church of Greenwood. In short order, they found a home in Arlington, Virginia, near the tony enclave of Yorktown—a neighborhood filled with veteran lawmakers, lobbyists, government brass, and the most powerful families in Washington.

Karen, meanwhile, built a fortress around their family. "Whatever goes on out there doesn't affect what happens in here," Michael Jr. remembered her saying. And it was true. Other lawmakers might keep their families back home in their home state—out of practical and political considerations—but the Pences moved to DC as a family and would remain a family there. Mike stuck close to a schedule of making it home to their Arlington, Virginia, house for dinner each night and hewed to a new rule set by him and Karen, the Billy Graham Rule—no dining, drinking, or meeting alone with women other than his wife. He didn't follow the rule in Indianapolis, where he would regularly sit down to lunch alone with his radio colleague Kate Shepherd, but Washington was a perilous new land for the Pences. A friend and former adviser put it this way, "Nothing good happens after the second drink and after nine P.M."

One of the first things Pence did when he got to his new office in the Longworth Office Building was ask the House staff to run in an ISDN line. Pence was going to build a makeshift radio studio right there. The modest setup would let him talk to stations all throughout his district, almost like he never left his show. The sound would be perfectly clear almost like he was still there in Indiana. House IT staffer David Almacy and his team ran the radio line for him, and they also built him a new website that could play video of Pence's one-minute floor speeches from the House chamber. The web of plug-ins, and competing technology—pick Quicktime, Windows Media Player, or another option—made it convoluted, but Pence knew the benefit of speaking directly to his base via the web. Almacy marveled at Pence, "It was pretty forward-looking."

Pretty soon other lawmakers wanted fresh websites and radio

technology in their offices, too. The Republican leadership took notice; this freshman lawmaker from Indiana was awfully good at delivering a finely crafted message back home. Representative Dick Armey, the Texas Republican who had endorsed Phil Sharp over Pence a little more than a decade earlier, took a shine to the freshman from Indiana. He offered Pence another bit of technological advice. "After hours, when the switchboard is off, you ought to put a separate line in the office," Armey told him. The line was just for his family, so they would stay close with him even when he worked late. So Karen bought a bright, cherry-red antique-style phone and they had a separate phone line run straight to his desk. "Mrs. Pence is the only one who has the number, not anyone on staff," Pence said. "She occasionally shares it with the kids. But when this phone rings, I answer it."

Pence struck up a fast friendship with another freshman lawmaker, Jeff Flake of Arizona. They'd both been presidents of conservative think tanks, were similar in age, and like-minded on the need for fiscal restraint from both parties. The United States was sitting on a cash surplus from the last few years of the Clinton administration. A mixture of tax hikes, spending cuts, a booming stock market, and a dot-com bubble all contributed to square the federal budget in a previously unthinkable way. The federal government was no longer racking up debt. And with Republicans in control of the White House and Congress, the debate became not whether to cut taxes, but how to cut them. Flake laughed, "We were sitting on the floor one day and Mike joked that we were Minutemen who had finally arrived at the battlefront, only to be told that the revolution was over."

Pence also found a community in Washington's suburbs rich with Christian and fiscal conservatives and plenty of opportunities to speak and be seen. He spoke regularly at lunches organized by the Center for Christian Statesmanship and gained the attention of a young Republican staffer from Normal, Illinois. After listening to Pence talk faith and policy at four or five lunches, Matt Lloyd determined he was the real deal, a man of faith and principle. Lloyd heard him preach

Christian principles in Washington without the scalding brimstone and fire that had marked some other moralists and decided immediately he had to find a way to get on Pence's staff.

Around the same time as Pence's arrival, an evangelical minister active in the pro-life movement also moved to Washington. Reverend Robert Schenck made his name chaining himself to the doors of Planned Parenthood clinics in order to bar access—in extreme antiabortion protests—a decade earlier. By 2001 he had moved to Capitol Hill to minister to the nation's politicians. He set up shop in a townhome just across the street from the Supreme Court, with a small granite monument of the Ten Commandments on display out front. Schenck prayed with everyone from the Republican leadership to the rank-and-file membership. He quickly connected with Pence. The two men prayed on occasion in Pence's congressional office. But when they would talk about ambition and leadership, Schenck often noticed Pence looking down at the floor, as though he were conflicted. Schenck picked out a striking dichotomy in Pence. Pence had what Schenck called a "discipleship problem"—he couldn't give his whole life over to God. He still had areas that he wanted to control, like his political ambitions, and it created a split personality in the man— "There's a Christian Mike and there's a Secular Mike. And that ambition fits into the secular role."

THE MORNING EVERYTHING CHANGED

On the morning of September 11, 2001, a commercial airplane crashed into the North Tower of the World Trade Center in the center of Manhattan. For fifteen minutes sheer confusion reigned as the country tried to figure out what the hell just happened. And then another plane struck, this time the South Tower. A half hour later, a third plane crashed into the Pentagon. Minutes later a fourth plane crashed just outside of Pittsburgh, on its way to Washington. In forty-five minutes, commercial flights crossing the country had turned into terrorist missiles. Terrorists were attacking the United States, on a catastrophic scale. The FAA grounded all flights and President George W. Bush was hustled out of a visit to a Florida school. Meanwhile, steely and stoic Vice President Dick Cheney, often rumored to be secretly running the Bush administration, took control from the securely ensconced Presidential Emergency Operations Center below the East Wing of the White House.

Mike Pence said a prayer with his staff in his office in the Longworth Office Building, across the street from the Capitol, then he met with other lawmakers and walked to the Capitol Police Command Center. "I did not see any Democrats or Republicans there—only Americans," he said. Karen Pence was teaching at Immanuel Christian School in Northern Virginia when the planes hit; she watched the smoke pouring from the Pentagon. "It was amazing how God gave me peace," Karen said. Later that day, Karen and Mike gathered with their three children at their Arlington, Virginia, home and told them not to be bowed by the attacks. Mike Pence returned to work on September 12, 2001, to stand with other representatives and senators on the steps of the Capitol—a public show of unity and strength. But even before the towers collapsed, before a cancerous gray cloud engulfed downtown Manhattan, the United States entered the age of terror, the security and prosperity of the 1990s melted away immediately, replaced with fear, confusion, and visceral national anger.

Early signs were that this was the work of al-Qaeda, a radical terrorist group led by an estranged member of the Saudi royal family, Osama bin Laden. Despite that assessment, a small group of top-level Bush administration officials began trying to connect the attack to Iraqi dictator Saddam Hussein. And televangelists Pat Robertson and Jerry Falwell saw yet a different hand at work: God's. It was vengeance, they said, for decades of defeat in the culture war. "The ACLU's got to take a lot of blame for this [for] throwing God successfully out of the public square, out of the schools. The abortionists have got to bear some burden for this because God will not be mocked. And when we destroy forty million little innocent babies, we make God mad," Falwell said on Robertson's CBN, in the days after the September 11 attacks. "I really believe that the pagans, and the abortionists, and the feminists, and the gays and the lesbians who are actively trying to make that an alternative lifestyle, the ACLU, People for the American Way, all of them who have tried to secularize America, I point the finger in their face and say, 'You helped this happen.'"

The White House, other evangelicals, and scores of conservative leaders all denounced Falwell's wild claim and Falwell himself later apologized. But, for a certain slice of the hard Right evangelical movement, he got to the heart of the dark path they saw the United States traveling down, and how the country was paying for its sins.

As the country was regrouping, an unknown assailant mailed letters to national news outlets containing anthrax spores, just one week after the attack. Then a second batch of letters were mailed to the offices of Democratic senators Tom Daschle and Patrick Leahy. The powdered anthrax got into the Capitol complex's ventilation system from the mailrooms and spread, although not in large enough doses to be lethal. The Capitol was on lockdown again. Congressmen, staff, reporters all rushed to secure a supply of Cipro, the preferred antibiotic for treating anthrax. Speaker Dennis Hastert called Pence on Friday, October 26, 2001, and told him that staff dusting the Longworth Building found trace amounts of anthrax in Pence's office; they had to shut down and relocate while the building was on lockdown. "It brings this too close to home," Karen Pence said. Pence, meanwhile, was on-camera and on-air regularly, providing updates about the scare.

The nation was on edge, but also unified in a way it hadn't been since World War II. The United States invaded Afghanistan, with broad international support, hunting for bin Laden. A few months later, in his first State of the Union address, Bush laid out the idea of an "axis of evil," a group of nations he said was supporting terrorists and seeking chemical and nuclear weapons: Iran, Iraq, and North Korea. In short order, the administration revealed its rationale for targeting Iraq, instead of Afghanistan. Iraq, the Bush White House argued, had weapons of mass destruction. The public argument was based on shoddy intelligence and the work of a group of rogue conservative hawks. But very few knew this at the time—most of the Washington establishment and the mainstream media was on board with the Bush administration's deceptive assessment. In October 2002, shortly before the House was set to vote on whether to authorize Bush to send troops to Iraq, Pence threw his support behind Bush. "I grieve at the thought of the United States at war and am not anxious to see it," Pence said. "But Saddam Hussein is a threat to America's national security and to world security." Democrats and Republicans overwhelmingly banded together in the House and Senate to give Bush the power to declare war on Iraq. On March 20, 2003, the United States invaded Iraq, just eighteen months after the September 11 terrorist attacks, and shunted the effort in Afghanistan aside. And Mike Pence, like the rest of Washington, was 100 percent on board.

MIKE IN DC

Mike Pence did not hit the town like most of the other freshmen lawmakers. Washington, for the uninitiated and undaunted, could be a town of both dreams and sins, great promise and dashed ambition, dedication and temptation. The two forces pulled at each other—the holding of power and the yearning for power, and often the promises made at after-work outings for the newly minted lawmakers bound their hands later in official capacities. But they also helped form lasting bonds that assimilated newbies to the Washington culture, buttoned down and chummy.

But Mike Pence cut himself off from that world by design. He went home for dinner with the wife and kids at the end of the day, and largely avoided drinking. And when he attended an event where alcohol was being served, it was always with Karen. That herculean restraint and discipline sometimes led his colleagues to wonder if something was a little off. While they were out drinking for free at high-dollar joints like Charlie Palmer's Steakhouse and Johnny's on the Half Shell, Pence was safely in Northern Virginia with his family. It may have been a little dull, but it would turn out to be an incredibly fortuitous move on Pence's part.

The ringmaster of the partying, the unabashed über-lobbyist, was a man named Jack Abramoff. Abramoff rocketed through the ranks of the GOP, first as the chairman of the College Republicans in the early '80s and later as the head of various activist outfits. He built a partnership with another young, hard-charging conservative: Grover Norquist, an antitax activist. Norquist formed the ideological core of the modern conservative movement, hashing out both policy and strategy at his weekly meetings of the conservative intelligentsia, politicos, think tank leaders, and activists, every Wednesday at his offices in downtown Washington. But Abramoff became the inside man, greasing the rails in Congress for clients, particularly Native American tribes seeking approval to build casinos. By 2001, Abramoff had built a small empire—he even owned his very own upscale restaurant, Signatures, where he lured the powerful with free meals and drinks to the tune of thousands of dollars.

If Abramoff and his cronies were a paean to the unfettered power of money in politics, Republican senator John McCain of Arizona and Democratic senator Russ Feingold of Wisconsin were hard at work trying to limit money's corrupting influence. The pair spent the mid-'90s working fervently on measures to limit political contributions, specifically "soft money," the unlimited campaign donations routed through political parties. Pence may not have run in the same circles as Abramoff, basking in the unchecked money, but he wasn't a good government crusader either (that Pence persona had died with his twenty-point loss to Phil Sharp a dozen years earlier). Pence and the other conservatives on the Republican Study Committee saw an af-

front to the First Amendment in the limiting of campaign spending—
they viewed it as the government quashing free speech.

So Pence scouted for potential allies. California Republican Darrell Issa, a tall and tanned former business executive, entered Congress
the same year as Pence. As they got to work fighting against campaign
finance limits, Issa picked up on Pence's political savvy—the man
seemed to have his finger on the pulse of any room he entered, who to
approach, and when to jump in or stay out of a fray.

"He came in a Reagan-esque way, somebody who made an as-
sumption that he would turn people toward him with his willingness
to listen, and he is good at it," Issa said. "Pence walks into a room,
quickly scans the room, and determines who he wants to meet up
with—who he knows and who he wants to know. Now that doesn't
mean he jumps from person to person, he may enter the room and go
to one person and have a very specific conversation." Pence, he said,
was a master at an old saw in politics, the basis of all great retail—
one-on-one—politicking. "In politics, they tell you people don't care
what you know, they want to know that you care."

This turned out to be very effective for climbing in the ranks
among influential conservatives. The Republican Study Committee
was a small, but growing group of activist conservatives—many of
them unhappy with the leadership of House Speaker Dennis Hastert
and House majority whip Tom DeLay, thought to be establishment
Republicans who ruled over the House with a firm grip on power.
Pence quickly made friends with influential conservatives like Representative John Shadegg of Arizona and Representative Joe Pitts of
Pennsylvania, both members of the committee.

There was another reason that active listening turned out to be
such a great technique for Pence. As Issa said, "By listening and asking a lot of questions he didn't have to know as much as the guy who
was endlessly telling you what he knew, because, frankly, [Pence] was
still developing what would be his final decision." He didn't have to
stake a firm position himself if he was always listening. Pence was

learning Washington fast, and he knew one of his greatest strengths was knowing when to keep his mouth shut.

Pence also found an eager partner in Jeff Flake as they broke rank with the House Republican leadership and the Bush White House on critical items. They would camp out late at night in the Capitol, waiting to see if House Republican leaders would try a slick parliamentary maneuver to jam through legislation. Whenever the House leaders tried the stunt, either Pence or Flake would book down the halls and burst into the House chamber—Objection! The sprints were so comical, and admirable, that some staff began calling them Butch Cassidy and the Sundance Kid.

Butch and Sundance fought their party's leaders on expanding nationalized testing via the No Child Left Behind Act. They stood shoulder to shoulder in the back of the House chamber through the fall of 2003 against an expansion of Medicare sought by the White House. Bush beckoned Pence and a few other holdouts to the White House, wanting to know why they were so steadfast against supporting seniors. Pence mentioned that it was his daughter Charlotte's birthday and that he couldn't bear giving her and her future husband a country that was racked by debt.

Meanwhile, back in Indiana an opportunity arose out of tragedy. Democratic governor Frank O'Bannon died in September 2003, after suffering a stroke. O'Bannon's lieutenant governor, Joe Kernan, had stepped in to fill the rest of O'Bannon's term—but he didn't want to seek a full term himself in the upcoming 2004 race. The Democrats were vulnerable for the first time since Evan Bayh won in 1988. He'd only been in elected office for three years, but Pence floated his own name for governor to gauge interest. Pence ran into Ann DeLaney, the former chair of the state Democrats, at a panel discussion put on by Republican megadonor Christel DeHaan. DeLaney told Pence she heard he was thinking about running for governor. He looked at her and said, "I don't know. What do you think I should do?" DeLaney laughed; Pence was too green. Besides, the same GOP brass who got

Pence a ticket to Washington in 2000 had their eye on someone else: Mitch Daniels, the former Lugar aide who was now working as President Bush's budget director. Daniels had a quick wit, a sharp mind for boiling down policy, and, above all, better political instincts than any Republican in the state.

THE CONSERVATIVE MAN—2004 VERSION

By the start of 2004, Pence's showdowns caught the eyes of national conservative leaders. The Conservative Political Action Conference had been launched three decades earlier as a forum for true believers in the cause. New talent and some old faces took the stage at their annual conference, which served as one part organizing rally for the troops on the right and one part scouting mission. In January 2004, it was Pence's turn for a boost on the Right's big stage. He delivered a stern but hopeful speech about a Republican Party that had lost its way. He used the same analogy he had years earlier with Flake, about being a soldier who shows up late to the fight. But now he wondered if the fight was ongoing—the Gingrich Revolution washed over DC ten years earlier, but federal spending never flagged.

On February 24, 2004, Pence gave hard Right activists another reason to swoon over him. He took to the House floor to support placing the country's ban on gay marriage inside the Constitution. Bill Clinton had signed the Defense of Marriage Act eight years earlier, defining marriage as solely the union between one man and one woman. But Democrats were slowly changing their tune on gay marriage. Earlier that February, in Massachusetts, the Democratic leaders of the legislature attempted to split the difference, pushing for a constitutional ban on same-sex marriage but offering civil unions for gay couples as a compromise. In San Francisco, the newly elected mayor, Gavin Newsom, issued four thousand marriage licenses to same-sex couples in protest of that state's ban on gay marriage.

Now Pence stood with President George W. Bush, who sought a

stricter ban on gay marriage, "Mr. Speaker, after weeks of legal and moral confusion, from Massachusetts to California, today President George W. Bush called on this Congress to adopt a constitutional amendment defining marriage historically and culturally as it has ever been, as the union between a man and a woman. In so doing, President George W. Bush brought moral clarity to the debate by calling for this amendment banning gay marriage, in his words, preventing courts from changing that 'most enduring of human institutions.'"

Pence had established himself as a champion of the issues most dear to the Christian Right, fiscal and social, and he soon received an invite to speak to a smaller, more exclusive group of conservative leaders—Tim LaHaye's Council for National Policy. That group, which included a coalition of fiscal conservatives, megadonors, Christian Right leaders like LaHaye, Jerry Falwell, and former Reagan administration officials, formed a modest intelligentsia of the Right. And even though the press was barred from attending, word often leaked out. The more important goal of the group was that it brought together major names from the broad spectrum of conservatism, from mainstream to extreme, to push a shared agenda.

On March 6, 2004, Pence stood before the Council for National Policy and delivered the same speech he had delivered at CPAC a month earlier, but it seemed to ring even truer before this more select group. "I am a Christian, a conservative, and a Republican—in that order. And I am deeply humbled to address CNP, the most influential gathering of conservatives in America," Pence said. "Not long ago, as I watched the children's animated movie *Ice Age* with my kids, I realized: I am the frozen man. You remember the frozen man, born in a simpler time, slips into the snow and thaws out years later in a more sophisticated age?" He hearkened back to his first run for Congress and a Democratic Congress stifling Reagan at every turn. Then he cited a "heroic band" of conservatives, referring to Gingrich's insurgent Republicans. And as Pence was "frozen" through the '90s, Gingrich and his conservative revolutionaries stormed Washington, ready to push through all the conservative efforts that had stalled before.

But, he said, imagine his surprise when he came to Washington and found liberalism had taken control of his movement. Bush was pushing to expand federal education programs, federal health-care spending . . . it was the symbolic death of everything that Reagan had stood for. The conservative intelligentsia loved it.

Then, three months later, the hero of the conservative movement literally did die. Ronald Reagan passed away on June 5, 2004.

THE HERO'S FUNERAL

An hour before the funeral procession for Ronald Reagan began, lines of onlookers stretched down Constitution Avenue to the Capitol. At 4:30 P.M. on June 9, 2004, an unidentified airplane hurtled toward the center of the nation's capital. From the ground, it looked like another September 11. Unsure of the nature of the aircraft, and with the procession carrying Reagan's body from the White House to the Capitol ready to roll, U.S. Capitol Police chief Terrance Gainer called for an immediate evacuation of the Capitol and the Supreme Court, just across the plaza. The North American Aerospace Defense Command scrambled F-16 fighter jets and Black Hawk helicopters with plans to shoot down the unknown aircraft.

But the small, twin engine Beechcraft was no terrorist weapon. It was piloted by Kentucky's new governor, Republican Ernie Fletcher. Fletcher, an amateur pilot, had alerted the FAA of his flight plans and his plane and flight were registered, but the transponder in his plane had gone dead shortly after he took off from Kentucky. Meanwhile, the Capitol police began a frantic evacuation of the Capitol—women's heels lined the first floor of the Capitol and the Hall of Statues, as they dumped their shoes or ran right out of them. It was a panic-inducing sight: hundreds of politicians running from the Capitol, pouring out of the building in fear. But one man walked, calmly, as all the others blasted by him. A reporter jogged over to this steady figure from across the congressional plaza and asked him why he was unfazed by the prospect of another terrorist attack. Mike Pence turned around, looked seriously at him, and said, "Son, I've always found the safest place is in God's good graces."

In the days and weeks afterward, the anecdote got a lot of laughs around the Capitol. But it also became a bit of a Rorschach test regarding Pence. Did they see a man of real faith and devotion, or the polished façade of so many other politicians? Or was Pence just completely out to lunch—like his Hill moniker "Mike Dense" implied? To his friends, however, it was the deepest sign of who Pence truly is—a man willing to let God be in control, no matter what the situation.

The evening of the funeral, Pence reflected on his idol. "President Reagan changed the course of my life. While youthful ambition led me to politics, it was the voice and values of Ronald Reagan that made me a Republican. The Bible says, 'If the trumpet does not sound a clear call, who will get ready for battle?' Ronald Reagan's gift was to sound a clear call to return our nation to the ideals of its founders."

THE FAMILY BUSINESS

Mike Pence was the only member of his family to enter politics. His brothers and sisters all stayed close to Columbus. His brothers rose as executives in the moderately sized city. Edward Pence, the second oldest, joined Cummins. Greg Pence, the oldest brother, took over at Kiel Brothers Oil Company after their father died in 1988. By 1998 he rose to president of the company—but small and midsize convenience store chains like the Pence's Tobacco Road stores were running into tough competition from large national chains.

Compounding the Kiel Brothers's problems was significant gas leakage from broken tanks at their gas stations—the state fined them $9 million to pay for cleanup costs. Then, in 2004, Greg Pence and Kiel Brothers filed for bankruptcy, unable to overcome more than $100 million in debt.

Mitch Daniels, the newly elected governor of Indiana, offered to help Greg Pence—he found him work at Indiana's Department of Environmental Management. Greg was bailed out by the agency that said he owed them $3.8 million—he resigned after just two and a half months on the job.

And for the second time in his life, Mike Pence lost a small fortune because of one of his closest friends, this time his oldest brother. The collapse of Kiel Brothers cost Pence close to $700,000 in stock he held in the company. Mike and Karen Pence were not poor, at all, they lived a comfortable life on his congressman's salary—$158,000. But Karen didn't work a paid job, instead teaching art for free at Immanuel Christian School, where they paid to send their three children. And with the mortgage on a modest colonial house purchased at suburban Washington prices—almost double that of Indiana's real estate prices, Pence's congressional salary was stretched thin.

As their children, Michael Jr., Charlotte, and Audrey, grew older, they began aging out of the K-8 Christian school at Immanuel Bible Church. Michael was the first to go and transferred into Yorktown High School in Arlington, Virginia—widely regarded as one of the finest public high schools in America. Representatives, senators, cabinet secretaries, lobbyists all sent their children there. But Mike Pence was afraid Michael Jr. would lose something as he left the protected environ of the Christian school, so he set up a weekly bible study at their Arlington home for Michael Jr. and some of his friends. The boys would come over and play basketball a bit, then have dinner with the Pence family and retreat to the basement for bible study. "The guys cherished the opportunity to hide God's word in those young men's hearts," Karen Pence said.

Karen's job was to protect the family from the outside forces of politics and ambition, the trappings of Washington that led to success for those playing the game, but also led many outside Washington, particularly across the Midwest and the South, to view it as a godless swamp rife with corruption. But sometimes that Pence family fortress seemed a little too strong, oddly impregnable. A neighbor whose kids attended Yorktown High School with Pence's kids said the family seemed cloistered, tucked away from the rest of the community. Other families in the wealthy pocket of Arlington, Virginia, played sports together, went to community outings together. But nobody ran into the Pences at these events. When Mike and Karen attended Charlotte's high school graduation, other families milled about the crowd, mixing and mingling. But the Pences stuck together, not talking with any of the other families.

RUBBING IS RACING

At the end of August 2005, Hurricane Katrina plowed toward the Gulf Coast. New Orleans officials, the Army Corps of Engineers, and others had known for decades that the city's levees could be vulnerable to the impact from a serious hurricane, but nobody foresaw a storm the size and strength of Katrina. The winds struck, the waves poured in, and the levees fell—and New Orleans was destroyed. East to west along the Gulf Coast, southern port cities and small rural towns were decimated. Families climbed to their rooftops to beg for help, as floodwaters whipped like a wild river around them. Close to two thousand people died, and the disaster laid waste to an estimated $125 billion worth of homes and businesses.

In Washington, there was no question that Katrina was a national emergency and the White House and congressional Republican leaders moved fast to find money for the rescue and reconstruction effort. But midway through September 2005, just a few weeks after Katrina struck, the conservative House Republican Study Committee came up with a list of programs and projects they wanted cut from the federal budget to pay for the emergency spending. "Operation Offset," as it was dubbed, called for cutting $24 billion in highway projects across the country, slicing into social safety net spending and more to pay for $62.3 billion in emergency aid to New Orleans and the Gulf Coast.

Just as House Republican leaders like Denny Hastert and Tom De-Lay were readying to whiz through relief for the families of the Gulf Coast, Pence and the conservatives in the House GOP conference threw a wrench in the entire plan.

"One more expansion of the Department of Education, one more big expansion of entitlements, and that (Republican) coalition will be shuttered," Pence declared. "If Republicans keep answering every problem with an expansion of big government, eventually people are going to get the professionals (the Democrats)—the guys who do big government."

Hastert and DeLay chewed Pence out in private for the attack; they smelled a publicity stunt. "He clearly got called—aggressively called—on the carpet" by the Republican leadership, said Representative Mark Souder, a conservative Republican from Fort Wayne, Indiana. But "he moved the system. Before he got up there, there wasn't even a discussion. It was just shovel the money out." Conservatives loved Pence's move, "Mike is the tip of the spear for the small-government conservatives in Washington today," said Dick Armey, who had just retired from the House.

The *Chicago Tribune* profiled Pence as a new hero to the Right. The paper found a pious man, but one who also had presidential mettle. Pence said that he got up every morning, early, and read from the Bible before starting the day. That week he was reading Chapter 1 from the Book of Joshua in his study at home. Chapter 1 retells the Israelites' exodus and God's passing of the torch to Joshua, after Moses's death. God promises Joshua the Israelites will have their own land, as long as they maintain their covenant with him. "Be strong, be courageous and do the work" is the lesson from the reading, Pence said. "I'm not a supremely confident man, but I have faith in God and faith in these ideas."

Pence achieved his nirvana—he was living his principles and changing public policy. "To understand Mike Pence, you have to understand it took me twelve years to get to Congress," Pence told the

Tribune. "I try to get up every day and prayerfully approach my job in a way that people will say he did what he said he would do when he got here."

But his success also brought the allure of the presidency. "The party faithful and the conservative grass roots have been searching for the next Ronald Reagan. And Mike Pence has been mentioned as someone who could fill the Gipper's shoes, even though he's still young and a relative political newcomer," said Stephen Moore, a conservative economist who worked at the stalwart Heritage Foundation.

By the fall of 2005, Pence had lined up enough support to take over the Republican Study Committee. The influential conservative magazine *Human Events* named Pence "Man of the Year" at the end of 2005. "It has been Pence and his roughly 100 colleagues on the Republican Study Committee who have almost single-handedly stopped the chronic GOP overspending of the past five years," the editors wrote. "Pence and his pals have changed the thinking of their own House leadership, as well as the president himself."

Pence was a natural fit to lead a band of like-minded conservative lawmakers. He was skilled at bringing together disparate personalities representing various conservative pockets across the country. His genial attitude and self-effacing humor kept everyone working together in the same direction. "He's really good at what he does, he really enjoys it," said a Republican familiar with his leadership of the RSC. When Pence took the reins, the group had about a hundred members and was growing—but a lot of members were skipping meetings, making it hard to coordinate on their big battles with the moderate establishment. So Pence began running movie clips at the opening of each meeting, cracking jokes, inspiring the kind of fun that would get congresspeople bantering when they saw one another at House votes later in the day. And, being a congressman himself, he knew there's nothing his peers hated more than FOMO, fear of missing out.

Nothing defined wasteful spending via earmarks (aka "pork") more than the "Bridge to Nowhere," a roughly $400 million project planned to connect the outer reaches of Alaska. The project had the support of home-state politicians, including Senator Ted Stevens and an upstart candidate for governor, Sarah Palin. Pence enticed his troops in the RSC by running a clip from *Bridge on the River Kwai* with a soldier exploding the eponymous bridge! This generated plenty of laughs around the room and kept everyone buzzing. Now that he had their attention, he listened—a critical skill, said Issa, "He was never known for long speeches, but for conducting a meeting of the RSC where RSC members got to talk."

When they went to battle with the House leadership, Pence liked to remind his RSC members that "rubbing is racing." In car racing, aggressive bumping, or "rubbing," on the track is fair game if you don't go too far. It was a statement of Pence's philosophy that would bridge the hard Right bomb-tossing tactics of the old Republican Study Committee and the more genial tactics he adopted. Pence would regularly let Tom DeLay and other House leaders know if they were going to try and jam a bill on the House floor. It didn't stop them from fighting the leadership, but the courtesy "heads-up" went a long way to building goodwill.

But the more aggressive banging up against the Republican powers was a little more impish. Legislative leaders from Congress to the statehouses to city halls long abided an informal, plainly obvious rule of politics—don't push a proposal without the majority support of the majority party. "We decided to call it the Hastert Rule, [and] it was a brilliant play," said a Republican familiar with the effort. Hastert hated it. Any time reporters would ask Hastert about *his* rule he would say he didn't know where it came from and then lecture gently on the basics of lawmaking. As an explicitly stated rule, it became the latest example of hyperpartisanship tearing apart the country; it solidified the power of the majority bloc of conservatives within the House Republican Conference. It also blocked Hastert from cutting deals with Democrats—and best of all, he caught the blame for it.

Just as Pence was taking over the Republican Study Committee, Jack Abramoff's lobbying empire was falling apart—and he was dragging down some powerful House Republicans with him. A series of explosive reports in the *Washington Post* revealed the extent of Abramoff's corruption—and his close ties to House Majority leader Tom DeLay. DeLay, meanwhile, faced his own trouble for a ballsy plan he had hatched with Texas state lawmakers to redraw legislative districts outside the normal window tied to the U.S. Census to benefit House Republicans. It was a stunning power play, but one that ended up with him getting indicted by a local Democratic prosecutor in Texas. Abramoff's implosion and the resulting call for ethics reforms and the redistricting fiasco took down DeLay and opened a vacuum at the top of the House Republican leadership. House Majority Whip Roy Blunt stepped in as House majority leader for the interim, but a battle ensued for control of the House Republicans.

Pence saw an opportunity, not to run for leader himself, but to win some chits—political money in the bank. The Republican Study Committee hosted its annual retreat in Baltimore at the end of January 2006. Pence invited everyone running for Tom DeLay's old job, but it was really an invitation for one person: John Boehner. Boehner, an Ohio Republican who represented the district directly adjacent to Pence's on the other side of the Indiana border, had been on track to rise through the Republican leadership years earlier. But Boehner, McIntosh, Armey, DeLay, and some others launched an ill-fated coup attempt against Gingrich—Armey chickened out at the last minute and tipped off Gingrich to the plot. McIntosh left for Indiana, Armey survived, DeLay waited a few more years to climb the ranks, but Boehner was jettisoned to a position chairing the House Education Committee—a relative backwater.

He spent six years in exile, but in that time he developed a penchant, a talent, for something increasingly rare in Congress: cobbling together compromise legislation. By the start of 2006, with the Republican Party on the ropes, Boehner was ready to mount a comeback. And Pence was prepared to help.

The other two candidates running for House majority leader were invited as well, Representative Roy Blunt of Missouri and Pence's close friend on the RSC, Representative John Shadegg of Arizona. Blunt was filling in as the acting House majority leader and served as the connection to the old guard. He had all the relationships and political capital from scores of favors paid and owed across the Republican conference. But there was a broad unease among the Republicans. The continued ethics scandals were a stain on the party. And, worse, they were straying from the conservative ideals. "House conservatives should seek to marry fiscal and ethics reform," Pence said at the Republican retreat. "It is not enough for us to change the way lobbyists spend their money. We have got to change how we spend the money of the American people."

Boehner offered a clean break from that troubled past, and that's why Pence brought him to the gathering—but he didn't have quite enough support to win on the first round of voting. Boehner would have to hold off Blunt from getting a majority of votes on the first ballot, and the lowest vote getter, presumably Shadegg, would be forced to drop out. On the second ballot, Boehner would be able to cobble enough support to edge out Blunt in a head-to-head match. The strategy worked. Just a few days after the RSC retreat, on February 2, 2006, Boehner survived to the second ballot and beat Blunt, 122–109. He was now the House Republicans' new second-in-command, with a big assist from Pence.

Despite the new leadership, the ethics woes turned out to be worse than anything Pence or other Republicans could have imagined. House Democratic leader Nancy Pelosi turned the endless stories of Abramoff, Tom DeLay, and others into a catchphrase—"Culture of Corruption." The public had also soured on the Iraq War in a big way, and in turn on the Republican Party. Where the GOP seemed impervious in the wake of the September 11 attacks, it now looked vulnerable. It was hard to shake that image of President George W. Bush in the flight suit, declaring "Mission Accomplished!"

On November 7, 2006, Pelosi, with youngish Chicago representative Rahm Emanuel by her side, led a sweep at the ballot box. The gains of the Gingrich Revolution a dozen years earlier washed away, as Democrats picked up 32 seats and flipped the chamber in their favor, 233–202. The Democrats now held control of the House, its investigative committees, and the power to issue subpoenas.

After the drubbing, Pence felt a new tug to lead, believing he had to represent the conservative standpoint in the House Republican Conference. He and other conservatives saw that the party of Reagan had lost its way. Shortly after the election, the House Republicans regrouped to pick the team that would lead them through the wilderness as the newly disempowered minority party. Pence now felt he was called on by God to challenge Boehner, to run as a conservative voice to lead the party back to its core principles. "I mean, what we're doing isn't working," said a Pence aide. It was a big leap for Pence. He was popular across many different groups of Republicans, but challenging the top-ranking Republican was less about mere popularity and more about knowing the interests and ticks of every individual vote he would need.

"Congress is really a lot like high school," Pence told an aide. "You got your jocks, you got your nerds, you got your basketball team, the cheerleaders." Pence knew he had to play across a wide range of interests—conservatives from western Michigan were going to want to hear something different than legacy Republicans from Orange County, California. Boehner had more than a decade of relationships in the building, Pence had half that. Boehner had chits he could call in, Pence was just a nice guy—although a nice guy with a perch and some talent.

"We were trying to scrounge for votes for two-three weeks, and it was just exhausting," the Pence aide said. "I mean, he just got thumped." The vote was 168–27 for Boehner; Pence didn't even come close. Reporters swarmed Pence as he left the Republican Conference meeting, "How'd you do??" And Pence, beaten and worn out, flashed a smile and deadpanned, "Well, I didn't ask for a recount." The reporters laughed, his aides loved it. "It was truly one of the most Reaganesque moments I've seen [from] him. . . . He just got thumped and he's still on top of his game."

After the dust cleared, Pence got back on board with Boehner. And Boehner remembered that. What also emerged from the experience was more evidence of Pence's trademark chameleon style: he knew exactly when and how to blend into the background when necessary. In this instance, he made a big play, tried and failed, then knew exactly how to disappear. His time to shine would come.

CHAPTER 9

PENCE'S MOMENT

Eric Cantor was the clear rising star in the Republican Conference. He was young, forty-five years old, and popular with the old guard that had just been deposed by Boehner. Cantor was just a few years younger than Pence and came to Washington around the same time, but he had skyrocketed through House leadership ranks. The old guard, people like Representative Roy Blunt and former House majority leader Tom DeLay anointed Cantor as someone worth grooming. Blunt plucked Cantor out of the burgeoning group of upstart conservatives who came to Washington in 2000 and placed him in the top job as the point man on his vote-counting team, chief deputy Republican whip. It was a heady job for a second-term congressman, and one that created a lot of envy around the building. And just as he gripped the reins of power, Boehner sensed danger from Cantor on his right flank.

Pence opened the year helping Boehner, giving him entrée to the conservatives, and he ended 2006 by challenging his hold on power, with his long-shot bid to unseat him. But Pence did it all up front and didn't seem entirely set on unseating Boehner, but more on making a name for himself and pushing the Republican Conference further to the right.

Now Boehner saw a good use for Pence—he could protect Boehner's right flank from Cantor, keeping conservatives inside the big tent and on board with the establishment and moderates. But first, Boehner would have to draw Pence into the flock. Little by little, Boehner started working on Pence, helping to show him that, despite Pence's recent upbringing on the far right, the Republicans had a much bigger tent, one that held more people in the middle.

THE GRANDSON OF STRUGGLING IMMIGRANTS

Pence, meanwhile, started work on comprehensive immigration reform. It may have seemed odd for a hard Right conservative from the heartland, but Pence's own family story and memories of his Irish grandfather inspired him. And the GOP seemed to be moving toward being more accepting of immigrants—everyone from President George W. Bush to the U.S. Chamber of Commerce wanted a way to fix the country's backlog of legal immigrants and welcome those who had crossed in undocumented. In 2006, a fix seemed imminent and some lawmakers began working up their own proposals. Pence didn't think immigrants should be rewarded for breaking the law, but he also wanted something on the books. So he teamed up with a moderate Republican senator from Texas, Kay Bailey Hutchison, to find a path between the Right and center. Their staffs began hammering out a plan. Josh Pitcock, a youngish Republican aide from Anderson, Indiana, had recently joined Pence's team. He linked up with Matt Lloyd, who had found his way onto Pence's office staff a few years earlier. Texas senator KBH, as she was known around the Capitol, offered up Marc Short, a tall, balding legislative staffer in his midthirties with strong conservative connections around Washington. Short represented the blue-blooded world of conservative Virginia politics—he ran Oliver North's bid for U.S. Senate in 1994 and later moved with his wife to run the Reagan Ranch in California. In short, he had pedigree.

The group worked day and night through the summer of 2006 in KBH's Senate hideaway—a small, secluded second office inside the Capitol itself, away from the senator's main office across the street. The hideaway is a Senate tradition and highly prized real estate inside the building, each small suite valued for its history and lore. They emerged with a plan to increase border security, grant temporary work visas to immigrants—and encourage them to leave the United States after a few years by offering up lump sum payments from their Social Security contributions. It bridged the gap between Far Right conservatives angry at an influx of immigrants from Central America and moderate, pro-business Republicans, led by the Bush White House. But the politics between the two sides proved trickier than Pence ever imagined. Hard-line conservative groups, including the Far Right Federation for American Immigration Reform, ran attack ads against him back home in Indiana, dubbing the plan "backdoor amnesty." It was impossible to miss the whiff of racism, as some opponents complained of being forced to speak Spanish if more Latin American immigrants came in. As Pence took a trip to the Mexican border in Southern California, to garner support for the compromise plan, he marveled at the backlash. "I'm not a stranger to controversy," he said. "But the crosscurrents here have been challenging to me."

Pence and KBH eventually dropped the effort, after a long two years, when it became clear that no immigration measure of any stripe was likely to clear the House or Senate. Meanwhile, another, more pressing issue was about to overtake the immigration debate. The piping hot economy of the mid-2000s seemed a little too inflated, and families across the country were beginning to default on bad loans. Pence himself knew a bit about stretching.

In 2007, Pence voted for a congressional pay raise —"I fear Mrs. Pence more than I do the voters." He started in Washington earning $141,300 in 2001 and was earning $165,200 by 2007—the raise would eventually bump him up to $174,000 a year. Those salaries were far superior to what most Americans made—the median income nationwide was $59,000 when Pence entered Congress and crept up just slightly after a slump to $60,000 in 2007. Congressional salaries grew, untouched by the post-9/11 recession. But for a single earner living in an upper-middle-class Washington suburb with a family, he was barely scraping by. The Pences had three kids in private school, the mortgages on two houses—one in Edinburgh, Indiana, where they barely lived, but kept to maintain residency in Indiana, and their home in Northern Virginia—and Karen wasn't earning any money, despite teaching art at the Christian school.

By the end of 2007, the United States was at the start of an economic death spiral—spurred by high-wire financial tactics on Wall Street that embedded increasingly worthless mortgages into the very fabric of the nation's economy. And by September of 2008, a full-blown financial crisis was at hand. Banking giant Lehman Brothers went belly-up. Bush and his advisers stepped in to stanch the bleeding before the country was sucked into a full-scale depression. To do so, they used $700 billion to buy up or stand up the disintegrating financial structure.

Pence and a bipartisan crew fought the bailout; at the end of September the House voted it down—but stocks tanked right after the vote. Pence picked up on a growing resentment on the ground. Years of taking one caller after another, getting them talking about the easy stuff first—Bobby Knight and Daylight Saving Time—and then pushing toward the more complicated issues gave him insights into the nation's psyche. Pence saw a building crescendo of outrage and populist revolt from people who were losing their jobs while watching Big Government hand bailouts to Big Banks.

THE OBAMA WAVE

On November 4, 2008, Senator Barack Obama made history—almost 150 years after the end of the Civil War, the United States elected a black man president. And not by a fluke; instead it was a resounding victory for the freshman Democratic senator from Illinois—he bested Republican nominee John McCain by almost ten million votes and racked up almost two hundred more electoral votes than McCain. He won states that had not voted for Democrats in decades, even deep-red Indiana. The historic tide of Obama's election lifted all Democratic boats: they cemented control of the U.S. Senate, coming within a breath of an indominable supermajority. In the House, Democrats won surprising victories in rural districts with the help of moderate-conservative Blue Dog Democratic candidates. They built their majority into a powerful seventy-nine-seat edge.

If the Republican Party had a pulse, it was hard to find. John Batchelor, a syndicated conservative radio talker, took an oddly fatalistic approach to his party's demise: "The Republican Party's death doesn't really threaten anyone, and I puzzle why Democrats and independents who vote Democratic spend words and worry debating looking at the corpse. We few Republicans with long memories wander around the cemetery admiring the tombstones and enjoying the rain. I can hear you doubting this could truly be the end. The final stage of grief is acceptance."

For the House Republicans, the crushing defeat of the 2006 midterms was beginning to look like a troubling trend. Realizing that this second round of losses could imperil his grip on power, Boehner moved swiftly after the election to assemble a de facto slate of House Republican leaders who would stand with him in the upcoming closed-door conference where Republicans would choose who would lead them into the Obama Era. Boehner's second- and third-in-command, Representatives Roy Blunt and Adam Putnam, both stepped down immediately after the 2008 slaughter. Into the vacuum swooped Blunt's cultivated pick for leadership, Eric Cantor. Boehner's cultivation of Mike Pence for leadership proved prescient indeed; Boehner picked Pence for the third-ranking slot, right behind Cantor. And Pence, who had made his inroads with establishment and moderate Republicans under Boehner's tutelage, enjoyed universal backing across the House Republican Conference.

Boehner's team prevailed in short order, the vote never seriously challenged. Outside the GOP conference room, Pence's aides awaited final word. Already, their BlackBerry phones were buzzing incessantly—piles of emails came in, with résumés from ambitious Hill staffers looking for work for the newly empowered Pence. Quickly, they realized they needed someone who could handle this level of attention. They needed Marc Short, the Kay Bailey Hutchison aide—he had lived in this world before. Bill Smith was a great friend and good leader for Pence's smaller congressional office, but Pence's staffers knew someone with stronger Washington ties and more political sophistication was required. Pence got on board and hired Short to direct his leadership office. "Mike outgrew Bill Smith's counsel, probably starting in 2006," said one aide. But why did Mike keep Bill around? "Because Bill is in the Comfort Zone." Pence felt comfortable with who and what he knew. Bill Smith would never be pushed out of Pence World, but he was sidelined.

The leaders of the broader conservative movement, meanwhile, understood their downfall only too well. By placating the establishment and the middle, they had ended up with mush: John McCain. Mainstream Republicans supported all the expanded government they once fought and lost the trust of their voters. The Wall Street bailout in the midst of the financial crisis merely punctuated the end of the very bad joke that was the GOP's flip-flopping on fiscal constraint under Bush. And that apostasy didn't even touch on the moral failings of the party, racked by embarrassing revelation after revelation—Gingrich, former Idaho senator Larry Craig, former Florida representative Mark Foley. The very people who had led the charge for impeachment of President Bill Clinton for his Oval Office blowjob were guilty of the same transgressions and more.

Shortly after the election, the old bulls of the Council for National Policy gathered at Brent Bozell's country house in Virginia. Bozell, in his midfifties with stark red hair, made a name as the Right's watchdog against perceived liberal bias in the mainstream media. The CNP group feared the next batch of establishment mush, Massachusetts governor Mitt Romney. Romney's nomination looked like a fait accompli, backed by the megadonors of the establishment and a misguided notion that people of the party should be granted their turn after waiting in line.

Diana Banister, a veteran of Buchanan's 1992 and 1996 presidential races, recalled, "We said, 'Okay, we've got to fix this. We can't have a candidate like this again.' You cannot have this kind of defeat, again." Banister floated Pence's name: he was as rock-solid as they came. The executive team of the CNP invited Pence to address the group. His speech to them four years earlier was impressive; it was proof that he was one of them. But his performance before the speech this time around convinced almost everyone in the room he was their champion—he made the rounds, one by one, asking them about their families, their pets, and everything else special to them. "Mike Pence came, walked into the room, and he talked to everybody. This is a man of the movement. Mike Pence is with us. He's been with us. He's our man, we have to run him for president."

Pence had fought the White House and Republicans on expanded spending, and he was guaranteed scandal-free—as he never went anywhere without his wife. There would be no repeat of the "culture of corruption" charges from 2006.

Unstated was that Pence was playing the longest game in politics— running for president. Decades spent having lunches and dinners with the most important people in the party had made him a shoo-in with the crowd at Bozell's house. And he was about to get another boost. A national conservative uprising was building.

2009—THE TEAVANGELICAL MIKE

When Pence led the Republican Study Committee, his team was small and limited in power. Now Pence's bigger leadership team sat in meetings with the House minority leader's staff, in the upper echelons of power. Boehner's staff let Team Pence know the door was open. Short built out Pence's new Republican leadership operation fast. He brought on Josh Pitcock and Matt Lloyd from Pence's personal office to work in the more elite team. Pitcock, Short, and Lloyd were also devout evangelical Christians.

Pence had his band of loyal soldiers, quiet and discreet—but he still needed someone to hype him around Washington. Short had worked closely with a longtime GOP pollster and erstwhile scout of presidential timber, Kellyanne Conway. She had deep roots in the national conservative movement, having come up under the wing of Reagan's own pollster, Dick Wirthlin. She also knew how to work the national media for her clients, a product in part of her own success as a talking head in the 1990s.

The roster for Team Pence was now firmly in place.

That conservative populist backlash that Pence picked up on during the bailout debate a few months earlier was crystallizing. A growing tide of white conservative rage was building against Obama that began almost immediately after he took office. The $787 billion stimulus bill, negotiated to keep the country from pitching over a financial cliff from the mortgage crisis and ensuing Great Recession, fueled the fire of anti-Obama sentiment before he had even taken the oath of office. The plans for sweeping health-care expansion and tough new limits on climate-change-causing pollution from power plants only spurred the anger further. Feeding that fire was a mixture of veteran conservative activists with a new cause—Dick Armey now led a Tea Party activist training group, FreedomWorks.

Meanwhile, David and Charles Koch were beginning to pour their incredible oil fortune into the nascent uprising. They gathered conservative megadonors on the other side of the country to plot out how to stop Obama and the Democrats. They quickly decided that bankrolling an entire Far Right protest movement would be a better strategy than throwing in with any one candidate.

The two billionaire oil brothers had dipped their toes in politics before, both with clear libertarian bents that stood just outside the mainstream of the GOP—and not always to the right of the GOP either. David Koch shunned the social conservatism of the Christian Right, although his older brother, Charles, was somewhat more accepting of the culture warrior ideas. In 1980, David Koch ran for vice president on the Libertarian Party ticket. But after three decades, they had given up on third-party politics.

The trick for conservatives and Republicans in particular, who wanted to capitalize on this building Obama backlash, was to make it clear that their concern had nothing to do with Obama personally and certainly nothing to do with his race. Instead, the anger had everything to do with his policies being too expensive.

On Tax Day, April 15, 2009, planned protests sprouted up across the nation—it was a bellwether moment for the emerging movement known as the Tea Party.

In just a few months in leadership, Pence had become a popular voice on cable TV. As the Tea Party protests swept the nation, MSNBC invited Pence on to explain their popularity. Host Mike Barnicle, a veteran columnist from the home of the actual Tea Party, Boston, seemed somewhat incredulous as he interviewed Pence that evening. Barnicle asked Pence where these protests were when Bush and the Republicans were ramping up spending. "Isn't it somewhat, well, not inconsistent, but somewhat odd that today we have this big protest coast to coast?" Pence quickly parried it away, "I think it's a fair question, Mike. But candidly, now I know how the old settlers back in the West felt when the cavalry came riding over the hill." Barnicle cut in, "Lookit, I agree with you and yet this growth in spending did not start at noontime this past January twentieth (Obama's inauguration)." Pence took it coolly (one of the reasons he was so great on television). "I think it began with the bailouts," Pence said. "When President Bush responded to the economic crisis last year by transferring $750 billion in bad decisions on Wall Street to Main Street, I think Main Street got a jolt."

Pence played to this new movement, but he was still apprehensive about diving in headfirst with them—particularly when it came to immigration. The next day, April 16, 2009, Pence was back in Indiana, hosting a town hall meeting in Anderson. He leaned on the podium, with his light blue button-down, a tie, and his BlackBerry clipped into its holder on his belt. One Hoosier asked him how he planned to stop drug dealers pouring in from Mexico. A wall? A border fence? Pence touted the border fence already under construction, but also cautioned that walls wouldn't stop the real drug dealers. "I will tell you the border security fence is almost entirely completed, it doesn't get a lot of press. It's almost entirely completed. And judging from the Mexican drug gangs and their impact on the number of urban areas in the United States, you can see we're probably stopping the gardeners. The other guys know how to get in though."

The wilder elements of the Tea Party posed some clear risk to Pence, who picked his issues and stances carefully. Some Tea Partiers were dubbing Barack Obama the next Hitler and showing images of him with a Hitler mustache. The 2008 election and a "postracial" America were being met with hyperracist sentiment from the fringe Right and some Republicans. Conservatives angry at Obama's victory circulated a wild conspiracy theory, alleging Obama was born in Kenya—and therefore an illegitimate president. Even though Obama was demonstrably born in Hawaii.

Pence eyed how to corral this raw energy, while not getting sullied by the extreme elements—he settled quickly on sticking to fiscal austerity. There were great rewards to be reaped, in the form of highly charged and engaged conservative voters, by staying this course.

"There are some politicians who think of you people as 'astroturf.' 'Un-American.' I've got to be honest with you, after nine years of fighting runaway spending here on this hill, you people look like the cavalry to me," Mike Pence was addressing tens of thousands of Tea Partiers gathered facing the west front of the Capitol in September 2009. The crowd loved it, they roared.

By the end of 2009, Pence had fashioned himself into both a popular member of the House Republican leadership and a Tea Party star—a rare feat for someone who'd been in Washington for close to a decade. By straddling both those worlds without ever fully falling in to one side or the other, Pence drew increasing attention from activists looking for a challenger to Obama in 2012.

That November 2009, the Tea Party flexed its muscle for the first time in a very serious way, delivering the Virginia statehouse to Republicans, en masse, and even flipping New Jersey's governorship from Democrat to Republican. Conservatives rallied in Northern Virginia, where Obama had swept the Washington suburbs just a year earlier. Short, a Virginia native, quickly plucked up the man responsible for the GOP's effort in NoVa, Kyle Robertson. Short didn't know what Pence's next step would be, but he did know Pence needed some strong political operators to help him capitalize on this moment. Then they reached back to Indiana, into the moderate administration of Republican Indianapolis mayor Greg Ballard, and snagged Ballard's lead fund raiser, Marty Obst. As part of his leadership duties for the House Republicans, Boehner had tasked Pence with raising $1 million for the House Republicans as they headed into the 2010 midterm races. Pence made Obst his point man to the national donors.

Pence had captured lightning in a bottle, he was the it man in Washington, the next big thing. People outside the tight-knit group of conservative kingmakers began paying attention, the chatterers in Washington began watching to see if there was more to this guy than just talking points and a smooth delivery on-air. And Pence knew he was being vetted for his potential to rise to the next level.

JANUARY 2010—THE OBAMA CONFERENCE

At the start of 2010, the House Republicans prepared for their annual retreat, a couple of days when they got out of Washington and gathered to plot their agenda and strategy for the coming year. President

Barack Obama, who was pushing a monumental health-care overhaul, wanted to come speak and make his case to them. Normally lawmakers let the press stick around through the beginning of big exchanges between the president and lawmakers at such retreats. But Obama wanted the cameras to stay through his speech and question-and-answer session. The network cameras would capture his cool versus the Republicans' fire. It was a clear play by the White House to make them look bad. After some consulting, the House Republicans agreed to let the cameras stick around. The show was on. They all agreed that Paul Ryan, their lead lawmaker on budget issues, would be the one to get the first question. He was best positioned to nail Obama on runaway spending and crippling national debt.

On January 29, 2010, at Renaissance Baltimore Harborplace Hotel, Obama took the podium—smiling, barely a fleck of gray in his hair. He looked to Boehner, seated just down the stage from him, and joked: "You know what they say, 'Keep your friends close, but visit the Republican Caucus every few months.'" But seriously, Obama said he valued the loyal opposition, "Having differences of opinion, having a real debate about matters of domestic policy and national security—that's not something that's only good for our country, it's absolutely essential." Then he scolded the Republicans in the room for basking in the benefits of the stimulus bill he signed a year earlier—"Let's face it, some of you have been at the ribbon-cuttings for some of these important projects in your communities."

At the end of Obama's brief lecture, Pence, who was emceeing the event, opened the floor to questions, "The president has agreed to take questions and members would be encouraged to raise your hand while you remain in your seat." Representative Paul Ryan of Wisconsin prepared to speak, but Pence decided he was going to take the lead. "The chair will take the prerogative to make the first remarks." Pence recounted a touching story. "Several of us in this conference yesterday, on the way in to Baltimore, stopped by the Salvation Army homeless facility here in Baltimore. I met a little boy, an African American boy, in the eighth grade, named David Carter Jr. When he heard that I would be seeing you today, his eyes lit up like I had never seen. And I told him that if he wrote you a letter, I would give it to you, and I have. But I had a conversation with little David Jr. and David Sr. His family has been struggling with the economy. His dad said words to me, Mr. President, that I will never forget. He was about my age, and he said, Congressman, it's not like we were coming up. He said, there's just no jobs." Pence was on a roll. Then came the punchline: "The first question I would pose to you, very respectfully, Mr. President, is would you be willing to consider embracing—in the name of David Carter Jr. and his dad, in the name of every struggling family in this country—the kind of across-the-board tax relief we have advocated?"

Obama laughed. "Well, there was a lot packed into that question. First, let me say I already promised that I'll be writing back to that young man and his family and I appreciate you passing on the letter." Then he ticked through a defense of his tax cuts in the stimulus bill, the state of the economy when he took office, and other measures. The one thing he didn't mention, because he didn't have to: Why would a family living in a homeless shelter need a tax cut?

Pence's question sounded a lot like the same answer he had given on jobs a decade earlier, at the October 2000 congressional debate in Muncie: the unfettered free market would provide. But would it? It hadn't provided for this family in Baltimore, or recently for the families in Muncie, Indiana. Was there something Pence was missing?

Pence was a rock star inside the conservative movement, but he sounded tone-deaf outside that bubble.

DECISION TIME

The recruiters at the National Republican Senate Committee, tasked with filling the Senate, had been working on Pence for a few months to run against Evan Bayh, the popular two-term senator of Indiana. With the Tea Party wind at their backs, the Bayh Senate seat looked winnable for Republicans, but they couldn't win with an explicit Tea Party candidate—they needed someone who could clear out a field of Tea Party challengers and keep the conservative base happy. Pence declined the offer; there was just too much risk.

Then, on February 15, 2010, Bayh said he was done with the Senate. He wouldn't run for reelection. The Senate, and Washington, he said, was broken. "There are many causes for the dysfunction: strident partisanship, unyielding ideology, a corrosive system of campaign financing, gerrymandering of House districts, endless filibusters, holds on executive appointees in the Senate, dwindling social interaction between senators of opposing parties, and a caucus system that promotes party unity at the expense of bipartisan consensus."

Pence's heart was not in the Senate; he had his eyes on the big prize—but he was not yet sure if he should run straight through to president in 2012. He also had his day job to take care of, running the House Republican Conference. A few months later, in May 2010, veteran Indiana representative Mark Souder was mortally wounded in a bitter primary battle. One of his opponents leaked word that Souder had been cheating on his wife with one of his staffers. Worse yet, it was the same staffer with whom he had filmed a PSA promoting abstinence. As the news broke, it quickly bubbled into a full-blown scandal in the House.

The memories of sex scandals just a few years old still permeated the chamber. Republicans couldn't suffer any more embarrassments heading into the 2010 election cycle. Pence was the perfect man to deliver the message to Souder that he had to go. Shortly after the story of Souder's affair broke, Pence approached him with some advice: resign and avoid further embarrassment. A few days later Souder issued a statement: "I sinned against God, my wife and my family by having a mutual relationship with a part-time member of my staff," Souder said. "I am so ashamed I have hurt those I love." Pence was at the height of his powers.

As he plotted his course for 2012, Pence's supercharged political team started getting him out more around the country. Short plugged Pence into the aristocracy of the conservative movement, people who didn't necessarily associate with the dustier movement conservatives of the Council for National Policy and CPAC. Meanwhile, Pence hit the road with his new fund raiser, Marty Obst. While he was out courting donors, Pence began sensing the GOP was changing, becoming more accepting of gay marriage. The former chairman of the Republican National Committee, Ken Mehlman, had recently come out of the closet and he was leading a fight to overturn California's ban on gay marriage. The donors Pence needed on his team were more open to gay rights. Pence went courting Paul Singer, a New York billionaire and prolific Republican donor. Singer's grown son had come out as gay more than a decade earlier—and was now an influential supporter of LGBT rights. After years of fighting on the side of the Christian Right, Pence would have to show he wasn't a homophobe.

The higher Pence climbed, the more the earth seemed to split beneath his feet—the future of the Republican Party, with unlimited money and more socially progressive stances, was a new world to him. But the Christian Right still embraced him as one of their own. In September 2010, Christian Right activists gathered together at the Family Research Council's Values Voter Summit in Washington to cast informal ballots for who they wanted to see run for president in 2012. Pence beat the entire field, edging out former Arkansas governor Mike Huckabee, a favorite among evangelical voters. He even bested former McCain running mate Sarah Palin, despite her incredible popularity with the Tea Party. Tony Perkins, president of the Family Research Council, explained Palin's poor showing this way: "I think she's a great spokesman . . . she says what a lot of people think. But you know a lot of people sometimes realize we shouldn't say everything we think." Pence believed most of the same things the Tea Party and Christian Right did, but never had to say it out loud, because after a decade in Congress, they already knew he was on their side.

Two months later, in November 2010, the Tea Party swarmed Washington in a serious way, picking up sixty-three seats in the House of Representatives. They swept governors' mansions and statehouses across the country. The wind was at Pence's back; here stood proof that the Republican base would not suffer another McCain. But Pence still couldn't decide whether he was in for 2012. He kept holding informal meetings with different groups of advisers—with his family and friends from Indiana, with his political team in Washington, with old friends and new.

Karen and he prayed, a lot. But Pence couldn't make up his mind.

One thing Pence did know was that he wasn't staying put—the only path to power in the House was to the Speakership, and he would have to wait in line for years. His friend and ally John Boehner easily took the Speakership, as Republicans retook control of the House that November. Challenging Boehner was good strategy in 2006, but out of the question now with Republicans basking in the glow of victory. Boehner could be in there for years, maybe a decade or longer. Pence wasn't ready to wait, so he announced he was stepping down from the House leadership. If he decided to run for president, he wouldn't have time to run the House Republican Conference.

Pence's advisers told him he needed to build out his national network of donors more if he wanted to run in 2012. The conservative grassroots and movement crowd loved him, but they didn't exactly wield the type of money needed to run a serious presidential bid. On November 29, 2010, he flew to Michigan to speak before the Detroit Economic Club, an early test if he could win over the party's business types and megadonor crowd. He tempered his message and went deeper on policy than he did typically. He called for a flat tax, he called for a spending limits amendment to the Constitution, he dove into an explanation of how government regulation strangled the economy. He intoned Reagan and former British prime minister Margaret Thatcher and pulled from his days at the Indiana Policy Review Foundation and studies of Russell Kirk. "To restore American exceptionalism, we must end all this Keynesian spending and get back to the practice of free market economics. The freedom to succeed must include the freedom to fail. The free market is what made America's economy the greatest in the world, and we cannot falter in our willingness to defend it."

Pence struck the right notes, but the GOP donor class and the establishment had their eye on another Hoosier for president, Governor Mitch Daniels. Daniels had an impressive six years as governor under his belt and had driven conservative priorities through the statehouse with gusto. For the donors worried that Mitt Romney couldn't engage the conservative base of voters and was too aloof, Daniels offered a better alternative. He veered away from social issues and struck a hard line on spending through his tenure. He also showed Republicans that conservatives could succeed in the Rust Belt, something that helped Republicans win governorships in Wisconsin, Ohio, Michigan, and Pennsylvania in the 2010 Tea Party sweep.

As governor, Daniels wooed national media with reports that he had called a "truce" on social hot buttons like abortion—even as he continued to support new restrictions on abortion and stood by as a constitutional ban on gay marriage advanced in the legislature. But those issues didn't stick to him—Daniels was conservative without the stigma attached to the Tea Party and Christian Right. But in his nascent run for president, he hadn't lined up his most important supporters, his family.

The state constitution barred Daniels from seeking a third term as governor in 2012, so he had nothing to lose if he jumped in for president. Pence had everything to lose; his job and career were on the line if he jumped in for the wrong race.

Shortly before Christmas 2010, Pence gathered with his most loyal donors at the Ruth's Chris Steakhouse in Indianapolis. The moneymen who had been with him since his very first run for Congress—Fred Klipsch, Jim Kittle, Van Smith, Dan Dumezich, Bob Grand—sat at the table with him and Marty Obst and political operative Kyle Robertson. Pence went around the table, one by one, "What am I going to do?" he asked. Every fund raiser sitting around the table was already supporting Mitch Daniels for president. Even if Pence wanted to run for president, he wouldn't have his core team behind him. Mitch Daniels had gotten to them first.

The money men had a better idea—one that should keep everybody happy—Pence should run for governor. They would help clear the field for him, just like they had in Pence's 2000 Republican primary.

With Daniels heading for the exit, other ambitious Republicans had been teeing up runs for governor. Daniels's lieutenant governor, Becky Skillman, had the backing of an influential bloc of Republican women power brokers, and Indiana's powerful House Speaker, Brian Bosma, also wanted in. After eight years serving at Daniels's side, Skillman knew how to run government and was infinitely more versed in Indiana's issues and challenges than Pence. But facing personal health issues, for her and her husband, her heart was not in a grueling campaign and four more years of sixteen-hour days. Bosma desperately wanted the governorship, but the GOP donor class saw someone who was too willing to buck them on priorities. And both Bosma and Skillman lacked the name identification with voters that Pence clearly had. Skillman was ready to leave the field, but Bosma never forgot being boxed out of his ambitions by Mike Pence.

"He was never really serious about running for president in 2012, I think he knew 'I need to have a little more experience, I need a little more time,'" said one Pence adviser. "He didn't have a political and fund-raising network at that point. He would have been an insurgent campaign."

But Pence still couldn't make up his mind, and he wasn't ready to slam the door shut on the White House.

At the start of 2011, some of the conservative intelligentsia took their recruitment effort public. Conservative mail vendor Richard Viguerie, Morton Blackwell, and a few others formed an explicit committee to draft Mike Pence. "Lincoln declared, 'this nation cannot endure half-free and half-slave.' So, it cannot, when we threaten to enslave ourselves and our posterity to debt and to massive expansion of the state," they wrote on January 17, 2011, in an open letter to Pence. "We believe that you, Mike Pence, must answer your country's call."

Marjorie Dannenfelser, president of the antiabortion group Susan B. Anthony List, adored Pence. Other Republican presidential contenders often came knocking on her door, looking for the pro-life seal of approval, but had never been interested in her group before. But Pence had been with them for years, from his very start in Washington. Pence may have wetted his finger and placed it in the wind to test which way to go on other issues, but never on pro-life measures. Now it was Dannenfelser doing the knocking; she wanted to know if Pence was jumping in. And his answer was always the same: He and Karen were praying about it.

She understood what he meant. In religion, she had gone the opposite route of Pence, leaving the evangelical faith for the Catholic Church, but she still knew all the intonations. They wanted to wait until God told them which way to go. One of their mutually favorite authors, C. S. Lewis, put it this way, in one of Pence's favorite passages, "But there must be real giving up of the self. You must throw it away 'blindly' so to speak. Christ will indeed give you a real personality: but you must not go to Him for the sake of that. As long as your own personality is what you are bothering about, you are not going to Him at all. The very first step is to try and forget the self altogether. The same principle holds, you know, for everyday matters. Even in social life, you will never make a good impression on other people until you stop thinking about what sort of impression you are making. . . . Give up yourself, and you will find your real self. Lose your life, and you will save it. Submit to death, death of your ambitions and your favourite wishes every day and of your whole body in the end: submit with every fibre of your being, and you will find eternal life."

On January 27, 2011, Pence made his decision. "In the choice between seeking national office and serving Indiana in some capacity, we choose Indiana," Pence wrote in a letter to his supporters. "I have learned to follow my heart, and my heart is in Indiana." He all but announced he was running for governor—the biggest supporters of a 2012 White House run knew he made the right call but were still disappointed. "I was crestfallen," said Kellyanne Conway, who had been pushing him to seize the moment and make a big run in 2012. "And I'm not much of a crier—but I was very sad about it and not mad, just sad because I thought it was a huge missed opportunity."

If Pence was serious about making it to the very top, he needed to build a better money machine before launching for president—it also wouldn't hurt in his bid for governor. The Supreme Court's decision just one year earlier in the *Citizens United* case effectively abolished campaign money limits and was slowly changing the dynamic of political financing in a very big way. To be considered seriously, every candidate needed at least one megawealthy benefactor. And, better yet, a network. Pence had made some strong inroads with David and Charles Koch. Pence's staunch opposition to tough new environmental limits pushed by Obama had won their attention, and even more importantly, Pence's selection of Marc Short to be his chief political aide won him entrée with the Kochs. Not long after Pence decided to run for governor, the Kochs hired Short as the president of their political umbrella group, Freedom Partners, heading in to the 2012 cycle. Pence and his team were making sharp moves, even if they didn't pay off immediately.

Bob Tyrrell, the combative publisher of the conservative magazine *American Spectator*, held a monthly dinner in a private room at the swanky, midtown Manhattan French restaurant, Brasserie 8½, for the feting of up-and-coming politicians and would-be presidential contenders. The Spectator Dinner was mandatory for any Republican looking to win over conservative tastemakers and was typically packed with a mix of megadonors, thought leaders, and activist journalists, like John Stossel. At the start of April 2011, Tyrrell invited Congressman Mike Pence to come and address his group; they wanted to see if he was presidential timber—if not for 2012, then further down the road. About two dozen of the Right's moneyed elite packed in to hear Pence's vision for the future. Tyrrell sat Pence at the head of the long table, right between himself and David Koch.

Pence gave some brief opening remarks, then answered questions—and to a person, the question was, "Why don't you run?" And Pence's answer was always the same: he was humbled by the attention but wasn't ready yet.

With Pence out for 2012, Daniels held the spotlight. He'd conducted a sweeping, conservative overhaul of the state's education system—a landmark policy victory he could carry with him into the GOP primary. In March 2011, Daniels headlined Washington's annual Gridiron Dinner, a gathering of the nation's media elite and tastemakers. The only thing Mitch had left to do was get his family on board with the idea. In May 2011, Daniels's wife delivered a very rare keynote speech at the GOP spring dinner—a sure sign she was thawing on the idea of living with their family under the microscope. Mitch told political staffers they should keep their calendars open, be ready to fly to Iowa. It looked like a go.

On May 21, 2011, Pence hosted a small fund raiser to informally kick off his bid for governor. Late that evening, Daniels delivered his decision, in a statement he said, "On matters affecting us all, our family constitution gives a veto to the women's caucus, and there is no override provision. Simply put, I find myself caught between two duties. I love my country; I love my family more." Just hours after he announced, Real Clear Politics published an exposé on how his wife split from him and their girls and ran off with her high school sweetheart in 1996, but returned to Daniels and their family years later. It was a deeply painful, and private, moment in their lives, and the searing article was just a taste of what Daniels would have endured if he hopped in.

With Daniels out, Pence was ready to ascend as the chief political star from Indiana. David Brody, the chief political correspondent for Pat Robertson's Christian Broadcasting Network, foresaw a merging of the old Christian Right and the new, libertarian-leaning Tea Party movement. The two factions overlapped in ideology and also made a nice portmanteau. Brody dubbed them "teavangelicals." And the likely ringleader of this movement? Mike Pence, by a mile. "I believe with all my journalistic heart," Brody told conservative blogger Matt Lewis, "that Mike Pence has a real chance to be the first teavangelical president of the United States."

This may have been true, but Pence was dropping the culture warrior schtick for something more palatable to the power brokers and moneymen who would finance any future White House bid. He entered the next major evolution of his career, turning into Mitch Daniels 2.0.

CHAPTER 10

BACK HOME AGAIN

On June 11, 2011, about one thousand friends, neighbors, Republican activists, and Pence campaign volunteers packed into Columbus's Commons in the center of downtown. Inside, the event seemed more like a kickoff for a presidential run than for governor. Pence, Karen, and the kids, walked out onto center stage to cheers—and a Hollywood-style film crew captured every moment. Videographers darted across the stage, grabbing multiple shots of the family—another camera, mounted on a crane, swooped down from above on stage right, capturing a grandiose view of a decidedly nongrandiose family. "These are my people!" he exclaimed. "This is where I'm from!"

Pence delivered a true stem-winder, filled with fire aimed at Washington. "We need to be willing to say 'Yes,' to Indiana and 'No,' to Washington!" Pence said. He riled up the crowd by promising to fight Obamacare and strict environmental regulations—all things that would be far easier to fight as a congressman than as a governor.

He got only tepid responses when he talked about the nuts and bolts of state government, like education spending.

In all of thirty minutes, Pence's kickoff seemed to hint more at his national aspirations than perhaps he meant to. That focus on running for president was exactly what the Democrats planned to use against him. The Democratic candidate for governor, John Gregg, previewed his attack on Pence the night before in downtown Indianapolis: "We need a leader who understands Washington, Indiana, not Washington, DC! We deserve a leader that will not use our governor's mansion as a stepping-stone!" Washington, Indiana, wasn't far from where Gregg had grown up—in a small town in the southwest pocket of the state, right where Illinois, Indiana, and Kentucky meet. If the cornfield in Pence's backyard was simulacrum, the cornfield in Gregg's backyard had been a reality. Gregg didn't need to put on any rural airs to prove his bona fides, they came through just fine in his gravelly voice and ribald humor. And with his bald pate and giant walruslike mustache—he was a dead ringer for Wilford Brimley.

Gregg's attack wasn't that far off the mark—to run for governor, the Pences had to uproot their family again. It'd been a dozen years since they last picked up and altered their lives so Pence could run for office, but the change wouldn't be as tough this time. Michael Jr. was already at Purdue University in nearby Lafayette, Indiana; Charlotte was on her way to college; and their youngest, Audrey, had one year left of high school to finish up. They found a nice place in Geist Reservoir—a ritzy enclave in the northwest pocket of Indianapolis, home to many corporate executives and upper-class families. Next, Pence got a campaign vehicle, a Chevrolet Z71 pickup truck, cherry red, with plenty of room on the flatbed for delivering campaign speeches.

Pence returned to Indiana a changed man, stiffer, more plastic, than when he left. The easygoing, warm personality from radio and television had been tempered into something polished and wooden— like Al Gore with better delivery. But his bank of goodwill from a decade on-air was profound. And his support came from some unlikely places. Former representative Mark Souder, who Pence helped push out of Congress over his affair with a staffer, wrote a glowing assessment of Pence as he entered the race for governor. "He's insufferably nice and smiley whether he's just one-on-one where a media person could not possibly be present, in a small group, or speaking to a crowd," Souder wrote. "At first I thought it was a fake. In politics there have been known to be a few. But Mike's style is not. He somewhere decided that if he was going to err, he'd err to the side of exaggerating the good side of people. You could have a worse bad trait."

Indiana Democrats knew they'd be in for a tough ride in 2012, but Gregg seemed like a pretty good get for a party with a shallow bench of talent statewide. He was pro-life, pro-gun, and, as he liked to point out, could go verse for verse on the Bible with Pence any time. Gregg liked to play up his country roots, but he'd risen to power in Indianapolis at about the same time Pence was starting out in the '80s. He became Indiana House Speaker through the late '90s. Pence and Gregg also shared something else; Pence handed off his Saturday call-in show on WIBC to Gregg when he ran for Congress again in 2000. Gregg and Pence had a personal connection—but it didn't mean they wouldn't take some shots at each other, it was the race to become governor after all.

Australian Gold

Pence and his team knew they would have to work the ground across the state to get Pence reintroduced to voters. But they also had to keep their eyes focused on the bigger goal, building their national base for an eventual White House run. At the start of November 2011, Pence and his team spent a few days in New York City courting high-dollar national donors. Kellyanne Conway, the pollster and pitchwoman he had picked up a few years earlier, came through for Team Pence, setting up meetings with some big names, including one of her other clients: Donald J. Trump.

On November 8, 2011, Pence entered Trump Tower on Fifth Avenue in Manhattan and took the elevator up to Trump's office. Marty Obst, Kyle Robertson, and Pence sat with Trump and his main political operative, Michael Cohen. The meeting was cordial, but barely memorable. Neither man made much of an impression on the other, it was just business. Trump cut a check for $2,500 to Pence. Trump had not met Pence before this and barely recalled the meeting later. Trump was closer to another Hoosier, his old foil from the 1996 Indiana Gridiron Roast, Steve Hilbert. The two had grown closer since then.

In the late '90s, Hilbert was the king of the insurance industry, lording over the Conseco insurance company, valued at $52 billion. He made hundreds of millions of dollars before running the company into ruin. Hilbert also helped Trump out in a pinch in 1998, entering a deal to buy the General Motors building in Manhattan for $800 million. Trump repaid the favor in spades more than a decade later. In 2011, Steve and his wife, Tomisue, paid $100,000 for a spot on Trump's *Celebrity Apprentice.* "We turn down many sponsors, I mean everybody wants to be on the 'Celebrity Apprentice,'" Trump said.

As Mike Pence was in New York that April, courting Republican tastemakers, Trump was in the studio with his own tastemakers, Gary Busey, La Toya Jackson, and Mark McGrath. On April 11, 2011, NBC aired episode 6 of Season 11 of *The Apprentice*—"Australian Gold." The competing celebrities had to come up with a marketing line for the Hilberts' product. La Toya Jackson won, with a gem of a slogan, "Live the gold life."

The only problem was Australian Gold didn't turn everyone's skin gold, sometimes they turned orange.

CHRISTIE, ROMNEY, LUGAR, AND THE ROAD TO THE MANSION

Pence and his team were cranking, making all the national connections they could. Two stars of the Republican Party were the governors of Virginia and New Jersey, who had both won decisive victories in 2009, presaging the Tea Party wave of 2010. Virginia governor Bob McDonnell now chaired the Republican Governors Association, tasked with electing more Republicans to governorships across the nation, and New Jersey governor Chris Christie served as vice chair of the group. In that capacity, Christie picked up a handful of states he was responsible for, including Indiana. That November, Pence and Christie met at the Republican Governors Association meeting in Florida—and they hit it off immediately. Christie knew Pence had talent, and Pence was ready to launch into major fund-raising. Christie promised him, "Anything at all I can do, I'll do it."

A few weeks later, Christie flew to Indianapolis for a fund raiser for Republican congressional candidate Susan Brooks. Pence and his team couldn't believe it—Christie promised to help them but he flew into town without telling them. Christie couldn't believe that he had to tell Team Pence everything he did—Brooks was an old friend from their days as federal prosecutors and this was a special favor for her. The two sides quickly patched it up and hastily threw together a fund raiser for Pence. No harm, no foul.

Even as Pence's long game seemed to play out in his favor, it was hard for some of his top advisers not to look back and wonder if they'd missed their window with 2012. The angst of the conservative leaders who had tried to recruit Pence to run in 2012 had played out writ large in the Republican primary field. The conservative base seemed to search for anyone other than Romney. First came Tea Party stalwart Michele Bachmann, then came Texas governor Rick Perry. Both rose in the polls and led for a week or so, but quickly fell off in the heat of the national glare. Next up came the pizza man, Herman Cain— who had owned the national chain Godfather's Pizza about a decade earlier. His tax plan was simple—9-9-9, cut the income tax to 9 percent, cut the corporate tax to 9 percent, and levy a new, national sales tax at 9 percent. It also looked like it was cribbed from a video game, SimCity 4. Cain fell off, too—just another flavor of the week.

Nobody had sticking power, including Mitt Romney.

If the feeling among the conservative base was blasé on the national level, it was virulently fired up in Indiana, where Tea Partiers readied to bag one of the biggest "RINOs," or Republicans in name only, in the country. Senator Dick Lugar's was one of the Tea Party's most prized scalps. They were angry at him for befriending Barack Obama when Obama was a fresh-faced senator on the Senate Foreign Relations Committee. They were angry at Lugar for working with Obama, as president, to draw down nuclear weapons in Eastern Europe. They were angry at Lugar for voting in support of Obama's Supreme Court nominees, something that had long been a tradition in the more genial Senate of years past but was no longer in fashion.

Lugar's many apostasies over the years angered the conservative faithful, but for decades his goodwill and network among Indiana Republicans made him invincible. But in that time he became a creature of Washington. He stopped showing up for Lincoln Day fund raisers and working the party circuit in Indiana. A generation of Republican activists grew up knowing Lugar only as a man of the swamp, not of the state.

Indiana's various Tea Party groups learned their lesson in 2010, when establishment pick Dan Coats ran up the middle to beat out competing Tea Party candidates. For 2012, they organized early to unite behind one candidate, Richard Mourdock, the state's treasurer.

Pence didn't have to worry about a contested primary, but the GOP field-clearing did leave one lingering problem for him. Indiana's House speaker, Brian Bosma, never forgot how he had been boxed out of the primary for governor. Bosma—a tall, bald man with a wry smile and calm demeanor—seemed to enjoy wielding the gavel even more than his predecessors and he knew how to slam it down, when needed.

That winter, as the 2012 legislative session started at the Indiana statehouse, Representative Bob Morris wrote a dear colleague letter to the other lawmakers, urging them to oppose a resolution honoring the one hundredth anniversary of the Girl Scouts. The group, he said, supported "feminist, lesbian, and Communist agendas" and Morris recommended they all send their daughters and granddaughters to an alternative scouting group started by the Christian Right. Bosma didn't care much for his state and the House chamber looking foolish and wacky, so he bought dozens of boxes of Thin Mints, and other cookies and placed them around the House chamber. They were going to honor the Girl Scouts, and Morris could eat crow, or Thin Mints, as it were.

The incident provided all the comedy gold that was needed for the writers of that year's Indiana Gridiron Dinner. They placed boxes of Girl Scout cookies on the tables throughout the Indiana Ballroom Rooftop Theater ("Contents Radicalized" read the stickers on the boxes) and sprinkled in Girl Scout jokes throughout the program that night. But the main course was the candidates for governor, Gregg, Pence, and Libertarian candidate Rupert Boneham, a fan favorite from the TV show *Survivor*. The three men ran through their own bits onstage, gently ribbing one another. Pence offered a rare bit of dry humor. "I am humbled to be with you," he said. "In fact, I'm humiliated." Pence's tone was dead on for the occasion—roasting without peeling the paint off the walls.

Then Bosma took the stage; a well-built six-foot-tall man, he squeezed himself into the biggest Girl Scouts uniform he could find—and borrowed a sash from Troop 69 (a real troop from Northwest Indiana). Then he jumped into his routine, riffing on the latest statehouse debacles. Mike and Karen sat down in the audience, even though this was clearly not their type of setting. Bosma burned through a series of one-liners shooting at the misguided state lawmaker and his fixation on the Girl Scouts. Then he turned his fire on the Pences. The police arrived at the Pences' new house in Indianapolis the other day, he said, where they found a disturbing scene: the garage door was banging up and down, repeatedly; something was amiss. They went inside and found Mike and Karen Pence having sex. When they got up, there was a chalk outline around Karen.

Silence.

And then uproarious guffaws—about 75 percent of the room laughed their asses off. The other 25 percent gasped. Bosma, in his Troop 69 Girl Scout uniform, smiled. Pence was, in fact, humiliated. As he and Karen got up to leave, he looked pale, like someone had just shot his family dog.

Bosma wasn't sure if he'd gone too far. He asked some friends after the show if they thought he'd crossed the line. They all said he stopped short of offending them. But the fact he even had to ask said everything that needed to be said. He sent flowers to Karen the next day as an apology. But the damage was done. In that moment, the most important moneymen in Republican politics closed their checkbooks for Bosma; they couldn't support a man with that character.

The roast was mean and spiteful—Mike and Karen vowed never to return—and Bosma's insult was clearly personal. But there seemed to be another problem; nobody would dare make a joke like that about Mitch Daniels. The joke was a sign of weakness on Pence's part, after more than a decade in Washington, Pence had better standing in the nation's capital than he did in the state's.

Pence also had a stronger team in Washington, made of the core group he brought on when he became Republican conference chairman. But only half the team emigrated with him back to Indiana for the run—other key players, Short, Conway, Pitcock, stayed behind and took on more limited roles. Into the vacuum stormed Bill Smith, Pence's first chief of staff and close friend. Back from the sidelines, Smith presented himself as the gatekeeper to Pence.

Pence seemed to wall himself off as well—his close friends from WIBC and Network Indiana noticed he didn't joke with them anymore, and he didn't pal around. Washington seemed to have sucked the fun out of him, they said. Pence was even more closed off than when he was in Washington—he limited press access and talked in stiffer tones. Something else had changed; he was no longer talking about other politicians, now he was talking about himself.

And another problem emerged. Pence didn't seem to mind toiling in Daniels's shadow, but his campaign aides did. Over the course of months, Pence's team developed their agenda for how he would govern, and Daniels's team began preparing to hand off the reins. But neither side wanted to talk to the other. Daniels's aides accused Team Pence of being ideologues, doctrinaire, and unwilling to work with moderates. Team Pence accused Daniels's aides of worrying only about protecting Mitch's legacy. Neither side aired this dirty laundry in public and Pence and Daniels never seemed to have any animosity themselves, but the tension was unavoidable, almost like a sibling rivalry.

The rocky crags of Pence's run for governor were readily apparent to most Indiana politicos, but rarely made it out in public in part because everyone was preoccupied by another race: Dick Lugar was on the ropes.

National conservative groups swooped in to aid Mourdock, battering Lugar with millions of dollars' worth of television ads. And Lugar, perhaps unwittingly, played into it. Lugar hadn't lived in Indiana since he left for the U.S. Senate in 1977; that hadn't mattered much in previous races, but Lugar's opponents found a novel attack in there: Lugar, they argued, couldn't even vote for himself in his own race, because he didn't live in Indiana.

Lugar, of course, could vote for himself—because the law allowed for continued state residency while serving as a legislator in Washington. But Lugar's staff scurried to put out the political brushfire, reaching out to friends and longtime allies like Mitch Daniels—Daniels recorded a television ad for his old boss, which ran in the waning days of the campaign. They reached out to Pence for help, surely the guy who got his start working in Lugar's political machine could help. When Pence avoided them, Lugar's staff reminded him he had the same problem—he hadn't lived in Indiana for a dozen years—the same fire licking at Lugar's career could just as easily engulf Pence's. But Pence stayed silent.

On May 8, 2012, the Tea Party claimed one of its biggest trophies yet, Dick Lugar. Republicans nominated Mourdock, 61 percent to 39 percent. To some degree the loss was inevitable, but Lugar's loyal team was devastated nonetheless. In the weeks and months afterward, they simmered, mulling over all the Republicans who stood with them in their time of need and all the ones who went missing, especially Pence. Pence, meanwhile, coasted to his first victory on his march to the governor's office—he was the only name on the ballot in the Republican primary.

BORING IS HIS CAMOUFLAGE

It wasn't just the Lugar race Pence was absent from—he also seemed absent from his own race, almost like he was running as if he already won.

Throughout the race, Pence was boring in public—purposefully so. As one veteran Republican who had tracked Pence since the late '80s said, "Boring is his camouflage." Even if behind the scenes Pence knew how to fire up his base. That June, after the Supreme Court ruled to uphold Obamacare—the central focus of every conservative's ire—Pence, in a private meeting with House Republicans, compared the decision to the September 11 terrorist attacks. He later apologized, after the comparison was reported, "I certainly did not intend to minimize any tragedy our nation has faced, and I apologize."

But aside from the occasional screw-up in private, Pence was so dull it almost became possible to forget that he was a social crusader in the vein of the lawmaker who opposed the Girl Scouts, or at least he had been. In previous times Pence had opposed federal research funding for AIDS if it supported "dangerous lifestyles." He had argued that cigarettes didn't kill and said that neither gays nor women should be in the military.

But that was ancient Mike Pence; he didn't espouse those ideas anymore, right? He wouldn't say. Pence had morphed for the fourth time in his life, from a "teavangelical" heartthrob into the heir to

Mitch Daniels's technocratic reign of government. On August 23, 2012, Pence made a campaign stop at Marian University, a conservative Catholic institution run by a prominent Republican operative. He was there to pitch his plan for workforce development. This was the jobs and education part of his narrowly crafted platform; the only thing that would've made it stronger would've been tax cuts.

Jim Shella, a reporter for the paper covering the Chicago suburbs in Indiana, the *Times of Northwest Indiana*, asked Pence if he would tighten the window for having an abortion. Pence dodged, saying he was there that day to talk about education and jobs, but Shella, who had MC'd the Trump roast sixteen years earlier, pressed again. Pence hadn't talked about abortion at all in the campaign. "Let me be very clear on this, I'm pro-life. If the legislature sends me pro-life legislation, I'll sign it. But I think this election is about jobs and schools," Pence said. "People who know me know I say what I mean, and I mean what I say." Then Pence's spokeswoman cut off the questions—they were afraid. The opposition caught a whiff of it right away.

"I feel like I'm a game warden," Gregg said shortly after Pence's campaign stop, in his trademark gravelly voice. "I feel like I'm chasing a leopard that's changed its spots. You can't just all of a sudden say you're about jobs and disregard your past." Gregg, meanwhile, had been campaigning hard on a promise to protect Indiana manufacturing from unfair trade practices overseas—while Pence was at Marian University ducking the abortion question, Gregg had been out talking about establishing an office to help Indiana businesses locked in international trade battles.

A few days later, photos from a Pence campaign event and a Facebook post detailing the event appeared. The Pence campaign had never advertised the stop, and they caught the Indiana press off guard. Pence had launched a new strategy after the harrowing abortion question experience. He was going to hide. For the rest of the campaign, Pence touted campaign stops only in press releases and Facebook posts after the fact.

Pence's best bet was to hide, from the press at least, if he wanted to win. Just a few hours to the west, in Missouri, Republican candidate for Senate Todd Akin tripped over himself as he tried to explain that women can't get pregnant from "legitimate rape." Pence may have had similarly strident views, but it didn't mean that he was going to commit political suicide by explaining them in public. All he had to do was run out the clock.

By the start of September, with just a couple months until Election Day, Pence was running short on money. The race for governor should have been a slam dunk but Pence wasn't registering with voters the way his donor cabal had promised. Pence was frantically raising money to stay on-air. On September 15, 2012, he called up his buddy Chris Christie with an urgent request—could he get to Indiana that night? They had a megadonor lined up for a big event, but they would only do it if Christie showed up. But Christie had a conflict.

"Chris, please do this, I need the money. This is the only night the guy will do it," Pence told the New Jersey governor. "I'll make it up to you some way."

Christie went to his wife and said, "Pence really needs me to do this, can we do your birthday dinner the next night?" Mary Pat Christie said, "Yes, go ahead."

"I gave up my wife's birthday to be in Indiana for Mike Pence," Christie said. "That wasn't money for the RGA, that was money for the Pence campaign."

To show their appreciation, Karen Pence sent Christie back with a small birthday gift for Mary Pat. Did they not grasp the seriousness of canceling Mary Pat Christie's birthday dinner or were they just being earnestly, honestly, midwestern nice? Christie wasn't entirely sure.

Something God Intended

Late in the election, the candidates for Dick Lugar's seat met for their last debate—a showdown on October 23, 2012, at Indiana University Southeast, nestled in the suburbs of Louisville.

Republican Richard Mourdock, Democratic candidate Joe Donnelly, and Libertarian candidate Andy Horning took the stage. They ticked through a rote recitation of their positions, and then the moderator asked for their positions on abortion.

Mourdock stood at the podium, his eyes tearing up as they often did on the campaign trail—whether he was talking about babies and conception or taxes and fiscal restraint. "I know there are some who disagree, and I respect their point of view, but I believe life begins at conception. The only exception I have, to have an abortion, is in that case of the life of the mother. I struggled with it myself for a long time, but I came to realize that, life is that gift from God [and] I think even if life begins in that horrible situation of rape, that it is something God intended."

There was no flash of light, no boom, no mic drop—the debate kept going, and that last statement sank in.

What did he mean, "something God intended"? The rape? The life? The ranks of reporters and politicos on Twitter immediately picked out what it really was: a gigantic fuckup. They spotted a trend of hard Right conservative candidates with asinine ideas about rape and abortion. It sounded an awful lot like Missouri candidate Todd Akin's claim that women can't get pregnant from "legitimate rape." As campaign staff and reporters filtered out for the postdebate press conference, Mourdock felt good. If Twitter was on fire, it didn't seem to have registered in New Albany, Indiana, or with Mourdock himself. "Are you trying to suggest somehow that God preordained rape? No, I don't think that," Mourdock said when pressed on his comment. "Anyone who would suggest that is just sick and twisted. No, that's not even close to what I said."

The next morning, Mourdock called a press conference to explain himself. Reporters gathered in the Republican Party headquarters, right next to the Hard Rock Café in downtown Indianapolis. His point, Mourdock said, was that babies conceived in rape are a gift from God—because all life is a gift from God.

For Mourdock, this was catastrophic, although he seemed resigned to whatever the voters may choose. But now Pence would have to answer the abortion question, after avoiding it the entire campaign. It was easy enough for Pence to duck the hicks in the local press, but now the national spotlight—powered by the attention of everyone he needed to impress in Washington—would beat down on him.

For the moderate suburban Republicans who ringed Indianapolis, Mourdock and Pence were not an inspiring duo. Pence never dispelled the notion that he was the same guy who wrote, a decade earlier, that AIDS funding shouldn't be used to promote "homosexual" lifestyles. Or that Karen didn't still think the occasional children's section of the *Indy Star* was trying to turn all the Hoosier children gay.

In one gaffe, Mourdock undid all of Pence's careful tiptoeing and hiding.

Pence immediately requested that Mourdock apologize—but he wouldn't say what Mourdock should apologize for. Because if Pence pushed too hard for an apology he could start losing his support from the Christian Right. He just had to hide out for two more weeks and he was home free.

BENNETT

If abortion was the splinter issue, something else was boiling up just beneath the surface, realigning the old Left-Right split that had dominated politics for a century—education. Indiana's schools chief, Tony Bennett, was discovering that now in a serious way. Bennett was a political creation of Mitch Daniels, plucked out of a school system in the suburbs of Louisville and cultivated into his champion for conservative education changes. Their plan included a blend of privatization favored by conservative thinkers and nationalized standards favored by more moderate, corporate types, including Obama's education secretary. Under Daniels's tutelage, Bennett soared to become a national education reform star in the space of just a few years. Former Florida governor Jeb Bush recruited Bennett to be the front man for his national education reform group, Chiefs for Change. Bush's group, with Bennett as the lead, corralled money from Republican megadonors, including the founders of Amway, the DeVos family. And, with Bennett at the lead, Bush's Chiefs for Change pushed for nationalized education standards called Common Core.

It was precisely the style of federal education control that Pence and other conservatives fought against in 2001, when George W. Bush stood side by side with Senator Ted Kennedy and signed No Child Left Behind. But the Republican Party still had room for differing views, and on Election Day, November 6, 2012, Pence stood side by side with Bennett at the party held in the end zone of the Indianapolis Colts' stadium. Control of the governor's office, a U.S. Senate seat, the Department of Education, and more hung in the balance—along with the White House itself.

Pence and his campaign aides watched the TV screens as the results came in, steadily. Mourdock trailed Democratic Senate candidate Joe Donnelly throughout the evening. But the biggest surprise came when an unknown teacher from Indianapolis with a distinctive frizzy blond volcano of hair, Glenda Ritz, upended the national education star Tony Bennett. Bennett was slated for an easy victory, but instead he lost by six percentage points to the unknown Democrat. Pence's team was getting nervous.

Meanwhile, the damage from Mourdock's rape comment was becoming clearer for Team Pence—as the evening wore on, the returns looked tough for Pence. With Mourdock and Bennett flailing, Pence's initial returns were not faring much better against Gregg. Then, just before ten P.M., Pence slipped through to victory—49 percent to 46 percent—he was the first candidate in Indiana's history to win the governorship with less than 50 percent of the vote. He hadn't been a terribly inspiring pick for most voters. But he won.

Karen Pence gathered Mike and their three children together for a minute before they walked out to bask in the victory. They stood in the suite of Republican donor Forrest Lucas, in his namesake Lucas

Oil Stadium, home of the Indianapolis Colts. Karen pulled them away from the donors and other family, into the bathroom, the only place they could find some privacy as a family. "We wanted a moment, just the five of us, to hold on to each other," Karen said, tearing up as she recalled the meeting. "We wanted a moment to hold on to each other before that roller coaster went down the hill. . . . We huddled in the bathroom, it was the only place we could have any privacy, and we kind of clung to each other." Then their children gave her a framed print-out of their favorite aphorisms of hers. Michael, Charlotte, and Audrey each wrote a "mom-ism" down, Karen's most used sayings and words of wisdom. Audrey's favorite mom-ism was "I'm listening, and I hear you." Then she wrote, "Mom, we are so blessed to have you as our rock."

Good to Great—January 2013

Fortunately for Pence, nobody in Washington noticed how he almost blew a sure thing. National Republicans were busier licking their wounds after Romney fell hard to Obama—332–206 electoral votes. Republican National Committee chairman Reince Priebus commissioned an election "autopsy" to help figure out what went wrong. The report came back with some big recommendations, not least of which was the Republican Party could not survive as the party of old white men in a country that was increasingly diversifying. This meant toning down some of the social issues, playing up more fiscal policy, and veering away from the latent racism that seemed to sprout up so much in the immigration debate.

Pence was inaugurated governor on January 13, 2013. Standing in the cold, on the steps of the statehouse, he started with his thanks and gratitude—to his family, foremost, to God, and to the governors of both parties who came before him. He heaped plaudits upon Mitch Daniels, calling Indiana "the fiscal envy of the nation" under his watch. Then he promised that Hoosiers stood on the brink of "greatness" and he was ready to lead them there. His tone was his typical

Reagan-esque—in the wake of the Great Recession, Indiana, with its heavy base of manufacturing, had been particularly hard hit, with one of the highest unemployment rates in the nation just four years earlier, under Daniels's watch. But Pence promised that fiscal austerity would lead the way for the state out of the recession.

"We dare not squander this moment with complacency or self-congratulation. With so many Hoosiers hurting in this economy, we must meet this moment with resolve, determined to leave our state more prosperous, our children more prepared, and our communities and families stronger than ever before," Pence said. "With so many families and businesses struggling just to get by, we have no choice but to remain bold, optimistic, and relentless in our work until good jobs, great schools, safe streets, and strong families become the hallmark of every community in this state!"

Pence opened his governorship by trying to craft himself into Mitch Daniels 2.0—he shelved the social issues and Christian Right priorities. This would appeal especially to the national donor class he was trying to win over. But he had some competition for the helm of most Daniels-like. Wisconsin governor Scott Walker made his name busting Wisconsin's unions, much the same way Daniels had—but Walker caught the national spotlight and held it. Ohio governor John Kasich struck a more moderate tone, while still running the Daniels playbook. The problem for Pence was that he couldn't be a Mitch Daniels prototype—Indiana already had one of those; his name was Mitch Daniels, and Pence entered the statehouse squarely in his shadow. And, since Daniels had effectively appointed himself president of the state's premier engineering school on his way out the door of the statehouse, Daniels's shadow wasn't disappearing soon.

Pence had another Daniels problem, one less obvious and one he could never talk about, if he valued his career. Daniels left some significant messes for Pence to clean up. Daniels rushed the opening of a major highway, the I-69 extension from Evansville in the state's southwest corner to Bloomington, home of Indiana University. He used money from the sale of the Indiana Toll Road to pay for the long-awaited highway extension, and shortly before he left office, Daniels took a victory lap on his Harley-Davidson for the highway's grand opening. Then, a few months after Pence took office, state engineers announced the I-69 extension was literally sinking into the ground—they hadn't properly accounted for the strip mine underneath. Daniels had also revolutionized the state's Bureau of Motor Vehicles—turning a soul-sucking waiting line that residents used to identify the whole of governmental confusion into a modern, easy-to-use system with automated kiosks, online renewals, and stunning efficiencies. But Daniels's BMV had been quietly overcharging residents for their licenses. A few years later, a Daniels holdover at the BMV negotiated a contract with lucrative payments for the vendor—then left to take a job with that vendor. A culture of soft corruption had taken hold during Daniels's time in office, often unchecked. The multibillion-dollar contract to privatize Medicaid went to the former employer of one of Daniels's closest allies, a top state transportation official's family benefited from land sales surrounding the vaunted I-69 highway extension (before it began sinking), and Daniels himself appointed the members of the Purdue University board of trustees who later selected him president of the college in a secret meeting. However, Daniels also pushed the creation of a state inspector general, which often ended up investigating cozy arrangements made by Daniels administration officials.

What was Pence supposed to do, blast the state's most popular politician? He'd only won his own race by three percentage points, and the wags inside the Beltway in Washington saw Daniels as the very image of a "reasonable" Republican at a time when the rest of the party had gone over the edge. Pence would have to sweep up after his quite popular predecessor very quietly. He'd done plenty of quiet sweeping in Washington, and he would need to do more in Indiana while keeping his eye on the prize. In fact, one of Pence's campaign slogans had hinted at this very dynamic—he was going to take Indiana "from good to great!"

A few days after his inauguration, Pence hosted his first cabinet meeting as governor—about two dozen top-ranking officials and agency heads sat around a wooden table that had been hand-carved by state inmates, with gorgeously inlaid cuts of each one of Indiana's ninety-two counties. Sitting in front of each agency chief was a copy of Jim Collins's *Good to Great.* Hardbound in a bright red cover, the book was an intensive study of how some companies like Kroger grocery stores, Circuit City, Fannie Mae, and Gillette exploded in growth, while others languished. Collins and his team identified critical elements for successful management. Pence believed that these were the same principles needed to run a successful state government. Unstated at the meeting, and perhaps one reason that book was parked in front of every agency chief, was Pence's critical lack of executive experience.

Pence had been the public face of a small think tank, a radio host, a failed politician, and a successful politician. All these experiences had made him stellar at navigating difficult situations, taking the pulse of the electorate, and learning how to climb, steadily, through vicious political terrain. But none prepared him to manage a massive organization with more than 130,000 employees, stretching over all facets of public life—from road and bridge construction to natural disaster management.

Sometimes his White House ambitions directly collided with running the state. Early in the administration, Pence's economic development team floated the idea of poaching some insurance companies from Iowa—a natural move and one where some of them already had some leads. But word came back from the governor's office that they were not to target any companies in Iowa. Unstated in the note from Pence's office, but one that the staff read between the lines, was that they weren't allowed to piss off voters in an important presidential primary state.

He also faced another challenge, not quite as obvious—balancing his family life.

As he set up in the governor's office on the second floor of the statehouse, Pence had some reporters in to meet with him. Things had thawed now that he won the race; he didn't need to hide anymore. They all gathered around the governor's desk in the sweeping office—portraits of Indiana's past governors hung on the surrounding walls; one of Pence would soon be placed there, too. On his desk, an antique-style cherry-red phone stood out. One of the press corps asked Pence what it was for. That, he said, was Karen's direct line to him—only she had the number. Jim Shella, the veteran reporter, asked Pence about rumors that Karen would also be close by, in the building. Karen, he said, was indeed getting an office inside the building, she was the first First Lady of Indiana to have a workspace directly across the statehouse atrium from her husband. That raised eyebrows among the press corps as they left Pence's new office.

Karen would often work out of the new First Lady's office and spend the day on the phone with Pence—she could've easily walked across the hall to his office, but she preferred the phone—fewer prying eyes from the statehouse to watch her as she worked. The relationship between Mitch and Cheri Daniels had been famously distant, but nobody expected that Mike and Karen would be quite this close.

Soon those prying eyes of the building, the lobbyists who filled the third floor, saw Karen's invisible hand at work. They liked to stash their coats and briefcases in the nooks dedicated to the former governors of Indiana. Busts of the former governors were saddled with workwear and sometimes donned caps. One day, they showed up to find velvet ropes blocking off each nook, and statehouse guards there telling them not to set their stuff by the former governors anymore. Karen, the lobbyists said, felt it was disrespectful of her husband to deface the busts like that. There was a new sheriff in town, and it wasn't Mike.

Karen also set some less visible barriers around Pence himself. The governor's office started closing often at 5:30 P.M., sometimes leaving nobody in the office, giving him time to get home for dinner. Pence had to clean up Daniels's messes, climb out from his lengthy shadow, deal with every random new occurrence around the state, cut a figure on the national stage crowded with other stars, and still make it home for dinner.

Meanwhile, as they surveyed the prospects for a 2016 White House run, Pence's team quickly decided he needed a few big trophies to tout. They immediately landed on a goal, "the largest tax cut in state history." The cuts would have to stand up to some strong competition in the prospective 2016 field; Ohio governor John Kasich proposed cutting his state's income tax by twice as much as Pence was calling for in his 2013 budget plan. And to the northwest, Wisconsin governor Scott Walker was also pushing an income tax cut as part of a broader package. In short, all the possible 2016 candidates were squaring up for the so-called Koch primary, the battle before the actual Republican race to win the incredibly lucrative backing of the Koch brothers.

Pence's proposal was minimal at best—he sought a 10 percent cut in the state's already low income tax. The average return from Pence's proposal would be under $100 per year.

Daniels, Bosma, and the statehouse Republicans had already passed some serious cuts in the last few years—there wasn't much left for Pence. Pence could've secured the goal he wanted by chopping into the state's sizable 7 percent sales tax.

To achieve his political goals, Pence needed to be able to market one of the smallest tax cuts the state had ever seen as its biggest. He faced a lot of practical obstacles to get to that point: Evan Bayh had already passed the largest tax cut in state history, chief among them how the state taxed cars. And the man who had to approve all this was Pence's archnemesis, House Speaker Brian Bosma.

Pence was lost inside the statehouse. And it showed. On the day he announced his most important proposal, the one he would use to till the ground for a White House bid, Pence's office called the lawmakers who would have to help him push the measure to invite them to the announcement . . . thirty minutes before they were set to roll it out. A few weeks later, when the tax cut came up for a hearing in a critical state senate committee, nobody from Pence's staff showed up to testify. Meanwhile, rather than directly asking legislators for their support, Pence went around the state to local Republican fund raisers, asking Republican activists to lobby for him.

And then it got stranger.

When the tax cut failed to catch on, he called in support from Washington, via the Koch brothers. Americans for Prosperity Indiana, the state-level version of the Kochs' political outfit, began targeting statehouse Republicans in television ads. The ad ticked through a series of newspaper headlines before sending viewers to a website, FightForIndiana.com, where they could send prewritten messages to their lawmakers.

Pence disavowed any knowledge of the ads. They may not have technically violated Pence's vaunted pledge not to run negative attacks, since they weren't technically his, but the stance didn't fool Bosma. He wouldn't budge. He'd suffered far worse during the fight against Indiana's unions. "You're looking at a guy that's had death threats, people camped at my front door and participated in millions of dollars of paid advertising on both sides, so my focus will be on making the right decision and not succumbing to one side or another."

With the clock winding down on Pence's very first session as governor, he looked like he might lose his most important policy measure, and his best argument for a presidential bid.

That March, he returned to the place where he cut his teeth three decades earlier, the Marion County Republican Party and the home of John Sweezy, the party boss who first recruited him to run. But this was not a warm homecoming. The Marion County Republicans were far more moderate than the rest of the state, and generally far more skeptical of Pence. And Bosma, who held a district representing the southside of Indianapolis, was one of their ringleaders.

As they gathered for their annual fund raiser at the Crowne Plaza Hotel in downtown Indianapolis, the tension was thick. Pence took the stage to mild applause—everybody knew why he was there. Pence was coy, "As we work through these challenging issues at the statehouse, whether you're 'fer it' or you're 'agin it,' or if you're somewhere in between, let me say from my heart, especially to my friends and allies near and far: We will not build up our state by tearing each other down. It is essential that we stay positive in advocating our positions."

The GOP operatives in the room watched Bosma as he delivered polite golf claps, light and gentle—and followed suit. They all felt that the Washington-style pressure tactics Pence had brought back with him—television advertisements and a flood of money from a national special-interest group—would tear down their more genial state culture. Pence did not stick around to shake hands, or schmooze, or attempt to win over any votes. That wasn't his purpose.

Bosma ripped off his genteel veneer when he took the stage after Pence left. He snickered at the Koch brothers' attempt to push him into a tax cut, "I would have said this with the governor here still, 'I'm from Americans for Prosperity and I'm just here to help.'"

Just as the feud between Pence and Bosma looked like it could sink Pence's very first session, cooler heads inside the Republican Party, including the leader of the state senate, David Long, intervened. One month later, peace was achieved, and Pence got his tax cut. It was pretty small, a 5 percent cut stretched out over four years. But that was all that he needed, now he could go around the nation telling everyone he got the largest tax cut in Indiana history—even if that statement was false.

Pence, Bosma, and everyone else declared the session a great victory—and then Pence and all his staff went on vacation. There was a lot of work left to do, like spending days and weeks reviewing the legislation. But Karen wanted a vacation.

CHAPTER 11

GOVERNOR PENCE
FOR PRESIDENT

Martin Lomasney, a legendary ward heeler from the West End of Boston in the 1800s, once said, "Don't write when you can talk; don't talk when you can nod your head." In other words, don't leave any evidence. But that lesson never entirely took hold in Indiana, where Democrats and Republicans maintained a gentleman's agreement of not releasing public records when requested by the press or others. It created a culture where politicians didn't mind writing some very interesting things in email.

Lomasney's old saw was on the mind of an AP reporter in May 2013 when he went hunting for emails from the Indiana Department of Education. The change in guard from Democrat to Republican gave a rare opening to the otherwise closed world of government decision making. The Democrats, still smarting from a lashing at the hands of Daniels and Republicans, seemed like they may be willing to break that gentleman's agreement and honor a public records request. The AP reporter went searching for emails from Mitch Daniels and struck gold in the first batch of responsive records he received. Daniels had secretly tried banning Howard Zinn's liberal take on American history, *A People's History of the United States*, from Indiana classrooms. In an email to his staff, Daniels wrote, "It is a truly execrable, anti-factual piece of disinformation that misstates American history on every page. Can someone assure me that it is not in use anywhere in Indiana? If it is, how do we get rid of it before more young people are force-fed a totally false version of our history?"

The reporter had also heard some stories around the statehouse, hallway chatter, that Tony Bennett, the former schools superintendent, had used his state staff and office to campaign for reelection and to fund-raise—a criminal violation of the state's ghost employment law, meant to curb corruption. Bennett was still a major star in conservative education reform circles, having secured a job as Florida's schools superintendent after he lost his 2012 reelection bid in Indiana. With a presidential run for Jeb Bush in the wings, Bennett was also widely discussed as a possible education secretary.

This time, the AP reporter went to the Department of Education and requested evidence of Bennett using his resources for his campaign. The reporter had also heard a rumor that Bennett had re-written a critical education policy to suit one of his biggest campaign donors. He asked for those emails, too. Then the Democratic DOE staff did something astonishing, they turned over Bennett's entire Microsoft Outlook file.

Bennett's emails were stunning. He had been mixing campaigning and his state business seamlessly—hundreds of entries from his calendar showed scheduled fund-raising calls packed in between official education meetings in his statehouse office. His staff had also downloaded fund-raising call lists to the state computer; one spreadsheet was dubbed "Big Hitter List" and another called "Red Meat List." They listed the names of major donors—many of the same ones who helped run Pence for governor—how much they had given Bennett, and their cell-phone numbers.

Also buried in Bennett's emails was a detailed account of how he and his staff scrambled to overhaul the state's school-grading system to protect one of his biggest donors, Christel DeHaan. Bennett secretly promised DeHaan in 2012 that when they wrote the new formula for evaluating schools, her Indianapolis charter school would be given an "A." But when they ran the school-grading formula a few months later, DeHaan's charter school got a "C"—due to poor math scores. "Anything less than an 'A' for Christel House compromises all of our accountability work," Bennett wrote in an email to his chief of staff. "This will be a huge problem for us." Bennett's chief of staff replied, "Oh, crap."

At the core of the conservative education reform movement stood an argument that public schools in the country had been unaccountable for their performance for decades—and the answer from a wide range of groups, from Bush's all the way to Bill Gates's philanthropic foundation, was more accountability in the form of grading the schools themselves on how many students they graduated, how the students scored on tests and other standardized metrics. The collaboration of conservative groups and corporate philanthropists also argued that charter schools and school vouchers were the best solution to what they deemed "failing" public schools. The Bennett scandal threatened far more than any single superintendent's career; it threatened the very basis of their movement—Bennett had rigged the accountability system to protect a wealthy donor's struggling charter.

And as the AP reporter was scouring the emails, Bennett was busy rewriting the school grading formula in Florida.

The AP published its first article in the investigation on July 29, 2013. Bennett was forced out as Florida's schools superintendent two days later. Bennett's career was done, but Pence's education problems were just beginning.

Indiana's public schools had always been modestly strong on the national level, with decent high school graduation rates matched against low per capita spending on education. The quality of schools varied widely, like in most states—from high-performing, gleaming schools in tony suburbs like Carmel, Indiana, to struggling institutions in the core of Indianapolis and Gary. Like the state itself, Indiana's education quality was very much in the middle. But what Indiana was famous for was being a testing ground of conservative policy ideas.

The same Indiana GOP donors who had put Pence in the governor's office wanted revenge for the fall of their education champion, Tony Bennett. Now Pence had to not only clean up Bennett's mess, but also drive an even more aggressive conservative overhaul. Pence started by pushing out his chief lobbyist, who had been Bennett's chief of staff. Then two weeks after the Bennett scandal broke, Pence opened a second education department to compete against the Department of Education.

The fighting between Pence and Indiana schools superintendent Glenda Ritz only escalated from there. State Board of Education meetings became monthly fiascoes—Ritz chaired the board, but Pence appointed the rest of its members. Ritz and the Pence board members wrote competing agendas for every meeting, and they yelled over one another in the proceedings. Pence's board hired staff to fight against Ritz's staff—and so they did, sometimes literally elbowing each other out of the way at the podium.

Fortunately for Pence, he didn't have the problem Bennett had with his emails. He couldn't, because he had been using his old AOL email account to conduct state business, instead of his government address.

READING THE FIELD

As the 2014 legislative session opened that January, Pence began work pushing a pilot program that would have the state pay a limited amount for preschool. He determined the modest program would cost $10.6 million. But expanding, or even starting, a new government program caught Pence's fiscally minded Republican colleagues off guard. This did not sound like the same man who proposed deep cuts in the state budget and rallied Tea Partiers in the nation's capital. Not only was he pushing a new program, Pence even testified before a legislative committee for the first time in his tenure as governor. Indiana's poor children were falling behind in kindergarten, Pence reasoned, "They arrive in kindergarten and spend too much time trying to catch up, and when that fails, they spend too much of their lives dropping out—out of school, out of work, and out of our communities." The man who didn't like to announce whether a proposal was on his agenda until it had crossed the finish line was suddenly putting his name on the line like never before. But why?

A small group of Republican lawmakers discovered the answer after they stripped out the money for the preschool program—Pence had been so absent from the statehouse for so long that his own testimony did little to change their minds. To counter, Pence kicked his lobbying up a notch. He invited a small group to the governor's mansion to watch basketball and have some snacks. One of the lawmakers, a stalwart conservative, asked the governor what was going on. Pence shrugged off the question, saying, "Karen's interested in this. She was a teacher, you know."

For more than a year, lobbyists, legislators, operatives, and others had all puzzled over how precisely Karen moved Pence on critical policy decisions. Now, for the first time, they had a definitive example. Pence had revealed the heaviness of Karen's hand, perhaps unwittingly.

Meanwhile, inside the statehouse, a massive battle ensued over the effort to place Indiana's statutory ban on gay marriage inside the state constitution. Christian Right groups in the state wanted to strengthen the state's ban, in anticipation of federal court action that could invalidate the law. Marriage bans across the country were being struck down, and other states were legalizing same-sex marriage— the national sentiment was clearly moving in favor of more support for LGBT couples. In Indiana, to amend the constitution, lawmakers would have to approve the measure in back-to-back, two-year sessions of the General Assembly. Legislative Republicans cleared the first hurdle in 2011, during the 2011–12 session, as Mitch Daniels stepped aside on the issue. Republican leaders punted on the issue in 2013, the first year of Pence's governorship.

Pence stood aside, too—the marriage ban, he said, was the province of the legislators and the voters in a referendum.

Meanwhile, a collaboration of the state's business leaders, moderate Republicans, and LGBT groups launched a coordinated effort to stop a marriage ban. Activists packed the halls outside the House and Senate chambers, chanting and waving signs, while premier Republican lobbyists worked the back rooms of the building. In a stunning turn for deeply conservative Indiana, the measure failed.

As the session wound to a close that March, Indiana's LGBT community cheered their surprise victory. But the state's small corps of Christian Right lobbyists vowed they were not finished; they were already hard at work on an alternative measure, a stopgap they said would protect the religiously devout from having to participate in same-sex wedding ceremonies.

Pence, meanwhile, was out actively testing the waters for a 2016 presidential bid. The year before gave him enough ammunition to make a case that he should at least be in the mix. Now he needed to build some buzz inside the Washington Beltway. His old Washington pitch team was working hard to sell Pence's governorship as a tremendous success. This was a hard sell. Pence had only been in one year, his vaunted tax cut was a pittance for the average Hoosier and just half of what he initially sought, and his competition had been far more successful. Pence was running in the shadow of New Jersey's Christie, Wisconsin's Walker, and Ohio's Kasich, in the "governor lane" of a GOP primary. And that didn't include far more dynamic politicians like Texas senator Ted Cruz and Florida senator Marco Rubio who had won the hearts and minds of Tea Partiers and conservatives.

With the domestic policies arena boxed out by other governors, Pence tried a novel move that spring, touting his foreign policy chops. He'd spent about eight years on the House Foreign Affairs Committee in Congress—work on the panel was never a priority for him, he focused his attention in Washington on climbing the rungs of House leadership instead, but it did provide him a base of understanding about world affairs that his would-be opponents lacked. The only thing he had to work on was convincing the national press why the governor of a landlocked state would be highly attuned to global affairs.

First, he had to tee up some interest, so he sent Matt Lloyd over to Fox News. "Chris Wallace wants to take me up on my pitch to feature you and Indiana's success story. Know you're leaving for Germany Saturday, so we can look at another date to make it work. Just wanted to make sure you knew you're back on their radar," Lloyd wrote on April 10, 2014. Pence replied almost immediately, "Excellent. Let's shoot for a few weeks out."

A few days later, Pence flew with a delegation of Indiana business leaders, political donors, and politicos to Berlin. The formal announcement from the governor's office was that this trip was about trade and nothing else, and he offered Indiana reporters interviews on the condition that they only asked about his plans for international trade and nothing else. Nothing. Else. He didn't want any questions about 2016, even though that's precisely why he was flying to Berlin. Meanwhile, in Washington, Pence's team pitched the Berlin trip as something else. The national press corps bit.

"I believe the United States and the EU must respond with deeds more than words to strengthen our economic and strategic defenses," Pence said in the prepared remarks his team leaked to Fox News. "I believe we must take immediate steps to deploy a robust missile defense in Europe—especially in Poland and the Czech Republic—to protect the interests of our NATO allies and the United States in the region. Stronger economic ties and stronger defenses is the strategic response to Russian aggression."

Fox News's digital news director, Chris Stirewalt, noted this was "an area he'd likely showcase if he ran for president in 2016." There was little surprising in Pence's stance; it was the standard Republican position on Russia and response to Obama's naïve approach to Vladimir Putin, who was clearly presenting as a dictator in the old Soviet mold of Joseph Stalin. The more surprising thing was watching Pence strain to build an image as both a nuts-and-bolts Midwest governor and global foreign policy hawk. He made no mention of any trade measures for Indiana, new jobs, or investments in the speech.

A few weeks later, Team Pence nabbed another big fish, the *Washington Post*. A front-page, May 9, 2014, headline read, "GOP Woos Mike Pence for 2016, and Indiana Governor Says He's 'Listening'"— the best part was that the story was about others trying to draft Pence to run, and not his own machinations. Nothing sounds better than being drafted in politics. *Post* political reporters Phil Rucker and Bob Costa noted Pence's maneuvering, "The moves bear all the hallmarks of a potential run for president in 2016." For his part, however, Pence brushed off the talk in public with one of his classic one-liners, "I'm a small-town kid who grew up with a cornfield in his backyard and dreamed of serving my country in public office. . . . The future will take care of itself."

The burst of national attention for Pence spurred the interest of Indiana's press corps. *What is this guy up to? Is he actually running for president? He hasn't been here more than a minute.* The guy with the record worthy of a presidential campaign was a forty-five-minute drive northwest of Indianapolis, presiding over Purdue University (Mitch Daniels). After an event on the second floor of the statehouse one day, a reporter for the Associated Press found Pence on his way to his office. The international jaunts, fund-raising trips to New York, and speeches targeted more at Barack Obama than Indiana manufacturing made it all so obvious. So "Are you going to run for president?" the reporter asked. Pence replied, "It is the greatest honor of my life to serve the people of Indiana as governor." The reporter pressed again,

"Right, I got that, but are you running for president?" Pence laughed a little, then answered again, "It is the greatest honor of my life to serve the people of Indiana as governor." The reporter went a different way. "If called on to serve the country as president, would you refuse?" Same answer: "It is the greatest honor of my life to serve the people of Indiana as governor." Not getting anywhere, the reporter tried yet another tack: He looked straight at Pence's eyes, with a somewhat surprised look, and said, "You are running for president, aren't you?!" Then Pence laughed, smiled, and his face flushed red—his well-known tell . . . and he repeated the exact same answer.

Pence wasn't ready to let the locals in on his plans, but his split personality—trying to half run for president while building a record worthy of running for president—was taking a toll at home. Bill Smith had successfully reasserted himself as the main gatekeeper to Pence, but Smith wasn't putting in enough time on the job. He maintained a residence an hour outside the city and some weeks would only show up to the building three or four days. Pence was also hobbled by major staffing problems. He lost his main liaison to the legislature, Heather Neal, in the Tony Bennett scandal. Lawmakers openly mocked his lack of a network inside the building. His most loyal, and proficient, lieutenants had stayed behind in Washington—Marc Short and Matt Lloyd were both working for the Koch brothers' political group.

That spring, Pence and Smith had a come-to-Jesus moment— Smith just wasn't cut out to be an executive chief of staff, a job that requires close to one hundred hours of work each week and constantly being on. Smith was better as a senior adviser and what he had always been to Pence, a close friend. And Pence himself was too preoccupied outside the state, chasing the big goal. They both needed someone who could keep the lights running at the statehouse and who understood how Indiana worked. Quickly they settled on a veteran Republican with a quiet disposition, an encyclopedic knowledge of Indiana government, and a tireless work ethic: Jim Atterholt.

Atterholt had been a state representative more than a dozen years earlier and was now running the state's utility regulatory commission. He was also a devout evangelical Christian, someone who lived the same faith as Pence and Smith. That May, Smith called Atterholt to the governor's office—Atterholt arrived carrying binders of printouts from the utilities commission. He had a whole presentation prepared. Nobody had told him why he was summoned. Smith laughed when he saw the binders; their instincts were spot-on—Atterholt was the perfect man for the job. The three men sat down and Pence stated that he needed a new chief of staff, someone who could commit to the job and effectively run the government. Atterholt demurred, but Pence pressed—he invited Atterholt to a round of golf, his standard interviewing tactic for the most important jobs around him. Finally, after eighteen holes, Atterholt agreed to take the reins.

That summer, Pence met an old adviser at the statehouse. The adviser asked him what he thought of the gay marriage battle in the statehouse earlier in the year, and the push among Christian Right activists for a new state-guaranteed protection against having to serve gay couples. Pence told him he'd rather not worry about it—cases were winding their way through the federal appellate courts, clearly on a track to the Supreme Court. And if the highest court in the land was going to decide the issue, why should he stick his neck out and have his head lopped off by the other side? Better to dodge the bullet, he said. There were some tweaks and protections to be had, for sure—after a federal judge struck down Indiana's state ban on gay marriage, Pence directed the state not to acknowledge the marriages of gay couples, while the ruling was being appealed. But gay marriage was too much of a flashpoint in the culture wars to be finessed—there was no middle ground on the issue between the Republican megadonors he needed for a White House bid and the Christian Right base he had been cultivating for decades. Pence had ducked it earlier in the year, but he couldn't duck it forever. The activists of the Christian Right were shifting their attention to a new front in the gay marriage battle, "protecting" businesses from being forced to serve gay couples in their

GOVERNOR PENCE FOR PRESIDENT   199

weddings. So-called religious freedom laws were being pushed in statehouses across the country as marriage was increasingly legalized for same-sex couples.

Pence would have to come to grips on the issue sooner or later.

PENCE ADVANCES HIS POSITION, MAYBE?

That fall of 2014, President Barack Obama flew to Southwest Indiana to tout manufacturing investments.

The trip by Obama was auspicious for a number of reasons—he had won the state in 2008, part of a remarkable turn for a Democrat, which hadn't won Indiana since Lyndon Baines Johnson ran in 1964. And his first trip as president was to Elkhart, Indiana, just outside South Bend, where he trumpeted the stimulus bill as a remedy for the state's ailing RV manufacturing industry. But by 2012 that political love affair had soured: in the wake of the Tea Party uprising, Obama avoided Indiana altogether; he was viewed as a liability that Indiana Democrats were quite glad to have stay away.

In October 2014, with Obama entering the final years of his presidency and no big-ticket races up in Indiana, the fires had cooled enough for Obama to return. On October 3, Obama flew in to celebrate National Manufacturing Day, with a visit to Millennium Steel in Princeton, Indiana.

Pence waited to meet Obama on the tarmac, although he had no plans of joining Obama for the event. He wasn't there to support him; he was there to lobby Obama on expanding Medicaid in Indiana. Pence reviewed his notecards as he sat in the holding room, waiting for Obama to land. The talking points were no different from the arguments he had made in public speeches and letters to the president before. But Pence studied them nonetheless. Then as Obama strode off the plane, Pence met him on the tarmac and welcomed him to Indiana. Then he delivered his rote talking points—Obama listened politely. There was nothing special in the words, but that's not what

Pence had been studying up on. The television crews rolled and, far away from earshot, all they picked up were images: Mike Pence was standing up to Obama! Or at least that's the way it appeared. Pence didn't jab any fingers, but the governor looked firm and confident. Then, after Obama left for his event, Pence stuck behind and held an impromptu press conference—mission accomplished. Pence may have fumbled at their last head-on meeting in January 2010, but this time, four years later, he used the cameras to his advantage and it worked.

Even if Pence hadn't fully committed to running for president, he did know what he had to do if he did want to run, and that was keep building out his network of donors. Two thousand fourteen proved a good opportunity. Pence and Christie were just two of a handful of Republican governors not on the ballot that year. Christie had just won his own reelection bid the year prior, and Pence wouldn't face reelection until 2016. With their peers preoccupied by their elections, the two formed the core of the RGA's fund-raising efforts. There may have been some sore feelings after Pence's big ask on Mary Pat Christie's birthday back in 2012, but they had all washed away in the heat of the election cycle.

With Election Day 2014 rolling up soon, Christie noticed some surprising polling in Maryland—a state as traditionally Democratic Blue as Indiana was Republican Red. Larry Hogan, the Republican candidate, was running an incredibly tight race with Maryland's Democratic lieutenant governor Anthony Brown, down by only two or three percentage points according to the RGA's internal tracking polls. Christie called up Pence and asked if they should take out $2 million from the RGA's line of credit to pay for a last-minute ad blitz to help Hogan. Pence said sure, and he would refill the coffers.

Christie wanted to hand off the RGA chairmanship, so he could run for president in 2016—and Pence was ready to take it over. By the end of 2014, Pence had made up his mind. He shouldn't run for president in 2016—there was no clear lane to victory for him, and the field was getting crowded with some very talented and powerful

Republicans. Pence waved off his staff for a White House bid and told them to start focusing on his reelection as governor in 2016.

Something shifted soon after, however. At the start of 2015, Pence changed his mind. He told Christie he needed to get ready for his own reelection bid that year and couldn't take over the RGA. Meanwhile, Pence told his top staff that he thought he saw a window for president—"I don't think we've exhausted all the options yet"—and so he sent some staff to Iowa to begin testing the waters for setting up an operation there.

Pence had run headlong into the same decision he faced four years earlier: Does he run for president or governor?

President still looked like a long shot, even with the major improvements he'd made in building his national donor network and his own profile in Washington. As he pondered his shot in 2016, he also had to gear up for a reelection bid in Indiana. He'd likely stand on better footing than he had in 2012, running as an incumbent, but he shouldn't leave anything to chance.

The only question on anyone's mind was whether he was staying or going. The clearest indication of that was likely to come in his 2015 State of the State address. Reporters and the public alike wondered if it would sound more like Pence's Berlin speech from a year earlier, or if it was going to be squarely aimed at home, with talk of domestic triumphs. The answer was the latter. Pence delivered a safe, narrow speech that focused squarely on his time as governor, and it seemed crystal clear that he was staying in Indiana. And, as part of that decision, he had to take a tighter grip on the reins of power.

Pence was staying put.

Even as Pence directed him to scout the field in Iowa, Marty Obst knew they had a problem back home. Pence's team was a mess. His administration was a "house of cards" as Marty put it—not as in Machiavellian machinations, but as in a stiff wind might knock it over at any moment. Obst decided to call in some help.

Nick Ayers was a Republican wunderkind. He had taken over

operations of the Republican Governors Association in 2009, one of the youngest operatives ever to amass such power. His pedigree in GOP politics was impeccable; he worked his way up under the tutelage of former RNC chairman and former Mississippi governor Haley Barbour and had married into Georgia governor Sonny Perdue's family. Ayers oversaw a wave of success in the 2010 elections, and in 2012 moved even further up, taking the reins of Minnesota governor Tim Pawlenty's 2012 bid for president. Pawlenty didn't last more than four months on the trail—but nobody blamed Ayers for the collapse; the campaign's troubles lay elsewhere. By the start of 2015, Ayers had graduated to advising gubernatorial candidates as a private consultant—and making millions of dollars. He was a confirmed, Washington, DC, power player. And certainly someone that the incumbent governor of a deep-red state would *not* need to spend any money on in a reelection.

Obst and Ayers met up on January 18 at the AFC Championship game between the Indianapolis Colts and the New England Patriots. As they talked, Obst had a bit of an odd request—Pence needed Nick's help. Ayers brushed him off, "I love Mike Pence, man. If you need me to help raise money, I'll raise money, but he doesn't need *me*. I'm not the cheapest political consultant on earth, I have a bunch of other opportunities."

But Obst insisted, "Mike's a great man. He's a good governor. He gets a lot of great ideas, but the structure which is built is a house of cards and at some point, it is going to come down. I have no idea how. I need people that are smart like you to help me see where we can prevent problems. Who can go in to fight to make sure that we're protecting him. I don't think he's being protected."

Obst was right—between the animosity from Daniels's top staff and the inexperience of much of Pence's inside the statehouse, trouble seemed imminent. Replacing Bill Smith as chief of staff with Jim Atterholt had started to correct the issues, but his troubles ran deeper—Pence's team never seemed to get a pulse on what was happening, politically, inside the statehouse. And Pence himself never seemed particularly dialed in. On top of all that, the state's powerful House Speaker, Brian Bosma, fought Pence at every turn—and Bosma knew all the levers of power inside the statehouse.

Obst, with his keen political instincts, knew it was just a matter of time before something blew up. Nick was worried how it would look if he came on board, because it would signal that Pence was trying to run in 2016, "I'm staying out of this presidential race." Marty shot back, "This has nothing to do with presidential. I'm helping this guy govern. The president thing doesn't matter if you don't help this guy govern."

"He's a function of who he surrounds himself with, and he can be phenomenal, or he can struggle, and he's struggling right now," Marty said. "They just don't realize it right now, because his poll numbers are a mile wide and an inch deep."

THIS JUSTIN—PENCE NEWS SERVICE

The morning of January 26, 2015, a reporter for the *Indianapolis Star* emailed Pence's press secretary, Kara Brooks—he wanted to know some more about the "JustIN" news service. Based on documents obtained by the reporter, Mike Pence had an ambitious plan to start a state-run news service, one that would turn the state's press secretaries and public staff into editors and reporters competing with the free press. This *Indy Star* reporter had some questions. The plan was stunning, as much for its seeming attack on the independent press as for the ham-handedness in which it was stated. "At times, JustIN will break news—publishing information ahead of any other news outlet. Strategies for determining how and when to give priority to such 'exclusive' coverage remain under discussion," Pence's communications staff wrote in a Q and A sheet sent to agency communications directors.

Jack Ronald, the publisher of a small paper in Northwest Indiana, called the proposal "ludicrous." Ronald had spent the late '80s and early '90s training journalists in the former Soviet state of Moldova on how to run an independent press, after decades under the rule of a totalitarian government. "The notion of elected officials presenting material that will inevitably have a pro-administration point of view is antithetical to the idea of an independent press."

Pence's team was floored; they avoided the *Star* reporter and instead began telling other reporters they planned to reveal a massive overhaul of the state's press release system. The only problem was that the sample items in the packet for the big rollout of the news service included draft articles and details of the "editorial boards" that would make news decisions. Niki Kelly, a longtime reporter for the *Fort Wayne Journal Gazette*, asked the nagging question that most of the other working stiffs in the corps had been pondering, "So what happens if I ask a state agency for specific information? Do they write my story before I do?"

The next morning, Pence rolled out his big announcement—not the one about a new press release system, the one about the expansion of Medicaid he had won from the Obama administration. Pence had assembled a major rollout of one of his most important policy achievements in office, a conservative version of expanded Medicaid that included health-savings accounts and a minimal payment requirement from the state's low-income residents. When he was confronted by reporters after the Medicaid announcement, he seemed shocked—he didn't realize that the state-run news story had gone viral. He brushed off any concerns, saying that if the site was indeed a state-run outlet, he would cancel it.

A veteran national reporter, Lloyd Grove, called up Bosma to get his take on the news service. Under the headline "'Pravda' on the Plains" Bosma got in a dig, "I understand the governor has indicated he's going to be issuing some clarifying remarks, so I'm withholding final judgment until that occurs. In the meantime, just in case, I have had my staff contact Rosetta Stone and I do have a new Russian version that will be coming out shortly."

Meanwhile, Pence's split-media strategy, of telling statehouse reporters one thing and national political reporters something else, was beginning to backfire. Pence had done such a good job teeing up interest in himself by then that national reporters were keeping closer tabs on him. MNSBC host Rachel Maddow dove in. "The government of Indiana, under Governor Mike Pence, really was in the process of launching a state-run news outlet, you know, like 'Press TV' in Iran, 'Russia Today' in Russia, or the Chinese news agencies that we all turn to," she said. "Mike Pence may want to be a Republican candidate for president in 2016; so far he is not setting himself up for that very well."

But why was Pence, with so many problems and such lackluster leadership, constantly in the mix for 2016? Maddow waved on-air at both of them: David and Charles Koch.

The damage mounted, but Pence seemed uncertain of what to do—he was indecisive, as ever. Pence had known about the plan months ago and had seen the language before it went out. An adviser had also raised these concerns with him, telling Pence that the language could be viewed as an affront to the free press. Pence said he was sure it would be fine. On January 28, two days after the story first broke, Pence's communications team finally called a press conference to further explain their plans. As the press conference got under way, it was clear the communications team didn't have much of a strategy—it quickly turned into a venting session, with many of the reporters complaining about how evasive Pence and his team had been for almost four years now. It was a disaster.

Two days later, on his old friend Greg Garrison's radio show, Pence apologized again, sort of. "I'm just telling you that I regret the confusion, and I'm telling you that that memorandum, however well intentioned, used language that was inappropriate." He couldn't understand how people had gotten him so wrong—he had sponsored a Media Shield law in Congress, after all, that would have protected *New York Times* reporters from having to reveal Scooter Libby's name, as well as all other journalists. "We don't have editors in state government, for heaven's sakes. We don't have editorial boards in state government."

Finally, on Thursday, after three days of national humiliation—Pence relented and said he would disband the news service. But Pence's brand had already been dented by days of indecision.

Washington had gotten a peek inside the real Pence operation, and it was something far more damning than theocratic, ideological, or extremist. It was amateur.

Mother Knows Best

The next day, Pence's mother went to hear him speak at an event in Terre Haute, on the west end of the state. Afterward, a reporter asked her if she wanted her son to run for president. "When people ask me if he should run for president, I say, 'No.' I want him as my governor. My feeling is he is a good governor," Nancy Pence Fritsch said January 27, 2015. "He's doing a lot of the right things, I want him to maintain where he's at right now." Mike offered up only this, "She's just the most courageous, amazing person that I know. And I never take issue with anything she says."

CHAPTER 12

NOW, GEORGE

The state-run news service plan had trampled what was supposed to be Pence's signature achievement: the expansion of Medicaid in Indiana. More than any middling tax cut, the Medicaid expansion would be a major win for his governorship and also was supposed to be a Hail Mary—one last long ball to see if he could drum up some interest in running for president.

While Pence was out courting national donors, testing the waters for president and struggling to mend the needless wounds of his state-run news outlet, Christian conservative lawmakers worked behind the scenes on legislation that would allow Indiana businesses to refuse to participate in same-sex weddings on religious grounds. The Religious Freedom Restoration Act was sold as a protection of First Amendment rights of practice, but Democrats in the statehouse—wildly outnumbered by Republicans—said the bill amounted to legalized discrimination. So where was Pence on this thing? He was the governor after all. Well, nowhere. Like the rest of the legislation that moved through the statehouse, he kept his hands off it until it looked like it could be a win. ◦

In reality, the Religious Freedom Restoration Act didn't amount to much—it barred localities from trying to enforce their own antidiscrimination statutes. And legal scholars testified they doubted the law would hold up if tested in court. It seemed symbolic, more than anything, a token prize to the Christian Right for their loss a year prior. And for three months at the start of 2015, it got zero attention—helped along by Pence's ambitions and his gaffe involving the almost comical state-run news service proposal. It took the vast sci-fi community and Indiana's massive comic book convention, GenCon, to change that.

GenCon brought about sixty thousand gamers, superfans, and CosPlay enthusiasts to the Indianapolis Convention Center each spring, a few blocks from the statehouse, where the marriage debate was under way. The event brought in an estimated $50 million in total revenue for the city and surrounding businesses, and they were signed up for Indianapolis through 2020. George Takei, the original Mr. Sulu on *Star Trek*, knew exactly what this law was—it was the same kind of law that resulted in his Japanese American family being put in internment camps during World War II, the same type of bigotry he had fought his entire life. And it was all the more pertinent since he had come out. "I am outraged that Gov. Pence would sign such a divisive measure into law. He has made it clear that LGBT couples, like Brad and me [referring to his longtime partner], are now unwelcome in his state," Takei wrote in a Facebook post that would ultimately be shared close to twenty-one thousand times.

GenCon's event organizers intimated that they needed to pull up stakes from a state that openly discriminated against gays.

Pence may have stayed out of the RFRA debate at the start of the 2015 legislative session, but now it looked like an easy win. It had sailed through the House and Senate with none of the chanting protesters who had packed the halls just a year earlier. It looked like it was safe to poke his head out.

Early on Thursday, March 26, 2015, Pence gathered a small retinue of monks, nuns, rabbis, and other religious figures together in his office. At hand were the three Christian Right lobbyists who had successfully pushed through the Religious Freedom Restoration Act. Pence had gathered them there for a special signing of the legislation. Other signings were hosted in public, in schools where new money would go, in factories where new jobs would be made—but Pence closed the doors for this signing. "This bill is not about discrimination," Pence told reporters afterward. "And if I thought it legalized discrimination, I would have vetoed it."

Despite Pence's assurances, businesses bore down—discriminating against gay people wasn't just bad business, it was passé. Salesforce threatened to end plans to make Indianapolis its second headquarters. Apple CEO Tim Cook said he would have problems doing business with Indiana. Connecticut governor Dannel Malloy, a leader in the ever-dwindling ranks of Democratic governors, saw a rare chance to pounce—he called Pence a bigot and said his state would not cover the cost for any employee traveling to Indiana. (He didn't mention whether very many Connecticut employees flew to Indiana on official business, likely because they didn't.)

The NCAA began squirming, too, as Indianapolis was set to host the Final Four in just a few days. The NCAA had won a sweetheart deal for its national headquarters in Indianapolis—$1 a year lease for a beautiful new building, paid for by the city, as long as it promised to host the Final Four there every four years. But it was becoming harder to justify doing business in a state that openly discriminated against gay folks.

The major problem Pence faced was that one of the men photographed with him at the bill signing, Eric Miller of Advance America, had told his supporters specifically that this new law would let businesses discriminate against LGBT residents.

"Churches, Christian businesses and individuals deserve protection from those who support homosexual marriages and those who support government recognition and approval of gender identity (men who dress as women). SB 101 will help provide the protection!" Miller wrote in his letter to supporters praising the bill. "Here are just three examples where SB 101 will help: Christian bakers, florists and photographers should not be punished for refusing to participate in a homosexual marriage! A Christian business should not be punished for refusing to allow a man to use the women's restroom! A church should not be punished because they refuse to let the church be used for a homosexual wedding!" ◎

Micah Clark, the executive director of American Family Association of Indiana, one of the main Christian Right lobbies in the state, was exasperated. Miller hadn't helped their cause with his statement. The reality, Clark said, was that the new law wouldn't allow businesses to refuse service to gay couples—but it would allow them to refuse to participate in a same-sex wedding. The difference, he said, was important—a conservative Christian baker shouldn't ban gay couples from buying something in their store, but they also shouldn't be forced to handmake a cake and deliver it to their wedding. This was the line.

But national LGBT rights groups, Democrats, and business leaders saw a distinction without a difference—it was discrimination whether the cake was premade and bought or made specifically for and delivered to the wedding.

By Friday, March 27, Pence had two offers to appear on television and explain the controversy—one from Megyn Kelly of Fox News Channel and another from George Stephanopoulos, host of ABC's Sunday talk show *This Week*.

A local business leader turned to Pence and asked him how he would answer the questions if he went on-air. Mimicking a reporter, he posed the question: "Governor, would you say that Indiana promotes discrimination?" Pence froze—it wasn't clear whether he was thinking or just didn't know what to say. "We're fucked," said the businessman.

Pence didn't want to change the bill—he didn't think it needed to be changed. Why would they change something that clearly didn't discriminate? he argued.

Pence's response had the feel of just a few months ago, with his state-run news service hairball—he was unclear and digging in his heels. And just like before, he insisted that everyone else had it wrong.

On Saturday morning, Mike Pence's chief of staff, Jim Atterholt, called up Marty Obst, who had just gotten to the gym for a run on the treadmill: Was he coming to the governor's for the meeting? "What meeting?" Obst asked. He was told, the strategy meeting that started in twenty minutes; Pence had called a strategy session for ten o'clock that morning. Nobody had invited Pence's own campaign manager, but the Christian Right lobbyists who'd helped land Pence in this mess were at the governor's mansion in force. Obst hopped off the treadmill and booked it to the mansion.

More than a dozen of Pence's top staff and advisers, from throughout his career, sat in the common space in the mansion, around a U-shaped table: his old chief of staff and a key connection to the Christian Right, Bill Smith; his longtime friend and adviser, Jeff Cardwell; pollster and messaging maven Kellyanne Conway. There was Chris Crabtree, the legislative aide who had invited the Christian Right lobbyists into the private bill-signing ceremony, and also Robert Vane, a former aide to Indianapolis Republican mayor Greg Ballard and a line to the more moderate voices in the party.

Pence sat at the head of the table. He was angry. "You could tell he was unraveled," said one attendee at the meeting. "He was angry because of how the state was being portrayed, he was angry at the thought if he had anything to do with it."

And he was also angry at his staff, for letting him get blindsided by this—the same people who had told him it wouldn't be a big deal now sat around the conference table watching Pence's anger spill out in a way they almost never saw. "Where were all of you on this?" he demanded.

"You could see a man who had meticulously built a successful career," said one attendee. "I was angry at most of the people in that room because they had led him off a cliff and then they couldn't help him. . . . They walked him off a plank and then said it wasn't that bad."

Some wanted him to go on-air and stick to his guns. Crabtree came up with a novel argument: Would the government try and force the popular Jewish deli downtown, Shapiro's, to serve up ham sandwiches? Others, like Vane, urged him to simply state that he would never support discrimination—and that he was certain this bill did not discriminate.

Marty Obst knew Karen was overseas and not there to keep Pence calm. He told the governor not to go on television. How could he, a stalwart Christian conservative, even begin to explain to Bill Clinton's former press secretary, Stephanopoulos, that this law was even close to the federal law Clinton signed two decades ago? The game was rigged from the start, Obst argued.

"Don't go on TV with a guy who is really smart, who is really good, and was there when they signed the law," Obst said. "Give it time."

Cardwell, one of Pence's oldest friends, sensed a different danger. Cardwell helped bring Pence into the fold of Republican politics three decades earlier, and he had never seen Pence this angry. Pence was livid that the trolls of social media were mocking him and his family—he was enraged, although with his collected and tight demeanor that wasn't apparent to everyone in the room.

Pence hated the Facebook and Twitter trolls who posted photos of him with penises pointing at his face, rainbows in the background, and called him a bigot. Weren't these anonymous assholes being hateful and spiteful by not respecting his religious views? The Bible clearly stated that marriage should be between one man and one woman, and while he might not want to force others to abide by that principle, wouldn't it be equally harmful to force believers to violate their faith and their conscience?

And then there were the online commenters who went after his children, the ones who mocked Michael, Charlotte, and Audrey, for being born of a bigoted father. He could take the attacks on himself, that was expected in the rough-and-tumble world of politics, but not the attacks on his children. Cardwell urged him to decline the offer—he was in no position to go head-to-head with someone who was clearly ready to take him apart on live television.

After about two hours of going around the room, they broke. Some advisers thought they had an agreement: Pence would go on Stephanopoulos and tell the nation that Indiana doesn't tolerate discrimination. Others were convinced that Pence agreed not to do Stephanopoulos, it was a terrible idea. Only Pence could know exactly what would happen.

Sunday, March 29, 2015— The Stephanopoulos Disaster

The next morning, Sunday, Pence sat in a small, one-room studio in Indianapolis, with a green screen of the city skyline behind him. Pence peered into the black lens of the camera, like he had a thousand times before, the opening music of ABC's *This Week* piped in through the small earpiece.

Obst found out Pence was booked for the show just a half hour before he was set to go live. He called the governor's security detail to try and get through to him, but Pence was already mic'd up and waiting to go on-air. It was too late.

The nation may have seen a flat, boring, midwestern conservative. But the small circle of Pence advisers saw a tense, angry man. Angry at the attacks on him. Angry at the attacks on his family. Angry at the attacks on his religion.

"So this is a yes or no question," Stephanopoulos started, after dispensing with niceties. "Is Advance America right when they say a florist in Indiana can now refuse to serve a gay couple without fear of punishment?"

"Well, let me explain to you, the purpose of this bill is to empower and it has been for more than twenty years," Pence replied. "Frankly, George, there's a lot of people across this country who, you're looking at Obamacare, you're looking at the Hobby Lobby decision, looking at other cases, who feel that their religious liberty is being infringed upon."

Stephanopoulos attempted to cut in, but Pence continued to steam-roll his way through the question ". . . empowering people . . ." Eventually, Stephanopoulos ran him over: "So yes or no, if a florist in Indiana refuses to serve a gay couple at their wedding, is that legal now in Indiana?"

"George, this is where this debate has gone with, with misinformation," Pence tried to reason. The "George"s began to take on less a tone of politeness and more one of exasperation.

George fired back, "Yes or no?"

Pence kept going, "You've been to Indiana a bunch of times. You know it. There are no kinder, more generous, more welcoming, more hospitable people."

"Governor, Governor, I—" Stephanopoulos tried to edge in.

". . . It's not based in any way . . ."

"I completely agree with you about the good people."

"I think people are getting tired of it, George, I really do."

"Perhaps," Stephanopoulos said.

"Tolerance is a two-way street," and then he broke. "I really believe, George, it has been breathtaking to many in Indiana . . . we have been under an avalanche of intolerance . . . I'm not going to take it lying down."

Pence walked out of the small studio. He had just defended discriminating against gay folks on a Sunday talk show. He was the new face of discrimination, perfectly coiffed and slightly stilted.

Cardwell knew exactly what happened, "He didn't go on there as the governor; he went on as a father."

Marty Obst poured himself a bourbon. He never drank before noon, but this was an astounding moment. His phone exploded, texts, phone calls—Pence's career was over! crowed Washington operatives and Indiana donors. Marty immediately called the campaigns of likely presidential candidates, Senators Ted Cruz and Marco Rubio, former Florida governor Jeb Bush—anybody he could find. Mike Pence needed help, ASAP!

What Pence and his advisers couldn't quite capture, or didn't seem to understand, was that their stance was hateful to the long-maligned LGBT community. The rest of the country was finally accepting gay people, deserving of all the rights and protections straight couples enjoyed.

Veteran activists from the wars of decades past cried as they remembered the fallout from hateful campaigns like Pat Buchanan's 1992 run for president. Rick Sutton, the founder of Freedom Indiana, remembered the friends who had committed suicide decades ago because they couldn't be open with their family—the stigma and fear of spending a life in hiding drove some of them to the worst possible conclusion.

This was what no one ever counseled Pence about in that Saturday-morning messaging meeting just two days earlier. The online trolls never drove any of his friends or family to a fatal end—this paled in comparison to what many persecuted gay people had endured.

The Christian Right lobbyists saw a trap, they believed national LGBT activists were waiting to make an example for all the other states considering similar bills. To them, it seemed all too convenient that the national outrage didn't crop up until after the bill was signed.

In Pence's insular world, the anger and rage at the coastal elites mingled with a dire fear over what that interview did to his career.

THE CLEANUP

On Tuesday, March 31, 2015, the *Indianapolis Star* declared what most of the state wanted: "FIX THIS NOW"—the rare all-caps headline topped an editorial calling for protections for LGBTQ Hoosiers. The religious freedom protections could stay, the paper's ed board argued, if the state could ensure there would be no discrimination. "Half steps will not be enough. Half steps will not undo the damage." ௐ

Behind the scenes, the Indiana legislators who started the whole mess had been working furiously to find a way to split the baby—prove that a bill that would allow businesses to refuse gay couples did not count as discrimination, while also protecting those businesses from being forced into endorsing something they considered to be a grave sin, same-sex marriage. Lobbyists for the business community and the state's biggest employers ferried between the offices of the House Speaker and the state senate leader—their point was simple, the legislators couldn't just explain away a law that protected discrimination, they had to change it.

Pence was left out of the discussion almost entirely. He'd taken the credit for the bill a week earlier, and now he reaped the fallout. But the great irony was he had almost nothing to do with it before or after. And when he told lawmakers he wouldn't support any change or "fix" to the legislation, they moved on without him. Some of the governor's staff were kept abreast of the negotiations, but that amounted to little more than courtesy.

Pence still had cleanup to do on his own demolished image. His friend Chris Christie advised he try and get out in front of the debacle—he knew a bit about damage control from his own governorship. So Pence called a press conference at the state library across the street from the statehouse. Reporters packed the room, Pence's staff filled the perimeter, camera crews from the national cable networks prepared to air the conference live—a major move. A tall, trim, older gay rights activist walked into the room, his tiny dog in tow, to watch. But one of Pence's aides kicked him out—they didn't want any trouble during the governor's big moment. Pence opened with a defense of the state and himself and then trained fire on the national press and coastal elites.

Across the street, Bosma and some of his deputies watched the press conference from his office. One of Bosma's aides watched as Pence's staffer kicked the gay rights activist out. Quickly, she asked him to come join Bosma in the Speaker's office. Team Pence had just kicked out Olympic gold medal winner Greg Louganis. Bosma adored Louganis; he remembered watching the star diver in the '80s. His dog was welcome, too. Louganis settled in at Bosma's office and Bosma played with his dog. "Personal sports hero to me," said Bosma, the man who helped start the whole RFRA mess in the first place. "I watched him dive many times and he shared with me the hurt he felt when he heard the incorrect message that Indiana supported discrimination."

Across the street, Pence kept on shoveling. "We've got a perception problem here, because some people have a different view. And we intend to correct that. After much reflection and in consultation with leadership of the General Assembly, I have come to the conclusion that it would be helpful to move legislation this week that makes it clear that this law does not give businesses a right to deny services to anyone," Pence said. He wasn't calling for a change to the law, he was calling for a formal explanation laying out how everyone else had gotten Indiana, and him, completely wrong.

Inside the *Star*, the longtime editorial cartoonist Gary Varvel, a friend of Pence's for more than a decade, seemed to capture the governor's troubles best: On a zoomed-in picture of the governor's desk, Pence's neat and very recognizable signature stood at the bottom of the RFRA bill. The pen, labeled "Politics," had fallen over below the paper, and a quite small Pence had been smashed underneath.

Pence's image was fast being cemented in the nation's mind. David Letterman, booster of his beloved home state since he had become a household name, hated how Mike Pence was destroying Indiana's reputation. "This is not the Indiana I remember as a kid. I lived there for twenty-seven years. And folks were folks, and that's all there was to it," Letterman said. So he made a special "Top Ten" list that night— Top Ten Guys Pence Looks Like:

10 The guy at the bar who sends your girlfriend a drink

9 The guy who makes his dog sleep outside

8 The guy whose wife has to tell him he's "getting a little loud"

7 The guy who greets a roomful of other guys with, "Morning, ladies"

6 The guy who has a little too much fun on "audience get acquainted" night

5 The real estate agent whose photo is on a bus stop bench

4 The guy who keeps a baseball bat in his trunk

3 The guy who won three national championships as head coach of Indiana University (that's a Bobby Knight joke)

2 The guy who arrives at his high school reunion in a rented Ferrari

1 The guy fishing in a Cialis commercial

Pence was the guy getting his head kicked in on national television—and he wasn't smiling.

The Cleanup, Part Two

The following morning, April 1, Pence and his team were back in the governor's office for a quiet and somewhat awkward meeting with Greg Louganis. Rick Sutton, Freedom Indiana's gay rights activist, escorted Louganis into the room. Pence smiled, welcomed Louganis warmly, and they chatted for about ten minutes. Pence chief of staff Jim Atterholt called it a warm reception and gracious exchanging of ideas. Sutton said it was obvious that Pence didn't want to be there. Pence asked for a photo with Louganis at the end of the meeting. Louganis said no.

Team Pence saw progress for an embattled, but good and decent man. Sutton saw a guy who would never get it.

The following morning, Bosma announced the fix for the notorious bill at a press conference. The "fix" changed little, it only "clarified" that the legislation could not be used as a safeguard in court to support any discrimination of LGBT people.

"Is the damage able to be turned back?" Bosma asked rhetorically. "That remains to be seen." He was talking about the damage to Indiana's reputation, but it just as easily would have applied to Pence's reputation.

Pence and all his staff were glaringly absent from the announcement.

Then Bosma set the gears of government cranking at breakneck speed—first up was a spontaneous committee meeting to vet the change to the law. The original bill took months to reach Pence's desk, now it would just take hours. And he wasn't sure what he would do.

So much like they had at the start of the whole mess, the legislature stormed ahead without Pence. And now they had another present for him. One week after he celebrated the signing of the RFRA bill, Pence had another bill to sign.

Pence was steadfast he wouldn't sign any changes to the bill. But then Paul Singer called him, the New York hedge-fund billionaire who Pence had been courting for a possible White House run. Singer was part of a new club of megadonors, unleashed by the Supreme Court decision to remove limits on campaign donations. He would be a formidable supporter in any campaign. He was also one of the most ardent supporters of LGBT rights inside the GOP, ever since his son had come out. He told Pence to sign the fix.

By Thursday, Pence wanted desperately to move on. He was tattered, exhausted, and hiding from the press. Pence's staff had leaked word to a conservative pundit that Pence was holed up at the mansion, but that was a calculated lie—a distraction to buy Pence some space. Finally, around two P.M., a clutch of the governor's security detail entered the second floor of the building. A *Star* intern got up to go ask the governor if he would sign the "fix," and suddenly a second gaggle of security walked in behind him—Pence had sent in a decoy security team! He slipped into his office before anyone could corner him.

Pence had until about six P.M. to make his decision; he had a flight to catch to Israel to meet his family. Inside his second-floor office, Pence retreated. He may not have believed the legislation discriminated and made him a bigot, but a large swath of the country certainly saw it that way.

Reporters circled the entire building, covering every exit. Pence's oldest brother, Greg, walked the perimeter of the building over and over—looking for a safe exit for his brother. A statehouse veteran spied some reporters near the statue of Civil War–era governor Oliver Perry Morton and asked them if they had every exit covered. The reporters laughed, saying this time they did. Then she laughed. "No, you don't. You're missing the governor's secret exit." The governor had an exit that led to the north side of the building, from his private bathroom through a janitor's closet. One of the reporters ran over to the secret bathroom exit, and sure enough, there were state troopers waiting to escort Pence to his car. Once they saw the reporter, they began talking into the mics in their shirt cuffs and jogged away. But little by little, the reporters watching the exits dropped off as deadlines loomed.

There was no photograph this time, no celebration. All he left in his wake was an obtuse statement that hinted at the forces that led him to change his mind, quietly, "In the midst of this furious debate, I have prayed earnestly for wisdom and compassion, and I have felt the prayers of people across this state and across this nation. For that I will be forever grateful. There will be some who think this legislation goes too far and some who think it does not go far enough, but as governor I must always put the interest of our state first and ask myself every day, 'What is best for Indiana?' I believe resolving this controversy and making clear that every person feels welcome and respected in our state *is* best for Indiana."

With that, the culture warrior, the once shining star of the GOP, exited through the secret door in his bathroom.

CHAPTER 13

AT PEACE

Marty Obst and Pence's core team of advisers scrambled to put out the fires lit by the Religious Freedom Restoration Act. While Pence was abroad in Israel with Karen and the kids, Obst caught wind of new troubles.

Many of the Indiana GOP's most powerful donors acted as a sort of town council for the state writ large, setting policy—largely conservative—and picking winners and losers. Pence's status as their favorite son hung in the balance. And other Republicans who had long chafed at Pence—because of his ineffectiveness and his allegiance to the Christian Right—began talking up challenging him in the Republican Party gubernatorial primary.

Mitch Daniels's former campaign manager, Bill Oesterle, began calling donors, saying he might run against Pence. Oesterle and Obst met at the home of Pence fund raiser Jim Kittle for two hours. Oesterle told them Pence needed to get out of the race for reelection or he'd lose the governor's office for the GOP. Obst told Oesterle to knock it off. Bosma tested the waters as well—he told GOP donors that Pence was damaged beyond repair. The irony of this insult was not lost on Pence's team; Bosma was more responsible than Pence for the whole RFRA mess, but Pence took all the heat. ✍

In just four months, Pence fell from a possible White House bid to battling for his own job in the statehouse. The last time he fell hard like this was twenty-five years ago, in the 1990 election. And like then, he seemed lost—to himself and to others. How could anyone ever view him as a bigot? He was a loving man. Perhaps the rest of the country was full of bigots who didn't respect his religion!

Pence's team struggled to figure out how it all went haywire so fast. Some tried to figure out why he reversed course and went on Stephanopoulos. Did Karen get to him after they all left the governor's residence that Saturday? Was it Bill Smith? Some blamed the religious Right, saying they misled him. Pence's Christian Right advisers smelled a conspiracy among the LGBT activists and the national media—they had been waiting for any governor to step forward and sign RFRA legislation; Pence was just the first one to walk into their trap.

Nick Ayers called up Obst. Laughing about his earlier assessment of the Pence operation, he said, "Wow, when you said house of cards, you weren't kidding. You know how to do things with a bang." While Pence was in China on a trade mission, Obst spent two weeks meeting one-on-one with donors. In fourteen days, he sat down with sixty of the GOP's most important rainmakers, and forty of them said they couldn't support Pence for reelection, or they weren't ready to just yet.

After Pence returned from his international trips, first to Israel and then China, Obst sat down with him for a heart-to-heart.

"Do you really want to do this?" he asked Pence. "You could go off and make lots of money, you don't have to do this." Then Obst laid down the brass tacks: "If you want to be governor, you have to do this. You've got to start to govern 6 million people and not just your base. You've got to throw this notion of being president away and go run the state."

Pence himself was heartbroken. His dreams of running for president were destroyed. Now he was the new face of anti-LGBTQ discrimination—and fighting for his very survival. He was in, of course, but they had some major repair work to do.

After two months, Pence's team called in Tennessee governor Bill Haslam, the chairman of the RGA, to do a fund raiser for Pence in Indianapolis—the event itself delivered the message that Obst and Ayers had been looking for: The RGA was on board with Pence, and would squash anyone who tried to run against him in a primary.

While Obst worked to keep Pence's career afloat, his operations man, Jim Atterholt, decided the governor ought to understand the gay community just a little bit better. Pence's own children had told him as much—even if he couldn't ever support gay marriage and equal rights for gay couples. Atterholt reached out to some old friends from the statehouse, veterans of the gay rights battles back in the '80s when barely anyone paid attention to them. He asked Kathy Sarris and Christopher Douglas to help set up some meetings for Mike Pence with LGBT workers in state government. They did one better, they brought in a transgendered state worker to meet with the governor— when the transgendered worker revealed himself to the governor, his boss was even surprised. This, noted Douglas, was the point—the worker was "passing" as a man, constantly fearful of being outed in public. This diligent, hardworking employee shouldn't have to live his life in the closet.

Pence was stunned and hurt. How could the rest of the nation see him as a monster? He wanted God's love for all people, especially LGBT folks—he just couldn't understand how defending other Christians from being forced to perform services in same-sex weddings could be viewed as bigotry, much less discrimination.

New Messaging in Pence World

Marty decided to drop Pence's longtime ad maker Rex Elsass. Elsass wasn't getting the right message across for a sitting governor. "We felt like we didn't have the messaging nailed on how to explain RFRA, and some other issues," Obst said. "How do we rebrand and repackage the message?" Ayers wanted to bring in his own team for polling and television ads—he had a reputation as an overly expensive consultant, but his candidates seemed to win more than they lost and Pence's team was fighting for their lives. Certain people in Mike's world got wind of this, namely Bill Smith, who sold it to Kellyanne Conway as though she were being pushed out, and Kellyanne erupted. "And then the genie was out of the bottle."

"Guys, what are you doing?" Pence asked Obst and Ayers. They wanted to pay for two pollsters, one who would be paid from the Pence campaign, the second from money directed by the Republican Governors Association, which Ayers managed. They would get different missions and different questions, then Pence's team would "compare notes in the middle." "It wasn't an effort to push Kellyanne out," they told him. And he said, "That's not how it was explained to her."

Conway wanted to keep helping Pence, and she also wanted to keep Elsass as his TV ad maker and buyer. She didn't like Ayers's inflated consultant fees. Kellyanne Conway flew to Indianapolis for a tête-à-tête. Bill Smith and Pence's oldest brother, Greg, joined. After going back and forth for a bit, the team decided not to hire Ayers's ad-buying firm or keep Rex Elsass but settled on a third alternative that would keep everyone happy, a firm run by veteran operative John Brabender. Ayers and Conway assured Pence that everything was fine between them, but two of the biggest egos in Pence's orbit had started off their relationship with a phenomenal fight.

On May 19, 2015, Pence made clear what just about everyone took for granted: he wasn't running for president. Unlike his big gubernatorial kickoff four years earlier, with the Hollywood-style film crew and hundreds of adoring friends and family, this announcement was issued simply. Pence's longtime friend and confidant and the Indiana GOP chairman, Jeff Cardwell, delivered the message, "Gov. Mike Pence is a conservative leader and dedicated public servant who always puts Indiana first. We are excited the governor will formally announce his plans to seek reelection during our annual Spring Dinner."

The polling that was coming back was terrible. Hoosiers, like many midwesterners, tended to think well of their elected leaders—being more forgiving of transgressions than their counterparts in more rambunctious climates like New York and California. But the first-round polls showed Pence underwater—45 percent approved of his performance, but 46 percent disapproved. Voters said, by a 2–1 margin, that the RFRA bill was not needed. Pence's team dismissed them out of hand in public, but their internal polls were showing the exact same numbers. They paid $750,000 to a crisis PR firm, Porter Novelli, ostensibly to rehabilitate Indiana's image. But it wasn't the state's image that needed fixing.

Meanwhile, Pence's national political team broke off for other candidates—they were still loyal members of Team Pence, but 2016 beckoned. Kellyanne Conway hopped on board with Tea Party favorite Ted Cruz. She went to run a super PAC for Cruz bankrolled by reclusive billionaire Robert Mercer. Conway's PAC paid millions of dollars to a specialized data firm based out of Britain that Mercer liked, Cambridge Analytica, which promised big results by building psychological profiles of voters across the country. The firm didn't mention that it had obtained personal data from Facebook users for academic purposes only—not political profiling for profit, nor that its political modeling was of questionable value at best. In fact, some Cruz campaign advisers considered it no more than a scam. Meanwhile, longtime Pence confidant Marc Short kept working with the Koch brothers' national political network—their money and influence was highly sought after by the dozen or so Republicans jumping into the presidential race with abandon.

The man to beat was Jeb Bush—2016 was almost guaranteed to be a dynastic showdown between Bush on the Republican side and Hillary Clinton on the Democratic. With Pence officially out, Indiana's network of moneymen, many of whom supported the Bush family over the years, were free to sign on with Jeb Bush in 2016. Indiana was Bush country, at least on paper. ❧

Then, on June 16, 2015, bankrupted casino magnate and reality TV star Donald Trump descended the gold-colored escalator at his Manhattan tower. Throngs of paid extras, brought in off the streets of Manhattan, hooted and hollered. And then he lit himself on fire: "The U.S. has become a dumping ground for everybody else's problems. When Mexico sends its people, they're not sending their best. They're not sending you. They're not sending you. They're sending people that have lots of problems, and they're bringing those problems with us. They're bringing drugs. They're bringing crime. They're rapists. And some, I assume, are good people."

This was a joke, right?

THE TRUMP TRAIN

Even though he had launched his campaign by branding an entire nationality rapists and drug lords, Trump seemed to be mounting a serious bid. One month later, he sat onstage at the Family Leadership Summit in Ames, Iowa—a gathering of the most important Christian Right leaders and activists, the types of people who could make or break a campaign in this critical early state. Veteran Republican pollster Frank Luntz asked Trump what he thought of 2008 nominee John McCain. Trump said McCain was a failure because he was captured in Vietnam. Pundits across the board wondered how Trump, who had dodged the draft five times citing bone spurs in his foot, could have the gall to say something so outrageous. The closest he ever got to Vietnam, by his own account, were the STDs he got, "It was my own personal Vietnam."

Surely that spelled the end of Trump's campaign, right?

Trump refused to apologize, for anything. He was clearly hypo-
critical and making things up, but something was building beneath
him, a volatile political concoction that appeared just as likely to
launch him to the White House as it was to launch him into obscu-
rity. Trump was working on a steady diet of seven P.M. ET rallies. He
would fly in on his personal plane, rally for about an hour, then fly
home to New York and get a quality eight hours of sleep. His rallies
were odd, more like circuses or rock concerts than political events.

And cable television ate 'em up—paid programming was replaced
with wall-to-wall coverage of Trump's rallies. Networks like CNN
staffed up to talk about what was happening, keeping a camera shot
of the Trump rally in the corner of the screen all the while. Trump
wasn't even there in many cases, but that empty podium was a big per-
former, almost as big as Trump himself. Trump said ridiculous, hurtful things and whipped up a big slice of the country into a frenzy—but
it was impossible to look away. Working hand in hand with the press,
no one could.

In his decades crawling up the ladder of New York's cutthroat
real-estate business and the world of celebrities, Trump had developed
a special way of manipulating the press. He would call up one of the
gossip sheets, often the legendary *Page Six*, and offer up some titil-
lating rumors about one of his competitors or even himself. Then he
would call the competition, sometimes posing as his own spokesman,
"John Barron" or "John Miller," and tell them the exact opposite. Did
it matter that he was lying? In a moral sense, yes, of course. But he
quickly figured out there was no downside to lying, only positives—
unless he was under oath. After decades of being used by him, some
New York outlets finally took action—Ben Smith, editor of BuzzFeed,
noted that the *New York Observer* blacklisted Trump because nothing
he said was based in fact. Accuracy, as a news value, extended as much
to what was written as to what was being quoted. But unlike their
peers in New York, the Washington press wasn't quite sure what to do
with him, other than play along.

Oddly, it seemed like the only person not breaking a sweat was

Trump himself. Reporters went to sleep sometime after midnight, long after his rallies ended and they filed their stories, and woke up to his tweets—which were followed immediately by his phone calls to all the major morning shows, starting promptly at seven A.M. Other candidates had to show up in studio, but Trump got the royal treatment—he could sit in his bathrobe and dial in. Why? Because his every move made news. Always.

Raging nationalists like him had appeared on the national political stage before—Buchanan and Pat Robertson, with their wild accusations; Ross Perot, with his sweeping populism; Ron Paul and Michele Bachmann more recently. But Trump had three things they lacked—limitless time, free money, and no shame. Also, he had a clear strategy: he picked out whoever was leading in the polls and aimed his shots squarely at them until their lead started to fade.

Trump's only weakness was his glass jaw—he couldn't take a hit. He could dish out abuse all day long, but when he got scraped, he lost his mind. A few weeks after he attacked McCain, Trump showed up for the first Republican debate, hosted by Fox News in Cleveland—future site of the Republican nominating convention, one year away, a veritable lifetime in politics. Debate moderator and Fox News host Megyn Kelly got straight to why Trump seemed to be getting steam in the field, "Mr. Trump, one of the things people love about you is you speak your mind and you don't use a politician's filter. However, that is not without its downsides, in particular when it comes to women. You've called women you don't like 'fat pigs, dogs, slobs and disgusting animals.'"

Then Trump cut her off, "Only Rosie O'Donnell." The studio audience, mostly Republican honchos and their guests, loved it. Kelly quickly corrected him, "No, it wasn't." But the audience kept laughing and applauding. "Thank you," Trump said. Kelly waited a breath and then hopped back in, "For the record, it was well beyond Rosie O'Donnell." Trump waved her off, "Yes, I'm sure it was." This time, Kelly kept on rolling, "You once said to a contestant on *Celebrity Ap-*

prentice, 'It would be a pretty picture to see her on her knees.' Does that sound to you like the temperament of a man we should elect as president?"

Then Trump launched into a tirade. "I don't frankly have time for total political correctness. And to be honest with you, this country doesn't have time either. This country is in big trouble. We don't win anymore. We lose to China. We lose to Mexico both in trade and at the border. We lose to everybody." He spun his wheels a second, before a threat slipped out, "And frankly, what I say, and oftentimes it's fun, it's kidding. We have a good time. What I say is what I say. And honestly, Megyn, if you don't like it, I'm sorry. I've been very nice to you, although I could probably maybe not be, based on the way you have treated me. But I wouldn't do that."

The next day, on CNN, Trump carried through on the threat—sort of. "You could see there was blood coming out of her eyes, blood coming out of her wherever. In my opinion, she was off base." Had Trump just accused Megyn Kelly of attacking him because she was menstruating? It sure sounded that way, but the nuances could be debated for forever—and they were. And all the while, it kept the spotlight on Trump.

EVANGELICALS FOR TRUMP

One by one, Trump's foes fell—they fell in the polls, and then, as their money dried up, they folded up shop. First was Wisconsin governor Scott Walker—at one time a favorite of the Koch brothers, but whose "burn rate"—the amount of money he was spending on his primary campaign—was completely untenable. He dropped out in September of 2015 with a prescient warning: unite against Trump or die one by one. Slowly, and methodically, they got picked off right down to Jeb Bush, the scion of the Bush dynasty. He called himself a "disruptor" because the term was trendy, but it only papered over the malaise of his candidacy. One Republican operative joked that his campaign finally made Jeb a four-letter word when they added an exclamation to the campaign materials, "JEB!" Trump insulted him endlessly, dubbing him "low energy" and it stuck, right until he dropped out in February 2016. The last ones standing were Texas senator Ted Cruz, with his bulwark of support from the Tea Party and Robert Mercer, and the more moderate Ohio governor John Kasich, who hung on by a thread following a solid performance in New Hampshire.

The Christian Right began taking notice of Trump as well. There was, it turned out, a biblical archetype for the Donald—and even the possibility that he could help bring back Jesus. Trump, said evangelical leader Lance Wallnau, is a "modern-day Cyrus." Cyrus, the Persian king, held the Jews in captivity in Babylon, but promised to free them to return to Jerusalem after seventy years of captivity. Among Dispensationalists, Christians who believed the end of the world was near, that seventy-year figure was prophetic, as was rebuilding Solomon's temple in Jerusalem. Restore Jerusalem to Jewish control, rebuild the temple, and Jesus would begin his return to Earth, the interpretation went.

On the surface, Trump seemed an awkward candidate to get behind, to put it mildly—he wasn't a hearty practitioner, something he made clear when he once cited "Two Corinthians" and accidentally tithed in a communion plate. His multiple marriages, affairs, cheating (in love and business), and support for gambling, *Playboy*, and all other manner of sin seemed obviously antithetical to a pious lifestyle. But Wallnau and some other modern-day versions of Falwell and Robertson, like Robert Jeffress, noted that God often used ungodly men to pursue divine ends. (They never mentioned why Clinton, or Gingrich, or anyone else didn't meet this metric before, despite their ungodly dalliances.)

This rationalizing of Trump struck many evangelical theologians and historians, who had been wary of the mingling of religion and politics for decades, as a little too convenient. John Fea, a professor of evangelical history in the United States at Messiah College in Pennsylvania, was one of those skeptics. He pointed to an old Baptist saying that seemed to sum up the Trump problem, "You can mix horse manure and ice cream, and the horse manure will be just fine." The latest mixing of politics and the evangelical movement was increasingly reeking to more and more evangelicals.

Pence Ticks Up

Pence's lieutenant governor, Sue Ellspermann, had never been fully welcomed into his tight circle of friends and advisers, but she was considered an important asset for Pence as he headed into a tough election. Ellspermann held a PhD in engineering and was viewed as a natural liaison to the Mitch Daniels wing of the Republican Party, which had always been suspicious of Pence's religiosity and social crusading. As a more business-minded Republican, she hadn't supported his stance on the Religious Freedom Restoration Act, and even broke with him publicly, calling for protections for LGBT residents.

But the final straw came when Pence said he would need her to go on the attack for him in the 2016 election—he had to maintain his pledge of positive campaigning, so she would have to lob the bombs for him. Ellspermann refused. She couldn't defend his opposition to LGBT rights, and to her mind Pence never explained how having her launch attacks by proxy for him didn't amount to a violation of his pledge to never go negative. She was pushed off the Pence ticket. This fixed another problem for the GOP kingmakers, they could pull Eric Holcomb—one of Daniels's close confidants, out of the Republican U.S. Senate primary and place him with Pence on the 2016 ticket for governor. It rewarded one of their finest soldiers, Holcomb, and also helped clear the field for their preferred candidate for the Senate, U.S. representative Todd Young.

By the start of 2016, things had started improving significantly for Pence, and he was prepared for a successful—if tight—reelection bid. Trump's presidential bid had wiped away all discussion of RFRA on the national stage, along with anything else that didn't have his name on it. And the results showed for Pence's team—the "undervote," the number of people they expected to support the Republican nominee for president but skip voting for Pence in the governor's race, was narrowing markedly.

The Cruz Campaign v. the Trump Circus

As March began, Ted Cruz's team looked down the schedule of primaries—they were doing great in states from the West, but less so in the South. Of the campaigns, Cruz's was by far the best organized—fueled by unlimited money, like the super PACs run by the Mercers, and stocked with movement conservatives. Ironically, it looked a lot like what would have been an ideal Pence campaign if he had run for president in 2016, right down to Kellyanne Conway's guiding hand. But Cruz had a vexing problem. If Trump compensated for his lack of organization with an abundance of personality and dynamism from the top of the ticket. Then Cruz dampened his own excellent campaign with flat performances, a diminutive character, and general squishiness.

Lacking for personality, the Cruz campaign leaned on the strength of its organization, and launched an impressive effort to yank the nomination out from under Trump's nose using the very rules of the Republican Party. Better organized and touting a more dedicated activist base, they began locking in delegates to the national convention, in states across the country—the strategy was arcane indeed, built on a layered understanding of state-level party rules and the very structure of the Republican nominating convention itself.

Trump's popularity with a slice of the Republican electorate was undeniable, but it was not expansive. Trump was pulling in pluralities, not majorities, in most early contests. Cruz's team filtered out ahead of Trump's, beating him to organize in states further down the schedule. Indiana's late primary date, at the start of May, typically left it out of contention—the party nominations were typically locked up by March or April. But the Republican contest looked like it could stretch all the way to the convention itself, and Indiana could be a deciding factor. Indiana's primary was still six weeks away, but Cruz's campaign managed to secure a guarantee from Pence that he would endorse them and help them beat back Trump.

Meanwhile, some of the veteran Republicans supporting Trump pushed him to professionalize his campaign. Trump was entering a world where seven P.M. rambles wouldn't cut it, and the constant scandalizing wasn't winning converts. Trump's daughter and son-in-law, Ivanka Trump and Jared Kushner, began taking a more active role in the campaign, pushing out the combative campaign manager, Corey Lewandowski. Old hands, led by California billionaire and former Reagan administration official Tom Barrack, pushed Trump to hire a real operator who understood party machinery and could keep the Cruz uprising at bay.

The answer to stopping the Cruz conservative insurrection, they figured, lay with Paul Manafort, a grizzled old Washington hand who made his name four decades earlier doing precisely what the Cruz campaign was doing now, scrounging for Republican delegates. At just twenty-seven years old, Manafort had helped put down an insurgent bid against sitting president Gerald Ford by the former governor of California, Ronald Reagan. When Reagan took office four years later, Manafort helped form the most powerful lobbying shop the nation had ever seen, with Republican operatives Charlie Black and Roger Stone. But after a decade or so, the partnership dissolved, and Manafort took on a new breed of client, foreign dictators. By 2014, he was earning millions working for the Ukrainian president backed by Vladimir Putin, Viktor Yanukovych.

Manafort brought on his chief aide, Rick Gates, and they were immediately tasked with stanching the delegate uprising that threatened to upend Trump's campaign. One of the first people Trump asked them to call was his good friend Steve Hilbert.

A few weeks later, on April 5, 2016, Cruz won a stunning victory in Wisconsin. For the first time in months, Republicans and conservatives saw a path to stopping Trump. They just had to hold him off until the nominating convention in three months. ♠

While Manafort was at work putting down the Cruz insurrection, Corey Lewandowski and Barry Bennett, a former adviser to Ben Carson, had started the search for a running mate for Trump. Fresh on their minds was the debacle of eight years earlier, when John McCain picked Sarah Palin—Palin was supposed to represent an olive branch to the conservative movement and a fresh new face that would help an old establishment bull, McCain, generate enough excitement to carry him over the finish line. Palin did generate plenty of excitement, for herself, and became an outright star after they lost in 2008. Now, after decades of the GOP establishment passing olive branches to the ascendant conservative base, the Trump camp faced an interesting problem. Trump had leapfrogged the Tea Partiers locked in with Cruz; he had his own base. Ironically, he needed to do some conservative outreach as well, but not because the movement was growing, but because it still held sizable power at its pinnacle. Their ranks seemed to be diminishing, in the face of Trump's rampant populism, but they still held enough control to deny him the nomination.

As Trump barreled through the Republican electorate, his supporters co-opted Pepe the Frog into a racist meme and circulated a favorite comic among the "MAGA" crowd. In it, the worried conductor shouts out, "Mr. Trump, the brakes won't engage!" Then Pepe the Racist Frog appears, wearing a white MAGA hat, with a sweep of blond comb-over slipping out from underneath. He pokes his head out the window of the speeding train with a flat smirk and says nothing. The conductor asks again, "Mr. Trump?" The answer is written in all caps: "THERE ARE NO BRAKES ON THIS TRAIN." But while Trump barreled through the Republican Party, most polling showed the Trump Train crashing up against the general electorate, where voters didn't take a shine to his plans to ban Muslims from entering the country, build a wall along the border with Mexico, start a nuclear showdown with North Korea, or any of the endless insults he hurled through the campaign. There were no brakes on that train.

The RNC had one job, to pick a winner, and Trump did not look like a winner—he looked like the kind of guy who would smirk as he crashed the GOP train. Paul Manafort had to convince the 168 members of the Republican National Committee—representatives from all fifty states and six U.S. territories—that the Trump Train really did have brakes, or at least someone who knew how to use them.

The RNC gathered that April at the Diplomat Resort and Spa in South Florida to decide how they would handle Trump. Operatives for Cruz, Kasich, and Trump mixed among the RNC members, pleading their case to the people who would decide the Republican nomination. Manafort pulled the RNC members together into a small room, jamming them in so tight that they were sweating. He had an important message: Trump was just putting on an act on the trail, he would become presidential once he was elected. And he would be elected because they would sweep the Rust Belt. "The part he's been playing now is evolving into the part you've been expecting. The negatives will come down, the image is going to change, but 'Crooked Hillary' is still going to be 'Crooked Hillary,'" Manafort said, drawing some laughs. The difference between Trump and Clinton, he said, was that Clinton's faults were "character" defects, but Trump's were limited to "personality" and easily assuaged.

Better than waiting for Trump to start using a teleprompter more often, Trump's aides knew they could win over converts with the right running mate, someone who would instill confidence in the party bigwigs and maybe even bring some disenchanted Republicans and conservatives back into the fold. Women topped their early lists, an implicit nod that Trump screwed up with the Megyn Kelly menstruation gambit. Governor Mary Fallin of Oklahoma, Governor Susana Martinez of New Mexico, and Senator Joni Ernst of Iowa were Trump campaign favorites. The vicious Republican primary, the competing factions in Trump's orbit, and Trump's own impulsive tastes made the task hard. Trump and his family liked the politicians who had jumped on the Trump Train when few other Republicans would, former House Speaker Newt Gingrich, New Jersey governor Chris Christie, and Alabama senator Jeff Sessions.

But as they began reaching out to prospects, they suffered stunning rebuttals—the people he had been insulting for almost a year straight wanted nothing to do with him. Would-be running mates like Ernst ran away from reporters in the Capitol who wanted to know if she would join Trump's ticket.

Meanwhile, Back in Indy

As the Indiana primary approached, Pence's aides weren't sure exactly who he had promised what. Pence told the Cruz campaign he'd endorse Cruz, but he never told his staff. On April 20, 2016, Trump flew to Indianapolis to meet with Pence at the governor's residence—Pence told him he was staying out of the primary.

On April 27, Pence flew north to Wrigley Field in Chicago for a fund raiser for his reelection, hosted by Todd Ricketts, owner of the Chicago Cubs and leader of a last-ditch effort to block Trump from getting the nomination. Some of the donors pulled him aside; they had a message from former president George W. Bush, "Please stop Trump and save the Republican Party." Pence took it under prayerful consideration.

But Pence's chief political advisers, Obst and Ayers, didn't want any heroics from Pence—he was almost out of the woods in his own reelection, and they didn't want him lining up with either Trump or Cruz. He had his own election to worry about.

On April 29, Pence walked back into his old stomping grounds, the WIBC offices just off Monument Circle. He had made his decision about who he would support in the Indiana primary, "I'm not against anybody, but I will be voting for Ted Cruz in the upcoming

Republican primary," Mike Pence said, before showering Trump with praise. "I particularly want to commend Donald Trump, who I think has given voice to the frustration of millions of working Americans with a lack of progress in Washington, DC."

Trump and Corey Lewandowski immediately lit up Christie's phone: "Did you get a heads-up that Pence was going to endorse Cruz??" yelled Corey Lewandowski. Christie didn't know, nobody had told him this was coming. Then Trump called up Christie: "I can't believe you didn't get a heads-up he was going with the other guy!" Now Christie was mad at Pence, so he called Nick Ayers, who was in his office in Georgia. Nick put him on speakerphone, Christie yelled, "You know how this game works! I brought Trump out there for you, he made a special trip just to see Mike. It doesn't mean you had to endorse us." Ayers breathed slowly and explained it was because he didn't know Pence was endorsing Cruz.

Cruz's campaign staff was equally livid. What kind of endorsement was that? It wasn't an endorsement at all! Had Pence gone soft on them? Marty Obst agreed to let Cruz's campaign cut a radio spot from the quasi-endorsement. Cruz's staff then told him Pence needed to do a rally in Indianapolis with Cruz to try and salvage this race. Obst responded that Pence only had time for one stop in the suburbs of Chicago. Meanwhile, Lewandowski had been dialing up Marty, asking Team Pence to stay on the sidelines—Obst promised they would stay out of it. In retrospect, it was hard to tell if Pence screwed them both, or neither of them. "He doesn't really make his own decisions," a Cruz aide said of Pence. "He's very empowering of staff, to the point where he gets manipulated by them." A Trump adviser had a more withering assessment. "He's not confident enough in himself," the adviser said, noting that Pence gets yanked around by his advisers. "I don't know why he doesn't trust in himself more."

Cruz's campaign suspected it was a case of Nick Ayers trying to position Pence as a running mate for Trump. Meanwhile, Manafort and his team took credit for pulling Pence back from the brink of a full-blown Cruz endorsement. A Trump campaign aide said, "Even if he couldn't support Trump, he should at least not slam the door in his face."　●

With the Indiana primary just four days away, the Cruz campaign was barely standing. That weekend, Cruz flew to California for the state's Republican convention, as did Kasich. At the convention they met to take their pulse. Kasich told Cruz he was going all the way to Ohio, his home state and home of the Republican nominating convention. Cruz had a better shot at beating Trump, but his chances diminished infinitely as long as Kasich stayed in the race. On his way to the plane to fly back to Indiana, Cruz's staff showed him some internal tracking polls; he was about to lose Indiana by twenty points to Trump. Kasich would suck out the remaining oxygen, so Cruz decided it was time to quit. He would make the announcement Tuesday night after the primary results were tallied.

The first hint he was done came Monday, when he decided he would debate a Trump supporter. The Trump voter pointed at Cruz and laughed, saying, "You are the problem." Another heckler jumped in, "You're the politicians that killed America!"

Cruz tried rationalizing with them. "Of all the candidates, name one who had a million-dollar judgment against them for hiring illegal immigrants." The voter cut him off, "Name one that's self-funded." Cruz shot back, "So you, you like rich people who buy politicians." The voter cut him off at the knees. "Where's your Goldman Sachs jacket? We know your wife works there."

"Sir, with all respect, Donald Trump is deceiving you, he is playing you for a chump," Cruz said. That was true, Trump was lying, but the message couldn't make it through with Cruz delivering it. The Trump voter hit him in the gut—"You'll find out tomorrow, Indiana don't want you."

The next day, Tuesday, May 3, the Republican voters of Indiana took Trump over Cruz, 53 percent to 37 percent.

Standing at the Crowne Plaza Hotel, in a converted train station, in downtown Indianapolis, Cruz wept as he announced he was leaving the race. His wife and daughters stood by him and also cried. Trump effectively won the Republican Party nomination that night. The next day, Kasich got in his campaign plane in Columbus, Ohio, to fly to the next stop—he was technically the last man standing against Trump—but the plane never left the runway. Kasich called a press conference and announced he was dropping out as well.

THE RUNNING MATE SEARCH CONTINUES

The May primary victory more or less sealed the nomination for Trump. Resistance remained within the party, led by a band of moderates and conservatives who argued Trump could still be blocked on the floor of the convention itself. This would create convention chaos the likes of which hadn't been seen since Reagan first ran in 1976. But the party leaders began making their decisions—sit it out or get, reluctantly, on the Trump Train.

The Trump campaign, meanwhile, ramped up its running mate search. One of the team members joked that the best running mate for Trump is Trump, and then, second only to himself, was Ivanka. Fittingly enough, then came word that Trump wanted his team to consider Ivanka seriously. They debated her as an option, and in certain ways she made sense—name recognition, favorability ratings, as a complete counterbalance to her father in age, gender, and ideology. But she was his daughter. Trump's advisers gently explained to him why nepotism would look bad for them, and he backed off the idea.

The problem that Trump faced was that he kept getting snubbed by would-be contenders. On May 26, 2016, Senate Foreign Relations Committee chairman Bob Corker was summoned to Trump Tower in Manhattan. Corker, a centrist Republican known for his compromises and genial manner, could not be more un-Trump. On his way up the elevator to Trump's office, Corker tried to downplay himself, saying they shouldn't consider him because he wouldn't be the right fit. Corker and Trump met briefly, and Corker said he didn't want the gig. Meanwhile, the press got word he was up there and gathered in the lobby of Trump Tower. Trump told him, "You go down there and tell them you're my pick."

Corker didn't go down there and say he was the pick, because he knew lying would come back to haunt him. But Trump had no issue with it.

Manafort and RNC chairman Reince Priebus had been hammering on Trump to look seriously at Mike Pence. Trump was not a fan—Pence looked like he was about to lose reelection in a solidly Republican state. This made him, in Trump's mind, a loser. And Trump hated losers. Pence also had endorsed Cruz a few weeks earlier, although it was a shitty endorsement.

Trump had been watching a lot of the cable news coverage of his vice presidential search, and the talking heads all told him that traditionally a nominee selects someone to be the attack dog while the nominee himself stays above the fray. Trump said he wanted an attack dog. He liked Chris Christie and Newt Gingrich. Trump's pollster, Tony Fabrizio, had run some crosstabs on who would get Trump more votes in November, and neither of them did anything for him. Trump needed a complement who would repair his standing with conservatives and more quiet, evangelical types who didn't align with the televangelists already backing him.

Trump's aides also told him they didn't need a ship with "two pirates" on it. Besides, Manafort reasoned, why the hell would Trump need an attack dog. He *was* the attack dog! Anyone else would just compete with him for airtime. Trump liked this latter argument, so he dialed up an old friend for some help.

The night of June 10, 2016, Pence was hosting a party for state Republicans, in town for their state convention, at a converted industrial warehouse, just down the street from the Colts' stadium. Pence saw his chief of staff, Jim Atterholt, across the room, and beckoned him over. Pence asked him if he could show him something in private.

They walked out to the alley that led to the football stadium. Pence's state security detail was there waiting for them, along with Karen Pence. Then Pence waved off his security. He pulled out his phone and showed it to Atterholt. It was a text message from Steve Hilbert: "If you were to be considered for vice president, would you be open to it?" Atterholt got goose bumps on his arms, he said, "Oh my gosh, Governor, it's vice president of the United States!" Pence nodded solemnly; it wasn't time to start counting his blessings—but it was time to get ready.

Pence hired an old friend from his very first congressional race, Republican fund raiser Bob Grand, to begin handling the necessary paperwork and working with the Trump legal team.

Meanwhile, the Trump campaign began a serious vetting of Pence. They dug into his personal financial history—they unearthed his debt problems and big financial losses from 1986 and 2004. That didn't bother them too much. They eyeballed his performance one year earlier, in the thick of the RFRA debacle, and that was disappointing but also forgettable in the moment. Former Indiana senator Evan Bayh once quipped, while being vetted for Barack Obama's ticket in 2008, that it was like getting a proctology exam with the Hubble Space Telescope. The Trump campaign quickly found it could have shoved the Hubble Space Telescope and the International Space Station in there and not find anything on Mike . . . at least not anything as scandalous as Trump was used to.

Trump marveled at Pence. He couldn't understand him. As he was driving one day to a campaign stop, he picked through the executive summary of the vetting packet on Pence—and then he tossed it in the back seat. It was boring! There was nothing on the guy, nothing at all. They heard the stories about fighting with his brothers growing up—yawn. His drinking in college (Where's the hard stuff??). His staff watched the infamous 1990 Arab sheik ad—Pence's team had included two takes—and nobody blinked. That was racist? Hard to tell. This was the Trump campaign. They dug into all his major races for office and his disasters as governor, all the way down to his fights with Brian Bosma. What did that matter?

No, Mike didn't bother them. But Karen did. The Trump camp had heard horror stories about Karen, the same ones that percolated through the halls of the statehouse. But just as in those halls, Trump's team couldn't quite place a finger on her power—she was like a ghost, like a shadow governor. ◦

THE MIRACLE FLAT TIRE

That Fourth of July weekend, Trump invited Pence to a round of golf and a weekend stay at his course in Bedminster, New Jersey. Pence hadn't played a round in at least a year; he was an okay player, but not great. Trump often shot two or three strokes above par, according to campaign aides. Halfway through their round, Trump pulled aside one of his aides. "He's really bad," Trump said. Pence told the assembled reporters afterward, "He beat me like a drum."

Trump didn't particularly like Pence—he carried the whiff of a loser. Here was a man who should be coasting to reelection in a solid Republican state, but instead was bailing out water in a rematch with the Democrat who almost romped him just four years earlier. Pence's team said their polling was strong and had improved greatly since last year's "religious freedom" disaster. But Trump pollster Tony Fabrizio saw something beyond Pence's job prospects; Pence was the only candidate he'd run the numbers on who helped lift Trump with evangelical voters and conservatives. Pence felt a lot like the medicine Trump didn't want to choke down.

The contest for vice president was quickly narrowing—the long shots and aspirational picks that the campaign had considered months earlier never got anywhere. The two who seemed most likely to get the nod were Pence's old pal Chris Christie and his quasi-mentor Newt Gingrich, the man he had learned from in a lifetime in politics without ever being directly under his tutelage. Trump had a years-long friendship with Christie from their work together around New York, and the most influential members of Trump's family—Jared Kushner and Ivanka Trump—were big fans of Gingrich, because he meshed well with Trump, performed well on TV, and also was a big thinker in a way that Trump wasn't.

Manafort and Priebus had both been pushing hard for Pence—both for their own reasons. Manafort saw an immediate crisis at the nominating convention in Cleveland: delegates could deny Trump the nomination if the uprising spurred by Cruz carried through. And Priebus saw another problem: Republicans could lose even more seats down the ballot with Trump at the top of the ticket if evangelical Christians and stalwart conservatives stayed home rather than vote for either Hillary Clinton or Trump.

Steve Hilbert also pushed hard for Pence behind the scenes—Trump came to him regularly with questions about Pence and Hilbert assured him he would be a good selection. When Trump asked if Pence could raise enough money for the ticket, Hilbert went to Marty Obst, who worked up a quick memo of their fund-raising efforts in Indiana and for the RGA and their biggest donors.

While Marty Obst and Nick Ayers worked the phones on Pence's behalf, in the great shadow-campaign for running mate, Pence laid back and didn't lobby directly. "Running" for running mate had always been a passive-aggressive exercise in wanting it while looking like you don't want it. But Pence seemed awkwardly placid, even to his aides. Obst asked him how he could be so calm, and Pence said it was because "God has a plan." Whatever God's answer was, Pence would be okay with it.

The decision would have to be made soon. The nominating convention in Cleveland started July 18 and the running mate was set to be nominated Wednesday, July 20, 2016. And Pence had his own deadline—if Trump was serious, he would have to make it clear before noon on July 15, because that was when Pence would have to pull his name off the ballot for governor if he was picked for vice president.

With the leaders of the establishment on his side, and no connections to Trump World, Pence was at the bottom of the small list of finalists—but he was still in the mix.

Trump was scheduled to do a fund raiser in Indianapolis Tuesday, July 12. Hilbert had helped set it up months earlier with the heads of Trump's campaign in Indiana, former GOP chairman Rex Early and veteran Republican operative Tony Samuel, long before Pence was seriously considered a running mate. Happenstance seemed to smile on the Indiana governor. ๑

Trump Force One, as it was known on the trail, was about as Trumpy as it got—the plane was a massive Boeing 757, which he'd bought for $100 million five years earlier when he was considering a run for president in 2012. It included a bedroom, guest room, galley, shower, and gold-plated fixtures throughout. But, like much of Trump's empire, there was quite a bit of wear underneath the gold plating. The plane was built in 1991 and ran as a commercial airliner for a few years before going into private use.

When it landed at a private airfield just outside Indianapolis that Tuesday afternoon, it popped a flat tire on the landing gear on the right side of the plane. Trump's Secret Service detail scrambled to figure out what to do—meanwhile Trump's campaign team rushed to downtown Indianapolis, because they were already late for the fund raiser. Trump spokeswoman Hope Hicks, bodyguard Keith Schiller, and personal assistant John McEntee rode in the car with a former aide to Rex Early, Kevin Eck. Eck could hear Hicks in the back setting up meetings for Trump in California the next day. Trump planned to spend July 12 in Indianapolis, do a fund raiser and rally with Pence, and then fly on to California for another fund-raising event.

About twenty-five high-dollar donors from Indiana showed up to the fund raiser late that afternoon at the Columbia Club. After brief remarks from Trump and Pence, they set up for photos with Trump inside the Crystal Terrace, a large, elegant ballroom with sweeping views of downtown.

When Pence's good friend Jeff Cardwell got to the front of the photo line, he introduced himself to Trump. "I understand you've known Mike a long time," Trump said. Cardwell nodded. They chatted a bit about Pence's qualifications, then Trump pulled him aside—"I want to talk to you more about this." Trump said, "Listen, it's down to two people: I'm looking at Newt Gingrich or Mike Pence." He wanted to know why Pence should be picked. "I don't think you need another lightning rod at the top of the ticket," Cardwell said, echoing the exact argument that Priebus and Manafort had been making for months. "Mike Pence will deliver the evangelical vote, he will deliver the Rust Belt. And because he is a member of the Republican Governors Association, he's got good relationships with all the surrounding governors, Kentucky Governor Matt Bevin, Michigan Governor Rick Snyder." The Rust Belt twist helped, since the Trump campaign long knew it would have to sweep the Rust Belt to win the White House.

The Secret Service agents assigned to Trump motioned for him to get moving, but Trump waved them off. Then Cardwell, a small-business owner for decades, remembered that he was talking with a businessman, so he made a finer point, which played to Trump's ego and inclinations, "The two of you would be the best public-private partnership in history." Trump smiled and asked for Cardwell's cell number.

Trump's team ran out the back of the Columbia Club to the alley where his motorcade was waiting to take him just north of the city to a rally in Westfield, Indiana. Eck sat in the car, idling, when Hicks, Schiller, and the rest of the team jumped in. Eck noticed the cool, collected chaos of the typical campaign style had been replaced with franticness—Hicks hopped between texting and phone calls, canceling every California meeting she could. The flat tire on Trump Force One would take a long time to fix. The brake on the right-side landing gear had broken and caused the tire to pop. They could fly up the replacement brake from Florida immediately, but that would cost $30,000, and Trump didn't want to spend that much. So he had a campaign aide drive the part from Florida to Indiana.

Some aides saw God's hand at work, others saw Paul Manafort's. Regardless the reason, Trump was stuck in Indianapolis overnight.

"The Trump family had pretty much made up their mind; they were getting ready for the next week, the convention," Cardwell said. "The family was all on board with Newt." ◊

That night, Mike and Karen Pence dined with Trump and his son Eric at the Capital Grille. Trump was gregarious. He told Pence, "You've really got a lot of muscle around here. Everybody has these good things to say about you." Pence had been scheduled to fly to New York the next day to meet with Jared Kushner, Ivanka Trump, and Donald Trump Jr., a formality as part of the VP vetting process. But Trump and he decided at dinner to have the Trump family fly into Indianapolis first thing in the morning for a family breakfast at the governor's mansion. Trump and his son Eric had already booked rooms for the night at the Conrad Hotel.

That night gave Pence the "home court advantage," Obst said. "If you think about Mike walking into Trump Tower with all the gold, and going up to the residence, it's really disorienting, and then sitting in this bizarre chair, having everybody fire questions at him. The interaction would have been very different."

Pence walked out of the dinner after a few hours with a giant smile on his face. Cardwell couldn't believe what was happening, "That's the night a flat tire changed the course of American history."

Mike and Karen Pence spent the night picking flowers for the breakfast in the backyard, using the light of their iPhones.

Eck got up early to drive out to the private airfield and pick up Trump's children from the airport—Kushner, Ivanka Trump, and Donald Trump Jr. One Trump aide said that Jared and Ivanka flew out to Indianapolis to meet Pence as a part of doing their due diligence in vetting running mates. Christie saw a last-ditch effort to block him from becoming Trump's running mate, a product of Kushner's long-standing hostility against Christie for sending his father to jail years ago.

Early that morning, Karen drove to the local boutique grocery store to pick up breakfast for them. It seemed so fitting that this played out on their home turf, in the neighborhood she grew up in—Broad Ripple, near Butler University. This was the same neighborhood where she and Mike first met, the same where they lived together after they were married and where Mike Pence launched his political career in 1986. With one busted tire, Pence had gained the home court advantage.

Karen served breakfast for the Trumps and Pence's small team. After the meal, Trump and Pence sat down with a small group in the "bunker"—the furnished basement of the mansion. They got down to brass tacks.

Trump looked at Pence and held up his cell phone. He had several missed calls from Chris Christie. "I need killers, I want somebody to fight. Chris Christie calls me nonstop about this job. He calls me every ten seconds; he'd do anything for his job. He is dying to be vice president. And you, it's like you don't care," Trump said. "I need killers! Do you want this thing or not?"

Pence was calm, preternaturally calm. Obst knew why; it was because he was resigned to whatever answer God would deem and he had a peace about how the dice would fall. Pence could only be himself.

"Look, Donald, if you want somebody to be a killer, if you want somebody to be a constant attack dog, I suggest you go find someone else. I'm not that guy. I'm going to enjoy myself, I'm going to be respectful. I'm going to do things with my own style because that's how I'm comfortable," Pence said. He was on a roll. "If you want somebody to help you govern, if you want somebody to help run that place, if you want somebody to help get bills passed through Congress. If you want somebody to build and maintain relationships with donors and elected officials and governors, I'm your guy. If you want somebody to do that, I could do that as well as anybody else you're talking to. So to your question, I like being governor. I like running for reelection.

I'd love to do this for four more years. I really enjoy this. If you're telling me you want me to do this, I'm in because I believe it's important for our country. I believe you'll change our country. I believe you can win. So, if you want me to do it? I'm going to say, 'Yes.' If you don't want me to do it, I'm gonna work really hard for you and the other guy. It doesn't matter. It really doesn't matter."

"Well, then why are you going through this process?" Trump asked, perplexed by Pence's dismissive answer.

"Well, you're in my home, you tell me," Pence said. "Your whole family came here to see me. Obviously, the feeling is mutual, right?"

All Trump could say was "Wow."

After Trump and his family left, Marty Obst looked over at Pence. "What was that? That was awesome!" Pence smiled.

Trump hopped back in his motorcade to have lunch with Newt Gingrich at the Columbia Club. In twenty-four hours, Gingrich had fallen from the pick to the bottom of the pack. Sean Hannity had flown Gingrich into Indianapolis at the last minute, but Gingrich was stuck waiting as Pence held court. The man who trained generations of Republicans and set the angry tone of Trumpism with his campaign school and instructional cassette tapes was trumped by a flat tire, some Hoosier hospitality, and masterful political timing by Pence.

Meanwhile, Eck drove Jared Kushner, Ivanka Trump, and Eric Trump back to the plane to leave. Eric Trump rode shotgun. Christie had been calling their father for hours, and it wasn't fair to just leave him hanging. Eric asked Ivanka if they should call him up, and she answered that it was a good idea. Eric got on the phone with Christie, and he assured him no decisions had been made yet. "Our families have been good friends for years," Eric told him, "we wouldn't make a decision without telling you." He hung up after a few minutes, "That was good," Ivanka said.

Trump Force One still sat on the tarmac, unmoved from the day before. It would be a while before the flat was fixed. But the Secret

Service had arranged for an auxiliary plane to fly Trump from another airfield nearby on the west end of the city.

That evening, Mike and Karen Pence gathered together with their central team, chief of staff Jim Atterholt, Marty Obst, and Nick Ayers, at the guest house next to the governor's mansion. The small house formed a de facto campaign headquarters, for only the innermost of Pence's circle. They talked out logistics, and there were plenty of logistics to consider—they needed to know before noon on Friday whether Trump was picking Pence or not.

They tried to stay focused on the race for governor, but it was hard. Trump was mercurial indeed, and an excellent encounter could be wiped away with another flat tire or impressive showing by Christie or anyone else. Nothing could be truly cemented until one week from then, in Cleveland, when the Republican delegates approved Trump's anointed running mate.

As they were debating their next steps, Ayers received a call from the Trump campaign: Pence should get ready for a call from Trump in thirty minutes. They did not know what was coming, but they had a feeling. As they grabbed one another's hands in a circle, Pence asked Atterholt to lead them in a prayer. Jim Atterholt, a devout evangelical like Mike and Karen, chose a "hedge of protection" prayer. "I prayed to put a hedge of protection around Mike and his family, I prayed for peace and wisdom and for God to protect his family." Atterholt, Ayers, and Obst then left—and Mike and Karen ran inside to the study to take the most important call of their lives.

THE DECISION IS MADE

Trump had just told Pence that he was his pick, but then he called up Chris Christie and asked, "Are you ready? . . . I want to know that you're ready and that Mary Pat is ready." Christie replied, "If you want me to do this, we're going to be ready." Trump said, "Stay by the phone tomorrow, because I'm making this call tomorrow."

So Trump's offer to Pence had been as ambivalent as Pence's endorsement of Ted Cruz a few months earlier? And what about Gingrich? Kushner and Ivanka liked Gingrich, but Trump told an adviser that Gingrich's vetting packet was terrifying. The dirt Trump's people had dug up on Gingrich "makes mine look tame," Trump told the adviser.

The previous Saturday, Trump had told a roomful of donors that he liked Chris Christie for vice president. That Tuesday, he told Pence's good friend, Cardwell, that the choice was down to Pence and Gingrich. And just yesterday, July 13, he'd called Pence and told him he was it. A former Trump aide laughed, hearing that. "He tells everybody yes."

The Pence family woke up on Thursday, July 14, believing that they had the nod from Trump locked up. They called in Lt. Gov. Eric Holcomb to tell him the news, and that they would support him in his bid to replace Pence on the ballot for governor. They would fly to New York for an announcement at Trump Tower that evening.

Mike, Karen, and Charlotte, their middle child, ducked into an SUV to ride to the airport. They hid in the back, heads down, so the television cameras assembled across the street wouldn't spy them. Before leaving, they sent a decoy, Greg Pence, chauffeured in a black SUV just like the governor's—the journalists ran after him, he looked just like Pence from far away. Greg Pence waved and smiled. They also had a decoy plane ready—the private jet owned by Pence's younger brother, Tom, was set for takeoff to New York. Pence flew on the private plane of one of his closest advisers and fund raisers, Fred Klipsch.

They'd fooled the press, but they didn't fool Christie. One of Christie's state troopers told him a private flight was coming in from Indianapolis and landing at Teterboro, New Jersey. Christie called up Trump and chewed him out, "You picked Pence?" Trump hated confrontation, so he played it down, "Nothing is final, Chris." Christie leveled with him, "I will do this for you, Donald, but I don't need this." But Trump assured him he was still in, "Chris, Chris, just be ready. Are you ready?" "Ready for what?" "Ready, I need you to be ready for this." "Mary Pat and I are ready, just tell us when."

News reports emerged that Pence was the running mate pick. The *Indianapolis Star* reported shortly after noon that Trump had settled on the Indiana governor. Pence and his family huddled at Trump Tower, waiting for the big rollout. That flat tire really had changed everything—he was supposed to be there a day earlier, meeting Ivanka Trump and Jared Kushner for the first time. It would've been a stiff formality, a courtesy call to preface Gingrich's or Christie's selection. But Pence and his family arrive a day later, and now he was the nominee for vice president. Incredible.

Then CNN reported that not long after Trump made his verbal commitment to Pence, he was already asking aides if it was too late to back out of the decision. The announcement was supposed to be made on Thursday, but the Trump campaign delayed. Trump said this was in deference to the terrorist attack in Nice, France, that had killed eighty-six people. This rang odd, since global events rarely seemed to make any impact on Trump.

A few hours later, Trump called in to Greta Van Susteren's show on Fox News to talk about the terror attack and the running mate process. "I haven't made my final, final decision," he said. "I've got three people that are fantastic. I think Newt is a fantastic person. I think Chris Christie is a fantastic person."

Nick Ayers and Marty Obst smelled trouble. They knew how Trump worked—he could change his mind a thousand times more between now and the convention and nothing would be locked in until the Republican delegates voted on a running mate. Ayers and Obst weren't about to have Pence and his family go through this only to have the football yanked at the last minute. They knew they had to lock Trump in. And the clock ticked for them, but not for Trump.

Manafort told them that Trump wouldn't announce Pence as his pick until Saturday, which would be one day after Pence had to remove his name from the ticket for governor. If Trump changed his mind and went with Christie or someone else, Pence wouldn't be running for governor or vice president. He'd be out of a job. They yelled at Manafort: If Trump doesn't make the announcement publicly before noon Friday, the deadline for Pence to decide if he would stay on the ticket for governor, they were going with their backup plan and Pence was running for governor. Trump called them at one a.m., after a fund raiser in Beverly Hills, he said, "Guys, I told you not to worry about it."

But they were worried, they were freaking out.

The morning of Friday, July 15, 2016, one of Pence's deputies stood ready to deliver the papers to the Indiana secretary of state's office that would remove Pence's name from the ballot for governor and legally allow him to run for vice president. They had until noon.

Trump called up Obst and Ayers and said, "Guys, what do you need me to do?"

Trump had to make it official, or they were backing out. Trump asked if a tweet would do, and they screamed, "Yes!" With just an hour left before the deadline struck on Pence's future, Trump tweeted: "I am pleased to announce that I have chosen Governor Mike Pence as my Vice Presidential running mate. News conference tomorrow at 11 a.m." ₉

And then the campaign revealed the new logo, the intermingling of Trump and Pence—literally. The "T" looked like it was penetrating the "P" in a suggestive manner. The internet quickly had its way with the blunder and the logo was turned into a GIF, the T repeatedly bobbing up and down through the hole in the P. Brad Parscale, the campaign's digital director, eventually took responsibility for the error and the logo was quickly scrapped. "What is the T doing to that P?" asked John Dingell, the Michigan Democrat who, at the age of ninety, seemed to understand trolling better than any other person in Congress.

But at least Pence knew what he was doing.

On Saturday, July 16, 2016, Donald Trump walked onstage with

Mike Pence—here it was, finally, the big moment. As they took the stage, Trump said he wanted to introduce his running mate—but first he had a few remarks. One minute, then two minutes, then five minutes. He rambled for twenty-five minutes. Finally, he landed on the first hint that this might be about Pence. "When I won that state in a landslide, and I learned that when Governor Pence, under tremendous pressure from establishment people he endorsed somebody else, but it was more of an endorsement for me!" Trump swung his arms wide, oh the schadenfreude. "He talked about Trump, then he talked about Ted, who's a good guy by the way and who's going to be speaking at the convention—he's a good guy—but he talked about Trump, Ted, and then he went back to Trump. I said, 'Who did he endorse?' So even though he was under pressure, because I'm sort of outside of the establishment, it was the single greatest non-endorsement I've ever had in my life. So, with that"—Trump looked down at his talking points again—"I would like to introduce a man who I truly believe will be outstanding in every way and who will be the next vice president of the United States, Governor Mike Pence." Pence opened by thanking God, then Karen and his kids, and then Trump, "I come to this moment deeply humbled and with a grateful heart."

After the announcement, Mike, Karen, and Charlotte hopped in a booth at a Chili's in New York. Karen looked exhausted, Charlotte was beaming, and Mike Pence looked elated, with his royal blue tie undone and a plate of nachos in front of him. He tweeted, "Busy weekend in NY! Enjoying a quick dinner with the family @Chilis. Looking forward to getting back to Indiana."

PENCE FINALLY ARRIVES

On Wednesday, July 20, 2016, Mike Pence prepared for the biggest moment of his life—accepting the Republican Party's nomination to be vice president of the United States of America. He took the stage at the convention in Cleveland and delivered the speech of his life, a heartfelt paean to everyone who got him there, mixed with an earnest promise to help Trump win the White House.

But one of the first people to encourage Pence into public speaking, more than four decades ago, heard something else, something distressing. "You know, Hillary Clinton wants a better title. And I would, too, if I was already America's secretary of the status quo," Pence said in his speech. It didn't come anywhere close to Trump's promise to "lock her up." But Sister Sharon Bierman, who taught Pence in the seventh and eighth grades at St. Columba's, and first picked out his talent for public speaking, had to turn off the television. "He was great until he started bashing Hillary. I did not like that at all," she said. "I think in the beginning he concentrated on what he was going to do as the vice president. I loved that part. He was very clear, and his values came out, but then when he started bashing Hillary, I did not appreciate that. So, I just turned it off."

But just like his official rollout four days earlier, Pence seemed to be an afterthought in one of the biggest moments of his life. As Pence accepted the Republican Party's nomination for vice president, the entire convention hall buzzed about Ted Cruz, who stole the show earlier in the night by refusing to support Trump. The national press corps collectively yawned at Pence's momentous arrival. As speeches went—and they'd heard plenty—this was just bad. Flat, boring, lacking in sweep and vision at the top end and rhythm and cadence throughout. He garnered more buzz and excitement when he was flirting with running.

After thirty minutes, Donald Trump walked onstage to embrace his new running mate. He walked up to Mike, beaming, glowing. He shook his hand, he held it firmly, he got closer, he pulled him in. Trump placed his left arm on Mike's back, Mike braced his right arm as Trump moved in. Trump puckered his lips, he went in for the kiss. Mike blushed, his smile never drooped, he turned the other cheek. Trump deadpanned for the cameras, he smiled and patted Mike on the back. Smoocheroo.

Pence had no plans to get sucked into the Trump Circus com-pletely. He had a fine line to walk for the next few months—all he had to do was survive through the election and he would be perfectly positioned to run for president in 2020.

On Thursday, July 21, 2016, Donald Trump accepted the Repub-lican Party's nomination.

Ronald Reagan's sunny vision of Morning in America was re-placed with the setting sun over an American hellscape. Trump warned of a lawless America where immigrants murdered innocent children and the patriotic law enforcement were under siege. And, he said, "I alone can fix it."

The Republicans from California to New York and all points in between chanted "Lock her up!" and "Build that wall!" The delegates from West Virginia whooped and hollered, underneath their coal miners' helmets. But just behind the coal miners for Trump sat the old Republican Party stalwarts from Indiana. They watched solemnly, quietly, as though a dear friend had just passed away.

CHAPTER 14

GOD'S PLAN

The Russians Are Coming—Trump Tower

A month before the convention, on June 3, 2016, a British PR maven, Rob Goldstone, reached out to Donald Trump Jr. with a proposition—he knew someone who had some valuable dirt on Clinton. Would Junior and the team be interested in meeting this guy? Goldstone represented Russian pop superstar Emin Agalarov. Agalarov's father, Aras, was a developer in Russia and Eastern Europe and one of Russian president Vladimir Putin's most valued oligarchs. Emin, the pop star, was the featured guest when Trump hosted Miss Universe in Moscow in 2013. Now Emin Agalarov had something enticing to share. "The Crown Prosecutor of Russia met with his father Aras this morning," Goldstone explained in his email to Trump Jr., "and in their meeting offered to provide the Trump campaign with some official documents and information that would incriminate Hillary and her dealings with Russia and would be very useful to your father. This is obviously very high level and sensitive information but is part of Russia and its government's support for Mr. Trump."

Trump Jr. replied just fifteen minutes later, "If it's what you say I love it."

A few days later Emin helped arrange for Trump Jr. to meet with his contact with the Clinton dirt, Natalia Veselnitskaya. On Thursday, June 9, Veselnitskaya and her small entourage met with Trump's most senior advisers: Trump Jr., Jared Kushner, and Paul Manafort. Stories varied wildly about what was said in the meeting, but everyone seemed to agree that adoptions were discussed. Why adoptions? Because Putin had suspended adoptions by U.S. couples in retaliation for U.S. sanctions against him and his oligarchs. It was a code word for the issue of ending U.S. sanctions. Trump Jr. has said the dirt on Clinton never materialized.

The sanctions were in response to years of transgressions by Russia, ranging from incursions into Ukraine to the murder of an accountant named Sergei Magnitsky. If the end of the Cold War spurred a veritable bromance between Bill Clinton and Boris Yeltsin in the late '90s, Putin's subsequent rise to power marked the return of a form of tzarism—a heavy, monarchical presence coupled with an effort to return Russia to its days as a global superpower. George W. Bush may have seen through Putin's eyes into his soul in 2001, but Obama saw past that guise as Putin led a takeover of Ukraine and violent consolidation of power. But the Obama administration, and then secretary of state Hillary Clinton, had always been reluctant to declare Russia an outright enemy, the result of diplo-politics that led America's foreign policy intelligentsia to believe that Russia could still be welcomed in to the broader world of Western democracies.

But by the summer of 2016, American intelligence had picked up on some troubling actions by Putin and his operators in Russia. Behind the scenes, Russian hackers and operatives had been hard at work the year before laying the groundwork for an elaborate attack on the very roots of American democracy—an army of internet trolls, working out of Moscow, not only spread propaganda and disinformation online, but also actively recruited and paid Americans to protest. In May 2016, they set up opposing Facebook groups, one called "United Muslims of America" and another called "Heart of Texas." Both fake groups advertised a protest for May 21, 2016, outside an Islamic center in Houston. And on May 21, 2016, the Russian trolling jumped from the internet to the streets of Houston—hundreds of protesters lined opposite sides of the street, some carrying signs reading NO HATE and others carrying Confederate battle flags.

Russians even set up real American bank accounts and actively recruited Americans to perform for them. The troll farm paid one man to build a wooden cage, and another woman to dress up in a Hillary Clinton costume—and then she rode in the cage at pro-Trump protests, to chants of "Lock her up!"

Meanwhile, Putin, the old KGB spy, was testing Trump and his campaign, putting out feelers to see if they might be open to working with him. Russians used more traditional spycraft to groom a pair of Trump campaign advisers who claimed to have top-level access to Trump, Carter Page and George Papadopoulos. Russia's ambassador to the United States, Sergey Kislyak, met with other top-level Trump advisers, including Alabama senator Jeff Sessions, the very first U.S. senator to endorse Trump. The contacts all seemed innocuous as there were legitimate policy reasons for coordinating with Putin. As Trump often liked to point out—they had a mutual enemy in ISIS and the war in Syria.

Trump seemed none the wiser to any of this; the man who had made a fortune in casinos, real estate, and television was visibly outgunned in the cloak-and-dagger world of international diplomacy, brinksmanship, and spycraft.

By the start of October, Pence had been crisscrossing the United States for Trump for a few months, delivering the toned-down version of a wild Trump rally. He wasn't exactly a top adviser to Trump; that role stayed with Jared Kushner and increasingly fell to newcomer Steve Bannon. Pence was more like a trusted hand—he could be counted on to go out and carry out whatever task was assigned him without fail, and maybe even smooth over some problems along the way. The Trump campaign had a very definitive role for Pence. "We're gonna run you for governor in five states: Pennsylvania, Michigan, Wisconsin, Ohio, and Iowa. And every now and then we pull you out and run you through Jesus Land," one senior Trump campaign adviser told Pence, and that's precisely what they did. "One thing about Pence is he's a loyal soldier; you tell him what to do and he does it."

"Pence just did an incredible job of soothing Republicans," a Trump adviser said. By the time Pence and Clinton running mate Tim Kaine headed to Longwood University, in rural Virginia, to debate, he was well established as Trump's explainer-in-chief. Some of the wags had a more colorful name for him, "pooper-scooper-in-chief," because he was cleaning up so many Trump messes. Pence prepped with Wisconsin governor Scott Walker playing the role of Kaine in mock debates, preparing for the real face-off. The preparation would pay off.

The VP Debate, October 4, 2016

The last Hoosier running mate to take the national debate stage made history. In 1988, Dan Quayle had been toying with some rebuttals to the expected knock on his youth and inexperience, including a reference to John F. Kennedy. His advisers, including a very young Mitch Daniels, cautioned against the retort. But Quayle went ahead anyway. "I have as much experience in the Congress as Jack Kennedy did when he sought the presidency." His opponent, Democrat Lloyd Bentsen, held back a grin and shook his head slightly but waited his turn. "Senator, I served with Jack Kennedy, I knew Jack Kennedy, Jack Kennedy was a friend of mine," Bentsen said, as he turned to look at Quayle.

Quayle only looked straight ahead, his hands fidgeting—he knew exactly where this was going. "Senator, you're no Jack Kennedy." The audience at the Civic Auditorium in Omaha, Nebraska, burst into applause. And Dan Quayle was etched in the history books before ever taking office.

Pence wasn't looking to make history, exactly, but he did hope to elevate himself as presidential timber. Inside the Pence operation, his political team had been planning on a Trump loss in just one more month. Pence's small band of advisers had let Republican donors know that if the Trump campaign went down in flames on November 8, Pence planned to be the first one out of the gate for the 2020 nomination. But Pence also had his current job to think about, and Trump hadn't made it any easier for him in the six weeks since they linked arms in Cleveland.

On Tuesday, October 4, 2016, he took his seat across the table from Virginia senator Tim Kaine, Clinton's running mate. Longwood University in Farmville, Virginia, hosted the sole debate of the running mates; Elaine Quijano of CBS News moderated. The meeting between Pence and Kaine was later dubbed "The Dad Debate" because, frankly, both men seemed like such nice guys. But Pence would have no problem tearing apart his opponent, even while keeping up the polite demeanor. The man who shredded former representative Phil Sharp on a debate stage twenty-six years earlier had wizened greatly since then, but kept some of that innate timing and parrying skill that made him such a threat.

Quijano cut straight to the chase with her first question—why should either man be qualified to fill the role of president should tragedy strike? "What about your qualities, your skills, and your temperament equip you to step into that role at a moment's notice?"

Pence used the answer to deliver a brief portrait, "I have to tell you, I'm a small-town boy from a place not too different from Farmville. I grew up with a cornfield in my backyard." Then he continued, "I would hope that if the responsibility ever fell to me in this role, that

I would meet it with the way that I'm going to meet the responsibility should I be elected vice president of the United States. And that's to bring a lifetime of experience, a lifetime growing up in a small town. A lifetime where I've served in the Congress of the United States, where I've led a state that works, in the great state of Indiana. And whatever other responsibilities might follow from this, I would hope and, frankly, I would pray to be able to meet that moment with that lifetime of experience."

As Pence answered the question, he looked straight into his camera and delivered his answer directly to the viewers. He was at home on the debate stage, comfortable in the Herman Miller Aeron chair, one foot resting against the base of the chair, the other a little bit forward as he clasped his hands together. Kaine was stiff, with his feet crossed beneath his chair, his back straightened out, and his chest puffed out a bit. ✎

Kaine did not wait long, however, to land his first hit on Trump. "As a candidate, he started his campaign with a speech where he called Mexicans rapists and criminals and he has pursued the discredited and really outrageous lie that President Obama wasn't born in the United States. It is so painful to suggest that we go back to think about these days where an African American could not be a citizen of the United States. And I can't imagine how Governor Pence can defend the insult-driven, selfish, me-first style of Donald Trump."

But Pence threw it back in Kaine's face, "Let me say first and foremost that, Senator, you and Hillary Clinton would know a lot about an insult-driven campaign." The quip sounded great in the moment, even if it was a non sequitur.

Kaine shot back with the big guns, "You guys love Russia! You love Russia!" Kaine wasn't entirely off with the statement; in an odd (even for this campaign) blip the last month, Trump mentioned that he thought Russian president Vladimir Putin was a strong leader, stronger than President Barack Obama. Pence was asked about Trump's assessment at the time, and he echoed it—What else could he do? Contradict his new boss?

"These guys have praised Vladimir Putin as a great leader," Kaine shouted, as Pence attempted to answer the question. Pence snipped back, "I must have hit a nerve here."

But the Russia piece was a little odd, even for Pence, and later in the debate he distanced himself from Trump on one of the most important foreign policy questions he might face if he ever became president. "You know there's an old proverb that says the Russian bear never dies, it just hibernates," Pence said, citing an aphorism he'd just coined onstage. "And the truth of the matter is the weak and feckless policy of Hillary Clinton and Barack Obama has awakened an aggression in Russia that first appeared few years ago with their move in Georgia, now their move into Crimea, now their move into the wider Middle East, and all the while, all we do is fold our arms and say we're not having talks anymore."

Veteran *Los Angeles Times* political correspondent Doyle McManus read into the significance of that break from Trump in his post-debate analysis. "On Syria and Russia, Pence wandered way off the Trump reservation, calling for a US-guaranteed safe zone in Syria (and possible US airstrikes against the Syrian army) and denouncing Vladimir Putin as a threat to the West," he wrote. "Those positions both break with Trump's—but they're squarely in the GOP mainstream, leading plenty of pundits to wonder whether Pence is running for the 2020 nomination already."

AND THEN, *ACCESS HOLLYWOOD*

A few days later, that chance seemed to appear as Mike Pence stood around admiring hot dog buns; all he had to do was say "Yes."

It was Friday, October 7, 2016, a surprisingly warm fall afternoon in Toledo, Ohio. Pence stood at the counter of Tony Packo's Café, chatting up diners at the legendary hot dog joint. The sleeves of his white shirt were rolled up, but his collar was still buttoned and the red-striped tie still perfectly knotted. This stop, the look, the energy in the place was all vintage campaign trail stuff and Pence was totally in his element and riding high. He thrived on the pomp and circumstance, he loved working a room. Donald Trump had been through Packo's earlier and completed the tradition of signing the hot dog bun that would join the dozens of other famous buns hung on the walls inside the restaurant—Barack Obama, George W. Bush—it was a campaign rite of passage for presidential contenders. Now it was Pence's turn. The assembled reporters from all the major networks huddled just down the bar, waiting for their shots. Pence was not exactly a compelling, news-making running mate.

On the rare chance that Pence did get some press, it usually went well for him—his surprise selection as running mate just a few months earlier reinserted him in the national conversation; his stellar performance on the national debate stage against Kaine had raised his profile even higher. Pence appeared a sane salve to the disaster of Trump: the insults; the bullying; his history of cheating, on his wives, on contracts—Pence magically shook it all off. If anything stuck, it stuck to Trump, but Pence just squared his shoulders a bit, took a breath, nodded slightly—just like Ronald Reagan used to do—and delivered his lines. He was remarkably good at it; he even took the fatal flaws of Trump and made them into a tale where Trump was the scrappy underdog. "Invariably they'll say, 'This time we got him, right?'" Pence said. "This time we found that there's another tweet that's come out or something. This time we got another thing, another issue that's come forward. Then they turn on the television the next morning, and Donald Trump is still standing stronger than ever before."

But halfway through the hot dog stop, the script stopped rolling. The reporters suddenly stopped looking at Pence and began checking their phones—all of them. "He appeared to grow suspicious," NBC reporter Vaughn Hillyard noted. Pence's aide Marc Lotter ducked in the back where Pence had been shuffled away with several other aides and showed the candidate his phone. Lotter returned a few minutes later and told the reporters to get out. Pence wouldn't be stopping in to see the hot dog bun Trump had signed, he wouldn't be signing his own, and there wouldn't be anything more to see here.

The Washington Post had just revealed a tape of Donald Trump bragging about abusing women. It was a hot mic moment from a 2005 episode of *Access Hollywood*. Trump bantered with show host Billy Bush, the nephew of former Florida governor Jeb Bush, about how easy it was for him to get whatever he wants from women because he's rich and famous. As Trump and Billy Bush rode on their *Access Hollywood* tour bus en route to the studio, they spied their cohost in the parking lot—tall and slender soap star Arianne Zucker. Trump said he better get ready, "I better use some Tic Tacs just in case I start kissing her. You know, I'm automatically attracted to beautiful— I just start kissing them. It's like a magnet. Just kiss. I don't even wait. And when you're a star, they let you do it. You can do anything." That's right, Billy Bush said, "Whatever you want." Yeah, Trump said, "Grab 'em by the pussy. You can do anything."

As Pence booked it out the back of Tony Packo's, the twentysomething-year-old campaign embeds from the networks looked around. Now, they had some tougher questions than the mechanics of signing spongy white hot dog buns. Did Pence support a womanizer for president? Someone who, by his own words, had molested women.

Meanwhile, within a half hour of the news breaking, WikiLeaks began posting thousands of emails from the Gmail account of Clinton campaign chairman John Podesta. The emails had been stolen in a hack that Democratic cybersecurity experts traced to Russia—it seemed awfully convenient that when the biggest "October surprise" to land in modern American politics dropped on the head of Trump, a half hour later an equally startling "surprise" landed at the feet of the Clinton campaign. It was whiplash for the American public.

The Pence campaign entourage began blocking and tackling, shuffling the reporters away. Pence only had one more public event to survive on his Friday swing, down the road in Rossford, Ohio, then he was home free—he could vanish without having to cancel any events and raise even more questions. On the rope line in Rossford a few hours later, a reporter demanded an answer—Did he still support Trump? Pence ignored the question.

And then he vanished.

A REQUIRED RESPONSE

The first calls from the RNC donors started coming into Marty Obst around 6:30 P.M. The Republican Party had a contingency plan, to remove Donald Trump from the ticket and replace him with Mike Pence as the nominee. Pence didn't even have to say yes, the RNC would just do it, to protect the party.

Reince Priebus and a small group of his top deputies had been preparing for just an event such as the *Access Hollywood* tape. Rumors of incredible comments Trump had made in other tapings had swirled through the election season, and Priebus and his team were certain one of them would eventually make it out into the open. So, when the *Access Hollywood* tape aired, the RNC was ready.

As a practical matter, it would be impossible to throw another party nominating convention on such short notice, and ballots had already been printed in most states—hell, in many states voters had already started casting early ballots. It would be impossible to change those votes and may even be impossible to remove Trump from the printed ballots, a matter the GOP's seasoned election lawyers were already chewing through on Friday night. But this measure was not about winning the presidency, it was about salvaging the party down ballot—saving the rest of the races that they would have to pry from under the wreckage of Trump's Tic Tac strategy. The Party of Reagan and Lincoln would be known as the Party of Grab 'Em by the Pussy.

The mechanism was convoluted, but not technically impossible—Pence had been nominated by the full convention of delegates in Cleveland, so he was approved already. This would give the RNC political cover. But the actual decision could be made solely by the 168 members of the RNC selected to represent the 56 states and territories—they wrote the rules of their party and could rewrite the rules at any time to designate another nominee.

A few select donors were designated to deliver the message to Pence, using backchannels, a standard practice in sensitive matters, to give Priebus and his team complete deniability if word ever leaked out. Marty listened as the calls came in, and he beat them back. He said, "Mike is too loyal for that. We made a commitment to this guy, he goes down, we go down. That's how this works."

Christie called up Pence that evening to see how he was doing. Pence said he just wanted to focus on getting Trump ready for the presidential debate coming up that Sunday. Pence said he was keeping his head down and focusing on the work.

Mike and Karen hadn't said what they were doing; all they had said was they had to pray. But the truth was, they didn't even know what they were going to do.

Helping remove Trump from the ticket would be political suicide for Pence—he'd lose the general election in a blowout by Clinton and he'd be known by the new base of the Republican Party, Trump's base of supporters, as a traitor and a snake. It would end his career.

No, the Pences had to consider another option, maybe they should resign from the ticket. It wouldn't be surprising, given Trump's comments. And Karen was livid—how could they face their daughters, and son, if they supported such defiling behavior by the man who wanted to become the most powerful man in the world? But dropping off the ticket also felt impossible—they had already hitched their fortunes to Trump; for so long, this was what they had prayed for and hoped for.

Pence's small team of advisers had to plot out the weekend—they huddled. There was a rally the next day in the critical swing state of Wisconsin, so making any move there was off the table, but the private, closed-door fund raiser in Newport, Rhode Island, Saturday night might be workable. They decided Pence should put out a statement saying he was "disappointed" in Trump, but not go any further than that—neither supporting nor condemning—until after Trump's debate performance Sunday night. Nobody wanted Pence to take over the Republican nomination from Trump, but his team of advisers were split on whether he should leave the ticket or stay.

While the Pences hunkered down at the governor's mansion Saturday morning, Trump gathered his team at his residence in Trump Tower in Manhattan. Reince Priebus confronted Trump and told him to step down from the ticket or lose in a landslide—he never mentioned the contingency plan the RNC worked out to remove Trump and replace him with Pence. Steve Bannon told Trump to stick to his guns. ☉

Republican senators who had suffered through a soul-crushing campaign finally cracked. "Donald Trump should withdraw and Mike Pence should be our nominee effective immediately," Republican senator John Thune tweeted. New Hampshire Republican senator Kelly Ayotte said that she would not support Trump or Clinton but would write in Mike Pence. Former Utah governor Jon Huntsman joined the chorus, as did former candidate and Hewlett-Packard CEO Carly Fiorina.

Priebus's chief of staff, Katie Walsh, tried to get Priebus, House Speaker Paul Ryan, and Senate Majority Leader Mitch McConnell to sign a joint statement calling on Trump to step down, but McConnell balked at the idea.

Shortly before noon, Pence put out a carefully hedged statement—he found Trump's comments reprehensible, could not condone any of them, and was praying for Trump.

Friends and colleagues called Pence repeatedly; they texted their pleas. "Please leave the ticket, save yourself," they begged. But Pence knew that Trump was the future of the Republican Party; the yowling from the politicians and elites inside the Washington bubble were the past. He had picked up on the rumbling of Trump support in rural white America a year ago, as he fought for his own reelection, and his sense that Trump owned the Republican Party base only increased once he joined the ticket and saw the passion of Trump's legions for himself.

Finally, after eighteen hours of trying to get through to Pence, Trump connected with his running mate around noon on Saturday. He apologized, he said that wasn't the man he was today. Then he asked to speak with Karen. Trump paused a second, waited for Mike to hand the phone to Karen, and apologized profusely to her. He couldn't be sure if it worked; Mike and Karen were still praying.

A few hours later, Mike and Karen Pence and Marty Obst boarded the campaign plane to fly to Rhode Island for their fund raiser. They were staying on the ticket. Still, to be safe, Pence would stay out of public view at least another twenty-four hours until the storm passed. Pence's traveling press corps were cordoned off inside a separate plane, unable to squeeze in a single question.

Mike and Karen Pence sat with Marty on the flight to Rhode Island and laughed. "Well, here we are again." Supporters got cold feet with Pence after the RFRA blowup, and now there were suddenly fewer campaign staff and fans who wanted to fly with him to a Trump fund raiser. Things got hot and the fair-weather friends disappeared.

Marty looked to Karen, whom he'd worked as closely with as Mike for the last decade, and asked her straight up, "Tell me how you feel about this, between you and me, as friends." Karen answered, "You know what, Marty, I told Mike that we knew we were signing up for something unique. We knew there'd be times he'd say and do things we'd never do. We understood that. All the trepidation about—well, he says things off the cuff—we settled in our hearts before we decided to do this. Obviously, it's disappointing, but it doesn't change the mission."

Pence fired up the Rhode Island crowd that night. He said that Trump was a good man, that people make mistakes, and that he was proud to stand with Trump. Pence sensed that Trump's "grab 'em by the pussy" comment might not be as big a deal to voters as it was to the chattering class in Washington. Trump's comments certainly didn't seem to matter to the New England blue bloods in Newport.

The Pences flew back to Indianapolis and hid out in the governor's mansion. They may have been willing to tell friends they were sticking with Trump, but they weren't ready to tell the public.

The calls from Republican donors and operatives promising to make Pence the nominee if he would help push Trump off the ticket continued coming in, but now they were easier to ignore.

PENCE LOCKS IN

The Trump campaign, meanwhile, cooked up a novel attack: Trump's words might be bad, but Bill Clinton's actions were worse. To prove their point, they invited Juanita Broaddrick, Paula Jones, and Kathleen Willey to join them at the next presidential debate. All three women had accused former president Bill Clinton of either sexually assaulting them or forcing himself on them. Trump and his team tried to have the women walk in the debate hall the same time as Bill Clinton himself, but the Presidential Debate Commission blocked that. Still, the broader stunt worked—if Trump had bragged about sexual assault, here was proof that the husband of the Democratic nominee was an actual assailant.

Mike and Karen and a few close aides watched Trump's performance intently in the study of the governor's mansion. This was their last exit ramp if they wanted off. But they liked his performance; they were still on board. After the debate Trump called up Pence and said, "You know, Mike, I was just telling everyone how loyal you are. I was telling Jared how loyal you are. A lot of people who were supposed to be my friends were trying to get me out of this race. A lot of people were trying to plot my demise. And you know what Mike Pence did? He got on a fucking plane to Rhode Island and raised money."

Pence looked over at Obst and beamed.

Monday morning, three days after the *Access Hollywood* tape exploded, Pence finally reappeared in public. "Last night my running mate, he showed the American people what was in his heart and he showed humility to the American people, and then he fought back and turned the focus to the choice that we face, and I am proud to stand with Donald Trump." Had Pence considered leaving the ticket? Not at all. The truth he didn't state was that it would have been political suicide to ditch Trump; he had gotten himself within sight of the big prize and he wasn't about to head back into the political wilds now. Steady Mike Pence didn't have to usurp Trump to become president, he was already on his way to winning the Oval Office by playing a cunning long game while exercising Herculean discipline. It was a strategy he'd been perfecting for four decades.

Pence was savvy enough to know that the ground had shifted beneath the feet of Republicans since Trump entered the race. There was a conservative, white, populist anger that had been building for decades—visible in campaigns like Pat Buchanan's—and it could no longer be ignored. This was the new base of the Republican Party, and to kill their king would have been ruinous. Besides, Pence only had to wait one more month and he could run for president in 2020 in his own right.

In the waning weeks of the campaign, Mike Pence tried a new message, one that captured the tone of the moment—and why he was selected as Trump's running mate in the first place. "I want to submit to all of you, it's time to reach out to all of our Republican and conservative friends and say with one voice: 'It's time to come home and elect Donald Trump as the next president of the United States,'" Pence said on October 24, at a campaign rally in Salisbury, California. "It's time to come home and come together and do everything in our power to make sure that Hillary Clinton is never elected president of the United States of America."

On October 28, 2016, FBI director James Comey delivered the unlikeliest of gifts to the Trump campaign. He wrote in a letter to House Republicans that investigators had discovered a new cache of Hillary Clinton emails. With about one week left until the election, it sounded as though the FBI was reopening its probe—politically, it was gold for the Trump campaign. The chants of "Lock her up!"; the woman paid—unwittingly—by Russian trolls to dress up as Clinton, locked in a fake prison cell; even Trump's own (half-joking) insistence that Russian hackers find the emails Clinton had wiped from her server—it all played into one central story line, that Hillary Clinton could not be trusted. And now the FBI director of a Democratic administration had just reinforced that narrative—and swept away any lingering coverage of Trump's *Access Hollywood* comments once and for all.

THE COMPLICATIONS OF WINNING

On Election Night, November 8, the Pences gathered with the rest of Trump's brass at the Hilton in midtown Manhattan. Pence told some Trump aides he was confident they would win, but nobody seemed to believe him—they took it more as natural optimism than any sort of insightful analysis. Indeed, everyone who had done serious analysis had more or less called the race for Clinton at the start of the evening. National polling aggregator and analyst website FiveThirtyEight—a nod to the total number of electoral votes at stake—closed its books on 2016 giving Clinton a 71.4 percent chance of winning. Key to that assessment were sunny forecasts for her in states like Florida and Virginia.

Then Trump did the impossible—he swept the Rust Belt, and he won every swing state he needed—from Pennsylvania to Florida. The win was a little awkward for Pence, how was he supposed to run in 2020 if he was in the White House as vice president? Trump losing would have meant a win for Pence, because he would have gained a strong footing for his own in 2020. Pence was going to have to spend at least another four years doing this dance, playing cleanup and acting as though Trump's foul mouth didn't bother him. Trump's aides universally credited Pence with putting them over the top, bringing home the conservatives and bringing in the evangelicals just as he was supposed to.

Early in the morning of Wednesday, November 9, Hillary Clinton called Donald Trump and conceded. After Trump took the call, Mike Pence leaned in to kiss Karen, but she rebuffed him. "You got what you wanted, Mike. Leave me alone." Upstairs, at the Pence's private suite—separate from the Trump's—he tried again for a victory kiss, and again she told him to back off.

Later Wednesday, after they had all gotten a few hours of sleep, they gathered at Trump Hotel for a briefing about transitioning to full-blown Secret Service protection. When Trump said he wanted to fly a helicopter from his New York office to Washington, DC—some of the Secret Service agents turned pale. The new president didn't get it. As the agents briefed them on what would happen, Karen burst out, "What are we going to do, Mike?? We don't have any money! Who's going to pay for my inaugural gown??" Mike got up and walked with her out of the room. But she was right, they were stuck. They didn't have much money, certainly not enough to make a big move to Washington on their own. They had been making student loan payments for their three, now grown, children and living solely off Mike's salary as governor, which was not stellar—$112,000. They hadn't had to pay a mortgage for four years, a major boon, but now they would have to move back to Washington with almost no savings. Worse yet, they looked poor standing next to Donald and Melania Trump. Pence carried $30,000 in credit card debt a decade earlier; a Trump aide joked that Trump didn't know what $30,000 in debt was, but probably had that much cash on him at any time.

Chris Christie had been directing the Trump presidential transition since the summer, and the other brass in the Trump campaign had barely given it notice—because they were supposed to lose. But after they won, the power centers circling Trump began vying for control of the new administration. At the top of the pyramid sat Trump's son-in-law and senior adviser, Jared Kushner, RNC chairman Reince Priebus, and campaign adviser and conservative nationalist Steve Bannon. All three represented various warring factions of the unique coalition that formed to elect Trump: Kushner, the Trump family, and New York elite; Priebus, the Republican establishment, and national megadonors; and Bannon, the reactionary nationalist base of white anger embodied by the Tea Party and other nationalist precursors to Trump. The director of the transition was a strong position indeed, an opportunity for each respective power base to get its own people in to hold the reins of government—from the State Department to the Interior Department and all agencies in between. Of the three, Kushner and Bannon were not particular fans of Christie, and they wanted him gone.

That Friday morning, November 11, Christie chatted with Pence as they plotted out next steps for the administration. A few hours later, Bannon called Christie, saying he was replacing him with Pence. They had found someone who Christie couldn't argue with, someone affable and respected. But why hadn't Pence told his old friend earlier in the day that this was coming? Did he not know himself? Was he hiding it? Christie didn't know. In just four months, Pence had cock-blocked Christie a second time—first it was for the spot as Trump's running mate, and now for the director of transition. But Trump's aides knew that Pence wouldn't actually direct the transition, instead he was a marginal figurehead—one with important ties to the conservative movement, but one with limited influence over Trump himself.

After a few weeks, Karen went to Marty Obst and demanded money for them. Obst went to the presidential inaugural committee to ask for help; initially they wanted $1.5 million transferred to the fund that pays for the VP's residence at the U.S. Naval Observatory. Karen argued with Mike, until finally he asked Trump for help. Trump found a way, transferring $750,000 from the Presidential Inaugural Committee to the Vice President's Residence Foundation. Normally the foundation was a staid affair that furnished the home at the U.S. Naval Observatory, but workers on the inaugural committee suspected the money was to help the Pences out in their financial pinch. The inaugural committee also paid for a ball gown for her, but when she got it, she didn't like it—so she had her favorite tailor in Indianapolis craft another one from the original gown and new materials. She submitted two invoices to the inaugural committee, one for $110 and another for the full cost of the original gown.

The Pence family prepared another move back to Washington. And this time with more help and quite a bit more stature. They rented a home in a wealthy Washington neighborhood, just across the border from Maryland—and were promptly welcomed by pro-LGBT protesters. After close to two years of being a national target, this didn't faze Pence much anymore; besides he was going to the White House. Their children were grown and moved out—Michael Jr. serving in the Marines, Charlotte in film school in California, and their youngest, the liberal rebel, Audrey, was attending Yale Law School. Mike and Karen had to settle back into Washington, but it was just the two of them—as it had been three decades earlier when they moved for Mike's first run for Congress. They looked for a place to worship, and quickly settled on an evangelical Anglican church with a popular national rector, the Falls Church, in the Northern Virginia suburb, not far from where they lived when Mike was a congressman.

A lot was happening. Their oldest son, Michael Jr., had proposed not long before to his college sweetheart and they were preparing to get married before he shipped off. It would be a small wedding, for now, because they needed to legalize their union so she could live on base with him and also receive military benefits. They would have a larger wedding ceremony later, when the couple wasn't pressed for time. Also, Michael Jr. and his fiancée had to approach Mike and Karen with a tough question: Could her gay best friend be the Man of Honor in their wedding? Of course, Mike and Karen agreed.

Mike and Karen had a long history of opposing LGBT rights, and making some vituperative statements about gay folks, but the world was changing, and they were evolving. Did that mean they now supported marriage rights for LGBT citizens and protections against hate crimes? They wouldn't say; this only meant they don't hate gay people for who they were. One friend explained their stance this way, "Love the sinner, hate the sin." Which, of course, meant they still saw love between gay couples as a sin. They weren't ready to acknowledge marriage for same-sex couples and protections for LGBT residents, which would violate their conservative evangelical religious beliefs, but they also wouldn't stand in the way of their children as they decided how to live their own lives. The greater reality was that no matter what, the world was watching Mike and Karen's every move.

A DIFFICULT TRANSITION

Just before New Year's 2017, as it became clear that Russia had successfully pulled off a stunning propaganda and disinformation attack on the 2016 election, Obama finally delivered the forceful response his supporters had been yearning for. Obama expelled dozens of Russian diplomats from the United States—many suspected of being spies—and shuttered some Russian compounds, including one not far from Washington on Maryland's Eastern Shore. That same day, December 29, 2016, retired lieutenant general Michael Flynn, Trump's designated national security adviser, called Russian ambassador Sergey Kislyak and determined he should raise the possibility of repealing sanctions on Russia. The call immediately drew the attention of American intelligence concerned that Flynn may be undermining the United States.

Michael Flynn had a distinguished military career—but exited the armed services under a cloud. By 2014, American intelligence had worried that Flynn, the head of the Defense Intelligence Agency, was being corrupted by Russia. He was forced out months later, and he quickly set up an intelligence consulting firm. In 2015, Flynn was honored as a special guest for Russia's state television—RT—paid $45,000 for the event, and seated next to Russian president Vladimir Putin at the dinner.

By the time Flynn joined the Trump campaign, he had morphed into one of Obama's sharpest critics, targeting Democrats on their handling of ISIS and the war in Syria. When Trump pulled off the win, Flynn was one of the few campaign advisers with serious national security training on his team—and he was quickly brought in on classified briefings. Soon he became Trump's national security adviser.

Pence, meanwhile, continued pushing his picks for cabinet spots and influential posts in the incoming White House, although Kushner and Bannon clearly dominated in that arena. Pence carved out some early victories. Health and Human Services quickly became an outpost for Pence's operation. Pence's old ally from the House, Representative Tom Price, was tabbed HHS secretary. The architect of Indiana's Medicaid expansion, Seema Verma, was picked to oversee the entire Medicaid program at the Centers for Medicare and Medicaid Services. Indiana's public health commissioner, Jerome Adams, was even selected to serve as the nation's twentieth surgeon general. And Pence's longtime communications expert, Matt Lloyd, was sent to HHS with the important task of helping coordinate the repeal of Obamacare.

But Pence also struck out. One of his old allies from the House, Representative Scott Garrett, was picked to run the Export Import Bank, but Republicans on the Senate Banking Committee broke rank and blocked Garrett's nomination after some intensive behind-the-scenes lobbying. Establishment Republicans didn't want Garrett running the trade bank that he was actively trying to eliminate.

The incoming Trump administration also continued parsing who would fill what roles in the new White House. Repealing Obamacare was their chief priority when they took office, and Trump recalled that Pence's biggest supporters, including Kellyanne Conway, had pitched him as a stellar emissary to Capitol Hill based on his years of experience in Congress. Trump and his top advisers quickly decided Pence should take the lead on health care, and Pence's close adviser Marc Short was tabbed as the chief White House lobbyist. But what nobody said, or very well knew, was that Pence had never been a vote-wrangler in Congress—he didn't know how to twist arms to win over tough votes. He was more like everyone's friend, and had never gotten into the nitty-gritty of vote-trading when he was there—that had been Eric Cantor's job, as the Republican whip.

In public, Pence was happy to have the role of transition director and did little to downplay stories of his lack of influence. This ended up being beneficial in certain cases.

On Sunday, January 15, 2017, just a few days before the inauguration, Pence went on CBS's *Face the Nation*. He knew a little by now about being ready for Sunday shows, and the day before he had called Flynn to ask for himself: Was it true that he had discussed lifting the sanctions on Russia with Kislyak? Flynn gave an unequivocal "No."

As he sat across from CBS's John Dickerson, Pence was confident nothing untoward had taken place. "I talked to General Flynn about that conversation and actually it was initiated on Christmas Day. He had sent a text to the Russian ambassador to express not only Christmas wishes but sympathy for the loss of life in the airplane crash that took place. It was strictly coincidental that they had a conversation. They did not discuss anything having to do with the United States decision to expel diplomats or expose censure against Russia."

Dickerson drilled down, "So did they ever have a discussion about sanctions on those days or any other day?"

Unlike his showdown with George Stephanopoulos three years earlier, Pence was completely unequivocal, "What I can confirm, having spoken to him about it, is that those conversations that happened to occur around the time that the United States took action to expel diplomats had nothing to do with those sanctions."

On January 20, 2017, Donald Trump walked through the west entrance to the Capitol building and peered out upon the National Mall—half filled with his supporters. Trump delivered an attack on the political establishment that sounded more like one of his campaign speeches than a presidential inaugural. "For too long, a small group in our nation's capital has reaped the rewards of government while the people have borne the cost," Trump said. "Politicians prospered—but the jobs left, and the factories closed. The establishment protected itself, but not the citizens of our country."

Mike and Karen Pence stood on the dais, looking out on the National Mall, with the departing President Barack Obama, First Lady Michele Obama, Vice President Joe Biden, and Second Lady Jill Biden. The vice president doesn't give an inaugural speech, but Pence enjoyed his own, quiet slice of history, taking the oath of office on Ronald Reagan's Bible, as administered by Supreme Court Justice Clarence Thomas. Trump's campaign advisers knew they would not be there without Pence; he had delivered the quiet evangelical vote, he had "brought home" conservative voters. Pence stood firm during the *Access Hollywood* debacle three months earlier and rebuffed efforts to remove Trump from the ticket.

"I don't think he would have won the election without Mike," said David McIntosh, Pence's longtime friend. And Pence seemed almost built for the Trump White House, the only one with the tools to survive it. "The discipline, on-message, and the steadiness that allow him . . . the chaos continues, right, in the West Wing. But Mike's very steady about it and Trump's come to appreciate that. But the humility lets him take the second seat and never deviate from that. And that, too, is necessary in a Trump presidency."

Inside the Capitol, Pence's family mingled with the leaders of the free world—the leaders of the new White House and of Congress. Greg Pence and his wife, Denise Pence, smiled for photos from the traditional lunch, hosted in Statuary Hall, just outside the House Chamber. There was already some chatter that Greg Pence might run for his brother's old congressional seat. Mike Pence beamed.

But chaos lurked beneath the surface.

A week after the inauguration, Acting Attorney General Sally Yates—an Obama holdover—alerted Trump's chief counsel of the results of an FBI interview with Flynn. Flynn had lied about his discussion with the Russian ambassador, Kislyak. The United States' national security adviser—an official privy to the nation's most sensitive intelligence who had the ear of the president—may have been compromised by the Russians. The Trump administration took the warning under advisement—and did nothing, until the *Wall Street Journal* broke the news of Flynn's calls. Then, on February 13, 2017, Trump fired Flynn—his reason? Because Flynn had sullied his vice president's honor by forcing him to lie on television. Trump later added that he fired Flynn because he had lied to the FBI—but who really knew? The answer could keep shifting and morphing until he was forced to deliver it under oath.

THE NEW VICE PRESIDENT'S OFFICE

Trump's White House aides quickly picked up on two things about the new vice president: he enjoyed the trappings of power; and he was awestruck by people with incalculable wealth, like the Trumps. Pence had always loved the pomp and circumstance of political office—the history, the regalia, the stagecraft. His ceremonial office, just across the street from the White House in the Eisenhower Executive Office Building, held one of his favorite new treasures—the Theodore Roosevelt desk. Roosevelt first used the desk in 1902, and it was used by other presidents, until the 1960s, when President John F. Kennedy brought the Resolute desk to the Oval Office. The Roosevelt desk was then moved to the vice president's office. Shortly after Richard Nixon took office, he began working out of the Eisenhower building—and a small hole appeared in the top left side of the desktop. Presidential historians surmised this was where Nixon ran the wires from his microphone to his hidden taping contraption.

Mike Pence did most of his work out of the smaller vice president's office in the West Wing—just down the hall from the Oval Office, where Trump would take many of his meetings. This allowed him to be present for almost every meeting—his chief of staff, longtime aide Josh Pitcock, helped ensure Pence was in the room as often as possible. But when Pence sat through those meetings, he hardly said a word—he nodded and smiled in sync with Trump's proclamations. White House aides began to wonder precisely what Pence was doing—he kind of resembled a coatrack at times, there but not entirely present.

It was a tough job being number two to a man like Trump. And the warring factions vying for influence over Trump only made it harder. Steve Bannon tried to pull Trump toward more radical nationalism, Chief of Staff Reince Priebus tried to keep him in line with the Republican Party's donor class. And Pence stayed quiet. There was a reason for this, said one former aide—Pence was taking some advice from former vice presidents he had consulted before taking office: always be the last man in the room with the president, save your comments for him, and don't take sides in staff fights—and there will be plenty of staff fights. Pence, who tended to take things by the book a little too literally, thus blended in with the furniture.

Pence had another role in the nascent administration—selling Congress on Trump's priorities. The first order of business for Pence was repealing Obamacare, something every Republican in the chamber had run on year in and year out since the plan passed, and something they all promised was a top priority. Still, it was much easier to rip on Obamacare when they knew Obama would veto any effort— now they had to figure out a way to replace key pieces of the legislation if they repealed it, or at the very least ensure that markets didn't crumble and millions of Americans lose their insurance as the result of any kind of Republican dismantle. And Pence was there, chief lobbyist for the White House, to ply his former colleagues.

On the first floor of the Capitol building, tucked down the hall from House Democratic whip Steny Hoyer's office, was Mike Pence's new office in the Congress. It faced south, with a nice view of the Mall and the Washington Monument. Every vice president has had quarters just off the Senate floor, because the vice president is the technical leader of the Senate. And Pence immediately drew attention for his role as the Senate's tiebreaker, casting decisive votes in favor of Trump's cabinet nominees who would've gone down in flames without his vote. But Pence's House office gave him another kind of access to his favorite chamber. It was conveniently located one floor below the House chamber, a quick hop down a marble staircase. Some weeks, especially as things got heavy that spring, Pence would pop into the office for a few days straight and camp out. The lobbyist was in and he was seeing new clients. House Republicans ducked in for a half-hour chat, and then back out. Pence would wave to the throngs of Capitol Hill reporters every day, never uttering a word about the conversations he'd had.

Pence and his small band of advisers had sold Trump on his impeccable skills working the halls of Congress. But Pence had two problems that were not apparent to most people: he had never successfully passed a piece of legislation in his twelve years in Congress, and many of the Republicans he called colleagues had long since been replaced or vacated the chamber. Furthermore, Pence was no longer the most conservative member of that chamber. The group he used to chair, the Republican Study Committee, had become the effective center of the House Republican Conference. The "new" Republican Study Committee, the new hard Right rabble-rousers, were the members of the House Freedom Caucus. And Mike Pence, conservative icon, hardly knew any them.

Republicans had spent eight years trashing the Democratic healthcare overhaul, but now that they were in power, they ran up against the same political winds that forced Obamacare to look like such a political Frankenstein's monster to begin with. Conservatives wanted a complete and total repeal of the law, moderate Republicans wanted to protect certain pieces of it—and the House GOP leadership couldn't figure out how to find the 218 votes needed to pass the House.

In private meetings at the White House, Pence consistently reassured Trump that they would have the votes needed to do away with Obamacare, create a new health-care plan, and put a bill on the president's desk. But Pence's own longtime adviser and confidant, Marc Short, consistently delivered a more pessimistic message to Trump—that the votes would be almost impossible to come by.

Short was right.

THE RUSSIA INVESTIGATION HEATS UP

Pence's big whiff on health care hurt him with Trump—they'd only been working together less than a year at that point, and had never truly developed a close relationship. Trump's anger at the loss drove a wedge between the two, Trump advisers noticed.

However, even with the Obamacare repeal failure, Trump had already been a boon for conservatives. Conservative stalwarts, who opposed environmental regulations, who opposed access to abortions and a whole host of other key items, were now at the table with the president—they were his cabinet. Had he not been discovered in the grade-change scandal four years earlier, Indiana's Tony Bennett may have even been the national education secretary. Instead that job fell to the woman who bankrolled Bennett and scores of other conservative activists, Betsy DeVos. Conservatives even got a justice on the Supreme Court—scot-free—Coloradoan Neil Gorsuch. And Senate Majority Leader Mitch McConnell did away with the filibuster for Supreme Court nominees, five years after his Democratic predecessor, Harry Reid, had removed that obstacle for lower-court nominees. The Trump administration—or more specifically, conservatives—were filling the courts.

But the Russia question just nagged, and nagged, and nagged.

Every week seemed to reveal more contacts, more involvement, more insinuation. Just a few weeks after Trump fired Flynn, the *Washington Post* reported that Trump's own attorney general, Jeff Sessions, had also had multiple meetings with Kislyak—none of them disclosed. Sessions held a press conference to announce that he was recusing himself from any investigation into relations between Russia and the Trump campaign that may or may not exist. (He wanted to be clear he wasn't confirming or denying the existence of any investigation.) In reality the FBI had been investigating contacts between the campaign and Russian operatives since July of 2016. And it was one of Trump's closest allies who inadvertently let the cat out of the bag.

In March, a few weeks after Sessions stepped aside, House Intelligence chairman Devin Nunes hosted FBI director James Comey for a rare public hearing of a panel that otherwise worked in secret. This panel was conducting their own investigation of Russian meddling. Packed into the giant joint hearing room in the Longworth House Office Building—it was stunningly cold in the room, almost as though the air-conditioning were on overdrive—on March 20, 2017, Comey shocked the world: the FBI had been investigating possible collusion between the Trump campaign and Russia since the preceding July. (The next night, Nunes, who had been vying for the job of Trump's CIA director months earlier, took a secret trip to the White House to begin paying his penance: he was about to launch the counterinvestigation that would help deflect attention away from the Russia ties.) ⍩

The constant revelations, the drip, drip, drip was driving Trump mad. He had already withstood plenty of attacks on his fragile ego—the crowd sizes on the inauguration, the popular vote victory by Clinton—to have his legitimacy questioned constantly was too much.

Not long after Sessions's number two, the man who would eventually oversee the Russia probe, was confirmed by the Senate, Trump asked him to fire Comey. The president had had quite enough. The very next day, Trump hosted Russia's foreign minister and Kislyak in the White House—and he revealed highly sensitive intelligence to them.

On Tuesday, May 9, Deputy Attorney General Rod Rosenstein recommended to Trump that he fire FBI director James Comey, based on his handling of the Clinton email investigation. Rosenstein noted that the release of details about the investigation that past October, which helped propel Trump to victory, violated Justice Department standards. And, suddenly, Trump became very concerned about the rule of law and treating Hillary Clinton fairly. So he fired Comey himself. The next day, Wednesday, Pence ran defense for the president, "The president's decision to accept the recommendation of the deputy attorney general and the attorney general to remove Director Comey as the head of the FBI was based solely and exclusively on his commitment to the best interests of the American people and ensuring the FBI has the trust and confidence of the people of this nation."

Then on Thursday, May 11, Trump changed his tune: he fired Comey because of the Russia investigation. Trump hung Pence and everyone else involved in the firing out to dry. But more than any political hack, Trump had crossed the career prosecutor now overseeing the Russia probe. Two weeks after Trump used Rosenstein to fire Comey, Rosenstein appointed a special counsel who would be independent of the Justice Department—and outside Trump's control; he picked former FBI director Robert Mueller to investigate the possibility of Russian collusion in the 2016 campaign.

In an instant, Pence got one step closer to the big job—if the last few months had proven anything, it was that Trump's team had been recklessly close with Putin, and Mueller was likely to unearth more. "Impeachment" had been tossed about by liberal activists since the day Trump won last November, but now it seemed like a real possibility. This was not how Pence wanted to get to the Oval Office; he was too sophisticated and driven to try and win the presidency on a technicality. Also, what was to say that removing Trump via impeachment or a forced resignation wouldn't irrevocably tar him as well? No, Pence's path was for Trump to win—or at least do the best job possible to keep him winning. Besides, he had his chance to push Trump off the cliff in October 2016 during the *Access Hollywood* blowup and decided against it—it was best to stick with the plan.

CHAPTER 15

PIETY & POWER

The closer Mike Pence got to becoming president, the more he seemed to lose himself. Standing with Trump had forced him to flip-flop on his most core principles (with the distinct exception of his opposition to abortion). Negative campaigning, presidential philandering, profligate federal spending, free trade—he bent completely to Trump's positions that stood opposite his.

David McIntosh, his old friend and ally, saw some biblical allegories for Pence's predicament.

In the Book of Daniel, the Jewish people, cast to exile in Babylon, live under the thumb of a Persian dictator, Nebuchadnezzar. One of the Jewish slaves, Daniel, rises to become Nebuchadnezzar's chief adviser and foresees that Nebuchadnezzar will one day be driven mad as his kingdom falls before the might of God. The Book of Daniel is packed full of prophecies—almost all ending with the destruction of foreign tyrants lording over God's chosen people. And God's faithful are tested time and again, Shadrach, Mezach, and Abednego are cast into the fire, but saved by God. Daniel is thrown to the lions, but protected. ◊

In another allegory, cited by McIntosh and some of Pence's former aides, Pence represents Joseph, the favorite son of Jacob. As told in Genesis, Joseph, one of twelve children who start the twelve tribes of Israel, wins the favor of his father and is given a special "coat of many colors." (Inspiration for the musical *Joseph and the Amazing Technicolor Dreamcoat*.) Joseph's brothers become jealous and sell him into slavery under the pharaoh. It is there, as a slave, that Joseph's talent for interpreting dreams is uncovered and eventually he rises to second-in-command as he helps the pharaoh prepare for a seven-year famine. Was Pence cast out by his brothers, sold into slavery? Hardly, but according to this interpretation, he is helping keep the United States on track—Trump may not see a coming famine, but a godly man like Pence certainly would.

There is a thread that runs through all these stories—aside from God's use of ungodly men. It is the Jewish prophet's ability to survive persecution for decades with the promise of redemption at the end. As Jeremiah made clear in the verse that Karen had framed for Mike sixteen years ago, Jeremiah 29:11, God would provide for those who remained faithful to him in trying times. But it would not happen immediately.

But was it really God who had placed Pence next to Trump? Wasn't it Pence himself who had reached that point? Pence deftly engineered his own climb through the ranks of House leadership, moving from bomb-tossing conservative antagonist to influential bridge between the establishment and the conservatives. Pence was as cautious as ever as he plotted his course for the White House, and his methodical approach seemed to point in one direction—when an important national donor called him and urged him to back down from his support for the Religious Freedom Restoration Act, he acquiesced. And when the nominating contest hung in the balance, with one hour before he had to decide whether to run for governor or risk taking Trump's word, Pence's team forced Trump to make a public declaration locking Pence in as the pick. ❧

The time that he spent away praying, as he made the most important decisions of his life, seemed to be the most formative to him. McIntosh noted that hearing God, feeling his answer, was different and unique to each person, but usually came with a sense of peace and calm. McIntosh said he only felt peace after he decided against running for office again, after a failed bid in 2012, and opted to recruit and train new candidates instead. The trick was not to confuse your ego with God's will, he said. "God had to take me through a lot of wringing out the ego and the desire to be the guy out front, to get me to this position," McIntosh said. "Mike similarly, and he'll often quote scriptures about this, believes whatever he serves in should only be what God's called him to." So who was telling Pence to make all the right moves to end up in the White House? Seemed a fair question to McIntosh, and one only Mike Pence could answer.

Pence kept climbing the mountain. The air got thinner the further he climbed, the contradictions more apparent to those watching him the closer he got to the summit. The young man who once pondered how to apply Christian teachings in the political arena seemed further and further away. And the battle-scarred veteran who emerged three decades later looked more willing than ever to make the compromises needed to win.

THE PENCE POLITICAL SHOP

Pence and his team had almost no expectation of being ushered into the White House via impeachment and removal of Trump. The odds seemed long, and he seemed more likely to bow out on his own after one term than being removed by the Senate. Instead, they set their sights on 2024, which would be his best chance to win the White House outright. The best option was following eight years of a successful Trump presidency, he could ride Trump's coattails the same way Bush rode Reagan's. But, barring that, 2024 would still work if Democrats ousted Trump in 2020—Pence would just run to face the Democrat.

But Washington Republicans noted that Pence didn't seem very strong in either scenario; there were plenty younger, more vibrant Republicans waiting to run after Trump finished. Pence had an edge, as the vice president, but he had to use it. At the start of the summer of 2017, he began hosting selective donor dinners at the vice president's residence, at the Naval Observatory, ostensibly raising money to help with their reelection effort in 2020. But it also afforded him the chance to make better connections with the donors he would need for his own White House run.

After the *New York Times* published a report on the Pence donor dinners, Trump became enraged, and suddenly Pence was in hot water with the president. The casualties of Trump's anger already included Reince Priebus, former White House press secretary Sean Spicer, Priebus deputy Katie Walsh, and more. Even though Trump couldn't force him out of office, he could still drop him from the ticket in 2020, which would be fatal to his career.

❧ Later in the summer of 2017, Pence shook up his operation inside the White House—some of Trump's people, including Steve Bannon, had been pushing Pence to get smarter about how he worked inside the building. Pitcock didn't seem to understand how to best manage Pence's time. Bannon urged him to take on someone with sharper elbows and a more aggressive style, so Pence selected Nick Ayers, a more political operative and one who knew how to throw elbows inside the White House. But Ayers had a penchant for leaking sensitive details out of White House meetings, something Trump's longtime advisers chafed at. One time, over the summer, Ayers leaked the details of a messaging meeting for the communications team. Fingers shot toward Ayers, but Pence's spokesman Marc Lotter took the bullet and left the White House.

Not everyone thought Ayers was a smart selection for Pence in the White House. His old advisers from Indiana saw an ambitious Republican hack who wanted to move up the ladder and would probably cause problems for their friend. Pence, they said, should stick to his strategy of keeping a low profile inside the administration— glorified coatrack wasn't exactly a bad thing for someone playing the long game. Ayers, meanwhile, began courting the power couple who many suspected of truly running the White House, Jared Kushner and Ivanka Trump. Ayers hit it off with Kushner in particular, and Kushner began grooming Ayers for a more important role in the White House.

Pence kept up his outreach to the inheritors of Jerry Falwell's fiery brand of televangelism. After Falwell's death in 2007, a new generation of televangelists had risen in power. Chief among them were Robert Jeffress, who had jumped on board the Trump Train early in the 2016 election, and John Hagee, who ran a group dedicated to repatriating Jews to the Holy Land. Implied in the effort of Hagee's Christians United for Israel was that Jerusalem must be held exclusively by Jews to promulgate Jesus's return.

In his speech to John Hagee's group on July 17, Pence cited a favorite passage among Dispensationalists, from Chapter 37 of Ezekiel— the prophecy of the dry bones. In the prophecy, Ezekiel sees God breathing life into the long-deceased Jews, resurrecting them to return and retake Israel. Pence lit up the room when he harkened to that prophecy, a favorite among Dispensationalists, "My friends, to look at Israel is to see that the God of Abraham, Isaac, and Jacob keeps his promises, keeps the promises He makes to His people and to each one of us. Ezekiel prophesized: 'Behold, I will cause breath to enter into you, and ye shall live.' And the State of Israel and her people bear witness to God's faithfulness, as well as their own."

Hagee's group, Christians United for Israel, formed the core of a large group of Christian Right Dispensationalists dedicated to repopulating Israel with the Jewish people. Did Pence believe the Second

Coming of Jesus was at hand? That as soon as the temple was rebuilt and the Jews were restored to complete control of the Holy Land, the Rapture would occur? Of course not, said longtime Republicans who knew him in Indiana and Washington. But why was he talking this way? The same reason Trump did, he needed to keep the support of a critical bloc of voters. "Who doesn't pander?" said one Pence friend.

The deeper problem he faced, a political problem, was that he might not have a firm lock on evangelical voters when he decided to run for president in his own right. He could face trouble in 2024 from popular Republicans like UN ambassador Nikki Haley or even Senator Marco Rubio if he chose to run again.

PENCE GOES TO A FOOTBALL GAME

In late September of 2017, seemingly unrelated events converged on the White House—increasing news coverage of the disastrous hurricane fallout in Puerto Rico and Trump's failed response met with Alabama senator Luther Strange's loss in Alabama to hard-core culture warrior, Trump-backed Roy Moore. These events were unrelated on their face, save for one thing: both were prime examples of Trump failing. So Trump responded by launching a culture war against the NFL and players who took the knee in protest of police shootings. This new effort offered Pence the perfect chance to make amends for getting too aggressive with the donor courtship.

Pence had become known inside the administration and was doing the grunt work that most previous presidents did, but Trump shunted him aside almost entirely. Sometimes Pence looked too presidential, easily more so than Trump. On Friday, October 6, Vice President Pence flew to Puerto Rico to tour the hurricane damage. He shook hands, hugged victims, and sermonized. The power to the entire island had been almost completely out for weeks—the leaders of the small island accused the Trump administration of ignoring them. The next day, Pence flew to California to assess wildfire damage and then flew to LA for a Republican fund raiser. (Trump, on the other hand, spent the morning at his golf club just outside Washington.) That Sunday, October 8, Pence flew all the way back to Indianapolis—a roughly five-hour flight—to attend a Colts game. They were playing the San Francisco 49ers, whose former quarterback Colin Kaepernick had launched the NFL protests that so enraged Trump.

Mike and Karen Pence teed up their excitement that morning with a tweet showing them at the game, ready to help retire the jersey of the Colts' second-greatest quarterback—Peyton Manning, number 18. (The greatest Colts quarterback remains Johnny Unitas.) They stood, placed their hands over their hearts at the singing of the anthem, and when almost every player on the field took a knee, they walked out.

This didn't seem like a spontaneous act of courage to honor his president. Aides told assembled reporters they would have to wait in the press vans, because there would likely be an early exit. Next, Twitter sleuths picked out that the tweet Pence had sent that morning was three years old. In the tweet he was wearing a Colts cap and jersey, and Karen was wearing number 50. But on Sunday, Pence was wearing a blazer and khakis, and Karen was wearing number 18.

They had staged the entire thing.

At 1:08 P.M., Pence tweeted, "I left today's Colts game because @POTUS and I will not dignify any event that disrespects our soldiers, our Flag, or our National Anthem." Peyton and his thirteen seasons of award-winning play leading the Colts were washed away on national television by Pence's need to placate the president. As the day wound through the 1:00 P.M. games, then the 4:15 P.M. games, Pence's early exit was all anyone could talk about—from James Brown, Neon Deion Sanders, and Boomer to the nonstop cable panels booked full of pundits. But Trump couldn't let the spotlight hang too long on his number two.

"I asked @VP to leave stadium if any players kneeled, disrespecting our country. I am proud of him and @secondlady Karen,"

President Donald Trump tweeted. Pence had paid his penalty with complete emasculation by Trump.

A few weeks later, Special Counsel Robert Mueller struck, indicting former Trump campaign chairman Paul Manafort and his chief deputy, Rick Gates, on counts of conspiracy and tax evasion for payments on their work for a key Putin ally, former Ukraine prime minister Viktor Yanukovych. Two of the people most integral to Pence's landing in the White House were carted off to jail.

ROY MOORE

On November 9, the *Washington Post* dropped a bombshell in the race to fill Attorney General Jeff Sessions's old Senate seat in Alabama. When Republican Senate nominee Roy Moore was a young prosecutor, in his early thirties, he had pursued underage girls more than half his age—seeking their phone numbers, taking them out, and, in some cases, sexually molesting them. Little by little, more started to trickle out about Moore's predatory behavior—he had become so notorious in the late '70s that the teenage girls knew to watch out for him at the local mall in Gadsden, Alabama. Moore denied all the accusations and said he did nothing wrong.

Trump was in Asia when the Moore stories exploded into the news. Pence and his team had the reins for handling the Moore response, and they got on board with a last-ditch plan to save the seat from falling into Democratic hands. They would have Trump go to Alabama governor Kay Ivey and try to get Moore revoked as the party's nominee and removed from the ballot. But the effort was waylaid after Trump made a call from overseas. Moore lost to Democrat Doug Jones a month later, a stunning loss in deep-red Alabama.

Pence's role in the Trump White House evolved over the course of their first year in office, sometimes expanding and in other ways contracting. White House aides largely credited Pence, with supercharged operative Nick Ayers in place inside the building and Obst working the donors across the country, with effectively running the White House political operation—deciding which races to get involved in, when to get involved, where to allocate resources and more.

But Pence's power diminished as well. After the failure of the Obamacare repeal effort, Pence was largely kept out of the drive for sweeping tax reform. Tax cuts and tax policy were priorities for him when he was governor, but Trump chafed at his handling of health care, and gave the reins to his economic team, including economic adviser Gary Cohn and Treasury secretary Steven Mnuchin.

New Year, New Strategy

The Pence team's approach to life in the White House had flipped 180 degrees in just one year. If 2017 had been all about getting Pence in the room for every meeting Trump held, 2018 became all about getting him out of there. Even when Pence wasn't saying anything, he was still getting pulled into some bad situations, for example, Trump's firing of FBI director James Comey. And those meetings were catching the attention of the special counsel, Robert Mueller, something Pence needed to avoid to protect his own White House chances.

As much as Trump and his team screamed "witch hunt," it was impossible to ignore the very real results—plea deals from Michael Flynn and George Papadopoulos, intensive trials for Manafort and his deputy Gates—which would both end in plea deals and convictions. Sure, Pence was lawyered up to protect himself in the Russia probe (with better counsel than the president, many noted), but that was no reason to tempt fate. One former White House aide joked that Pence was being kept behind protective glass, "Break glass in case of emergency"—a nod to the establishment's backup plan for if and when the Trump presidency collapsed.

At the end of January 2018, Pence flew overseas on a long-awaited trip to Israel, to tour the Holy Land. But Donald Trump's scandals were inescapable, and they mounted. During Pence's trip the *Wall Street Journal* uncovered that Trump had paid a porn star, Stormy Daniels, $130,000 to stay quiet about the affair they had while Melania was pregnant with his fifth child. ❧

Reporters with Pence wanted to know, what did he think of the allegations that Trump cheated on his third wife with a porn star? "I'm not going to comment on the latest baseless allegations against the president," Pence said. Two decades earlier, Pence had determined that presidential philandering was an impeachable offense, but now he wasn't so sure. The man who held the moral high ground through a long career in Washington—clean enough that he had asked his own friend and colleague, former representative Mark Souder, to resign over his affair—now believed the president over the accuser.

Robert Schenck, the evangelical pastor who had prayed with Pence in his office when he was a congressman, had undergone his own transformation in the years since they last saw each other. He had largely left the confines of the Christian Right movement. His first break with them was over their support for unchecked gun sales amid the mounting mass shootings. His final break was when leaders of the Christian Right, like Jerry Falwell Jr. and Robert Jeffress—the heirs to the movement started four decades earlier—went all in for Trump.

As he looked at Pence, Schenck noticed something he saw in other people he pastored, in other leaders in public life who seemed ambivalent at times. He saw the push and pull between Pence's faith and his ambition.

"So, in the deal with Trump, I felt like I was watching Mike sell his soul on the global stage, certainly on the national stage. And I thought, as a pastor, 'This will take a very long time to repair—in his own soul, in his interior world.'" If Pence delivered the evangelical votes in return for Trump helping him fulfill his ambitions, "then that is the Faustian bargain, [and] that is spiritually dangerous, perilous for anyone who does that transaction with something as serious as one's commitment to Christ and his people."

On February 2, 2018, Schenck saw Pence again for the first time in six years. Pence stood at the front of the Indian Treaty Room of the Eisenhower Executive Office Building, a gorgeous room with high ceilings, white marble, and a wraparound balcony. By his side stood Pence's longtime Christian conservative warrior—former U.S. senator Sam Brownback of Kansas. The vice president was swearing Brownback in as the U.S. ambassador for religious freedom. Here stood one of their own; this moment was the promise they foresaw in the bargain they made with Trump. Endure the indignities, the insanity, and the godly will have their hands on the reins of government.

Schenck stood there, applauding Brownback's swearing in, surrounded by all his old friends in the movement. Most of the conservative evangelical leaders had acquiesced to Trump—at first they thought Trump would be pushed out of office early, either by the limitless scandals or his own exasperation at the job. And then they would have President Mike Pence! Slowly, this magical thinking shifted into something more rational. They were stuck with Trump, but at least their man Pence would be able run the show from the inside.

Sitting there that day, Schenck was filled with woe and worry. The latest nightmare was a secret memo that Trump's allies in the Capitol had produced that would, allegedly, prove that the federal probe of Trump was built on political spying by Democrats and a shadowy conspiracy of intelligence agency bureaucrats and "Deep State" illuminati aligned against him.

Schenck knew there was a good man tucked inside Pence's heart, he just needed to pry him back out. Pence needed some courage, "If he could spend enough time in his interior world, I think Mike could find a conscience." After the ceremony, Schenck walked up to his old friend and confronted him, "You know, Mr. Vice President, more than anything, we need you to find your conscience, the country desperately needs you to find your conscience." Pence stopped smiling, he looked down at the floor, just like he used to when the two men would pray together in his old House office, and he said, "It's always easier said than done." And then he walked away.

THE 2018 GRIDIRON ROAST

The man with stark principles kept slipping away, clouded by his ambition and political maneuvering. Trump only made Pence's machinations more obvious to those who had watched him for decades.

One month later, Pence sat at the front of the ballroom of Washington's Renaissance Hotel with Karen—Trump was at the podium. In the audience sat column after column of top-level journalists and their guests, senior Trump administration officials, veteran Washington luminaries, and, in total, the most powerful people in the country (and possibly the world). There they all were in full formal dress—the men in tuxes with white bow ties and long tails, the women in fine, formal dresses. Pence had done the 2017 Gridiron Dinner in Trump's place, and got in a few zingers, but this year Trump opted to attend. Still, Pence wanted to be in the room for the festivities.

Pence and Karen had been seated to Trump's left, smiling, and continued to smile as the president took the podium. Trump was doing well, better than he had at previous roasts—he seemed to get the idea this time, taking as much as he dished out, "My staff was concerned heading into this dinner that I couldn't do self-deprecating humor. Nobody does self-deprecating humor better than I do." The self-awareness got some uproarious laughs, especially from the press in the audience. "But I have to tell you, in preparation, I did what any good late-night comic would do these days, I called Chuck Schumer and asked him for some talking points." Ba-zing. "I also spoke with some of the funniest people around the White House, starting with my number two: Mike Pence!" Some hoots and catcalls from the crowd. "Oh, I love you, Mike. Some of you may think that Mike is not a comedian, but he is one of the best straight men you're ever going to meet." The room erupted. The most powerful people in Washington couldn't stop laughing. Mike and Karen just looked up, smiles fixed, not moving, but very, very red in the face, Mike especially. Trump piled on, "He *is* straight! I mean it!"

Holy God, Trump was insinuating that Mike Pence was gay. At least when Bosma roasted Pence six years earlier, Pence was midcoitus with his wife, not another man.

The president plowed on, "Karen, I saw him the other day. We were in line shaking hands with men and a woman came over to shake his hand, and he said, 'I'm sorry, I can't do that, my wife is not here.'"

Then Trump's roast seemed to reveal some animosity: "Mike is doing a fantastic job as our vice president, he really is, he's doing a fantastic job. Could not have asked for better. I really am very proud to call him the Apprentice. But lately—it bothers me, I have to tell you—he's showing a particularly keen interest in the news these days. He starts out each morning asking everyone, 'Has he been impeached yet?'"

Mike and Karen were trapped in a humiliating spotlight.

THE PRICE OF POWER

Mike and Karen made no indication that Trump's personal insults had fazed them. Much as Karen said when they boarded the plane October 8, 2015, to fly to Trump's fund raiser in Rhode Island—"We knew what we were signing up for."

As part of their strategy they had to work to craft a strong, clean public image for Pence. Like all other things in politics, that got increasingly harder the higher he climbed. Charlotte Pence, now an aspiring filmmaker living in Los Angeles, decided to write a lighthearted children's book about their pet bunny, Marlon Bundo. Karen painted the pictures for the book, titled *A Day in the Life of the Vice President*. The book tells Pence's story from the literal ground up, as Marlon Bundo, hops between White House meetings and visits to the Capitol with Pence.

But HBO's John Oliver beat them to the punch—show comedy writer Jill Twiss wrote *A Day in the Life of Marlon Bundo*. The children's book, also filled with watercolor illustrations, told the story of BOTUS, as he was dazzled by another male bunny, Wesley. They quickly fell in love, but a mean stinkbug, who looked distinctly like Pence, tried to stop them from getting married. The book soared up the bestseller list, and the show gave the proceeds to LGBT groups that promote safe sex and work to prevent suicides among LGBT teens.

Charlotte Pence said she bought a copy of the Oliver parody. She played it off, "He's giving the proceeds of the book to charity, and we're also giving the proceeds of our book to charity, so I really think it's something we can all get behind."

Pence's humility and honor were the price for becoming vice president. The president of the United States called him gay. The mockery of his family jumped in three years from Twitter to the bestseller list. But power was the promise, that he would soon enough have the tools to run for president in his own right. And, because Trump was effectively a weak president, one without firm control of his own administration and an outright aversion to the mechanics needed to govern, Pence seized this opportunity. Chief among them was becoming the nation's most powerful fund raiser. ❖

A few weeks after Trump burned him onstage, Pence was out on the campaign trail. Trump hated fund-raising and retail politicking; besides, Trump's advisers said they wanted Pence out working with the donors. Pence gladly took up the cause. Donors loved talking with Pence and he loved listening, he had infinite patience for them and was unflinchingly cordial. But there was some danger in Pence's gambit. His aggressive fund raising the previous summer, sometimes asking donors to fork over upward of $75,000 a person to have lunch or dinner with him in small settings, appeared to have gone too far. Trump hated anyone stealing his spotlight and was especially sensitive to rumors that Pence was sharpening the knives, getting ready to oust him—rumors that were often spread by Trump loyalists who saw Pence and his operation as a competing force against their own interests.

Besides, Pence had long been more talented on the campaign trail than in executive offices. And the Republican Party writ large needed him—control of the House was at stake in November, and a flip to Democratic hands could definitely set up the possibility of impeachment. And control of the Senate hung in the balance as well, which could stifle the GOP's ability to appoint judges through the end of Trump's first term. Trump's stunning unpopularity—he had been "under water" or had higher negative ratings than positive, for almost all his presidency according to most national polling—was cascading down the ballot and hurting other Republicans.

If Pence and Trump were distant in private, the presentation in public was one of a tight-knit team fighting for America. The fundraising circuit gave Pence and the Republican Party ample chance to display the unified front. On March 27, 2018, Pence flew to Fargo, North Dakota, for a series of fund raisers for Representative Kevin Cramer, who was running against Democratic senator Heidi Heitkamp for Senate. They stacked a series of meetings from the morning through noon—different levels of donations bought different levels of access. Giving $50,000 would get you into the first meeting with the vice president, the most exclusive. This meant a few less than a dozen people, including oil tycoon and megadonor Harold Hamm; the state's other senator, John Hoeven, and his wife; and a few others. Getting in there got you Pence's ear while the White House was hard at work on the national farm bill, a critical spending measure for the country's agricultural sector. After that came the slightly larger fund raiser for Cramer, open to about a hundred donors. And finally, after that, came the campaign-style rally put on by Trump's affiliated political campaign, America First Policies. Every fund-raising trip was political money in the bank for Pence.

And Pence played it all off, with folksy charm, and stilted rhythm.

"What's that old adage? 'What's an expert? An expert is anybody who's from more than ninety miles out of town.' And I qualify," Pence said, to a few chuckles around the room in North Dakota. "I'm just telling you, the character, the quality, the vision, the values, the agenda that Kevin Cramer's going to bring to the United States Senate make this. One. Of. The. Most. Important. Races."

Behind the scenes, other ambitious Republicans played a shadow game of positioning—either for president, or for vice president. Pence understood that politics was as much preparation as action in the moment, and he was a master of preparation. As John Wooden, the legendary Hoosier who led UCLA to national championships, said, "When opportunity knocks, it's too late to prepare."

Inside the White House, that meant keeping up a team of loyal staffers who would prove useful in a future presidential run and also denying possible opponents their services. When Pence attempted to hire Jon Lerner away from UN ambassador Nikki Haley's office, it set off some alarm bells—Pence wanted him to serve as his national security adviser, but Lerner had almost no national security experience. Lerner was better known as a premier political pollster. Word leaked out that Lerner had worked with the Never Trump movement during the 2016 race. Trump became enraged and Pence's gambit to win over a key aide failed.

But Pence's long-standing reputation as a stable and solid Republican yielded its benefits. Republican operatives who worried what would happen to their careers if they were marked with the stain of working under Trump could apply to Pence's office, a relatively safe haven.

PIETY AND POWER COME TOGETHER

Standing in the Rose Garden on May 3, 2018, on the National Day of Prayer, Pence cited one of his favorite verses proudly. "You know, over the mantel of our home, for nearly twenty years, has been a bible verse that speaks of a promise our little family has claimed and Americans have cherished through the generations. In Jeremiah 29, verse 11, we read: 'For I know the plans I have for you, plans to prosper you, and not to harm you, plans to give you a hope and a future.'"

In Pence's history, the verse had been a promise that God would provide for their family at the end of the journey that started when Mike left his radio job, they moved their family to a new home, and he ran for Congress in 2000. And two decades after that provident decision, Pence now stood delivering a speech in the Rose Garden, just outside the Oval Office.

But the broader promise from Jeremiah, Chapter 29, harkened to returning the exiled Jews in Babylon to Israel after seventy years in captivity. In two weeks, the United States would officially move its embassy in Israel from Tel Aviv to Jerusalem, a monumental policy decision fundamentally supporting Israel as a state for Jews—and the Trump White House invited renowned Dispensationalists John Hagee and Robert Jeffress to bless the new embassy.

"You have called Israel the apple of your eye and Father, we are all so grateful as we think about what happened seventy years ago today, at this very moment when you fulfilled the prophecies of the prophets from thousands of years ago when you regathered your people in this promised land," Robert Jeffress, the Texas megachurch pastor, prayed at the opening of the embassy on May 14, 2018. Jeffress referred literally to the founding of Israel in 1948, but he also hinted at one of the requisites for bringing about Jesus's return.

Jeffress seemed an odd choice to send as an official emissary to the Holy Land on a day designed to return all of Jerusalem to the Jewish people. Just eight years earlier, he deemed that Jews, along with Muslims and Mormons, would all end up in hell unless they converted to Christianity. "You can't be saved by being a Jew," Jeffress had said. "You know who said that, by the way? The three greatest Jews in the New Testament: Peter, Paul, and Jesus Christ. They all said Judaism won't do it. It's faith in Jesus Christ."

Israeli prime minister Benjamin Netanyahu now sat next to Jared Kushner and Ivanka Trump in the front row, listening to Jeffress—he cocked one eyebrow and tilted his head slightly, as Jeffress hinted at the Christian Right's use for Jews, to hasten the return of Jesus. Netanyahu, in his own speech, praised the most powerful nation on earth for doing something that few others dared to do—and that previous White Houses had avoided—dive fully into the battle between Palestinians and Israelis on the side of Israel. He made no mention of prophecy or his people being used as cannon fodder in a perpetually imminent Holy War.

The fire that Pence and the White House seemed to be playing with was not a biblical one, but a very earthly one—the potential for massive war in the Middle East. Previous White Houses under both parties had attempted to cement the so-called two-state solution as a means of achieving actual peace in the Middle East. The United States had previously acted as a broker between the Israeli and Palestinian leadership because of the very real bloodshed that would occur if they didn't.

But Pence still saw the rails, the boundaries, and attempted where he could to keep Trump on track. War in the Middle East seemed a likely outcome down the road, but Trump had been playing a nuclear game of chicken with North Korean dictator Kim Jong-un on Twitter—and the test rockets that Kim kept launching were very real. So Pence gently inserted himself as a bulwark, not unlike a biblical Joseph to Trump's pharaoh.

On May 16, 2018, just a few days after the opening on the embassy in Jerusalem, Pence welcomed Jim Morris, vice chairman of the Indiana Pacers and one of Indianapolis's city fathers, to be sworn in as the U.S. representative to UNICEF. Morris invited his old friend Dick Lugar to the ceremony. Lugar and Pence had never been particularly close, but now, perhaps more than ever, Lugar's sage leadership on nuclear disarmament was needed. He had spent years working with former Democratic senator Sam Nunn to secure nuclear weapons stockpiles after the fall of the Soviet Union. Lugar kept in his office the well-worn table that he and Nunn used to negotiate many of the deals. He had been vilified in his 2012 reelection for his work in helping Obama extend another nuclear treaty with Russia, but in hindsight his work seemed incredibly valuable.

After the swearing in, Pence asked if Lugar could come by his office soon to talk. Lugar sent him a copy of the op-ed he and Nunn had written in the *Washington Post* just a few weeks earlier—it was a brief blueprint of how the United States worked with its old Cold War enemy, Russia, to draw down arms. Ten days later, Pence asked if Lugar and Nunn could come meet him at the White House—Trump was scheduled to head off to meet with Kim himself in just one week, in Singapore. Lugar and Nunn headed to the White House and were led into Pence's office tucked just down the hall from the Oval Office. Pence got up to greet them—then walked them into the Oval Office for a surprise meeting with Trump. There the men talked disarmament with the president for about twenty-five minutes.

The sense of duty, of the weight of the office, of the opportunity, clearly hung on Pence—in ways that he rarely mentioned. But that was hard to see from the outside, and Pence didn't tout all the times he tried to keep the country on the rails. He couldn't, Trump would have his head if he promoted his own work. So what the country saw was something else entirely.

Veteran conservative columnist George Will hopped on the Pence for President bandwagon in 2014—he was impressed by Pence's willingness to push a conservative expansion of Medicaid. To Will, it showed principle. But now he found the vice president to be "oleaginous"— which is to say, overexuberant with praise, greasily so. In contrast to Pence, he held up Abraham Lincoln. In 1838, an abolitionist newspaper editor had recently been murdered by a pro-slavery mob, Lincoln responded in a speech, deriding a "mobocratic spirit" among "'the vicious portion of [the] population.' So, 'let reverence for the laws . . . become the *political religion* of the nation.' Pence, one of evangelical

Christians' favorite pin-ups, genuflects at various altars, as the mobocratic and vicious portion require."

And Pence couldn't help but play into that assessment. June 6, at a meeting discussing emergency preparedness at FEMA, Donald Trump and Mike Pence sat at the head of the table. Trump listened intently, Pence kept his head bowed silently. As he listened, Trump took the water bottle in front of him and placed it on the ground, and Pence instantly followed suit.

Twitter destroyed him, again. Increasingly, the nation was building its image of Mike Pence and it was, as George Will stated, "oleaginous."

September 2018—The Lodestar

Perhaps one reason Pence was so obsequious was because a core group of former Trump advisers who regularly got through to the president were quite dubious about Pence—they didn't trust him. They figured that Pence would throw Trump to the dogs—or more specifically one pit bull, Mueller—at the very first chance. Shortly after Labor Day, they seemed to get some confirmation via an anonymously penned op-ed in the *New York Times*. The extraordinary decision to run an opinion piece on the *Times*'s pages seemed justified by the stunning headline alone, "I Am Part of the Resistance Inside the Trump Administration." "It may be cold comfort in this chaotic era, but Americans should know there are adults in the room. We fully recognize what is happening. And we are trying to do what is right, even when Donald Trump won't," wrote the anonymous author, who claimed to work inside the White House. Then the author seemed to slip a hint of who they were in the text, "We may no longer have Senator McCain. But we will always have his example—a lodestar for restoring honor to our public life and our national dialogue."

McCain had died just a few weeks earlier, and he asked, shortly before he passed, that Pence attend his funeral instead of Trump. But that's not what caught most operatives' eyes, as they tried to uncover the leader of the mysterious resistance—Pence loved to use the word *lodestar* in his speeches. "Lodestar" was his north star when it came to memorializing Republican giants like McCain and Jack Kemp. Pence immediately said it wasn't him.

The whole op-ed did sound a bit like the biblical allegories explaining Pence's role under the mad king, trying to keep the country on the rails. But it didn't seem like something he would do—why announce a secret conspiracy to the world? Besides, he was already quietly keeping Trump on the rails the best he could. Although McCain himself had sounded doubtful about that. Well before he died, he weighed in on his old colleague Pence's role keeping Trump in check. "I don't know, I don't know," McCain said when asked, as he laughed with a wry smile and twinkle in his eye. "I guess it varies from day to day."

PENCE AT THE DOORSTEP

By October of 2018, "impeach" sat on the tips of everyone's tongues—sometimes quite literally, as microbrewers had cooked batches of "I'm Peach" beer. Even a hard Right supporter of President Trump accidentally fueled the flames as he tried to protect the president. Republican representative Jim Jordan floated the idea of impeaching Rod Rosenstein over his handling of the firing of James Comey. The third-ranking Democrat, South Carolina representative Jim Clyburn, guffawed: "I believe it will be very instructive for us to find out whether or not they are willing to apply the same measuring stick to their own president." Implied in Clyburn's comment was that congressional members might very well get the chance to put that to the test. Over the summer, Trump had stood side by side with Putin at a press conference in Helsinki—he accepted a soccer ball from the Summer Olympics as a gift. Trump's intelligence directors, the heads of the CIA, FBI, and the director of national intelligence, had just issued a conclusive finding that the Kremlin meddled in the 2016 election. Putin told Trump at the summit, emphatically, that it never happened. Trump took Putin's word over that of his intelligence chiefs. "I have great confidence in my intelligence people, but I will tell you President Putin was extremely strong and powerful in his denial today," Trump said. He then invited Putin to a special summit in Washington. Had Trump been compromised? "I feel he has," Clyburn said. "When you've got this much smoke, there's fire somewhere."

On November 6, 2018, Democrats swept the Republicans out of the House, winning forty-one new seats and taking control of the House for the first time in eight years. The Democrats now had subpoena power to investigate, and the "I" word loomed even larger. Cracks emerged in the Rust Belt coalition that carried Trump in two years earlier: Wisconsin's public schools superintendent, a Democrat, ousted Republican governor Scott Walker. Democrats turned out in massive numbers and won both statewide contests in Michigan and Pennsylvania. And in traditionally red states to the south, Georgia and Texas, they came perilously close to upsetting Republican candidates for governor and the Senate, respectively.

The chaos of Trump World, which Pence had successfully insulated himself from for two years, began seeping in. Pence's chief of staff, Nick Ayers, had been "managing up" as one veteran Republican put it, focusing too much on winning his next job and not enough on helping Pence. Ayers got out too far in his courtship to become Trump's chief of staff, and some White House aides, including Kellyanne Conway, saw a chance to kill two birds with one stone—remove Ayers and limit Jared Kushner's influence at the same time. Stories began cropping up about Ayers's plans to become Trump's new chief of staff. In normal circumstances this would have been great news and a great boost for Ayers, but in this White House it meant he would have to oversee the responses to endless congressional investigations and a boss who would only become more paranoid with each new subpoena. The flow of stories was boxing him in, little by little. Ayers

asked Marty Obst and some others to help him knock down the spec-
ulation, but anonymous White House aides kept leaking details of his
meetings with Trump. Ayers was being forced into the role of Donald
Trump's chief handler and babysitter and he couldn't control it.

In their two years in the White House, Pence had never truly
connected with Trump. Their relationship, according to staff and campaign aides, never developed much beyond cordial respect. Some said
that Pence's piousness rubbed off on Trump, and that his message
discipline could be heard in Trump's increasing use of teleprompters
and written speeches. Pence's close friends saw Trump's spontaneity
beginning to rub off on Mike. Trump was forcing Pence to stay on his
feet in a way he hadn't since he was on-air six days a week in the '90s.
That forced spontaneity, they noticed, was breaking some of the stiltedness that had built up over close to two decades in national politics.

But the enigma of Pence seemed to gnaw at someone new after
the 2018 blowout, someone more important to Pence's future than the
public, the press, even his old friends and acquaintances from Indiana.
Now Donald Trump was asking just who Mike Pence was.

With threat of impeachment or indictment hanging over his head,
Trump grew more paranoid than ever. Could he trust Mike Pence?
Should he trust him? Pence sure would love to become president.
Trump stewed; he asked his friends if Pence would turn on him and
try to push him out of office. And a small coterie of Trump loyalists
wanted Pence gone. They preferred someone with fewer ties to the
Republican establishment and the conservative movement. Pence's
team brushed off reports of Trump's questions. Pence had been the
most loyal soldier of all, never questioning the president and only ever
gently pushing him toward policy ideas. How could the president not
trust him?

One day after the midterm shellacking, at a press conference in
the East Room of the White House, a reporter asked Trump if he
planned to keep Mike Pence on the ticket with him in 2020. Trump
looked across the room and laughed, "Well, I haven't asked him, but

I hope so. Where are you?" Trump looked over to his side, the pale white around his eye sockets accentuated even more than usual against his orange hue. "Mike, will you be my running mate? Huh? Stand up, raise your right hand." Pence began to stand, everyone laughed, Trump stopped him, "No, I'm only kidding." But Mike Pence was already standing. "Will you?" Pence smiled, waved his right hand, and nodded; he'd been through this dance once before, in July 2016.

Then Trump spoke for him, "The answer is 'Yes.'"

ACKNOWLEDGMENTS

Angelica—Of the many things I am grateful to Indiana for, you are foremost among them. I'm grateful your dad brought home a brochure with pictures of the beautiful IU campus in Bloomington. And I'm even more grateful you enrolled at the Indianapolis campus by accident. The fire of our very first meeting continues to burn—we have our family, we have our adventure, and we have so much more. I love you, mi cachorrita.

Maria Alessandra—Hola, baby doll. You are the best of us and have taught me more than anyone. Your eyes smile, your brain whirs, and you light up every room you enter. We started at "diggy diggy diggy" eighteen months ago, and now we're at "Octopus so big!" We talk to the ants, sing to the buses, and watch the helicopters fly. I love you.

Mom and Dad—I think about you every day. Mom, you inspired me with your perseverance and independence. Dad, you taught me to

ACKNOWLEDGMENTS

Angelica—Of the many things I am grateful to Indiana for, you are foremost among them. I'm grateful your dad brought home a brochure with pictures of the beautiful IU campus in Bloomington. And I'm even more grateful you enrolled at the Indianapolis campus by accident. The fire of our very first meeting continues to burn—we have our family, we have our adventure, and we have so much more. I love you, mi cachorrita.

Maria Alessandra—Hola, baby doll. You are the best of us and have taught me more than anyone. Your eyes smile, your brain whirs, and you light up every room you enter. We started at "diggy diggy diggy" eighteen months ago, and now we're at "Octopus so big!" We talk to the ants, sing to the buses, and watch the helicopters fly. I love you.

Mom and Dad—I think about you every day. Mom, you inspired me with your perseverance and independence. Dad, you taught me to

312 ACKNOWLEDGMENTS

love all the wonders of the world, from the trees to the stars. Joe and Chris—we're a long way from playing Ghostbusters and flashlight tag in the backyard, but not that far. Joe, you have courage. Chris, you have heart. I love you both. Uncle Chuck, Aunt Donna, Alicia, Andy, Charlene, Jeff, Caitlin, Josie, Tia Shannon, Abuelo Karl, I love you all.

A mis suegros, cuñados, y familia extendida, por su apoyo y comprension.

Bridget Matzie—Your skepticism at the start inspired me to think harder, your dedication throughout kept me strong, and your knack for prose and a sharp turn-of-phrase turned the raw reporting into a compelling read. Your savvy and strategy are impeccable and your patience ineffable.

Julia Cheiffetz—You believed in the idea and pushed me to think bigger. I hope this is something that people still read years from now and learn from.

Jonathan Allen—I asked you how to write a book, you showed me how.

And Amie Parnes for your ear and your wisdom.

Carrie Thornton—You lived the story with me; our late-night chats and brainstorming teased out the big ideas. Your questions elevated the story and were dead-on, and you synthesized my excited ramblings into the big thoughts that tied it all together. Thank you for helping me find the vision and craft it, and just being eminently badass.

Shannon O'Neill—When it was crash time, we crashed—and there were quite a few crash times. You picked out the gaps, were unflagging with what needed filling in, and always reminded me of the obvious.

Lynn Grady, Sean Newcott, Tatiana Dubin, Erin Reback, Anwesha Basu, Laurie McGee, and the entire Dey Street and HarperCollins team—thank you for unending support, enthusiasm, dedication, expertise, and world-class professionalism.

Mike Murphy—Your daily guidance and patience has helped me at all steps for years now. I told you the dream, you told me how to get it. You pushed open doors and we got to the closest version of the truth possible. You always answered and stuck with me through all the twists and turns.

Matt Lewis—You gave freely and candidly of your wisdom and insights, you heard me out and kept me on the rails. For our friends in the ignition group, who warmly welcomed my family and me and helped me better understand the contours of the Bible. My research team—Howard Fletcher Jr., Jane Ketzenberger, Erica Irish—your legwork in a pinch was invaluable. Your work let me fall down the rabbit holes we needed to dive down. I hope you walked out with something good. I know I did.

To the library and archives staff at Ball State University, University of Indianapolis, Hanover College, and Indiana University-Purdue University Indianapolis—thank you for both preserving history and making it available to the public. And also for the wonderful conversation.

Chuck Quilhot, David McIntosh, Jim Atterholt, Jeff Cardwell, Bob Massie, Marty Obst, Russell Pulliam, Chris Christie, Kellyanne Conway, Ryan Streeter, Kevin Eck, Sherman Johnson—You sat patiently and walked me through the hard stuff, you steered me away from some duds, and you helped me see the human behind the polish. I hope I have reflected that fairly and truly in these pages.

Craig Shirley, Jack Howard, Darrell Issa, Joe Gaylord, Cal Thomas, Terry Holt, and the many other veterans of Washington who helped me better understand the history and context of each political era throughout Pence's career—Thank you for your generosity and candor.

Jon Quick, Kate Shepherd, Steve Simpson, Scott Uecker, and the veterans of Indiana radio who helped fill in one of the most important eras in Pence's life.

To my sources I cannot name, thank you. Your unending generosity and wisdom brought me here as much as anyone. I hope that I respected the value of your insights and information.

Craig, for your hospitality; Wayne, for your unending knowledge;

James, for your insights. Rita Leiphart, for helping me run every leg of the marathon, start to finish.

Charlie, Jake, Sean, Stokes, Chandler, Lena, Melissa, Davis, and all our friends who listened through the long talks. . . . A brick. Witte, Julie, Annie, Kristen, Brody, Sears, Rosen, Lazarick, Tallman, Charles Robinson, Wagner, Rucker, Liam, Sarah, Disco, and all the faithful scribes of "One Maryland." Ted, Deirdre, Manu, Marshall, Levine, Berman, Jedd, Nobles, Rex, Kristin, Phil, Ashley, Merica, Landers, and all of my CNN friends and colleagues.

To my brothers and sisters in the Indiana corps, Chelsea Schneider, Tom Davies, Tony Cook, Eric Bradner, Mary Beth Schneider, Lesley Weidenbener, Niki Kelly, Brian Howey, Ed Feigenbaum, Adam Van Osdol, Jim Shella, Brandon Smith, Jeni O'Malley, Kusmer, Callahan, Murphy, Coyne (am I missing a Tom?), Weaver, Alvie, and many, many more. "Let me be clear." And John Ketzenberger and Doug Richardson, for always lending me your collective scribbler ears. Lawrence Jackson, John Krull, Jane Mayer, Trish Wilson, Desmond Butler, thank you.

To my friends in the national corps—our job has never been tougher, our necessity never greater, and our work never better. I'm honored to stand by your side.

To all my colleagues at the AP, CNN, *The Indianapolis Star*, *The Washington Times*, and my (many) other stops on this journey, thank you. I learned from all of you, something different, something new, always exhilarating, sometimes exasperating, always important and stubbornly fun. The Hill team, the Russia team(s), the basement in Indiana, the bullpen in Maryland, thanks for being there every day and proving journalism to be the best damn job in the world.

Adrianne Flynn, Rafael Lorente, Chris Frates, and the entire University of Maryland journalism community—I've leaned on you often, at many twists and turns on this grand adventure, and am forever in your debt.

Northeastern University professor Michael Dukakis—Your example, focusing on the smallest details of each transportation project and seeing the bigger possibility, has always helped me see past the image and the press release and remember there are humans who want to do good behind the caricatures often seen in public.

To all my friends at the National Press Club, my home away from home.

And to all the journalists who came before—I could not have written this draft without your hundreds and thousands of first drafts. I spent hours upon hours reading the archives and breathing easier working off your foundation.

And to Vice President Mike Pence—I hope I have presented as complete a portrait as possible.

NOTES

As part of my general research for this book, I relied on a handful of insightful books (and highly recommend them for anyone interested in understanding Mike Pence better). I'll start with Pence's two favorite books: the Bible, and Russell Kirk's *The Conservative Mind*. Additionally, I relied on John Fea's tour of evangelical history and the Trump campaign, *Believe Me: The Evangelical Road to Donald Trump*, as well as Cal Thomas and Ed Dobson's review of the start and disbanding of the Moral Majority, *Blinded by Might*. And for all Hoosier-philes, I highly recommend James Madison's *The Indiana Way*. I also feel like I found my own bible in this process, Jon Franklin's *Writing for Story*. (Thank you, Desmond.)

INTRODUCTION

The Pence White House—Gleaned from the entirety of reporting for this book

Antiabortion pregnancy centers—Author interview with Marjorie Dannenfelser, president of Susan B. Anthony List

Four Supreme Court appointments—Author estimate based on reporting, and age and health of sitting justices

"Is Mike Pence the shadow president?"—Question posed by various political operatives in Indiana and Washington, DC, to author

Smart lobbyists—Author interviews with Indiana and Washington Republicans from throughout Pence's career

"Now we're with you"—Author interview with a former Indiana official

"Porn star presidency"—South Bend mayor Pete Buttigieg, CNN Town Hall, March 10, 2019

"in awe of people who make money"—Author interview with former Trump campaign aide

Railroading questioners—Author's experience

"Out of the loop"—Mike Pence gaggle, February 8, 2018, C-SPAN, https://www.youtube.com/watch?v=SBv-94hns20

PROLOGUE

This chapter is built largely on author's reporting trips and experiences covering Pence.

"Forrest Gump kind of personality"—Author interview with Chuck Quilhot

"I've known him for thirty years and I still don't know him"—Author interview with former neighbor

Warm, funny, and open—Author interview with Scott Uecker

Zelig—Author interview with veteran Republican operatives from Indiana

Washington operators who worked for Ronald Reagan—Author interviews with Reagan biographer Craig Shirley and other Republicans on background

"I've become more myself on radio"—Nicole Roales, "Pence Hosts Show Here All Day," *Kokomo Tribune*, July 14, 1998

Trump began asking aides—Maggie Haberman and Katie Rogers, "Is Mike Pence Loyal? Trump Is Asking, Despite His Recent Endorsement," *The New York Times*, November 16, 2018

Views of different Christian groups, Pence's religion—Author interviews with dozens of Pence friends and former associates, research on history of Fundamentalism and Protestant Reformation

Kept attending a Catholic church—Author interviews with Republican staffers, Pence friends

Pence family church in Northern Virginia, Immanuel Bible Church in Springfield, Virginia—Michael Easley former pastor

Unshakably pious—Author interviews with former Republican aides

Rarely saw the public displays of religiosity—Author interviews with colleagues and acquaintances from the 1990s

Scrupulously avoided the soft corruption—Author's experiences covering Pence

Attends church as often as he can—Author interviews with Pence friends and former aides

CHAPTER I: IDYLLIC

Richard Michael Cawley—Pence family history, from the following:
Sheryl Gay Stolberg, "'I Am an American Because of Him': The Journey of Pence's Grandfather from Ireland," *The New York Times*, March 16, 2017

Harry McCawley, "The Road to the Governor's Office," *The Columbus Republic*, January 13, 2013

Boris Ladwig, "Pence Recounts How Hometown Shaped Future," *The Daily Journal*, January 14, 2013

The Columbus Republic, January 2013, special coverage of Mike Pence inauguration

"My mother and father were the American dream"—Mike Pence interview with Indiana journalist Craig Fehrman

Dunlappe Apartments—Author interview with former neighbor

Columbus Republic—2013 profile

Richard, took a shine to him—Stolberg, "'I Am an American Because of Him'"

"If you lied to him"—Jane Mayer, "The Danger of President Pence," *The New Yorker*, October 16, 2017

"Bubbles"—Ibid.

"My mom grew up in a Democratic family" —Pence interview with Fehrman

"In my early youth, I was very inspired by . . . JFK, MLK"—Ibid.

J. Irwin Miller—"A Man for All Reasons," *Esquire*, October 1, 1967

The new developments—Author interviews with former Pence neighbors, author interview of Columbus, Indiana, historian David Secrest

Miller's family filled it with—Author visits to Columbus, interviews, research, Wikipedia

without much to do—Mayer, "The Danger of President Pence"

"He was always talking" . . . *Nancy Pence*—McCawley, "The Road to the Governor's Office"

Sister Sharon Bierman taught him math—Seventh- and eighth-grade details from Bierman interview with Judith Valente, WGLT, August 1, 2016, https://www.wglt.org/post/catholic-sister-recalls-her-pupil-gov-mike -pence

he placed second in the Columbus Optimist Club contest—"Speech Winner Says Get Involved and Care," *The Columbus Herald*, February 11, 1972

"channel a lot of that anxiety"—John Schorg, "Pence Hopes to Overcome Outsider Role," *The Columbus Republic*, September 25, 1988

He wanted to raise a family someday—Valente interview with Bierman

"It wasn't just that it came naturally"—McCawley, "The Road to the Governor's Office"

THE FIRST RUN FOR OFFICE

Tom Hodek's place down the street—Ladwig, "Pence Recounts"

John Rumple—Ibid.

"I was the fourth-string center on the team" —Schorg, "Mike Pence Hopes to Overcome Outsider Role"

promptly ran for vice president—Columbus North High School yearbooks reviewed by author, 1975–1977

"Did I tell you I tried out for the girls swim team??"—Mike Pence, "The Adventures of Mortimer" comics, Columbus North, *The Triangle*, 1976–1977

"He had a bigger plan for himself"—Ladwig, "Pence Recounts"

"I think he became interested in politics in high school"—McCawley, "The Road to the Governor's Office"

Pence on guitar—Author interview with Tom Pickett

Additional Columbus background—Author interview with Columbus historian David Secrest

CHAPTER 2: CONVERSION

Hanover was a Presbyterian school and additional Hanover background—Author interviews with former classmates

It was like church service lite—Author interviews, news clippings from the *Hanover Triangle*, Hanover's yearbook, *Revonah*

In 1978, he picked Pence—Mike Pence speech, Church by the Glades, March 2017, https://www.youtube.com/watch?v=5BO6DxuxAFA

THE DISPENSATIONS

A century earlier; Christian split; Darwin history—Author aided by evangelical historian John Fea; for more see John Fea, *Believe Me: The Evangelical Road to Trump*, Eerdmans, 2018

Moral Majority background—see Cal Thomas and Ed Dobson, *Blinded by Might*, Zondervan, 2000

founder of Union Oil, Lyman Stewart—Ibid.

Reporting on Dispensationalists, types of evangelicals, Billy Graham—Author interviews with Cal Thomas, Russell Pulliam, John Fea. Additional research from PBS series *America's Evangelicals*; more here: https://www.pbs.org/wgbh/pages/frontline/shows/jesus/evangelicals/

ENTER THE DOOMSDAY PROPHETS

took a road trip from Washington down to Central Virginia—Matt Lewis, *Too Dumb to Fail: How the GOP Went from the Party of Reagan to the Party of Trump*, Hachette, 2016

"Moral majority"—Ibid.

Jerry Falwell wrote—Jerry Falwell, "Nuclear War and the Second Coming of Jesus Christ," *Old-Time Gospel Hour*, 1983

"According to my Bible"—Pat Robertson, "The 700 Club," March 28, 1980; accessed via https://www.youtube.com/watch?v=uDT3krve9iE

THE NEXT STEP

he didn't show it—Author interviews with multiple friends, Bob Massie, Jeff Cardwell, others

had little to do with—Author interview with Bob Massie

Hanover College was tucked away—Author visits to Columbus, Indiana, and Southern Indiana

Hanover was a dry college (Additional campus life)—Author review of *The Hanover Triangle* and *Renovah*, the Hanover yearbook, 1977–1981

Just then, a giant, beefy arm—Pence comic strips, obtained by author from Hanover College, published in *Hanover Triangle*

Phi Gamma Delta GPA, probation, presentation to university—*The Hanover Triangle*, various issues, Fall 1977—Fall 1978

"A Historical Note on the Alcohol Steering Committee"—Mike Pence, *The Hanover Triangle*, October 1978

"They really raked us over the coals"— McKay Coppins, "God's Plan for Mike Pence," *The Atlantic*, January/February 2018

By the fall of 1979—Author interview with Susan Brouillette, reviews of *Renovah* yearbooks

"I originally went because I was checking things out"—Mike Pence, *The Hanover Triangle*, 1979

MORAL MAJORITY INTERLUDE

Moral Majority stormed the Republican Party—Wallace S. Turner, "Group of Evangelic Protestants Takes Over the GOP in Alaska," *The New York Times*, June 9, 1980

Additional information—Kathy Sawyer and Robert G. Kaiser, "The Sunday-go-to-meeting white evangelicals have come away from the Republican convention singing 'What a friend we have in Reagan,'" The Washington Post News Service, July 19, 1980

"Why would you elect a movie star?"—Steve Kukolla, "Penance, Redemption Punctuate Life of Mike," *Indianapolis Business Journal*, January 31, 1994

"People latch on to the material"—Ibid.

"When I accepted your nomination"—Reagan victory speech, November 4 1980, C-SPAN, https://www.c-span.org/video/?418300-1/reagan-victory-speech

"The Religious Expressions of Abraham Lincoln"—Mike Pence, "The Religious Expressions of Abraham Lincoln," December 14, 1980; obtained by author via Hanover Library

delivered the student address—*Renovah* yearbook; author interviews

Mike's grandfather and namesake—Stolberg, "'I Am an American Because of Him'"

"I am an American because of him"—Ibid.

Tamler said the experience was very emotional—Ibid.

But Pence had a small cadre of close friends—Author interview with Pence friend

Karen Batten was just two years older—"39 Top Seniors in Marion County Plan Future," *The Indianapolis News*, May 30, 1975

Additional Karen Pence background—"Indiana's First lady Recalls Her Days at Park School," *Park Tudor Phoenix*, Summer 2013

She had married her college beau—Whittaker-Batten wedding announcement, *The Indianapolis News*, September 2, 1978

"Bulldog"— Shari Rudavsky, "She's Right at Home," *The Indianapolis Star*, December 9, 2012

Their romance was intense—Ibid.

"Oh, you're my number one"— Jenna Browder, "Indiana Nice vs. D.C. Vice— Karen Pence on Faith, Family and Her Heart for Healing," The Christian Broadcasting Network, April 10, 2017, https://www1.cbn.com/cbnnews /us/2017/april/indiana-nice-vs-dc-vice-ndash-karen-pence-on-faith-family -and-her-heart-for-healing

modest partyer—Author interviews with former acquaintances and former aides

Prof. William Harvey—Author interview with Pence friend; Kukolla, "Penance"

a similar everyman theme—Mike Pence "Law Daze" comic strips, obtained by author from Indiana University Maurer School of Law library

It was a screed against Ogden himself!—Author interview with Paul Ogden

"Wasn't serious about it"—Author interview with longtime acquaintance

THE GRAND OL' PARTY

rock-ribbed Republican mainstay—Oliver Perry Morton, Ku Klux Klan, general Indiana history—multiple author interviews. For more, read Indiana historian James Madison's *The Indiana Way*, Indiana University Press, 1990

"The South's Middle Finger to the North"—Author interviews

"The Mother of Vice Presidents"—Daniel Carden, "Indiana Is 'the Mother of Vice Presidents,'" *The Times of Northwest Indiana*, July 14, 2016

Indiana GOP machine—Author interviews with dozens of Indiana Republicans

"He studied up . . ."—Author interview with former adviser

But another Hoosier and Quayle history—Author interview with Greg Zoeller

she taught art at Acton Elementary School—Rudavsky, "She's Right at Home"

"Pence started knocking on doors"—Author interview with multiple Republicans

Cardwell met for lunch—Author interviews with Jeff Cardwell

Cardwell and some friends—Author interviews with Cardwell, others

"Where do you start?"—Author interview with Pence acquaintance

Pence's closest friend—Author interviews with former aide, Republican familiar with the loss

Toby McClamroch—Author interview with Toby McClamroch

Pence called Sweezy—Ibid.

went looking for a new house—Ibid.

CHAPTER 3 CANDIDATE SCHOOL

the Ball brothers—"The Ball Brothers," Ball State University website, accessed via the Internet Archive, https://web.archive.org/web/20120402180532/ http://cms.bsu.edu/Academics/Libraries/CollectionsAndDept/Archives /Collections/UniversityArchives/Exhibits/Beneficence/BallBrothers.aspx

To advertise their newfound bounty—Author interviews with Indiana Republicans

the Second District—Indiana Second District Map 1982–1992—Jeffrey B. Lewis, Brandon DeVine, Lincoln Pitcher, and Kenneth C. Martis. (2013) *Digital Boundary Definitions of United States Congressional Districts, 1789-2012*. Viewable via https://github.com/JeffreyBLewis/congressional -district-boundaries/blob/master/Indiana_98_to_102.geojson

very much like Columbus—Author interviews with Indiana Republicans and former Pence neighbors; author visits to Muncie and Columbus

SHARP POLITICS

Extensive research from the Phil Sharp archives at Ball State University, finding aid available here: https://lib.bsu.edu/archives/findingaids /MSS156.pdf; most of Sharp archives only available in person at Ball State

U.S. representative Phil Sharp—Phil Sharp biography, accessed via Sharp archives, Ball State University

Sharp beat back a retinue—Author interviews with former Sharp and Pence campaign aides

Ball family heirs spent decades—Author interviews with former Sharp aides, Indiana Republicans

NEWT'S CAMPAIGN SCHOOL

bumped into Pence—Author interview with Ogden

Gingrich ran twice unsuccessfully, and general Newt Gingrich history—"The Long March of Newt," PBS *Frontline*, January 16, 1996, https://www.pbs .org/wgbh/frontline/film/newt/

"trio of muggers" and additional Gingrich comments—Myra McPherson, "Newt Gingrich, Point Man in a House Divided," *The Washington Post*, June 12, 1989

GOPAC campaign school—Author interview with Joseph Gaylord; "The Long March of Newt"

"Fights make news; shyness doesn't"—Joseph Gaylord, *Flying Upside Down*, GOPAC, 1991

Colin Chapman—Author interview with former Pence campaign aide

list of preapproved operatives—Author interviews with former Pence and Sharp aides, Sharp archives, FEC records

"Mike, it looks like you've been living in Washington Township"—Author interview with Doug Richardson

Sweezy pulled in national fund raiser—Author interview with Jeff Terp

he met Chuck Quilhot—Author interviews with Chuck Quilhot

"I would say Mike characterizes himself more as a Hoosier"—Nathan Kennett, "Sharp Congressional Foe Awaits GOP Challenger," *The Daily Journal*, April 30, 1988.

Pence hadn't really thought through the details—Author interviews with former Pence and Sharp campaign aides and extensive research of 1988 campaign news clips, including coverage from *The Columbus Republic*, *The Muncie Star*, *The Daily Journal*, and other local newspapers in Indiana's Second District

PAT ROBERTSON'S RUMBLINGS

had misgivings; Moral Majority frays—Thomas and Dobson, *Blinded by Might*

televangelist Jim Bakker—Kelsey McKinney, "The Second Coming of Televangelist Jim Bakker," BuzzFeed News, May 19, 2017

Robertson announces own run for president—October 2, 1987, C-SPAN, https://www.c-span.org/video/?3191-1/robertson-announcement

we realize that 92 percent—George Stuteville, "Pat Robertson Still Marches Onward for Conservatism," *The Indianapolis Star*, April 17, 1988

Ryan White; Ryan White history—Dr. Howard Markel, "Remembering Ryan White, the Teen Who Fought Against the Stigma of AIDS," PBS, April 8, 2016, https://www.pbs.org/newshour/health/remembering-ryan -white-the-teen-who-fought-against-the-stigma-of-aids

He never had to pick a side—Exhaustive research by author and interviews with Republicans and Democrats active at that time

on April 13, 1988—"'Kiel oil exec dies,' Staff Reports," *The Columbus Republic*, April 14, 1988

Pence was crushed—Interviews with former aides

"This will not be a nasty, or mean-spirited campaign"—John Schorg, "On the Offensive," *The Columbus Republic*, May 4, 1988

Phil Sharp sent aide to Columbus—Staff, "Mobile office here Thursday," May 23, 1988, *The Columbus Republic*

THE SHARP EDGE

"Because people liked Sharp"—Author interview with Gaylord

"representing Texas's Twenty-Sixth District"—"Texas Congressman Applauds Sharp for Help," Dick Armey, *The Franklin Challenger*, October 20, 1988; Sharp archives, Ball State

hurdle of anonymity—Sharp campaign polling memo and call sheet, April 8, 1988; Sharp archives, Ball State

Pence debate letter—Sharp archive

Sharp debate response—Ibid.

Pence bike ride—Schorg, "Pence Hopes to Overcome Outside Role"

he must know some verse!—Author interview with Ryan Streeter

THE ATTACK

softie in the War on Drugs—Sharp archives

Sharp believes—Sharp radio ad script in Sharp archives

"Hitler youth"— Jim Jachimiak, "Even Third-Place Candidates Show Good Sense of Humor," *The Daily Journal* (Franklin, Indiana), November 14, 1988

ANOTHER INDIANA SURPRISE

Pence Reagan meeting—Mike Pence speech at Reagan Library, September 8, 2016, C-SPAN, https://www.c-span.org/video/?414899-1/mike-pence -delivers-remarks-reagan-library

Tuesday, August 16, 1988—Author interview of Jim Shella, Indiana Republicans

PENCE V. SHARP

October 11 debate—News clips, Sharp archives at Ball State

"Stop being defensive."—Scribbled note by Sharp aide—Sharp debate notes from Ball State archive

"I thought we had a good dialogue . . ."—Ibid., Sharp archives

"don't like Japanese coming to America"—Pence debate quotes; Sharp archives notes

the returns looked good—Author interviews of former Pence aides, advisers

withering growl—Author interview with John Schorg

"Pence proved to be a tireless campaigner"— Larry Shores, "Negativism Didn't Work Here," *The Muncie Star*, November 12, 1988

CHAPTER 4: BROKE—1990

Republicans at Acapulco Joe's—Author interviews with McClamroch, Quilhot, other attendees

"Pence didn't know which end was up . . ."—Author interviews with Chuck Quilhot

a real job and some regular income—Ibid.

trying to conceive—Melissa Langsam Braunstein, "Second Lady Karen Pence Opens Up About Her Struggles with Infertility," *The Federalist*, April 25, 2017, https://thefederalist.com/2017/04/25/second-lady-karen-pence -opens-struggles-infertility/

Approved by the Catholic Church—Ruth Graham, "Why It Matters That Karen Pence Pursued Medical Assistance When Trying to Get Pregnant," Slate, April 26, 2017, https://slate.com/human-interest/2017/04/karen-pence -used-an-obscure-catholic-friendly-alternative-to-ivf.html

hadn't been bringing in business—Author interview with Pence acquaintance

"I will freely admit my frustration"—Karen Terhune, "Pence Offers Congressional Campaign Preview," *The Muncie Evening Press*, February 15, 1990

habit of micromanaging operations—Author interviews with Republicans familiar with Pence congressional races

"always keep the candidate's wife happy"—Author interview with Sherman Johnson

launched a media tour—Author interview with Tim Bonnell

carved out a weekly spot—Darren Samuelsohn, "The Old Cassettes That Explain Mike Pence," Politico, July 20, 2016, https://www.politico.com /story/2016/07/mike-pence-talk-radio-225855

Pence letter to editors—Sharp archives

"I think you'll sense a different level of professionalism"—Terhune, "Pence Offers Congressional Campaign Preview"

THE MOVING GROUND

Dick Cheney—Shifting ground of GOP, history, based on multiple interviews with former longtime Republican staffers

Cheney, Bush, Gingrich—history based on multiple background interviews by author

Pence never took a side—Author interviews with Republicans in and around his 1990 race

Alan Secrest warned Sharp—Polling memo, Sharp archives

RUTHLESSLY SHARP

Billy Linville and Bob McCarson—Author interview with Brian Francisco

found "the silver bullet"—Author interview with Billy Linville

$222 a month for Karen's car—Details of campaign cash spending, FEC reports; author interview with Linville; author interviews with Indiana Republicans

"It's a full-time job to run a campaign"—Author interview with Johnson

red in the face—Author interview with Linville

"We will not deal with the character flaws of my opponent"—Tyrone Meighan, "Pence Urges Clean Campaign, Calls Opponent a Liar," *The Indianapolis Star*, July 25, 1990

"Pence Urges Clean Campaign, Calls Opponent a Liar"—Ibid.

television campaign fared better—Mike Pence campaign ads, accessed via Oklahoma University political ad archives

noticed him withdrawing—Author interviews with Republicans familiar with the Pence 1990 campaign

MUNCIE DEBATE

Pence and Sharp took the debate stage—Muncie debate video obtained by author from WIPB

THE ARAB AD

burning through more; Pence donation figures—Brian Francisco, "Pence Says Campaign Isn't Short of Cash," *The Muncie Star*, October 20, 1990

"Tea party"—Ibid.

Not long after the debate; Pence comes up with idea for the Arab ad—
Author interviews with Republicans familiar with Pence ad-making
decision

"Oh, thank you Phil Sharp!" and additional Arab ad details—Karen Terhune,
"Pence Won't Pull Controversial TV Ad," *The Muncie Evening Press*,
October 11, 1990, and Dan Carpenter, "Racial Stereotypes: We've Not
Come Such a Long Way, Baby," *The Indianapolis Star*, October 14, 1990

Columnist Dan Carpenter—Carpenter, "Racial Stereotypes"

"If I felt the ad was racist"—John O'Neill, "Pence Slings Oil, Not Mud," *The
Indianapolis Star*, October 10, 1990

protests cropped up around Indianapolis—Angela C. Allen, "200 Arabs Rally to
Protest 'Hurtful' Pence Commercial," *The Indianapolis Star*, October 14,
1990

surprised how passé Pence's choice was—Author interview with Jim Zogby

Pence and his team gathered—Author interviews with Cardwell, Sherman
Johnson, Republicans familiar with the campaign

CHAPTER 5: THE THINK TANK

"Mike burned a lot of bridges"—Mayer, "The Danger of President Pence"

he never said who he was—Author research from hundreds of news clips,
interviews with former campaign aides

Quilhot called Pence immediately—Author interviews with Quilhot

"We didn't tell anybody"—Braunstein, "Second Lady Karen Pence"

regulars at the Catholic church—Author interviews with Indiana Republicans

BEING CONSERVATIVE

wanted to move the dial right; Indiana Policy Review history—Author
interviews with Quilhot, Craig Ladwig

a central split on the Right—Author interviews with Quilhot

would bump into a veteran Republican—Author interview with Bill Smith

Indiana Family Institute stances—Author interviews, research of IFI website
obtained through Internet Archives

"In Defense of a Little Virginity"—Indiana Family Institute ad, *The Indianapolis
Star*, September 24, 1993

After Ryan White died; additional Ryan White history—Ken Kusmer, "1,500
Say Goodbye to AIDS victim Ryan White," The Associated Press,
April 11, 1990

On July 29, 1991—Info on Karen, gay teens, *Indianapolis Star* in *The
Indianapolis Star*, July 29 and August 11, 1991

Seven Habits of Highly Effective People—Author interview with Bob Massie

Doug Richardson—Author interview with Richardson

Pence, campaign cash, FEC rules—David L. Haase, "Campaign funds case dropped," *The Indianapolis News*, December 15, 1990

ran into Peter Rusthoven—Author interview with Peter Rusthoven

write a book—Author interviews with Bob Massie

"Confessions of a Negative Campaigner"—Mike Pence, "Confessions of a Negative Campaigner," *The Indiana Policy Review*, Fall 1991

"my opponent is really irrelevant"—Brian Francisco, "Pence Sorry for Negative Campaign," *The Muncie Star*, August 15, 1991

MOCKING MULLIN

the Republican councilman—Kathleen Johnston, "McGrath Urged to Quit Race," *The Indianapolis News*, June 7, 1991; author interviews with Indiana Republicans

Pence got to Southport Middle School—Author interview with Tim Mullin

ENTER PAT BUCHANAN AND THE BUSH TAKEDOWN

Pence picks his side in GOP split, emerges Christian conservative—Author interviews with numerous Republicans familiar with his rise

Buchanan history—Pat Buchanan Wikipedia entry, https://en.wikipedia.org/wiki/Pat_Buchanan

Buchanan and GOP primary results—"1992 Republican Party presidential primaries," Wikipedia, https://en.wikipedia.org/wiki/1992_Republican_Party_presidential_primaries

Buchanan gay ad—C-SPAN, February 18, 1992, https://www.c-span.org/video/?c4679699/pat-buchanan-ad-featuring-tongues-untied

Pence support for Buchanan 1992—Author interview with Quilhot, other Republicans

Pence comments supporting Buchanan—Author interview with Quilhot and Mary Beth Schneider, "Tsongas, Buchanan hustle to get in race," *The Indianapolis Star*, February 21, 1992

Pence Limbaugh anecdote—Author interview with Quilhot

Bush protest votes and GOP primary results—Buchanan Wikipedia entry

Effort to replace Dan Quayle—Author interviews and research, news clips

Pence defense of Quayle—Mike Pence, "How George and Jim might dump Dan," *The Muncie Star*, August 8, 1992

Pence—Clinton, No Tell Motel—Mike Pence, "America about to sign into no-tell motel with Clinton," *The Daily Journal*, October 21, 1992

David McIntosh background, start in politics—Author interviews with David McIntosh

Pence helps McIntosh—Ibid.

"I genuinely believe . . ."—Brian Francisco, "Talk radio suits former congressional candidate," *The Muncie Star Press*, March 7, 1994

CHAPTER 6: MIKE PENCE, INC. v. MICHAEL

"You couldn't talk to him about elected office"—Author interviews with Bob Massie

IPR invites Russell Kirk to a dinner—Author interviews with Quilhot, others

Kirk brand of conservatism—Author interviews, review of Kirk writings

Kirk in Columbus, Pence meeting—Author interview of Pence for *Indianapolis Star*

IPR short on money, Pence launching own career—Author interviews with Quilhot

The Pence Report $19.95—Steve Hall, "The Kind Conservative," *The Indianapolis Star*, September 11, 1995

Pence colonial, Karen break from teaching, broke—Author interviews with Pence friends, former acquaintances

Pence Catholic to evangelical church—Author interviews with former acquaintances

Jim Dodson, Greenwood Community Church—Ryan Trares, "Friends in Faith: Group Recalls Strong Roots that Helped Pence Thrive," *The Columbus Republic*, January 17, 2017

THE RISE OF RUSH

Limbaugh background, Bush campaign work on Rush—"Rush Limbaugh's America," PBS *Frontline*, accessed via Youtube, https://www.youtube.com/watch?v=tWD_F6sZ5dE

Pence Rush—Author interview with Quilhot

Network Indiana history—Author interviews with Scott Uecker

Pam Ferrin WNDE—McCawley, "The Road to the Governor's Office"

Gingrich 1993 GOPAC memo—Steve Gillon, "GOPAC strategy and instructional tapes (1986–1994)," The Library of Congress, http://www.loc.gov/static/programs/national-recording-preservation-board/documents/GOPACtapes.pdf

LEFT BEHIND—NOVEMBER 1944

Left Behind—Author review of *Left Behind* series

"We believe (the Tribulation) to be true . . ."—Bennie M. Currie, "Revelation launches yet another novel," The Associated Press, August 26, 2000

LaHaye, Robertson, Falwell, extreme—Author interviews with evangelical historians, Republican operatives

"If Hagee were urging his congregation"—Kathleen Parker, "Foreign Policy, Not Religion," Tribune Media Services, August 5, 2006

Pence tone on-air—Author interviews with Jon Quick, Kate Shepherd, Scott Uecker, Indiana Republicans, others

Ripken joke—Brian Blair, "Open Mike," *The Columbus Republic*, September 17, 1995

Larry King of Indiana—Author interview with Scott Uecker
"My obligation first as a Christian . . ."—Blair "Open Mike"
"The epicenter of our cultural decline . . ."—Judy Chatham, "Writing Around," *The Daily Journal*, September 26, 1995

GAMBLING IN INDIANA, TRUMP STYLE

"The Mike Pence Show," February 13, 1996—Samuelsohn, "The Old Cassettes"
Christian Right emergence in Indiana—Author interviews with Indiana Republicans
For more on Steve Hilbert—Evan West, "Dumpster fire of the vanities: John Menard, Steve Hilbert, and the Midwestern nouveau riche," *The Indianapolis Monthly*, February 26, 2016
1996 Gridiron Video obtained by author
"Hilbert has become Indiana's version of Donald Trump"—Dick Cady, "A Vendetta Against Hilbert? No, The Steve Has Become a Big Story," *The Indianapolis Star*, April 2, 1996
"Dinner with Mike Pence"—*The Indianapolis Star*, October 24, 1996

THE RADIO PRO—1997

Pollack showdown, Pence dead air—Author interview with Uecker
Pence radio show tic-toc—Author interviews with Dan Jensen
Pence radio voice—Author interview with Jon Quick
Simpson catches on to Pence—Author interview with Steve Simpson
For more Clinton background—Mike Isikoff, *Uncovering Clinton*, Three Rivers Press, 1999
Pence Clinton impeachment; *". . . the Constitution failed"*—Pence op-ed, *Indy Star*, 1999
Pence words matter –Author interviews with Kate Shepherd
McIntosh/Pence—Author interviews with David McIntosh

CHAPTER 7: RESURRECTION—2000

Mike Pence didn't live in the Second District—Second District map
Planted a new tree for each new child—Author interviews with Indiana Republicans
Wasn't sure he wanted to leave the media spotlight—Author interviews with Pence friends, including Massie, Cardwell, and others who spoke on background
"That's John Dillinger, folks"—The Mike Pence Show, October 30, 1999; video courtesy of the Bart Peterson archives at the University of Indianapolis
Take some working to get Karen to yes—Author interview with Rusthoven
McIntosh ran into his friends—Author interviews with McIntosh
Pence trip to Theodore Roosevelt National Park—Allison McSherry, "Popcorn and Mrs. Pence Shape Indiana Office," *Roll Call*, May 19, 2010. Note,

other versions of this story Pence has told place him in Colorado for the retreat. But this was the most detailed.

Draw down life savings to run—Ibid.

Framed Jeremiah 29:11—Ibid.

Jeremiah Chapter 29, verses 10 through 14—Accessed via Bible online

A DIFFERENT KIND OF EVANGELICAL—2000

For more on this topic:

"I was watching the debate with my wife and daughter in the room"—Hanna Rosin, "Bush's 'Christ moment' is put to political test by Christians," *The Washington Post*, December 16, 1999

W. was a different kind of evangelical—"America's Evangelicals," PBS *Frontline*, 2004

"They had a whole peace about running" —Author interview with Bill Smith

Shortly after Smith took over the campaign—Ibid.

Van Smith positioning—Author interviews with Indiana Republicans

November 9, 1999, he filed an "exploratory committee"—David Smith, "Talk show host forms committee to explore Congress bid," *The Palladium-Item*, November 9, 1999

Pence moved his family to Edinburgh, Indiana—FEC filings, residential records and Paul Minnis, "Pence plans 2nd District run; moving back here," *The Columbus Republic*, December 8, 1999

"I won't make a formal announcement until January"—Minnis, "Pence plans 2nd District run"

Linder argued that he and every other candidate—Staff, "Pence challenged over radio show air time," The Associated Press, January 8, 2000

"I do intend to run for Congress in the year 2000"—David Smith, "Radio host says he will run for District 2 seat," *The Palladium-Item*, January 11, 2000

Pence scheduled kickoff rallies—Advertisement, *The Columbus Republic*, February 15, 2000

May 2, 2000, Republican primary results—Gregory Weaver, "Robert Rock to face Mike Pence," *The Indianapolis Star*, May 3, 2000

THE TWO MIKES

"Our campaign has committed itself"—"Straight talk" Mike Pence ad via YouTube, https://www.youtube.com/watch?v=F9sIefTurj4

"Everything I know about public education"—"Education," Mike Pence ad via YouTube, https://www.youtube.com/watch?v=EII8vkbFhu0

"Greetings across the amber waves of grain, this is Mike Pence."—"Renewing the American Dream" Mike Pence ad via YouTube, https://www.youtube.com /watch?v=EII8vkbFhu0

"Guide to Renewing the American Dream"—Mike Pence campaign website,

MikePence.com/issues.html. Captured via Internet Archive: http://web
.archive.org/web/20010408125427/http:/mikepence.com/issues.html
Pence positions on gays and women in the military, HIV prevention, etc.—
Ibid.
For more on Dick Cheney vice presidential search—Adam Nagourney and
Frank Bruni, "The Selection: Gatekeeper to Running Mate" *The New York
Times*, July 28, 2000, https://www.nytimes.com/2000/07/28/us/2000
-campaign-selection-gatekeeper-running-mate-cheney-s-road-candidacy
.html?mtrref=www.google.com&gwh=EAED88F3B09B648B401D92DD
6FC2EE35&gwt=pay
and Barton Gellman, *Angler*, Penguin, 2008

THE 2000 DEBATE

Debate video obtained by author from WIPB
On Tuesday, November 7, 2000—FEC, https://transition.fec.gov/pubrec/2000
presgeresults.htm

CHAPTER 8: THE UNKNOWN

Seven years after they first met—Author interviews with David McIntosh
$30,000 in credit card debt—Pence personal financial disclosures, 2001–2012
Pence enrolled children Immanuel Bible Church—Interviews with Pence friends
*The church was nondenominational, but spiritually and culturally conservative
much like the Community Church of Greenwood*—Author interviews with
Washington and Indiana Republican sources
"Whatever goes on out there, doesn't affect what happens in here"—"Karen Pence—
Who's on Your Stool?" Truth at Work, 2013, https://truthatwork.org
/video/karen-pence-whos-on-your-stool-who-god-wants-you-to-mentor/
Mike stuck close to a schedule of making it home—Interviews with Pence friends
and former House colleagues
"Nothing good happens after the second drink and after nine P.M."—Author inter-
view with former aide
Ask the House staff to run in an ISDN line—Author interview with David
Almacy, former House IT staff
*"After hours, when the switchboard is off, you ought to put a separate line in the
office"*—McSherry, "Popcorn and Mrs. Pence"
"Mrs. Pence is the only one who has the number, not anyone on staff"—Ibid.
*Pence also found a community in Washington's suburbs rich with Christian and fiscal
conservatives*—Interviews with Washington Republicans on background
gained the attention of a young Republican staffer from Normal, Illinois—Author
interview with Matt Lloyd
an evangelical minister active in the pro-life movement also moved to Washington—
Author interview with Rev. Robert Schenck

THE MORNING EVERYTHING CHANGED

September 11, 2001, background via Wikipedia, "September 11 attacks," https://en.wikipedia.org/wiki/September_11_attacks

Mike Pence said a prayer with his staff—Rick Yencer, "Officials Call for Retaliation," *The Muncie Star Press*, September 12, 2001

Karen Pence was teaching at Immanuel Christian School—Ibid.

A small group of top-level Bush administration officials began trying to connect the attack to Iraqi dictator Saddam Hussein—Max Follmer, "The Reporting Team That Got Iraq Right," Huffington Post, March 28, 2008, https://www.huffpost.com/entry/the-reporting-team-that-g_n_91981

"The ACLU's got to take some blame for this"—Marc Ambinder, "Falwell Suggest Gays to Blame for Attacks," ABC News, https://abcnews.go.com/Politics/story?id=121322&page=1

Speaker Dennis Hastert called Pence on Friday, October 26, 2001—Alan Fram, "Anthrax Found in Three Lawmakers' Offices In House Building," The Associated Press, October 26, 2011

Bush State of the Union Address—January 29, 2002, via C-SPAN, https://www.c-span.org/video/?168239-1/2002-state-union-address

"I grieve at the thought of the United States at war and am not anxious to see it"—"Rep. Pence Discusses Iraq Debate," *Richmond Palladium*, September 29, 2002

MIKE IN DC

Mike Pence did not hit the town like most of the other freshmen lawmakers—Author interviews with Washington Republicans

That herculean restraint and discipline, sometimes led his colleagues to wonder if something was a little off—Author interviews with Washington Republicans

General Jack Abramoff background—*Casino Jack and the United States of Money*, written and directed by Alex Gibney, 2010

Pence and the other conservatives on the Republican Study Committee saw an affront to the First Amendment in the limiting of campaign spending—Author interview with former representative Darrell Issa, other Republicans

"He came in a Reagan-esque way"—Author interview with Issa

Pence also found an eager partner in Jeff Flake—Jeff Flake, *Conscience of a Conservative*, Random House, 2017. See also Tim Alberta, "How Donald Trump Became Mike Pence and Jeff Flake," *Politico Magazine*, January/February 2018, https://www.politico.com/magazine/story/2018/01/03/mike-pence-jeff-flake-republican-party-friendship-216208

Bush beckoned Pence and a few other holdouts—Author interview with a former Pence aide

Pence ran into Ann DeLaney—Author interview with Ann DeLaney

the same GOP brass who got Pence a ticket to Washington in 2000—Author interview with a former Republican operative

THE CONSERVATIVE MAN—2004 VERSION

He delivered a stern, but hopeful speech—Pence speech to CPAC, 2004, via Pence congressional archives at Indiana University

"Mr. Speaker, after weeks of legal and moral confusion"—Pence gay marriage ban 2004 comments, February 24, 2004, via C-SPAN, https://www.c-span .org/video/?c4659020/mike-pence-anti-gay-marriage-2004

On March 6, 2004, Pence stood before the Council for National Policy—Mike Pence speech to CNP, via Pence congressional archives at Indiana University

THE HERO'S FUNERAL

An unidentified airplane hurtled toward the center of the nation's capital—Spencer Hsu, "Plane That Caused Capitol Evacuation Nearly Shot Down," *The Washington Post*, July 8, 2004

Women's heels lined the first floor of the Capitol—Author interviews with former Republican aides

"Son, I've always found the safest place is in God's good graces."—Author interview with former Republican aide

THE FAMILY BUSINESS

Then, in 2001, Greg Pence and Kiel Brothers filed for bankruptcy—Michael Tackett, "As Another Pence Runs for Congress, His Business Record Raises Questions," *The New York Times*, April 22, 2018, https://www. nytimes.com/2018/04/22/us/politics/pence-brother-congress-business -record.html

Greg was bailed out by the agency that said he owed them $3.8 million—Ibid.

The collapse of Kiel Brothers cost Pence close to $700,000 in stock he held in the company—Pence tax returns, provided by Trump campaign

they began aging out of the K-8 Christian school at Immanuel Bible Church—Author interview with former Pence neighbor from Northern Virginia

"The guy's cherished opportunity to hide God's word in those young men's hearts"—Ibid.

the family seemed cloistered, tucked away from the rest of the community—Author interview with a former Democratic official

RUBBING IS RACING

Close to two thousand people died— Eric S. Blake, Christopher W. Landsea, and Ethan J. Gibney, "The Deadliest, Costliest, and Most Intense United States Tropical Cyclones from 1851 to 2010," National Weather Service, National Hurricane Center, August 2011, https://www.nhc.noaa.gov/pdf /nws-nhc-6.pdf

"Operation Offset," as it was dubbed—Mike Dorning, "One for the Gipper; Indiana Congressman, Talk Show Darling and Reagan Disciple Mike Pence Is Fast Becoming The Voice of Small-Government Conservatives," *The Chicago Tribune*, October 26, 2005

"One more expansion of the Department of Education"—Ibid.

"He clearly got called—aggressively called—on the carpet"—Ibid.

The Chicago Tribune *profiled Pence as a new hero to the right*—Ibid.

That week he was reading—Ibid.

Chapter 1 retells the Israelites—Joshua 1, The Bible

"Be strong, be courageous and do the work"—Ibid.

"To understand Mike Pence"—Dorning, "One for the Gipper"

"The party faithful"—Ibid.

"It has been Pence and his roughly 100 colleagues"—Lawrence Kudlow, "2005 Man of the Year: Mike Pence," *Human Events*, December 22, 2015

"He's really good at what he does"—Author interview with former Republican aide

Pence began running movie clips—Ibid.

"Bridge to Nowhere," a roughly $400 million project—Tom Kizzia, "Palin Touts Stance on 'Bridge to Nowhere' Doesn't Note Flip-Flop," *Anchorage Daily News*, August 31, 2008

Pence liked to remind his RSC members that "rubbing is racing."—"Pence Predicts 'Fender Rubbing' Between Administration, House Conservatives," *The Frontrunner*, December 21, 2004

Pence would regularly let Tom DeLay and other House leaders know—Author interviews with former Republican aides

"We decided to call it the Hastert Rule"—Author interview with former Republican aide

The Washington Post *revealed the extent of Abramoff's corruption*—Susan Schmidt and James V. Grimaldi, "The Fast Rise and Steep Fall of Jack Abramoff," *The Washington Post*, December 29, 2015, https://www .washingtonpost.com/archive/politics/2005/12/29/the-fast-rise-and -steep-fall-of-jack-abramoff/56987391-1b47-414d-866e-531bc2b0a603 /?utm_term=.e1c3454cb136

indicted by a local Democratic prosecutor in Texas—Terence Stutz, "Earlier Jury Declined to Indict DeLay," *The Dallas Morning News*, October 6, 2006, https://www.sun-sentinel.com/news/fl-xpm-2005-10-06-0510051155 -story.html

it was really an invitation for one person: John Boehner—Former Republican aide

Boehner, McIntosh, Armey, DeLay, and some others—James Carney and Karen Tumulty, "Attempted Republican Coup: Ready, Aim, Misfire," TIME Magazine/CNN, July 28, 1999, http://www.cnn.com/ALLPOLITICS /1997/07/21/time/gingrich.html

he developed a penchant, a talent—Author interviews with former Republican aides

"House conservatives should seek to marry fiscal and ethics reform"—Gwyneth K. Shaw, "GOP Urged to Return to Tenets; Lawmakers at Baltimore Retreat Back Conservative Values, Spending Cuts," *The Baltimore Sun*, January 31, 2006

Boehner would have to hold off Blunt—Author interviews with former Republican aides

and beat Blunt, 122–109—Ben Pershing, "Election Update: Do-over on First Ballot," *Roll Call*, https://web.archive.org/web/20060204102043/http://rollcall.com/issues/1_1/breakingnews/12015-1.html

House Democratic leader Nancy Pelosi—Patrick O'Connor, "DeLay Urges Conservative Vision in Farewell to GOP Colleagues," The Hill, June 8, 2006

Pence felt a new tug to lead—Author interview with former Republican aide

"I mean, what we're doing isn't working"—Ibid.

"Congress is really a lot like high school"—Ibid.

"We were trying to scrounge for votes for two-three weeks"—Ibid.

"It was truly one of the most Reagan-esque moments I've seen [from] him"—Ibid.

Boehner remembered that—Ibid.

CHAPTER 9: PENCE'S MOMENT

anointed Cantor as someone worth grooming—Author interviews with former Republican aides

Boehner sensed danger from Cantor on his right flank—Author interview with former House Republican aide

Boehner saw a good use for Pence—Ibid.

Boehner started working on Pence—Ibid.

THE GRANDSON OF STRUGGLING IMMIGRANTS

Pence immigration background—Author interviews with former House Republican aide

Short represented the blue-blooded world of conservative Virginia politics—Author interviews with former House Republican aides and Washington Republicans

a plan to increase border security—Ruben Navarette, "Downed by His Own," *San Diego Union-Tribune*, August 23, 2006

the Far Right Federation for American Immigration Reform ran attack ads—Ibid.

"But the crosscurrents here have been challenging to me."—Ibid.

"I fear Mrs. Pence more than I do the voters."—Maureen Groppe, "Pence in His Own Words: 24 Key Quotes," *USA Today*, July 15, 2016, https://www.usatoday.com/story/news/politics/onpolitics/2016/07/15/mike-pence-key-quotes/87100512/

Congressional salaries—"History of Annual Salaries—Members of Congress and Leadership," LegiStorm website

Median national income 2006 and 2007—Real Median Household Income in the United States, Federal Reserve Bank of St. Louis, https://fred.stlouisfed .org/series/MEHOINUSA672N

Pence financial status—Pence personal financial disclosures, tax returns, and real estate records

Pence saw a building crescendo of outrage and populist revolt—Author interview with former House Republican aide

THE OBAMA WAVE

On November 4, 2008—2008 election results, Federal Elections Commission, https://transition.fec.gov/pubrec/fe2008/federalelections2008.pdf

"The Republican Party death"— John Batchelor, "GOP R.I.P.," The Daily Beast, April 10, 2009, https://www.thedailybeast.com/gop-rip

Boehner moved swiftly—Author interviews with former aides and see Steven T. Dennis, "Boehner: Survivor Star," *Roll Call*, November 10, 2008

Pence's aides awaited final word—Author interview with former House Republican aide

They needed Marc Short—Author interviews with former House Republican aides

"Mike outgrew Bill Smith's counsel"—Author interview with former Pence adviser

gathered at Brent Bozell's country house—Author interviews with Diana Banister, Washington Republicans

"Okay, we've got to fix this"—Ibid.

"This is a man of the movement"—Ibid.

2009—THE TEAVANGELICAL MIKE

Now Pence's bigger leadership team—Author interviews with former House Republican aide

Pitcock, Short, and Lloyd were also devout evangelical Christians—Author interview with former House Republican aide

scout of presidential timber, Kellyanne Conway—Author interviews with former House Republican aide, Washington Republicans

Conway background—Ryan Lizza, "Kellyanne Conway's Political Machinations," *The New Yorker*, October 8, 2016, https://www.newyorker .com/magazine/2016/10/17/kellyanne-conways-political-machinations

David and Charles Koch background—For more on Kochs, see Jane Mayer, *Dark Money: The Hidden History of Billionaires Behind the Rise of the Radical Right*, Anchor, 2016

MSNBC invited Pence on—MSNBC Hardball transcript, April 16, 2009, http://www.nbcnews.com/id/30248197/ns/msnbc-hardball_with_chris _matthews/t/hardball-chris-matthews-wednesday-april/#.XLONi6fMzGI

Pence was back in Indiana—Town Hall clip via YouTube, April 16, 2009, https://www.youtube.com/watch?v=ZvlyG70qB8s

Some Tea Partiers were dubbing Barack Obama the next Hitler—Author experience watching Tea Party rallies

"you people look like the cavalry to me"—Mike Pence remarks at Tea Party rally, September 12, 2009, https://www.c-span.org/video/?c4610231/mike -pence-remarks-tea-party

quickly plucked up—Interview with former Pence adviser

snagged Ballard's lead fund raiser—Author interview with Marty Obst

JANUARY 2010—THE OBAMA CONFERENCE

the House Republicans agreed to let the cameras stick around—Author interviews with former House Republican aides

On January 29, 2010—Obama speech to House Republican Conference, January 29, 2010, C-SPAN, https://www.c-span.org/video/?291730-1 /presidential-remarks-house-republican-conference

DECISION TIME

The recruiters at the National Republican Senate Committee—Author interview with former House Republican aide

Bayh said he was done with the Senate—Evan Bayh, "Why I'm Leaving the Senate," *The New York Times*, February 20, 2010, https://www.nytimes .com/2010/02/21/opinion/21bayh.html

he had his eyes on the big prize—Author interviews with former House Republican aides, Washington Republicans

veteran Indiana representative Mark Souder—"Indiana Rep. Mark Souder Resigns After Affair with Staffer," The Associated Press, May 18, 2010, https://www.syracuse.com/news/2010/05/indiana_rep_mark_souder _resign.html

Pence approached him with some advice—Author interviews with Washington and Indiana Republicans

Pence hit the road with his new fund raiser Marty Obst—Author interview with Obst

Pence went courting Paul Singer—Author interview with Republican official

Family Research Council's Values Voter Summit—Michael Memoli, "Pence Edges Out Huckabee, Romney in Conservatives' Straw Poll for President," *The Los Angeles Times*, September 18, 2010, https://www.latimes.com/archives /la-xpm-2010-sep-18-la-pn-0918-values-voter-summit-20100918-story.html

"a lot of people sometimes realize we shouldn't say everything we think"—Ibid.

in November 2010—Jeff Zeleny, "GOP Captures House, But Not Senate," *The New York Times*, November 2, 2010, https://www.nytimes.com /2010/11/03/us/politics/03elect.html

Pence still couldn't decide—Interviews with former Pence advisers, Washington Republicans

Pence's advisers told him—Author interviews with current and former Pence advisers

speak before the Detroit Economic Club—Pence speech to Detroit Economic Club, November 29, 2010. Obtained via Pence congressional paper archive, Indiana University

GOP donor class and the establishment—Author interviews of Indiana and Washington Republicans

Daniels wooed national media—Author's experiences

Pence gathered with his most loyal donors—Author interviews of current and former Pence advisers

With Daniels heading for the exit—Author interviews with Indiana and Washington Republicans, current and former Pence advisers

"He was never really serious"—Author interview with a Pence adviser

"Lincoln declared"—Michael Falcone, "Draft Mike Pence Movement Gaining Steam Among Conservatives," January 19, 2011, https://abcnews.go.com /Politics/draft-mike-pence-movement-gaining-steam-conservatives/story ?id=12682362&page=1&fbclid=IwAR13xm_Z4nrP16vfbRVNUgie4_cKn FtKVxc8791QUixoA1r8LM_8p9Rnm8U

Marjorie Dannenfelser—Author interviews with Marjorie Dannenfelser

"But there must be real giving up"—C. S. Lewis, *Mere Christianity*, HarperOne, 2015

On January 27, 2011—Maureen Groppe and Mary Beth Schneider, "Pence Shuts 1 Door, Leaves Another Open," *The Indianapolis Star*, January 27, 2011

"I was crestfallen"—Author interview with Kellyanne Conway

held a monthly dinner—List of attendees, photos of dinner obtained by author

"Why don't you run?"—Author interview with dinner attendee

Pence hosted a small fund raiser—Author interview with Pence adviser

Daniels delivered his decision—Peter Hamby, "Indiana Gov. Mitch Daniels Says Sorry, Not Running for President," CNN, http://www.cnn.com/2011 /POLITICS/05/22/indiana.daniels.out/

Real Clear Politics published an exposé—Erin McPike, "Why Mitch Daniels Said No," Real Clear Politics, May 22, 2011, https://www.realclearpolitics .com/articles/2011/05/22/why_mitch_daniels_said_no_109948.html

Mike Pence has a real chance Teavangelical—Matt Lewis, "In 'The Teavangelicals' CBN's David Brody yearns for a President Mike Pence," The Daily Caller, July 24, 2012, https://dailycaller.com/2012/07/24/in-the -teavangelicals-cbns-david-brody-yearns-for-a-president-mike-pence/

CHAPTER 10: BACK HOME AGAIN

On June 11, 2011—Mike Pence campaign kickoff, author experience

"We need to be willing to say 'Yes'"—Tom LoBianco, "Pence Comes to Indiana to Fight Washington," The Associated Press, June 11, 2011

"We need a leader who understands Washington"—Ibid.

nice place in Geist Reservoir—Pence financial disclosure reports, Indiana campaign finance records

returned to Indiana a changed man—Author interviews with former acquaintances and colleagues from the 1990s

wrote a glowing assessment—Mark Souder, "Faults of Mike Pence," Howey Politics Indiana, June 16, 2011

Gregg and Pence had a personal connection—Author interviews with Gregg

AUSTRALIAN GOLD

a few days in New York City—Author interview with Pence adviser

Pence entered Trump Tower—Ibid.

Trump relationship with Hilbert—Interviews with Trump campaign advisers, Pence advisers, Indiana Republicans

Hilbert helped Trump out in a pinch in 1998—Charles Bagli, "Trump in Deal to sell G.M. Building," *The New York Times*, June 14, 2003, https://www.new yorktimes.com/2003/06/14/nyregion/trump-in-deal-to-sell-gm-building.html

"We turn down many sponsors"—Anne Marie Tiernon, "Steve Hilbert Touts Australian Gold on Celebrity Apprentice," WTHR 13, https://www.wthr .com/article/steve-hilbert-touts-australian-gold-celebrity-apprentice

NBC aired episode 6 of Season 11 of "The Apprentice"—Details via IMDB, https://www.imdb.com/title/tt1882984/

sometimes they turned orange—Author interviews with former Trump and Pence campaign advisers

CHRISTIE, ROMNEY, LUGAR,
AND THE ROAD TO THE MANSION

Christie picked up a handful of states—Author interview with Chris Christie

Christie flew into Indianapolis—Author interviews with Christie, Pence advisers

it was hard for some of his top advisers—Author interviews with Pence advisers

Tea Partiers readied to bag one of the biggest "RINOs"—Author coverage of 2012 Indiana Senate race

Lugar's many apostasies—Ibid.

organized early—Ibid.

Brian Bosma, never forgot—Author interviews with Cardwell, Pence advisers, Indiana Republicans

Bob Morris wrote a dear colleague letter—Niki Kelly, "Lawmaker Won't Honor 'Radicalized' Girl Scouts," *The Fort Wayne Journal Gazette*, February 21, 2012, via Internet Archive, https://web.archive.org/web/20120223025203/ http://www.journalgazette.net/article/20120220/NEWS07/120229974

Bosma didn't care much—Author's experience

"I am humbled to be with you"—Brian Howey, "Gridiron Returns with Humor, Cookies," Brian Howey, Howey Politics Indiana, February 23, 2012

Then Bosma took the stage—Author attendance at Gridiron

there was a chalk outline—Author interviews with more than a dozen attendees at 2012 Gridiron Dinner

Bosma wasn't sure if he'd gone too far—Author interviews with dinner attendees

The roast was mean and spiteful—Author interviews with Pence advisers, Cardwell

Washington seemed—Author interviews with former colleagues from the 1990s

neither side wanted to talk to the other—Author interviews with Pence advisers, Daniels advisers, Indiana Republicans

National conservative groups swooped in—Author's experience, news clips, LoBianco

Lugar's staff scurried—Author's experience

Lugar's staff reminded him—Author interviews with former Lugar advisers

On May 8, 2012—Indiana GOP primary results

BORING IS HIS CAMOUFLAGE

he also seemed absent from his own race—Author's experience

"Boring is his camouflage"—Author interview with a veteran Indiana Republican operative

Pence compared the decision—Jake Sherman, "Pence Likens Health Care Ruling to 9/11," Politico, June 28, 2012, https://www.politico.com/blogs/on -congress/2012/06/pence-likens-health-care-ruling-to-9-11-127628

He wouldn't say—Author's experience

On August 23, 2012—Author's experience

"Let me be very clear on this"—Tom LoBianco, "No Running from Social Issues in Election Battles," The Associated Press, August 26, 2012

"I feel like I'm a game warden"—Ibid.

Facebook post detailing the event—Author's experience

"legitimate rape"—Lori Moore, "Rep. Todd Akin: The Statement and the Reaction," The New York Times, August 20, 2012, https://www.nytimes .com/2012/08/21/us/politics/rep-todd-akin-legitimate-rape-statement -and-reaction.html

"Chris, please do this"—Author interview with Christie

SOMETHING GOD INTENDED

Mourdock stood at the podium—Tom LoBianco, "Mourdock: God at Work When Rape Leads to Pregnancy," The Associated Press, October 24, 2012; author experience

The next morning—Author coverage

Pence immediately requested that Mourdock apologize—Dan Caren, "Mourdock

Rape Remarks Draw Responses from Across Indiana, Nation," *The Times of Northwest Indiana,* October 24, 2012, https://www.nwitimes.com /news/local/govt-and-politics/elections/mourdock-rape-remarks-draw -responses-from-across-indiana-nation/article_8b252809-076b-52d2 -9941-3288ba9d9097.html

BENNETT

Bennett was a political creation of Mitch Daniels—Author interviews with Indiana Republicans
Pence and his campaign aides watched the TV screens—Author interviews with Indiana Republicans
Pence slipped through to victory—2012 election results, courtesy *New York Times,* https://www.nytimes.com/elections/2012/results/states/indiana.html
Karen Pence gathered Mike and their three children—"Karen Pence—Who's on Your Stool?"

GOOD TO GREAT—JANUARY 2013

election "autopsy"—"Growth and Opportunity project," The Republican National Committee, March 2013, http://s3.documentcloud.org/documents /623664/republican-national-committees-growth-and.pdf
"We dare not squander this moment"—Pence inaugural address, January 14, 2013, https://www.in.gov/governorhistory/mikepence/2571.htm
he shelved the social issues—Author's experience
Pence had another Daniels problem—Author interviews, author's experience
I-69 sinking—Kara Mattingly, "INDOT Says Part of I-69 Is Sinking," 14 News, January 31, 2013, http://www.14news.com/story/20877584 /indot-says-i-69-is-sinking/
BMV had been quietly overcharging—*Indianapolis Star* investigation, including, Tony Cook, "$62M BMV Settlement Means More Refunds," *The Indianapolis Star,* July 20, 2017, https://www.indystar.com/story/news /politics/2017/07/19/62-million-bmv-settlement-means-more-refunds -motorists/493201001/
A culture of soft corruption—Author interviews of Indiana Republicans, author's extensive experience
The multibillion-dollar contract to privatize Medicaid—Matea Gold, Melanie Mason, and Tom Hamburger, "Indiana's Bumpy Road to Privatization," *Los Angeles Times,* https://www.latimes.com/archives/la-xpm-2011-jun-24 -la-na-indiana-privatize-20110624-story.html
top state transportation official's family—Ryan Sabalow, "INDOT Official Troy Woodruff Resigns as Probe Ends," *The Indianapolis Star,* July 3, 2014, https://www.indystar.com/story/news/2014/07/30/indot-official-troy -woodruff-resigns-probe-comes-end/13384951/

and capped by Daniels's own appointees—Christy Hunter, "Daniels Has No Comment on Conflict of Interest Issue," *The Purdue Exponent*, June 20, 2012, https://www.purdueexponent.org/campus/article_94017752-3cb7 -567d-aaff-dc9ca89520ca.html

Pence would have to sweep up—Author interviews with current and former Pence advisers

Pence hosted his first cabinet meeting—Author attendance at first cabinet meeting

identified critical elements for successful management—Jim Collins, *Good to Great*, HarperCollins, 2011

Pence's economic development floated the idea—Author interviews with Indiana Republicans familiar with the proposal

an antique-style cherry-red phone stood out—Author's attendance at event

spend the day on the phone with Pence—Author interviews with Indiana Republicans

to find velvet ropes blocking—Author interview of Indiana Republicans, statehouse aides

Karen also set some less visible barriers—Author interviews of Indiana Republicans, statehouse aides

squaring up for the so-called Koch Primary—Author observations, interviews with former Republican operatives

FightForIndiana.com—Accessed by author via Internet Archive, https:// web.archive.org/web/20130328135824/http://www.kintera.org/c.9hK PI4MCIhI4E/b.7884733/k.8B82/Action_Center/siteapps/advocacy /ActionItem.aspx?c=9hKPI4MCIhI4E&b=7884733&aid=519235

"You're looking at a guy that's had death threats"—Maureen Hayden, "Tea Party Group to Spend to Support Tax Cut," *The News and Tribune*, March 8, 2013, https://www.newsandtribune.com/news/tea-party-group-to-spend -to-support-pence-tax-cut/article_23de0035-117b-5510-b8a0-c63de d6e2810.html

he returned to the place where he cut his teeth—Author attendance at dinner

"whether you're 'fer it' or you're 'agin it'"—Tom LoBianco, "Pence, Bosma Try to Keep Reins on Intraparty Battle," The Associated Press, March 25, 2013, https://www.ibj.com/articles/40362-pence-bosma-try-to-keep-reins-on -intraparty-tax-battle

"I would have said this with the governor here"—Ibid.

including the leader of the state senate, David Long, intervened—Author interviews

then Pence and all of his staff went on vacation—Author interviews with Indiana Republicans

CHAPTER 11: GOVERNOR PENCE FOR PRESIDENT

"Don't write when you can talk"—Albert D. Van Nostrand, "The Lomasney Legend," *The New England Quarterly*, December 1948, https://www.jstor .org/stable/361565?seq=1#page_scan_tab_contents

AP reporter in May 2013—The author

"It is a truly execrable, anti-factual piece of disinformation"—Tom LoBianco, "Daniels Sought to Censor Public Universities, Professors," The Associated Press, July 16, 2013, via Internet archive: http://web.archive.org/web /20150423161754/http:/www.huffingtonpost.com/2013/07/16/mitch -daniels-censor_n_3607065.html; emails available via Internet Archive: https://web.archive.org/web/20131205194936/http://hosted.ap.org /specials/interactives/documents/daniels1.pdf

The reporter had also heard some stories—The author

Bennett's entire Microsoft Outlook file—Author's experience

scrambled to overhaul the state's school-grading system—Tom LoBianco, "AP Exclusive: GOP Donor's School Grade Changed," The Associated Press, July 29, 2013, https://www.apnews.com/a82bdb0286c24d6e8 59872963d82e235

"Oh, crap."—Ibid.

argument that public schools in the country had been unaccountable—Author interviews

Bennett was forced out as Florida's schools superintendent two days later—Gary Fineout, "Ex-Indiana Education Head Bennett Resigns Amid Grading Scandal," The Associated Press, August 1, 2016, https://www.southbend tribune.com/news/education/ex-indiana-education-head-bennett-resigns -amid-grading-scandal/article_c635a55c-fab4-11e2-a74a-001a4bcf6878 .html

The same Indiana GOP donors—Author interviews with Indiana Republicans

State Board of Education meetings became monthly fiascoes—Author's experience

he had been using his old AOL email account—Pence emails obtained by author

READING THE FIELD

"They arrive in kindergarten and spend too much time trying to catch up"— Scott Elliott, "In Rare Legislative Appearance, Pence Touts Preschool," *Chalkboard Indiana*, February 12, 2014

"Karen's interested in this. She was a teacher, you know"—Author interview with Indiana Republican

lobbyists, legislators, operatives, and others had all puzzled—Author interviews with Indiana Republicans, state lawmakers

His old Washington pitch team—Author interviews with Indiana and Washington Republicans; Pence emails obtained by author

"Chris Wallace wants to take me up on my pitch"—*Fox News Sunday*, Matt Lloyd email to Mike Pence personal email account, April 10, 2014. Email obtained by author via public records request.

he offered Indiana reporters interviews—Author interviews with Indiana reporters

"I believe the United States"—"national press coverage," Matt Lloyd to Mike

Pence personal email account, April 16, 2014. Email obtained by author via public records request.

"GOP woos Mike Pence for 2016"—Robert Costa and Philip Rucker, "GOP Woos Mike Pence for 2016, and Indiana Governor Says He's 'Listening,'" *The Washington Post*, https://www.washingtonpost.com/politics/gop-woos-pence-for-2016-and-indiana-governor-says-hes-listening/2014/05/08/967 d0ece-d60d-11e3-aae8-c2d44bd79778_story.html?utm_term=.1fe510 0b18e3

a reporter for the Associated Press found Pence—Author experience

Bill Smith had successfully reasserted himself—Author interviews of Indiana and Washington Republicans

Quickly they settled on a veteran Republican—Author interviews with Jim Atterholt

Pence met an old adviser at the statehouse—Author interview of a former Pence adviser

PENCE ADVANCES HIS POSITION, MAYBE?

On October 3, Obama flew in—"In Indiana Visit, Obama Highlights Manufacturing Gains" The Associated Press, October 3, 2014, https://www.wfyi.org/news/articles/in-indiana-visit-obama-highlights-manufacturing

Pence waited to meet Obama on the tarmac—Author interview with Indiana Republican

Christie noticed some surprising polling—Author interviews with Christie, Pence adviser

At the start of 2015 Pence changed his mind—Author interview of Pence adviser

2015 State of the State address—Mike Pence, 2015 State of the State address, via C-SPAN, https://www.c-span.org/video/?323751-1/indiana-governor-mike-pence-r-state-state-address

Marty Obst knew they had a problem back home—Author interview with Obst

Ayers had graduated—Author interviews of former Trump aides, Washington Republicans, more

Obst and Ayers met up—Author interview with Obst

THIS JUST IN—PENCE NEWS SERVICE

Author's reporting, experiences

Documents obtained by author

"The notion of elected officials presenting material"—Tom LoBianco, "Gov. Mike Pence's State-Run News Outlet Will Compete With Independent Media," January 26, 2015, *The Indianapolis Star*, https://www.indystar.com/get-access/?return=https%3A%2F%2Fwww.indystar.com%2Fstory%2Fnews%2F2015%2F01%2F26%2Fpence-starts-state-run-news-outlet-to-compete-with-media%2F22370005%2F

"So what happens"—Twitter, Niki Kelly, *Fort Wayne Journal Gazette*, January 26, 2015, https://twitter.com/nkellyatJG/status/559858662555258881?ref
_src=twsrc%5Etfw%7Ctwcamp%5Etweetembed%7Ctwterm%5E5598586
62555258881&ref_url=https%3A%2F%2Fwww.indianapolismonthly
.com%2Fnews-and-opinion%2Ftweets-week-governor-pence-just-in
-news-agency

He brushed off any concerns—Author experience

"'Pravda' on the Plains"—Lloyd Grove, "'Pravda' on the Plains: How Indiana Gov. Mike Pence Wants to Make News," The Daily Beast, January 27, 2015, https://www.thedailybeast.com/pravda-on-the-plains-how-indiana
-governor-mike-pence-wants-to-make-news

"What in the name of Vladimir Putin . . ."—Matthew Tully, "Tully: Mike Pence's horrible idea," *The Indianapolis Star*, January 26, 2015

"Mike Pence may want to be"—MSNBC, *The Rachel Maddow Show*, transcript, January 27, 2015, http://www.msnbc.com/transcripts/rachel-maddow
-show/2015-01-27

On January 28—Author experience

"I'm just telling you" on Garrison show—Eric Bradner, "Indiana's Pence Spikes Government News Site," CNN, January 29, 2015, https://www.cnn
.com/2015/01/26/politics/mike-pence-launches-government-news-site
/index.html

MOTHER KNOWS BEST

I want him as my governor—Sue Loughlin, "Not So Fast, 'Michael,' Pence's Mom Says of Run for Presidency," *The Tribune-Star*, January 27, 2015, https://www.tribstar.com/news/local_news/not-so-fast-michael-pence-s
-mom-says-of-run/article_53be2e94-d366-57c0-99d3-bad71473b594.html

CHAPTER 12: NOW, GEORGE

one last long ball—Author interviews with current and former Pence advisers

The Religious Freedom Restoration Act was sold—Author interviews with Indiana Republicans, statehouse aides, more

GenCon brought in an estimated $50 million—Tony Cook and Mark Alesia, "Gen Con Threatens to Move Convention If Gov. Mike Pence Signs Religious Freedom Bill," *The Indianapolis Star*, March 24, 2015, https://
www.indystar.com/story/news/politics/2015/03/24/gen-con-threatens
-move-convention-gov-mike-pence-signs-religious-freedom-bill
/70393474/

"I am outraged that Gov. Pence would sign"—George Takei Facebook post, March 26, 2015, https://www.facebook.com/georgehtakei/posts/i-am
-outraged-that-gov-pence-would-sign-such-a-divisive-measure-into
-law-he-has-/1213705725325545/

"This bill is not about discrimination"—Tony Cook, "Gov. Mike Pence Signs Religious Freedom Law in Private," *The Indianapolis Star*, https://www .indystar.com/story/news/politics/2015/03/25/gov-mike-pence-sign -religious-freedom-bill-thursday/70448858/

The NCAA began squirming too—Author interviews; Luke DeCock, "NCAA Took Stand on Religious Freedom Law," *Charlotte Observer*, April 2, 2015, https://www.charlotteobserver.com/sports/spt-columns-blogs/luke-decock /article17238695.html

"SB 101 will help provide the protection!"—"Victory at the Statehouse!" Advance America blog post, March 28, 2016

new law wouldn't allow businesses to refuse service—Author interview with Micah Clark

Pence had two offers to appear on television—Author interview with Jeff Cardwell

"Governor, would you say that Indiana promotes discrimination?"—Author interview with Indiana Republican

"What meeting?"—Author interview with Marty Obst

More than a dozen of Pence's top staff and advisers—Scene composite of interviews with multiple attendees, including Obst, Cardwell, others

SUNDAY MARCH 29, 2015—THE STEPHANOPOULOS DISASTER

Pence sat in a small, one-room studio—Author interviews with Cardwell, Obst others

"So, this is a yes or no question"—ABC's *This Week* with George Stephanopoulos, March 29, 2015, video via ABC, https://abcnews.go.com/ThisWeek/video /gov-mike-pence-religious-freedom-law-29987447

"He didn't go on there as the governor"—Author interview with Cardwell

Obst poured himself a bourbon—Author interview with Obst

remembered the friends who had committed suicide—author interviews with Rick Sutton

THE CLEANUP

"FIX THIS NOW"—Editorial Board, "FIX THIS NOW," *The Indianapolis Star*, March 31, 2015, https://www.indystar.com/story/opinion/2015/03 /30/editorial-gov-pence-fix-religious-freedom-law-now/70698802/

Behind the scenes—Author interviews

one of Pence's aides kicked him out—Author interviews

"Personal sports hero to me"—Ali Slocum, "Louganis Played Key Role in Discrimination Debate," WISH TV, April 3, 2015, https://www.wishtv .com/news/politics/louganis-played-key-role-in-discrimination-debate _20180411103442668/1115083821

"We've got a perception problem here"—Transcript of Mike Pence RFRA news

conference, staff, *The Washington Post,* March 31, 2015, https://www
.washingtonpost.com/news/the-fix/wp/2015/04/01/david-letterman
-counts-down-the-top-10-guys-indiana-gov-mike-pence-looks-like
/?utm_term=.d5e109964df7

Gary Varvel—Varvel editorial cartoon, *The Indianapolis Star,* March 31,
2015

Top Ten Guys Pence Looks Like—Hunter Schwarz, "David Letterman Counts
Down the Top 10 Guys Indiana Gov. Mike Pence Looks Like," *The
Washington Post,* April 1, 2015, *The Late Night Show,* Tuesday, March 31,
2015, https://www.washingtonpost.com/news/the-fix/wp/2015/04/01
/david-letterman-counts-down-the-top-10-guys-indiana-gov-mike-pence
-looks-like/?utm_term=.d5e109964df7

THE CLEANUP, PART TWO

The following morning—Author interviews with Sutton, Atterholt

"Is the damage able to be turned back?"—Tony Cook and Brian Eason, "Gov.
Mike Pence Signs RFRA Fix," *The Indianapolis Star,* April 2, 2015, https://
www.indystar.com/story/news/politics/2015/04/01/indiana-rfra-deal-sets
-limited-protections-for-lgbt/70766920/

Bosma set the gears of government—Author experience

But then Paul Singer called him—Author interview with Pence adviser

Reporters circled the entire building—Author experience

"In the midst of this furious debate"—James Gherardi and Dan Spehler, "Gov.
Pence Signs RFRA Changes into Law, Issues Statement," Fox 59, April 2,
2015, https://fox59.com/2015/04/02/indiana-now-waiting-to-see-if-gov
-pence-will-sign-rfra-fix-into-law/

CHAPTER 13: AT PEACE

Obst scrambled to put out the fires—Author interview with Marty Obst

Oesterle and Obst met at the home of Pence fund raiser Jim Kittle—Ibid.

Bosma tested the waters as well—Ibid., and author interviews with Cardwell,
and other Indiana Republicans

Pence's team struggled—Author interviews with Atterholt, Cardwell, Obst,
Micah Clark, other Indiana Republicans

Nick Ayers called up Obst—Author interview with Obst

"Do you really want to do this?"—Ibid.

Pence himself was heartbroken—Author interviews, Obst, Cardwell, other Pence
advisers and Indiana Republicans

The RGA was on board with Pence—Author interview with Obst

Jim Atterholt, decided—Author interviews with Atterholt, other Indiana
Republicans

Pence was stunned and hurt—Dozens of author interviews

NEW MESSAGING IN PENCE WORLD

"We felt like we didn't have the messaging nailed"—Author interview with Obst

"Guys, what are you doing?"—Ibid.

Conway wanted to keep helping Pence—Author interviews with Pence advisers, Indiana Republicans

"Gov. Mike Pence is a conservative leader"— Michael Anthony Adams, "Gov. Pence to Announce Re-Election Bid," *The Indianapolis Star.*, May 18, 2015, https://www.indystar.com/story/news/politics/2015/05/18/pence-to -announce-reelection-bid-during-gop-dinner/27554571/

polls showed Pence underwater—Brian Howey, "Brian Howey: Historic Damage to Pence Brand," *The Times of Northwest Indiana*, April 19, 2015, https:// www.nwitimes.com/news/opinion/columnists/brian-howey/brian-howey -historic-damage-to-pence-brand/article_aa0731d2-0a2a-5fdd-8fd0-40d 5ec74183d.html

paid $750,000 to a crisis PR firm—Tony Cook, "Why Did Pence Abort RFRA- Related PR Contract," *The Indianapolis Star*, July 3, 2015, https://www .indystar.com/story/news/2015/07/02/indiana-cancels-pr-contract-tied -rfra/29628745/

Cruz bankrolled by reclusive billionaire Robert Mercer—Author interviews

The firm didn't mention—Paul Grewal, Facebook Newsroom, https://newsroom .fb.com/news/2018/03/suspending-cambridge-analytica/

on June 16, 2015—Trump campaign announcement via C-SPAN, June 16, 2015, https://www.c-span.org/video/?326473-1/donald-trump-presidential -campaign-announcement

THE TRUMP TRAIN

Family Leadership Summit in Ames, Iowa—Trump at Leadership summit, July 18, 2015, video via C-SPAN, https://www.c-span.org/video/?327045-5 /presidential-candidate-donald-trump-family-leadership-summit

"It was my own personal Vietnam."—Tim Mak, "Draft-Dodger Trump Said Sleeping Around Was My 'Personal Vietnam,'" The Daily Beast, https:// www.thedailybeast.com/draft-dodger-trump-said-sleeping-around-was -my-personal-vietnam

cable television ate 'em up—Author experience

"John Barron" or "John Miller"—John Cassidy, "Trump's History of Lying, from John Barron to @realdonaldtrump," *The New Yorker*, April 23, 2018, https://www.newyorker.com/news/our-columnists/trumps-history-of -lying-from-john-barron-to-realdonaldtrump; also see Chris Cillizza, "Donald Trump's 'John Miller' Interview Is Even Crazier Than You Think," *The Washington Post*, May 16, 2016, https://www.washingtonpost .com/news/the-fix/wp/2016/05/16/donald-trumps-john-miller-interview -is-even-crazier-than-you-think/?utm_term=.15ae9e150cfa

New York Observer blacklisted Trump—Ben Smith, "Why Donald Trump Cares So Much About the Media," BuzzFeed News, May 21, 2017, https://www.buzzfeednews.com/article/newsfeedpodcast/why-donald-trump-cares-so-much-about-the-media

only person not breaking a sweat was Trump himself—Author interviews of former Trump campaign aides, author experience

he couldn't take a hit—Author experience

"Mr. Trump, one of the things"—First Republican presidential debate, August 6, 2015, Fox News, https://video.foxnews.com/v/4406746003001/

"blood coming out of her wherever"—Paola Chavez, Veronica Stracqualursi, and Meghan Keneally, "A History of the Donald Trump-Megyn Kelly Feud," ABC News, October 26, 2016, https://abcnews.go.com/Politics/history-donald-trump-megyn-kelly-feud/story?id=36526503

EVANGELICALS FOR TRUMP

dropped out in September of 2015—"Scott Walker drops out of US 2016 presidential race," staff report, BBC, September 21, 2015. https://www.bbc.com/news/world-us-canada-34317758

"modern-day Cyrus"—Lance Wallnau, "Trump Is a Modern Cyrus," LanceWallnau.com, December 21, 2017, https://lancewallnau.com/trump-is-a-modern-cyrus/

a little too convenient—Author interviews of Fea, Schenck, and former evangelical Christians

PENCE TICKS UP

Pence's lieutenant governor, Sue Ellspermann—Author interviews of Pence advisers, Indiana Republicans

Pence said he would need her to go on the attack—Ibid.

She was pushed off the Pence ticket—Ibid.

the results showed for Pence's team—Author interviews of Obst, Smith, Cardwell, Conway, others

THE CRUZ CAMPAIGN V. THE TRUMP CIRCUS

As March began—Author interviews of former Cruz campaign aides, Trump campaign aides, Washington Republicans

Jared Kushner and Ivanka Trump—Author interviews

led by California billionaire and former Reagan administration official Tom Barrack—Author interviews; Franklin Foer, "Paul Manafort, American Hustler," *The Atlantic*, March 2018, https://www.theatlantic.com/magazine/archive/2018/03/paul-manafort-american-hustler/550925/

Manafort background—Author interviews, Ibid., Foer

Steve Hilbert—Author interviews of former Trump campaign aides

Corey Lewandowski and Barry Bennett—Author interview of Barry Bennett

"Mr. Trump, the brakes won't engage!"—Olivia Nuzzi, "How Pepe the Frog Became a Nazi Trump Supporter and Alt-Right Symbol," The Daily Beast, April 13, 2017, http://www.thedailybeast.com/how-pepe-the -frog-became-a-nazi-trump-supporter-and-alt-right-symbol

The RNC had one job—Author reporting, experience

gathered that April at the Diplomat—Author experience

"The part he's been playing now"—Philip Rucker, Dan Balz, and Robert Costa, "Trump Is Playing 'a Part' and Can Transform for Victory, Campaign Chief Tells GOP Leaders," *The Washington Post*, April 21, 2016, https:// www.washingtonpost.com/news/post-politics/wp/2016/04/21/trump-is -playing-a-part-and-can-transform-for-victory-campaign-chief-tells-gop -leaders/?utm_term=.2e32adbdb7f0

Women topped their early lists—Author interviews of former Trump campaign aides

MEANWHILE BACK IN INDY

Pence's aides weren't sure—Author interviews

"Please stop Trump and save the Republican Party"—Author interviews of GOP donors, Washington Republicans

"I'm not against anybody"—Eric Bradner, John Berman, and Phil Mattingly, "Mike Pence Endorses Ted Cruz," CNN, April 29, 2016, https://www .cnn.com/2016/04/29/politics/mike-pence-to-endorse-ted-cruz-friday /index.html

"What the fuck was that?"—Ibid.

Cruz's campaign staff was equally livid—Author interviews former Cruz aides, Pence advisers

"He's very empowering of staff"—Author interview of former Cruz aide

"Even if he couldn't support Trump"—Author interview former Trump campaign aide

"You're the politicians that killed America!"—"Ted Cruz Confronts Trump Supporters," Fox News, May 2, 2016, via YouTube, https://www.youtube .com/watch?v=EkCifM0kDd0

Tuesday, May 3—Election results

Standing at the Crowne Plaza Hotel—Author experience, coverage

THE RUNNING MATE SEARCH CONTINUES

ramped up its running mate search—Author interviews

wanted his team to consider Ivanka seriously—Author interviews

Bob Corker was summoned—Former Trump campaign aide

Manafort and RNC Chairman Reince Priebus—Pence adviser and former Trump campaign aides

Trump said he wanted an attack dog—Author interviews

Pence was hosting a party—Author interview with Atterholt

They dug into his personal financial history—Washington Republican familiar with Pence VP vetting

His staff watched the infamous 1990 Arab sheik ad—Ibid.

But Karen did—Ibid.

THE MIRACLE FLAT TIRE

"He's really bad"—Former Trump campaign aide

big fans of Gingrich—Interviews

scheduled to do a fund raiser—Interviews

Trump Force One—Benjamin Zhang, "Check Out Trump Force One—Donald Trump's Personal Boeing Airliner," *Business Insider*, July 27, 2015, https://www.businessinsider.com/donald-trumps-boeing-757-airliner-2015-7

landed at a private airfield—Author interview with Kevin Eck

About twenty-five high-dollar donors—Author interview with Jeff Cardwell

"I understand you've known Mike a long time"—Ibid.

Trump's team ran out the back—Author interview with Eck

The brake on the right-side landing gear had broken—Ibid.

"The Trump family"—Author interview with Cardwell

Mike and Karen Pence spent the night—Author interviews with Cardwell, Eck, others

One Trump aide said—Former Trump campaign aide

Christie saw a last-ditch—Author interview with Chris Christie

Karen drove to the local boutique grocery store—Former Pence aide

"I need killers"—Author interview with Obst

Trump hopped back in his motorcade—Author interview with Eck

Eric asked Ivanka if they should call him up—Ibid.

Mike and Karen Pence gathered together—Author interview with Atterholt

Pence asked Atterholt to lead them in a prayer—Ibid.

THE DECISION IS MADE

"He tells everybody 'Yes.'"—Former Trump campaign aide

Mike, Karen and Charlotte—Pence adviser

"You picked Pence?"—Author interview with Christie

The Indianapolis Star reported shortly after noon—Tony Cook, James Briggs, and Chelsea Schneider, "Indiana Gov. Mike Pence Is Donald Trump's VP Pick," *The Indianapolis Star*, July 14, 2016, https://www.indystar.com/story/news/politics/2016/07/14/report-pence-trumps-vp-pick/87075866/

CNN reported— Mark Hensch, "Trump Tried to Back Off Pence Pick: Report," The Hill, July 15, 2016, https://thehill.com/blogs/ballot-box/presidential-races/287951-cnn-reporter-trump-tried-to-back-off-pence-pick

"I haven't made my final, final decision"—On the Record with Greta Van Susteren,

Fox News, July 14, 2015, https://archive.org/details/FOXNEWSW
    _20160714_232000_On_the_Record_With_Greta_Van_Susteren
They knew they had to lock Trump in—Author interview with Marty Obst
they screamed "Yes!"—Ibid.
"I am pleased to announce"—Trump tweet, 11 A.M., July 15, 2016, https://
    twitter.com/realdonaldtrump/status/753965070003109888?lang=en
"What is the T doing to that P?"—John Dingell, Twitter, 11:09 A.M., July 15,
    2016, https://twitter.com/JohnDingell/status/753985891459297281?ref_sr
    c=twsrc%5Etfw%7Ctwcamp%5Etweetembed%7Ctwterm%5E7539858914
    59297281&ref_url=https%3A%2F%2Fwww.politico.com%2Fstory
    %2F2016%2F07%2Ftrump-vp-pick-mike-spence-logo-225612
Saturday, July 16, 2016—"Presidential Candidate Donald Trump Vice Presi-
    dential Selection Introduction," Trump, Pence announcement, C-SPAN,
    https://www.c-span.org/video/?412804-1/donald-trump-announces-
    governor-mike-pence-running-mate
"Busy weekend in NY!"—Mike Pence, Twitter, 1:14 P.M., July 16, 2016, https://
    twitter.com/mike_pence/status/754408867912622080?lang=en

PENCE FINALLY ARRIVES

Mike Pence acceptance speech, July 20, 2016—C-SPAN, https://www.c-span
    .org/video/?412401-101/governor-mike-pence-acceptance-speech
"He was great until he started bashing Hillary"—Ibid., Valente interview with
    Sister Bierman
hall buzzed about Ted Cruz—Author experience
he went in for the kiss—ABC News, "Trump, Pence Share Awkward Air Kiss at
    RNC," July 21, 2016, https://youtube/dPAPIVu3p_g
perfectly positioned to run for president in 2020—Author interviews with
    former Pence advisers, former Trump campaign aides
"I alone can fix it."—Yoni Appelbaum, "I Alone Can Fix It," *The Atlantic*, July
    21, 2016, Trump acceptance speech, https://www.theatlantic.com/politics
    /archive/2016/07/trump-rnc-speech-alone-fix-it/492557/
They watched solemnly, quietly—Author experience

CHAPTER 14: GOD'S PLAN

THE RUSSIANS ARE COMING—TRUMP TOWER

"The Crown Prosecutor of Russia met with his father Aras this morning"—Trump
    Jr. emails posted to Twitter, https://twitter.com/DonaldJTrumpJr/status
    /884789839522140166
On Thursday, June 9, Veselnitskaya—Jeremy Herb and Marshall Cohen, "The
    Trump Tower Meeting: A Timeline," July 31, 2018, https://www.cnn
    .com/2018/07/31/politics/trump-tower-meeting-timeline/index.html
by the summer of 2016—David E. Sanger and Eric Schmitt, "Spy agency

consensus grows that Russia hacked DNC," *The New York Times*, July 26, 2016, https://www.nytimes.com/2016/07/27/us/politics/spy-agency -consensus-grows-that-russia-hacked-dnc.html

Behind the scenes—Mueller indictment of Internet Research Agency, et al., February 16, 2018, https://www.justice.gov/file/1035477/download

opposing Facebook groups—Senate Intelligence Committee hearing on Russian social media influence, November 1, 2017, https://www.intelligence.senate .gov/hearings/open-hearing-social-media-influence-2016-us-elections

Russians even set up real American bank accounts—Mueller Russia indictment

used more traditional spycraft—Quinta Jurecic, "Document: Justice Department releases Carter Page FISA application," https://www.lawfareblog.com /document-justice-department-releases-carter-page-fisa-application; and Sharon LaFraniere, Mark Mazzetti and Matt Apuzzo, "How the Russia inquiry began: A campaign aide, drinks and talk of political dirt," *The New York Times*, December 30, 2017, https://www.nytimes.com/2017/12/30/us /politics/how-fbi-russia-investigation-began-george-papadopoulos.html

Pence was more like a trusted hand—Author interviews

"We're gonna run you for governor"—Author interview of former Trump campaign adviser

"One thing about Pence is he's a loyal soldier"—Ibid.

THE VP DEBATE, OCTOBER 4, 2016

a very young Mitch Daniels—Author interviews

"I have as much experience"—1988 vice presidential debate, C-SPAN, https:// www.c-span.org/video/?4127-1/1988-vice-presidential-candidates-debate

October 4, 2016—2016 vice presidential debate, NBC News, October 4, 2016, https://www.youtube.com/watch?v=mVXqNcW_-HA

"On Syria and Russia, Pence wandered way off the Trump reservation"—Los Angeles Times news staff, "We Scored the Vice Presidential Debate and Mike Pence Won," *Los Angeles Times*, October 4, 2016, https://www .latimes.com/projects/la-na-pol-vice-presidential-debate-scorecard/

AND THEN, *ACCESS HOLLYWOOD*

Tony Packo's Café—Author interviews, VP pool report Vaughn Hillyard

Packo's details—Mike Pence tweet, October 7, 2016, https://twitter.com /mike_pence/status/784499266786131968?lang=en; Tony Packo's tweet, October 7, 2016, https://twitter.com/tonypackos/status /784581885812936705

"This time we got him, right?"—Matthew Nussbaum, "Pence refuses to re- spond on Trump's comments," Politico, October 7, 2016, https://www .politico.com/story/2016/10/mike-pence-donald-trump-comments -women-229311

The reporters suddenly stopped looking at Pence—Michael Calderone and Nick
  Baumann, "Mike Pence's team boots reporters after audio of emerges of
  Trump saying he can grab women 'By the p***y,'" *Huffington Post*, October 7,
  2016, https://www.huffpost.com/entry/mike-pence-protective-pool_n_57
  f80a99e4b0e655eab43381?guccounter=1&guce_referrer=aHR0cHM
  6Ly93d3cuZ29vZ2xlLmNvbS8&guce_referrer_sig=AQAAAEGkme
  5icBPffBYECAIdFKG-wo_-bp5mJVuVTIwcYwjSII-rtlF8QRNjRDYP
  YK_exJQB-RBE-HFUq9vY3rf5629AtXKDORFCnKeF0prro1fY0cBB1
  Br1ERK07Xep721dZVSnujhrL82cQn1sUCLsfzSkCQMRwihUhQxMT
  nsK-8Zv
"I just start kissing them"—David Farenthold, "Donald Trump Recorded
  Having Extremely Lewd Conversation About Women in 2005," *The
  Washington Post*, October 8, 2016, https://www.washingtonpost.com
  /politics/trump-recorded-having-extremely-lewd-conversation-about
  -women-in-2005/2016/10/07/3b9ce776-8cb4-11e6-bf8a-3d26847eeed4
  _story.html?utm_term=.8da7d29b2803
WikiLeaks began posting—WikiLeaks Podesta emails, https://www.wikileaks
  .org/podesta-emails

A REQUIRED RESPONSE

The first calls from the RNC donors—Author interview with Marty Obst
Reince Priebus and a small group—Author interviews former Trump campaign
  advisers
A few select donors—Author interviews with Pence and Trump aides
"Mike is too loyal for that"—Author interview with Obst
Christie called up Pence—Author interview with Christie
Mike and Karen didn't even know—Author interviews of current and former
  Pence aides and former Trump campaign aides, others
maybe they should resign—Author interviews
Karen was livid—Ibid.
Pence's small team of advisers—Ibid.
Reince Priebus confronted Trump—Yahoo News Staff, "64 Hours in October:
  How one weekend blew up the rules of American politics," Yahoo News,
  https://www.huffpost.com/entry/yahoo-64-hours-october-american-politics
  _n_59d7c567e4b072637c43dd1c
Access Hollywood—Author reporting
"Donald Trump should withdraw"—Sen. John Thune tweet, October 8, 2016,
  https://twitter.com/senjohnthune/status/784798261781598208?lang=en
Priebus's chief of staff, Katie Walsh—Author interview with a Washington
  Republican and former Trump campaign aide
Friends and colleagues called Pence repeatedly—Author interviews of current and
  former Pence aides, Indiana Republicans
after eighteen hours—Author interviews of former Trump campaign aides

Mike and Karen Pence and Marty Obst boarded—Author interview with Obst
"we settled in our hearts before we decided to do this"—Ibid.
Pence fired up the Rhode Island crowd—Ibid.

PENCE LOCKS IN

cooked up a novel attack—Liam Stack, "Donald Trump Featured Paula Jones and 2 Other Women Who Accused Bill Clinton of Sexual Assault," *The New York Times*, October 9, 2016, https://www.nytimes.com/2016/10/10 /us/politics/bill-clinton-accusers.html

Trump called up Pence—Author interview with Obst

"Last night my running mate"—Vaughn Hillyard, "Mike Pence indicates he's all-in for Donald Trump," NBC, October 10, 2016. https://www.nbcnews .com/politics/2016-election/mike-pence-indicates-he-s-all-donald -trump-n663921

"It's time to come home and elect Donald Trump"—Vaughn Hillyard, "Mike Pence to GOP: 'It's time to come home,'" NBC, October 24, 2016

On October 28, FBI Director James Comey—Comey letter to House Oversight Committee Chairman Jason Chaffetz, October 28, 2016, accessed via Politico, https://www.politico.com/story/2016/10/full-text-fbi-letter -announcing-new-clinton-review-230463

THE COMPLICATIONS OF WINNING

Election Night, November 8—Author interviews of former Trump campaign aides

Mike Pence leaned in to kiss Karen—Ibid.

he tried again for a victory kiss—Ibid.

"What are we going to do, Mike??"—Ibid

November 11, Christie chatted with Pence—Author interview with Chris Christie

Karen went to Marty Obst—Author interviews with former Trump campaign aides

transferring $750,000—IRS 990 forms for Presidential Inaugural Committee and Vice President's Residency Fund

She submitted two invoices—Author interviews with former Trump campaign aides

welcomed by pro-LGBT protesters; Betsy Klein, "Pro-LGBT rights protesters dance to Mike Pence's home," CNN, January 19, 2017, https://www.cnn .com/2017/01/18/politics/mike-pence-lgbt-protesters/index.html

The Falls Church—Interviews with Washington Republicans

Could her gay best friend be the Man of Honor in their wedding?—Author interviews of Pence friends

"Love the sinner, hate the sin."—Author interview of Pence friend

A DIFFICULT TRANSITION

Obama expelled dozens—Mark Mazetti and Adam Goldman, "'The game will go on' as US Expels Russian Diplomats," *The New York Times*, December 30, 2016, https://www.nytimes.com/2016/12/30/us/politics /obama-russian-spies.html

December 29, 2016—Mueller indictment of Manafort and Gates

paid $45,000 for the event—Michael Isikoff, "Moscow Paid $45,000 for Flynn's 2015 Talk, Documents Show," March 16, 2017, https://www.yahoo.com /news/moscow-paid-45000-for-flynns-2015-talk-documents-show-165 404052.html

Representative Scott Garrett—Author interviews of former Trump White House officials

quickly decided Pence should take the lead; author interviews of former Trump campaign aides

"I talked to General Flynn"—Pence interview, CBS *Face the Nation*

taking the oath of office on Ronald Reagan's bible—Alex Gangitano, "Pence will be first to use Reagan's bible for swearing in," Roll Call, January 18, 2017, https://www.rollcall.com/politics/the-story-of-how-pence-is-getting -reagans-bible-for-the-inauguration

"For too long, a small group in our nation's capital"—Trump inaugural speech

"I don't think he would have won"—Author interviews with David McIntosh

Acting Attorney General Sally Yates—Sally Yates testimony before Senate Intelligence Committee, 2017

THE NEW VICE PRESIDENT'S OFFICE

Trump's White House aides—Author interviews

His ceremonial office—Vice president's website, https://www.whitehouse.gov /about-the-white-house/the-vice-presidents-residence-office/

vice president's office in the West Wing—Map of the White House, "Inside the real West Wing," Graphic by Doug Stevens, *The Washington Post*, http:// www.washingtonpost.com/wp-srv/politics/administration/whbriefing /whitehousemap.html

And Pence stayed quiet—Interview with former Pence aide

Pence had another role—Author interviews with former White House officials, Trump and Pence advisers

Mike Pence's new office in the Congress—Author experience

ADD Cheney office in House side—Maureen Groppe, "Mike Pence will wear lots of hats as Trump's vice president," *USA Today*, January 15, 2017, https:// www.usatoday.com/story/news/politics/2017/01/15/mike-pence-role-as -vice-president/96539046/

In private meetings at the White House—Author interviews with former White House officials, Washington Republicans

THE RUSSIA INVESTIGATION HEATS UP

Pence's big whiff on health care—Author interviews with former Trump aides, White House officials

it was stunningly cold in the room—Author experience

The Washington Post *reported*—Adam Entous, Ellen Nakashima, and Greg Miller, "Sessions Met with Russian Envoy Twice Last Year, Encounters He Later Did Not Disclose," *The Washington Post*, March 1, 2017, https://www.washingtonpost.com/world/national-security/sessions-spoke-twice-with-russian-ambassador-during-trumps-presidential-campaign-justice-officials-say/2017/03/01/77205eda-feac-11e6-99b4-9e613afeb09f_story.html?utm_term=.36f8c794450b

a rare public hearing—House Intelligence Committee hearing, March 20, 2017, transcript via *Washington Post*, https://www.washingtonpost.com/news/post-politics/wp/2017/03/20/full-transcript-fbi-director-james-comey-testifies-on-russian-interference-in-2016-election/?utm_term=.fd81d63d312b

The next night, Nunes—Author interviews with former House aides and Philip Bump, "The Nunes-White House Question Assessed Minute by Minute," *The Washington Post*, March 30, 2017, https://www.washingtonpost.com/news/politics/wp/2017/03/29/the-nunes-white-house-question-assessed-minute-by-minute/?utm_term=.0e9df939e9e6

Tuesday, May 9—DAG Rosenstein letter to Donald Trump, May 9, 2017, Justice Department website, https://www.justice.gov/oip/foia-library/moss/download

"The president's decision"—Mike Pence defends Comey firing, May 10, 2017, CNN, https://www.cnn.com/videos/politics/2017/05/10/mike-pence-entire-statement-on-james-comey-fbi-firing-sot.cnn

Thursday, May 11, Trump changed his tune—Trump interview with Lester Holt, NBC News, May 11, https://www.youtube.com/watch?v=5Wvuw_Zmubg

Pence's path was for Trump to win—Author interview Pence advisers

CHAPTER 15: PIETY & POWER

David McIntosh—Author interviews with McIntosh

In the Book of Daniel—Ibid.; the Bible

In another allegory—Author interview with former Pence aide

McIntosh noted that hearing God—Author interview with McIntosh

"a lot of wringing out the ego"—Ibid.

THE PENCE POLITICAL SHOP

Pence and his team had almost no expectation—Interviews of current and former Pence advisers, friends, Trump advisers, more

The best option was—Interviews of current and former Pence advisers

Washington Republicans noted—Interviews of former Trump campaign aides, Washington Republican operatives

New York Times *published*—Jonathan Martin and Alexander Burns, "Republican Shadow Campaign for 2020 Takes Shape as Trump Doubts Grow," *The New York Times*, August 5, 2017, https://www.nytimes.com/2017/08/05/us /politics/2020-campaign-president-trump-cotton-sasse-pence.html

some of Trump's people, including Steve Bannon—Interviews of former White House officials

Ayers had a penchant—Author interviews of former Trump campaign aides, former White House officials

Pence's spokesman Marc Lotter took the bullet—Author interview former White House official and former Trump campaign advisers

His old advisers from Indiana—Author interviews of Indiana Republicans

Ayers, meanwhile, began courting the power couple—Author interviews of former Trump aides, former White House officials

speech to John Hagee's group—Transcript of Mike Pence speech to Christians United for Israel conference, July 17, 2017, vice president's office

Of course not—Author interviews of Pence friends, advisers

"Who doesn't pander?"—Author interview of Pence friend

PENCE GOES TO A FOOTBALL GAME

Pence had become known inside the administration—Author interviews of former White House officials

Pence tweets—October 8, 2017, https://twitter.com/VP/status/9170488869 75500289, https://twitter.com/vp/status/917074120084516865?lang=en

Trump asks Pence to leave—Scott Horner, "Trump: 'I asked Mike Pence to leave stadium if any players kneeled,'" *The Indianapolis Star*, Oct. 8, 2017, https:// www.indystar.com/story/sports/nfl/colts/2017/10/08/vice-president-mike -pence-leaves-colts-game-over-protests-during-anthem/744277001/

Trump tweets—October 8, 2017, https://twitter.com/realdonaldtrump/status /917091286607433728?lang=en

Special Counsel Robert Mueller struck—Justice Department indictments of Paul Manafort and Rick Gates, October 30, 2017, https://www.justice.gov/sco

ROY MOORE

Washington Post *dropped a bombshell*—Stephanie McCrummen, Beth Reinhard, and Alice Crites, "Woman Says Roy Moore Initiated Sexual When She Was 14, He Was 32," *The Washington Post*, November 9, 2017, https://www .washingtonpost.com/investigations/woman-says-roy-moore-initiated -sexual-encounter-when-she-was-14-he-was-32/2017/11/09/1f495878-c29 3-11e7-afe9-4f60b5a6c4a0_story.html?utm_term=.10b8592c4ea3

Pence and his team had the reins—Author interviews of Republican operatives

White House aides largely credited—Author interviews with former White House aides

Trump chafed at his handling of health care—Author interviews

NEW YEAR, NEW STRATEGY

Pence team's approach to life in the White House had flipped 180 degrees—Ken Thomas and Tom LoBianco, "Pence has long pushed for Trump policies on Israel," The Associated Press, January 19, 2018, https://www.news-herald.com/news/pence-has-long-pushed-for-trump-policies-on-israel/article_4307f78b-ea6e-5db2-9838-97c2b6672ab9.html

"Break glass in case of emergency"—Author interview with former White House official

Pence flew overseas on a long-awaited trip to Israel—Author reporting

The Wall Street Journal *uncovered*—Michael Rothfeld and Joe Palazzolo, "Trump Lawyer Arranged $130,000 Payment for Adult Film Star's Silence," *The Wall Street Journal*, January 12, 2018, https://www.wsj.com/articles/trump-lawyer-arranged-130-000-payment-for-adult-film-stars-silence-1515787678

"I'm not going to comment"—Chris Cillizza, "The Big Question Mike Pence Didn't Answer About Stormy Daniels," CNN, February 13, 2018, https://www.cnn.com/2018/01/23/politics/pence-stormy-daniels-cnn/index.html

Schenck, the evangelical pastor—Author interview with Schenck

Pence stood at the front of the Indian Treaty Room—Sam Brownback swearing-in ceremony, VPs office

THE 2018 GRIDIRON ROAST

Audio, 2018 Gridiron Dinner

THE PRICE OF POWER

Marlon Bundo—Charlotte Pence, *A Day in the Life of the Vice President*, Regnery, 2018

HBO's John Oliver—Marlon Bundo with Jill Twiss, *A Day in the Life of Marlon Bundo*, Chronicle Books LLC, 2018

"He's giving the proceeds of the book to charity"—Judy Kurtz, "Charlotte Pence Says She Bought John Oliver's Marlon Bundo Book," The Hill, March 21, 2018, https://thehill.com/blogs/in-the-know/in-the-know/379538-charlotte-pence-says-she-bought-john-olivers-marlon-bundo-book

Trump's advisers said they wanted Pence out working with the donors—Author interviews with former White House officials, Washington Republican operatives

flew to Fargo, North Dakota—Author interview with GOP donor

"What's that old adage?"—Pence audio obtained by author

Jon Lerner—Author interviews of former White House aides

Republican operatives who worried—Author interviews with former White House officials

PIETY AND POWER COME TOGETHER

"You know, over the mantel of our home"—Pence remarks, Day of Prayer, May 3, 2018, vice president's office, https://www.whitehouse.gov/briefings -statements/remarks-vice-president-pence-national-day-prayer/

"You have called Israel"—Robert Jeffress, invocation, opening of U.S. embassy in Jerusalem, May 14, 2018, https://www.youtube.com/watch?v=jSGSSisCT7E

"You can't be saved"—Eugene Scott, "A Look at Robert Jeffress, the Controversial Figure Giving the Prayer at the U.S. Embassy in Jerusalem," *The Washington Post*, May 14, 2018, https://www.washingtonpost.com/news /the-fix/wp/2018/05/14/a-look-at-robert-jeffress-the-controversial-figure -giving-the-prayer-at-the-u-s-embassy-in-jerusalem-today/?utm_term=.b 30e7ccb08cb

Netanyahu now sat next to Jared Kushner—Jeffress invocation video

test rockets that Kim kept launching—List of North Korean missile tests, Wikipedia, https://en.wikipedia.org/wiki/List_of_North_Korean_missile _tests

Pence welcomed Jim Morris—Author interview with former senator Richard Lugar

There the men talked disarmament—Ibid.

"oleaginous"—George Will, "Trump Is No Longer the Worst Person in Government, Pence Is," *The Washington Post*, May 9, 2018, https://www .washingtonpost.com/opinions/trump-is-no-longer-the-worst-person-in -government/2018/05/09/10e59eba-52f1-11e8-a551-5b648abe29ef_story .html?utm_term=.a17abbb7858a

Trump took the water bottle—"Pence mirrors Trump clearing his water bottle from meeting table," NBC, June 7, 2018, https://www.nbcnews.com /video/pence-mirrors-trump-clearing-his-water-bottle-from-meeting -table-1250081347911

SEPTEMBER 2018—THE LODESTAR

op-ed in the New York Times—Anonymous, "I Am Part of the Resistance In-side the Trump Administration," *The New York Times*, September 5, 2018, https://www.nytimes.com/2018/09/05/opinion/trump-white-house -anonymous-resistance.html

that Pence attend his funeral instead of Trump—Jonathan Martin, "At his ranch, John McCain shares memories and regrets with friends," *The New York Times*, May 5, 2018, https://www.nytimes.com/2018/05/05/us/politics /john-mccain-arizona.html

"I guess it varies from day to day."—Author interview with John McCain

PENCE AT THE DOORSTEP

impeaching Rod Rosenstein—Author interviews and Sabrina Eaton, "Rep. Jim Jordan introduces articles of impeachment against Rod Rosenstein: Read them here," *The Cleveland Plain-Dealer*, July 25, 2018, https://www.cleveland.com/metro/2018/07/rep_jim_jordan_introduces_impe.html

"be very instructive for us"—Author interview with Jim Clyburn

With Putin at a press conference—Trump Putin press conference, July 16, 2018, https://www.youtube.com/watch?v=cwxqOoIyWm0

"When you've got this much smoke"—Author interview with Clyburn

On November 6, 2018—Election results

had been "managing up"—Author interviews with Indiana Republicans, former White House officials

kill two birds with one stone—Author interviews with Washington Republicans, Indiana Republicans, and former White House officials

Pence had never truly connected with Trump—Author interviews of Trump advisers and former White House officials

breaking some of the stiltedness—Author interviews Pence friends

Could he trust Mike Pence?—Haberman and Rogers, "Is Mike Pence Loyal?"

"Well, I haven't asked him"—Trump press conference, November 7, 2018, C-SPAN, https://www.c-span.org/video/?c4762041/president-trumps-november-7-2018-press-conference

INDEX

ABOUT THE AUTHOR

Tom LoBianco is a longtime Pence reporter who covered Pence from the statehouse to the White House at the Associated Press, CNN, and the *Indianapolis Star*. LoBianco is a regular political analyst on national television and radio, including Fox News, MSNBC, NPR, and more. In more than a decade covering politics, he has unearthed scores of stunning stories. He lives in the Washington, D.C., area.